Reinventing the Left in the Global South

This book offers a fresh appraisal of the nature and significance of the democratic Left in the Global South. The moral and intellectual leadership of the Left is shifting south from its European birthplace. It is in the Global South, most notably in Latin America, that one finds newly self-confident progressive movements. This "new" democratic Left includes parties and social movements that not only are avoiding the familiar pitfalls that ensnared socialists and social democrats in the twentieth century, but also are coping with the realities of the twenty-first century, especially neoliberal globalization. In analyzing and illustrating three innovative strategies – moderate social democracy, radical social-democratic transition to socialism, and Left populism – this study nudges the debate about the Left out of the well-worn grooves into which it has fallen in recent decades.

Richard Sandbrook is Professor Emeritus of Political Science at the University of Toronto and a Fellow of the Royal Society of Canada. Since 1968 he has focused his research on the Left's experience in the Global South, the relevance of social-democratic thinking to the reshaping of neoliberal globalization, the political economy of the basic-needs and market-oriented development strategies, the relationship of democratization to development, and the political role of workers and the urban poor in Africa. He has published over fifty articles and ten books, including *Social Democracy in the Global Periphery: Origins, Challenges, Prospects* (with Marc Edelman, Patrick Heller and Judith Teichman, Cambridge University Press, 2007).

Reinventing the Left in the Global South

The Politics of the Possible

Richard Sandbrook

Department of Political Science
University of Toronto

 CAMBRIDGE
UNIVERSITY PRESS

CAMBRIDGE
UNIVERSITY PRESS

University Printing House, Cambridge CB2 8BS, United Kingdom

Cambridge University Press is part of the University of Cambridge.

It furthers the University's mission by disseminating knowledge in the pursuit of education, learning and research at the highest international levels of excellence.

www.cambridge.org
Information on this title: www.cambridge.org/9781107421097

First published 2014

Printed in the United Kingdom by Clays, St Ives plc

A catalogue record for this publication is available from the British Library

Library of Congress Cataloguing in Publication data
Sandbrook, Richard.
Reinventing the left in the global South : the politics of the possible / Richard Sandbrook, Department of Political Science, University of Toronto.
   pages   cm
ISBN 978-1-107-42109-7 (paperback)
1. New Left – Developing countries.   2. Developing countries – Politics and government – 21st century.   3. Democracy – Developing countries.
4. Right and left (Political science)   I. Title.
JF60.S257   2014
320.5309172′4–dc23

                                                                    2014006985

ISBN 978-1-107-07278-7 Hardback
ISBN 978-1-107-42109-7 Paperback

All human beings are born free and equal in dignity and rights. They are endowed with reason and conscience and should act towards one another in a spirit of brotherhood.

Article 1, Universal Declaration of Human Rights

Politics is a strong and slow boring of hard boards ... Only he has the calling for politics who is sure that he shall not crumble when the world from his point of view is too stupid or too base for what he wants to offer. Only he who in the face of all this can say "In spite of all!" has the calling for politics.

Max Weber, "Politics as a Vocation"

Contents

Figures

Tables

Acknowledgments

Frankly, I never set out to write this book. If someone had suggested a dozen years ago that I write a book with the scope suggested by the title, I would have demurred. But one thing led to another. It dawned on me that we in the Global North, at a time when our Left has seemingly lost its way, have much to learn from the experience of the democratic Left in the Global South. And so the scope of my inquiry broadened. Yet whatever merit my readers ascribe to this study derives substantially from the advice and support provided by generous friends and colleagues.

Some of the commentaries and discussions helped me to establish the theoretical foundations and scope of this book. Particularly helpful in this respect were Atul Kohli (Politics, Princeton University), Frank Cunningham (Philosophy, University of Toronto), Ali Burak Güven (Politics, Birkbeck University of London), Mitu Sengupta (Politics, Ryerson University) and Marc Edelman (Anthropology, Hunter College, CUNY). The talented students in my graduate seminar on the Political Economy of International Development at the University of Toronto also helped clarify my thinking. There is no better crucible for developing ideas than a seminar in which one elucidates and defends various propositions.

Other friends and colleagues were kind enough to read chapters bearing on their geographical expertise to correct any errors of fact and interpretation, though some doubtless remain despite their best efforts. Judith Teichman (Political Science, University of Toronto) was very helpful on Latin America. Antoinette Handley (Political Science, University of Toronto) tried to steer me through the treacherous terrain of interpreting South Africa's political experience since 1990. Patrick Heller (Sociology, Brown University) and Anil Varughese (Political Science, Carleton University) shared their extensive knowledge pertaining to the leftist experience in Kerala and West Bengal. I would also like to acknowledge the contributions of three meticulous research assistants: Jennifer Fender, Sarah Ellis and Joelle Westlund. Inasmuch as the analysis of this book depends heavily on the experience of actual cases rather than abstract models, the contributions of these friends and assistants are clearly significant. But I am solely responsible for any remaining errors.

I wish also to acknowledge the contribution of Cambridge University Press's two anonymous reviewers. Their detailed, extensive and perceptive criticisms and suggestions were invaluable. Authors have mixed experiences with anonymous reviewers, but in this case John Haslam at Cambridge University Press selected readers who possessed both encyclopedic knowledge and open-mindedness. All three deserve high praise for their professionalism.

1 Reinventing the Left

Neoliberalism, the doctrine that assumed hegemonic status about 1980, made a bold promise. Liberalizing markets, by unleashing the wealth-enhancing forces of competition and risk-taking entrepreneurship, would produce greater prosperity and well-being for more people than any alternative. But this promise appears today as a chimera to the populations of Western countries who are still struggling to escape the aftershocks of the 2008–9 global crisis, a crisis rooted in the deregulation and liberalization extolled by neoliberals. The situation in the Global South appears to support a more favorable judgment of neoliberal development doctrine. In the countries of greatest neoliberal influence – in Latin America and sub-Saharan Africa – the neoliberal promise was not kept in the 1980s and 1990s. Yet, following 2002, these countries experienced high growth. Poor people consequently constitute a shrinking share of the populations of many countries while the middle class has expanded. This growth, instigated mainly by a commodity boom and inexpensive credit following the crisis-ridden 1990s, was interrupted by the world economic crisis that affected the Global South in 2009–10. The extent to which the earlier neoliberal reforms belatedly spurred the growth surge is debatable.[1] What is clear, however, is the high and continuing costs to society and nature of neoliberal development trajectories.

These costs, gleaned from critiques of the mainstream approach, would include some or all of the following. Privatization, cuts in the civil service, and trade and capital-account liberalization have often led to the loss of jobs in the formal sector since the 1980s, while precarious employment in the informal sector has expanded. Credible threats by large-scale global corporations to relocate production in lower-cost jurisdictions have driven down wages throughout the world. Globalization has thus generated millions of poor-quality jobs. Market crashes and harsh competition for the available jobs and economic opportunities have fostered widespread economic insecurity. Periodic financial crises in many countries have reduced even middle-class families to at least temporary poverty. The reduction or elimination of agricultural subsidies and tariffs to protect small farmers has driven many into bankruptcy. The privatization of land formerly governed by indigenous or collectivist land tenure rules has favored wealthy corporations and entrepreneurs seeking land for industrial activities or large-scale agricultural exports. Resurgent commodity speculation periodically drives the prices of basic foodstuffs dramatically higher, undermining food security for the poor in developing countries. User charges for educational and health services and/or the deteriorating quality of public services, together with the rising cost of private provision, confront even middle-class families with unpalatable choices. High and often growing economic inequality means that the gains from growth have been disproportionately appropriated by the wealthy, even while their evasion of income taxes has typically starved the public sector of resources. Inequality has also permitted the wealthy few to gain disproportionate political influence, vitiating democracy. Barely regulated industrial development, forestry, fisheries and export agriculture have despoiled the land, water and air. Growing carbon emissions from unregulated production and consumption propel climate change, evident especially in more frequent droughts and flooding, rising global ocean levels and shortages of fresh water. Individualism, especially the quest for personal material advancement, has weakened the bonds of community reciprocity, while social dislocation, unemployment and the juxtaposition of wealth and poverty have stimulated high rates of urban crime. These trends most adversely affect the poor and near-poor; they are forced off their land, housed in squalid, overcrowded and ill-serviced urban settlements, and exploited by employers or the conditions of self-employment in the informal sector. Many people live insecure lives plagued by uncertainty, despite economic growth since 2002.

Neoliberal doctrine, needless to say, has not remained static in the face of such trends. The lackluster socioeconomic record of neoliberal policies in the early decades, together with the East Asian financial collapse of 1997–8 and the 2008–9 global financial debacle, demanded policy reformulation. In addition, China's rapid and sustained growth has demonstrated anew the central role of the state in economic development, an unpalatable view for neoliberal hard-liners. And China, by offering commodity-exporting countries an alternative source of finance, aid, investment and trade to the West and the international financial institutions, has augmented the policy autonomy of many governments in the developing world. These governments, especially in Latin America, have used their enhanced autonomy to adopt heterodox policies. In response, the World Bank and other purveyors of the dominant model have shifted since the late 1990s from a market-fundamentalist "Washington Consensus" to an increasingly variegated and more centrist

"Post-Washington Consensus." These modifications have narrowed the rhetorical gap between the neoliberals and their critics on the Left.

If this sketch of the current conjuncture is largely accurate, it raises an important question: What has the Left in the Global South to offer in the way of desirable and realistic alternatives to even the refurbished Post-Washington Consensus? Granted, the Left's historical record is not encouraging. Economic failure and political oppressiveness discredited socialism in the 1970s and 1980s, especially its centrally planned versions. Nearly all of the communist and socialist governments collapsed. Social democracies in the Global South as well as the North also ran into economic difficulties in the 1980s and 1990s, though many soon recovered. Other regimes resembling social democracies dissolved into unsustainable populisms. In these circumstances, liberal-democratic capitalism came to be celebrated in the early 1990s as the acme of institutional development, an "end of history" (Fukuyama 1992). Soon after its triumph, however, this order too began to unravel. Now, when the failings of the neoliberal world order have starkly crystallized in the form of a West-based financial crisis with long-lasting effects, the moment is opportune to revisit the possibilities offered by the Left.

An overview of the argument

Can one identify a "new," democratic Left in the Global South today? A rejuvenated Left would include parties and social movements not only avoiding the familiar pitfalls that ensnared the Left in the twentieth century, but also coping with the realities of the twenty-first century. Foremost among these realities is neoliberal globalization. To meet the challenges and make progress in attaining greater equality, solidarity and democracy is a tall order. In the real world, progressive movements remain imperfect. Nonetheless, despite their inevitable imperfections, enough has been achieved to warrant an in-depth examination.

A dispassionate analysis of the democratic Left in the developing world may interest not only students of international development and the global Left, but also those in the Global North disheartened by progressive politics in their own countries. The democratic Left in the West is in disarray. Even in the context of the worst capitalist crisis since the Great Depression, the Left has been unable to seize the initiative in pressing for a new policy/political paradigm. Instead, many leftist parties in 2008–9 jumped on the stimulus bandwagon, and later vacillated on the necessity for austerity programs.

Socialist and progressive movements in general have made bold pronouncements during election campaigns, but, when elected, they have governed in a manner similar to the center-Right. In the European Union, the European Commission, the European Central Bank, the IMF, the credit-rating agencies and financial markets have shaped the economic and social policies of all governments regardless of ideological hue. The small Nordic social democracies have had the most success in negotiating the shoals of globalization without succumbing to high unemployment, crushing public debt and high inequality. Yet social-democratic parties everywhere have failed to forestall the rise of the far Right by channeling the resentments and fears of dislocated workers and the middle class. In Greece and Hungary, but also in France and the United Kingdom, the far Right has emerged to express the anger and insecurity of electorates resulting from austerity and high unemployment. In the United States, President Barack Obama, unconvincingly cast as a socialist and liberal by the American Right, was unable to rally support within Congress (or even his own party) for many of his modestly progressive policies. A major crisis of capitalism did not give rise to a coherent leftist alternative.

Meanwhile, the most publicized progressive protest movement – the Occupy movement – produced no coherent ideology or organization. Beginning with the Occupy Wall Street protest in September 2011, the youth-based movement sparked emulation throughout the world. Protests initially articulated the view that a small and wealthy coterie of corporate leaders and financiers controlled the capitalist system, for the benefit of a small minority (the "1 percent") and at the expense of the majority and meaningful democracy. But the lack of leadership and organizational framework led to a proliferation of grievances and demands. This incoherence undermined the movement's effectiveness. Although the Occupy movement did raise awareness of inequality and its detrimental consequences, it produced no alternative program for realizing its egalitarian and democratic goals.

Thus it is mainly in the Global South, most notably in Latin America, that one finds a newly self-confident Left with consistent strategies for dealing with recalcitrant global realities.[2] *The moral and intellectual leadership of the Left seems to have shifted south from its European birthplace.* If this is so, we in the North may have much to learn from the experience of leftist-governed middle-income developing countries.

What then is distinctive about the democratic Left in the Global South? Although this question animates Chapter 2, some foreshadowing is needed. The driving force of progressive movements remains the belief that capitalism perpetuates injustice and dislocations that must be rectified. Rectifying the ills of capitalism involves both an end – primarily the building of equal freedom – and the primacy of solidarity and participatory politics in attaining this goal. Equal freedom, in brief, entails a society in

which all citizens are accorded an equal opportunity to experience freedom. People should be able to live long and worthwhile lives of their own
choosing, rather than have their fates determined by circumstances of
birth, family standing or initial market position. "Social" liberals state
their goal in similar or the same terms: both social liberals and progressives focus on the development of individual capabilities. But the Left,
unlike even the social liberal, focuses on the importance of cooperative
means in achieving the *equal* development of human potential – a society
where "the freedom of each is the condition for the freedom of all," to
quote a famous line. Not individual competition and liberal-democratic
politics but cross-class solidarity, the collective organization of excluded
or marginalized groups and participatory political action are the means
needed to attain this radical goal. Decisive state action, propelled by a
popular movement, is crucial, from a progressive viewpoint, because
equal freedom will remain meaningless in societies where vast inequalities
in access to resources persist. The required measures involve the redistribution of all or most of the following: good-quality educational and
health services, social protection in the form (eventually) of universal
programs, income through progressive tax policies and generous minimum wages, the creation of good jobs and cash transfers, political power
in the shape of decentralized or participatory democracy, decision-making
power in economic entities, and assets where wealth is highly concentrated. Solidarity – manifest in autonomous interest-based organizations
and collective action – and participatory democracy are not only the
means by which the lower classes and strata overcome domination, but
also a way of experiencing freedom. The focus on collective political
action to achieve redistributive goals distinguishes the Left from social
liberalism and other ideological tendencies.

The degree of change that is needed or possible, however, is a matter of
dispute on the Left; today as in the past, we can distinguish three positions. One set of movements contends that capitalism, in wreaking social
and ecological damage, is irredeemable. Therefore, it will be necessary
eventually to transcend capitalism to deal with its defects. This socialist
approach involves confronting inherited power structures, the intergenerational transmission of privilege and existing property rights. A
second group, which is of more recent origin, holds either that a movement to displace capitalism is futile or that the real problem lies with
neoliberalism. In either case, the immediate goal is to replace neoliberalism with a more equitable and sustainable *variety* of capitalism – involving
at a minimum the movement toward a universalistic social-democratic
welfare state and a more inclusive politics – with more fundamental
change relegated to a more propitious future. A third current, while

acknowledging that certain neoliberal policies have had unfortunate results, retains faith in the ethical as well as practical superiority of the liberal-market economy. Hence, its proponents call, in effect, for humanizing neoliberalism, primarily by combining open markets with liberal democracy and an expansion of targeted safety nets and public services, so that markets benefit the poor and near-poor as well as the better-off. This is the position of the reform-oriented social liberals who have propounded, since the early 1990s, a "Third Way" between market fundamentalism and statist versions of social democracy. Each of these approaches pursues change at a different level.

Should we consider all three as variants of the "Left"? Any decision about where to draw the line is somewhat arbitrary because what is considered Left varies from culture to culture and over time. In the United States "liberals" (social liberals in my terminology) are widely regarded as progressives (and even "socialists," a term used by the far Right to heap opprobrium on their opponents). But I propose that social liberalism is more accurately conceived as a centrist doctrine. It is certainly to the left of classical liberalism insofar as the latter focuses on "negative" freedom – removing state constraints on individual action – rather than the "positive" freedom of the social liberal, who is intent on building individual capabilities to enjoy freedom. But social liberalism is not *of* the Left.[3] For one thing, leaders of this persuasion are ambivalent about inequality; they are keen to outlaw discriminatory practices, make tax systems progressive and direct more resources to public education and health services. But they do not want to interfere unduly with markets in the allocation of rewards, owing partly to reverence for the market, and partly to the view that inequality is necessary to reward individual entrepreneurship, skill and diligence. Some social liberals talk about "good" inequality and "bad" inequality, but it is unclear where one ends and the other begins.[4] They feel more comfortable addressing poverty reduction, which involves raising the poor above a certain income threshold, than inequality, which raises thorny issues of class relations and zero-sum struggles. They propose palliative (and often technocratic) means to achieve poverty reduction: accelerated growth, better services, improved institutions and targeted safety nets. They talk about social *needs* rather than social *rights*.

In light of these distinctions I make three related arguments in this book. First, I contend that the Left offers an alternative vision of development in the Global South, distinct from the inclusive growth or social liberalism of the Post-Washington Consensus with which it is sometimes confused (Chapter 2). Second, I substantiate the critique of neoliberalism sketched in the first two paragraphs of this chapter. I contend that neoliberal development doctrine, even in its more sophisticated recent versions, has failed as a policy guide to a socially and ecologically sustainable future (Chapter 3). If one accepts this view, the need for an alternative development vision is apparent.

The first two themes create a foundation for posing the central issue of strategy. In reality, the Left in the developing world pursues complex and diverse strategies. This diversity is fortunate because it allows the observer to learn what progressive models have succeeded or faltered, as well as what strategies might possibly work. Yet, to achieve a broad understanding, the social scientist necessarily reduces the complexity by creating a manageable set of categories. In devising Weberian ideal types, I have been aware of the inescapable dilemma that our concepts to some extent construct the world in the process of observing it. This dilemma is particularly acute when the field of study is as controversial as the new Left. What follows is thus one scholar's attempt, on the basis of forty-five years of study, to distil the essence of the democratic Left across the vast reaches of the Global South. My ambition is to help nudge the debate about the Left out of the well-worn grooves into which it has fallen in recent decades.

I maintain that three innovative and democratic approaches for attaining the leftist vision, partially avoiding earlier pitfalls, have emerged in the Global South (chapters 5–7). Escaping the earlier pitfalls, I suggest in Chapter 4, entails the Left's adherence to two assumptions: that progressive strategies must be democratic in means as well as an end; and that central planning, even if it could be done in a participatory manner, is unlikely to work, thus affirming the indispensability of markets in complex economies. I refer to the three models congruent with these assumptions as moderate social democracy, a radical social-democratic strategy for attaining socialism, and Left populism. I elaborate these strategies below.

Whether the Left emerges as a significant contender for national power and, if so, which of the three strategies comes to the fore, depends, as we shall see, on several factors. Historical experiences, both national and regional, are obviously important. Critical also are the global and national opportunity structures that constrain or embolden political actors, I consider these factors in Chapter 4.

Although I concentrate on progressive experiments at the national level, I do not ignore alternatives at the global and local levels. I emphasize the national arena because it remains the most inclusive level at which solidarity can most readily be mobilized behind a vision of equal freedom, solidarity and democracy. Cosmopolitanism, the sense of obligation one feels for people beyond one's national borders, remains rudimentary. However, at the national level, the global neoliberal order constrains the

Left by restricting the autonomy of national policy making and by locking in various neoliberal arrangements through multilateral and bilateral treaties and agreements. A realistic progressive national strategy must thus include (in addition to some protectionist measures) a complementary regional or global component – to change the global order or construct regional buffers and alliances. Also, many significant experiments in equitable cooperation have developed at the local level. Nevertheless, I suggest, few of these local experiments can survive without a sympathetic regional or national government. I consider alternatives at the global and local levels in Chapter 7.

To understand the quandaries facing progressive political organizations and the trajectories they trace, I employ a version of Karl Polanyi's model of the "double movement" as developed in his analysis of the first great transformation (approximately 1830–1940). Polanyi's model, I contend, cogently identifies the systemic roots of the acute dilemmas that confront the Left – whatever path it chooses to follow.

The Left and the double movement

An inherent conflict at the heart of capitalism – a double movement – presents progressive forces with difficult choices.[5] On the one hand, a liberal "movement," inspired by the ideal of the productive and liberating self-regulating market, seeks to achieve this end by "disembedding" the economy from restrictive social norms and regulations. Yet this movement is doomed to failure because the liberal project is "utopian," in the sense of impossible, owing to the devastation unleashed by any attempt to realize it. On the other hand, this social and environmental devastation inevitably arouses a disparate "counter-movement" of societal protection to mitigate the damage – by re-instituting institutional and normative checks on market forces or abolishing (some) markets altogether. But, Polanyi contends, the counter-movement, in seeking to protect society by "re-embedding" economy in society, unavoidably interferes with the logic of the market system. By undermining the conditions for efficient, productive and interconnected markets, the counter-movement unintentionally instigates an economic crisis that, in countries with weak political institutions, leads to an associated political crisis. Whatever solution the Left chooses to deal with this dilemma stakes out a route strewn with deadly pitfalls.

Before investigating these routes, we need to understand more precisely what is at stake in the double movement. Polanyi employs this concept in analyzing the conflicting forces that, in his view, led to the disastrous denouement of the first great transformation – the Great Depression, the rise of fascism and World War II. In the earlier non-capitalist systems, economy had been submerged in spiritual, political or social obligations and regulations; the latter provided some shelter for families and other social institutions. But the disembedding of the economy inherent in creating a self-regulating market courts danger by stripping away these social constraints. The liberal/neoliberal movement, in pursuit of its ideal, not only separates economy from society with the rise of markets, but also subordinates society and nature to economic imperatives, principally efficiency, commodification and profitability. The result of the process is to expose human beings and their habitat to the mercenary calculations of opportunistic actors.

Capitalism brings about a reversal of the earlier society–economy relationship because markets, according to Polanyi, must form an interlocking system to work efficiently, with prices determined solely by market conditions (Polanyi 1957: 249). Changes in market-determined prices then spur the necessary adjustments in the self-regulating system. What this means is that the markets for what Polanyi terms "fictitious commodities" – labor, land and money (to which we might add knowledge [see Jessop 2007]) – need to be as flexible as markets for commodities such as consumer goods, foodstuffs, stocks in public companies and capital equipment. But land, labor and money are not commodities like the others, Polanyi counters, and to treat them as if they were leads to disaster. In this sense, the self-regulating market, the ideal inspiring the Washington Consensus and even the Post-Washington Consensus, is utopian or unrealizable. "Such an [institutional arrangement] could not exist for any length of time without annihilating the human and natural substance of society, it would have physically destroyed man and transformed his surroundings into a wilderness" (Polanyi 2001 [1944]: 3).[6]

Although the disembedding of economy from society is central to the double movement, the key concept is not clearly defined in *The Great Transformation* (2001 [2004]) or elsewhere, and is often misunderstood. Some economic sociologists have objected that Polanyi overstates his case because markets are always and necessarily embedded in an institutional framework (Block 2003; Polanyi Symposium 2004). This proposition is clearly correct; markets cannot function without supportive institutions to protect property and enforce contracts, resolve conflicts and safeguard social order, manage a "sound" currency, arrange infrastructure and services, and oversee the rules of market competition. But accepting this view does not undercut Polanyi's conceptual distinction. Polanyi himself emphasizes that (paradoxically) "laissez-faire was planned" – that markets, far from being a spontaneous and natural development, were "instituted" through the power of the state (Polanyi 1957: 243–70). What disembedding the economy fundamentally implies is the subjection of society to the imperatives of the market, that is, the creation of a "market society." Hence, *formal or informal institutions that build a fully commodified market order are part of the liberal-market movement*. As the next chapter shows, structural adjustment in Africa and Latin America since 1980 has had just that goal; it has involved a state-directed effort to institute free markets through liberalization, commodification and the building of conducive political, judicial and administrative institutions.

The counter-movement also seeks institutional and normative change, but change that expresses a contrary logic to that of the liberal movement. The counter-movement, which can emerge at the local, national or global levels, reacts to the growing insecurity and dislocation by seeking to re-embed markets in society. A disparate set of social groups respond by way of social movements, civic associations, religious communities, lobbyists, protests, occupations, rebellions, coups d'état, revolutions, strikes and/or political parties, to forge regulations, legislation and social orders reflecting a protective logic of redistribution, welfare, cultural and religious revival and, above all, decommodification of the fictitious commodities.[7] Chapter 2 focuses on this side of the double movement too, emphasizing the distinctiveness of the Left's response even as the neoliberal movement – remaking itself as Post-Washington Consensus – co-opted popular concepts associated with the Left's critique.

The key issue, from the viewpoint of the Left's strategy, is whether Polanyi in the double movement identifies an ineluctable and ultimately irreconcilable contradiction in capitalism or only an inherent but potentially manageable tension. If the former, the only way out of the impasse between the movement and the counter-movement is a socialist transformation. Indeed, for Polanyi in *The Great Transformation* (2001 [1944]), the only meaningful stance of the Left was to displace market society with socialism, understood as a form of democratic and decentralized planning. "Socialism," he concisely observes in his magnum opus, "is essentially the tendency inherent in an industrial civilization to transcend the self-regulating market by consciously subordinating it to a democratic society" (Polanyi 2001 [1944]: 242). This "hard" position is probably the most accurate reflection of Polanyi's lifelong commitments and the logic of his theory (Lacher 1999; Adaman, Devine and Ozkaynak 2003; Mendell 2007).

Later in Polanyi's life, however, a "soft," or reformist position sometimes vied with this "hard" view.[8] If the double movement constitutes only an inherent tension in capitalism, we might expect that governments of the Left could successfully manage this conflict for a considerable time. That is, social-democratic governments, regardless of whether their long-term goal was socialist or not, might be able to tame the destructive propensities of markets while promoting the end of equal freedom. This possibility, from both historical and logical viewpoints, appears more persuasive than the "hard" position. Historically, we know from the vantage point of the twenty-first century that social democracies achieved enormous gains for the working classes and others during the golden age of capitalism between 1948 and 1975. And logically, it is unconvincing to hold, as Polanyi seems to do, that embeddedness either exists or not. He argues in *The Great Transformation* that the logic of a market system necessitates free markets/self-regulation (disembeddedness); anything less will lead to economic crisis and ultimately disaster. But the real world rarely produces such pure or textbook situations: disembeddedness is more accurately conceived as a continuous than a dichotomous variable (Hejeebu and McCloskey 1999: 301–2). If disembedding is *a matter of degree*, rather than an either/or condition, decommodifying and commodifying tendencies may coexist in the same society. They will wax and wane in tune with economic cycles and ideological currents.

Although the parties of the democratic Left form part of the counter-movement while in opposition, they must grapple with this tension when they assume power. Progressive parties must decide whether to seek a modus vivendi between the movement (what I call the accumulation imperative) and the counter-movement (the redistribution imperative), or transcend the dialectic altogether by abolishing market society. On the one hand, the liberal movement demands that markets allocate resources and rewards. It calls for some combination of protection of private-property rights, flexible labor markets, minimal regulation of natural-resource extraction and land use, market-determined exchange rates together with capital-account liberalization, a private banking sector, a monetary policy that keeps inflation under control, and trade liberalization. The champions of the liberal movement typically include large local firms oriented to, and potentially competitive in, export markets, especially those involved in commodity exports, the professionals associated with these firms, transnational corporations, technocrats in government, bankers at home and abroad, mainstream economists, and the international financial institutions and powerful Western governments. The claim is that, without these policies, investors will have less incentive to invest and thus economic growth and prosperity will suffer.

On the other hand, the disparate counter-movement seeks regulations, national ownership, subsidies and redistribution to protect society and nature from unleashed market forces. Businesses oriented to the local market or benefiting from governmental patronage and protection plead for continued protection and subsidies. Exporters expect governmental assistance to break into new markets. Small farmers protest import liberalization that allows often subsidized agricultural imports to undercut local producers. Indigenous groups seek to protect their traditional lands and ways of life from pressures to privatize land and exploit natural resources. Workers oppose privatization of state corporations and the pro-employer revisions of labor codes. Religious movements react against incursions of alien ideas and practices via the global mass media and the extension of the culture of possessive individualism. Conservationists arise to protest the destruction of habitats and species occasioned by the commodification of nature. And the organizations of the poor, the workers and much of the middle class assert that market-based rewards should be tempered by the entitlements stemming from social citizenship, especially universal social protections and universal access to high-quality public education and health services. Without protective action, it is claimed, economic insecurity and inequality will undermine social cohesion and the environment will degrade. The counter-movement has the numbers, but it is stymied by a cacophony of voices and divergent interests.[9]

Whatever path they choose in dealing with these conflicts, the organizations of the Left confront pitfalls and dilemmas.

Socialists confront a dilemma that Polanyi does not directly consider. Spearheading the counter-movement even after attaining power, they intend eventually to abolish capitalism's inherent conflict by forging a new society. It will be underpinned by such values as solidarity, equal freedom and participatory democracy, and it will feature non-market or quasi-market institutions that limit individual material incentives and promote cooperative production. But such a society can work only if new men and women, those imbued with the requisite values and orientations, inhabit it. Yet most people in the existing capitalist society are immersed in the culture of possessive individualism and the competition of one against all, not to mention divisive ethnic or religious identities and authoritarian traditions. How do progressive movements reconcile this disparity between the requisites of the good society and the dispositions of real people?

Polanyi (1947: 113, 114) holds the optimistic view that human dispositions are molded by the dominant institutions.

Single out whatever motive you please, and organize production in such a manner as to make that motive the individual's incentive to produce, and you will have induced a picture of man as altogether absorbed by that particular motive. Let that motive be religious, political, or aesthetic; let it be pride, prejudice, love, or envy; and man will appear as essentially religious, political, aesthetic, proud, prejudiced, engrossed in love or envy. . . . The particular motive selected will represent "real" man.

Market institutions thus accentuate the competitive, self-interested side of human character. Conversely, cooperative, participatory institutions would presumably draw forth the solidaristic dispositions of people. But, even if this is so, there is inevitably a lag: what happens in the interim, when people have yet to shed their market mentality?

A Leninist vanguard approach represents a potential solution. If people are not yet ready to assume self-determination in the new society, a vanguard comprising those with a more highly developed consciousness will guide the people toward the correct mind-set and institutional arrangement (as well as crush external and domestic enemies). This tutelary period will probably be authoritarian and certainly top-down, the better to forge socialist men and women and defeat enemies. When these goals are achieved, paternalism and authoritarianism are supposed to yield to expansive forms of democracy in the economic as well as political spheres. This approach, we now universally acknowledge, led to the Stalinist dead end and ultimately the demise of state socialism in the Soviet Union, Eastern Europe and elsewhere. There were always reasons why the vanguard felt it could not give way to a genuine democracy. Consequently, citizens of socialist countries attained neither political nor economic democracy. As I illustrate through the case of Nyerere's Tanzania in Chapter 6, even under relatively favorable conditions, a top-down approach to the promotion of socialism fails to achieve its goals. This state-socialist or bureaucratic-collectivist pitfall derailed socialist experiments in the (then) Third World in the 1970s and 1980s. But even today, in the context of "twenty-first-century socialism," the old vanguard notion creeps back in, responding as it does to a very real dilemma.

The other option is to avoid the authoritarian tutelary phase by accepting people more or less as they are and aiming for gradual changes in their values and attitudes. This approach, in which the progressive party or coalition competes for power within a liberal-democratic system, became the option of the moderate social democrats. Such parties aim incrementally to deepen social citizenship, democracy and solidarity within capitalist economies and electoral democracies. But moderate social democracy, like socialism, encounters distinctive pitfalls.

They arise from the inherent tension facing moderate leftist governments. To assert that it is conceivable to manage the clash between the "movement" and the "counter-movement" is not to suggest that it is easy to do so. The moderate Left's dilemma, to reiterate, is to advance decommodification of the fictitious commodities, equal freedom, solidarity and inclusive democracy (the equity/redistribution imperative), but without fatally impairing the economic viability of capitalism (the efficiency/accumulation imperative). On the one hand, the progressive party, to retain its popular support, must extend and deepen political and social citizenship in accordance with its ideological commitments. On the other hand, the moderate Left, to sustain itself in the long run, must attend to the efficiency/accumulation imperative because a party's continued success depends upon robust economic growth. Growth will generate the needed employment and revenues to abolish poverty, expand public services, and raise the prosperity of its constituencies. It is obviously difficult to pursue these two goals simultaneously.[10]

One pitfall to which social-democratic governments may succumb is a deadly embrace of the counter-movement, flouting the conditions for capital accumulation. Most instances in the Global South occurred in the Keynesian era of state-directed import-substitution industrialization, which was also the era of state socialism. Before 1980, the dominant development ideology and socialist theory accorded a central role to the state in modernizing society and building a more just world. Closely fought elections, while democracy survived, prodded leftist and populist parties to escalate their promises to attract support. If the new administration then yielded to the populist temptation – inflammatory rhetoric combined with redistributive programs and augmented clientelism, expansionary economic policies and increases in minimum wages while controlling prices – the result could be disastrous. The unpredictability and loss of profits would undermine business confidence, triggering capital flight and capital strikes. The consequent inflation, balance of payments deficits, growing unemployment and falling state revenues would generate economic breakdown, often accompanied by a political crisis. At the worst, "macroeconomic populism" (Dornbusch and Edwards 1990) could perversely victimize the very groups that the policies were supposed to help – usually organized labor and the urban poor.

Alternatively, the moderate Left, intimidated by the structural power of capital, may focus too single-mindedly on the efficiency/accumulation imperative (the liberal movement) at the expense of decommodification, equity and redistribution. Purportedly leftist governments may be so anxious to reassure the local business class, foreign investors, financial markets and the International Monetary Fund that they are co-opted. They implicitly move to a centrist position – a variant of what has become known as the "Third Way" (Giddens 2000). This acquiescence to neoliberalism involves a retreat manifest in the adoption of palliative measures (targeted safety nets, minor adjustments to the budgets for education and public health) that do not challenge inherited inequalities and injustices. Yet the party's rank-and-file and supporters, inspired by the earlier vision of a just society, react antagonistically to its leaders pragmatically accommodating capital and placating reactionary or opportunistic coalitional partners. When vast inherited inequalities of wealth and power persist unchallenged, the followers of the Left become disenchanted. Disenchantment may not surface during boom times, when prosperity trickles down; however, hard economic times precipitate a crisis as supporters defect or withdraw. Social-democratic governments might better be criticized for settling for too little – financialization, oligopoly and high inequality persist in Brazil and Chile, for instance – than for seeking a modus vivendi through a class compromise.

Many false starts have thus bedevilled the struggle for equal freedom, class solidarity and genuine democracy. Yet parties and social movements in certain countries have devised ways, provisionally at least, to avoid the various traps. To succeed, they must also overcome a variety of challenges posed by social and political structures at the national level and a mainly hostile international environment.

The realities of society

In Chapter 4, I develop the notion of "opportunity structures" (Block and Somers 1984) to evaluate how the possibilities for progressive change vary from one country or region to another. This conceptual tool focuses on the relationship among international factors, national states, and contending domestic social forces in political-economic change. The global opportunity structure constrains what national states can achieve by limiting the leeway a government enjoys in formulating economic and social policy. A government's room for maneuver depends mainly on the national economy's role within the international division of labor, its regional and international alliances and the impact of imperialism or geopolitics. The national opportunity structure, in turn, influences whether social and political movements can actually seize the opportunities presented by the global opportunity structure. Such national constraints as mass poverty, limited state revenues, fragmented class structures, weak institutions, limited history of democracy, absence of a tradition of mobilizational politics, communal or regional cleavages and cultural norms of quietism vary markedly from one country or region to another. The global and national opportunity structures set limits on the effectiveness of leftist social and political movements – assuming they exist and are well organized.

Yet even where extensive constraints obtain, the scope of the politically possible is never entirely clear. Strong and cohesive leadership, effective political organization, coherent and attractive ideology and contingent events make an important difference, as the case studies in chapters 5 and 6 illustrate. Nevertheless, the complex organizational requirements of instituting moderate or radical social-democratic arrangements virtually rule out these options in the many countries where multiple structural and cultural obstacles obtain.

Another challenging lesson the Left has learned, or should have learned, is that the substitution of central plans for markets does not work.[11] Even modern notions of "participatory" and decentralized planning are probably doomed to failure. Markets are essential in complex modern economies, I contend in Chapter 4, though market *systems* involving the fictitious commodities are not. But markets are not only economic institutions; they have a cultural impact as well. The market's ever deeper penetration of societies breeds an individualistic, consumer-oriented mentality inimical to the solidarity principles associated with the Left. Dealing with this dilemma involves difficult choices. If the Left is perceived as opposed to the rising material aspirations of growing middle and working classes, it will lose support. Yet unending accumulation through markets will strengthen the culture of possessive individualism, not to mention propel ecological ruin. An emergent middle class, though initially supportive of the Left, may become a conservative force as their material aspirations rise. This is another dilemma that is not readily resolved.

Moderates and radicals have developed their own strategies for navigating through this thicket of obstacles and snares. The moderate and radical Left agree that the road to equal freedom entails, at some point, tackling power structures and giving voice to the vulnerable and excluded. Only a powerful political movement can hope to redistribute income, public services, social protection, decision-making power, and perhaps assets. But should the agenda be the end of neoliberalism, a type of capitalism, or capitalism itself?

Avoiding the pitfalls? Strategies of the Left

My focus on dilemmas, pitfalls and hard realities is not an implicit argument for inaction. It is rather a recognition of the lack of certainty in undertaking progressive change owing to complexity and contradictory tendencies. Although no blueprint for success exists, we can probe in particular cases both the failures and the qualified successes in dealing with the contradictions. Such an analysis promises to expand the political imagination.

I propose (Figure 1.1) that we can distinguish the strategies of the democratic Left along two axes: the degree of institutionalization of the leftist party or parties and the degree of class conflict. Institutionalization

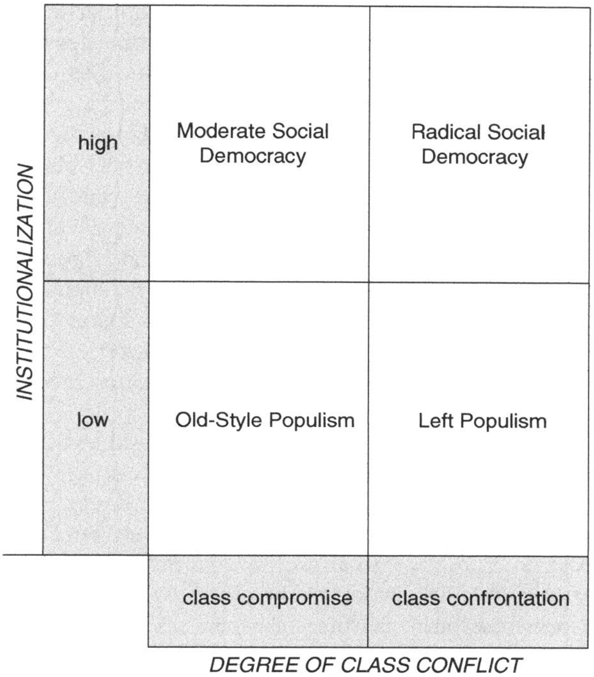

	class compromise	class confrontation
high	Moderate Social Democracy	Radical Social Democracy
low	Old-Style Populism	Left Populism

INSTITUTIONALIZATION

DEGREE OF CLASS CONFLICT

Figure 1.1 Varieties of the Democratic Left

is important because weakly institutionalized parties, by definition, are less cohesive, less organizationally competent, more dependent upon loyalty to the supreme leader, and thus less stable, consistent and powerful than highly institutionalized parties (Huntington 1968: 12–24). Insofar as struggles for equal freedom normally take place over extended periods and democratic continuity is central to the project of a democratic Left, well-institutionalized parties are more likely to achieve lasting redistributive success than their weakly institutionalized counterparts. The degree of class conflict is also a crucial distinction. Progressive movements divide, as mentioned, into two types. We can characterize this distinction in various ways. On the one hand, there are leftist parties with a moderate strategy that aim, or at least resign themselves, to implement redistributive programs with the acquiescence of the elites. On the other hand, one finds parties that believe that only unrelenting confrontation of existing power structures will bring the desired results. The division between class compromise and class struggle is thus fundamental. Employing these criteria, we arrive at four varieties of the democratic Left.

The *moderate social-democratic route* is especially popular in contemporary Latin America. This approach is innovative to the degree it avoids both macroeconomic populism and the full commodification of labor, land and money, while dealing effectively with neoliberal globalization. In other words, proponents find a progressive way to balance the imperatives of redistribution/equity and accumulation/efficiency. They reassure investors through orthodox monetary and fiscal policy and trade liberalization. They seek redistribution from growth via state developmentalist policies that, if they succeed, expand state revenues and "good" jobs and indirectly promote social citizenship through universal social protection, cash transfers and good public services. They also foster participatory institutions, though mainly at the local level. In Chapter 5 I employ case studies, particularly Brazil, to understand the underlying mechanisms of this resilient, hybrid approach.

The moderate Left, I suggest, has learned how to live with neoliberal globalization. Developmentalist states have taken advantage of the beneficial legacies of democratic reformism – advanced human capital, good social and physical infrastructure, stable and relatively effective government and industrial relations – to attract foreign investment and encourage local producers to fill lucrative niches in the global economy.[12] By orchestrating incentives and channeling resources to private firms and joint ventures, developmentally oriented states aim to stimulate innovation and competitiveness in select high-value-added exports. If successful, this strategy generates the remunerative employment opportunities and the expanded tax revenues to reduce both poverty and inequality. But living with globalization also means living with large private corporations and concentrated ownership of the mass media, an uncomfortable position for leftist governments bent on redistribution.

Moderate social democracy, however, may succeed in balancing the movement and the counter-movement only as long as growth continues. The commodity boom through much of the period 2003–13 served the Left well. But when growth recedes, the leadership loses its ability to promote both accumulation and redistribution of income (or, rather, redistribution *from* accumulation). The moderate Left's choices may then become stark: to champion the accumulation imperative, reverting to social liberalism, or to embrace asset as well as income redistribution, thus effectively moving to class confrontation. Either path will prove tumultuous.

A *radical social-democratic strategy of socialist transition* is a second innovation. I suggest in Chapter 6, against the backdrop of failed or disappointing socialist experiments, that, if there is a democratic path to socialism, this is what it looks like. The strategy promises an escape from the socialist impasse: namely, that attempts to transcend capitalism finish in an authoritarian cul-de-sac, thus contradicting the initial emancipatory aims. But it is a highly risky, turbulent venture.

The case for a radical social-democratic strategy proceeds along the following lines. Socialism is not a fixed destination, but an open-ended, long-term process of building equal freedom and democracy. Redistribution of income via progressive taxes, social programs and generating good jobs is important, but insufficient. Equal freedom requires dismantling inherited inequalities of class, caste, ethnicity and gender by redistributing not only income, but also physical and human capital and power as well. This task can be achieved only by challenging the power structures of capitalist society, that is, by engaging in class struggle rather than class compromise. Normally, this challenge will proceed from within inherited liberal-democratic institutions.

To have any chance of success, a radical movement requires certain political conditions. Nationally, a cohesive, left-of-center party or coalition must emerge, one which is capable of mobilizing a heterogeneous cross-class and, if required by circumstances, cross-communal coalition. This party must articulate a coherent ideology that convincingly portrays how a just society can be attained. And autonomous, encompassing movements of the subordinate classes (especially labor) and other groups (such as indigenous peoples' organizations, feminists, environmentalists, human rights organizations) are crucial to give voice to key constituencies and ensure political accountability. Ideally, radical social democracy involves a synergy between civil society (especially social movements), and the leftist party or coalition (see Chapter 4). Success entails avoiding the dead end of bureaucratic collectivism while building participatory and egalitarian institutions and undercutting the culture of possessive individualism among the Left's constituencies.

Obviously, this confrontational approach is very unlikely to survive within a single country alone, given the tightly integrated global market economy. Survival requires, at a minimum, the support of like-minded states and the buffer of regional institutions of solidarity, such as those that are appearing in South America.

This strategy harks back to the democratic revisionism of the German Marxist Eduard Bernstein, around the turn of the twentieth century (Bernstein 1961 [1909]). Social democracy, in this view, is an evolutionary, mainly peaceful and democratic route to socialism. Socialist movements can take advantage of parliamentary democracy, Bernstein believed, to build a trans-class (and, in today's world, trans-communal) coalition by appealing for support on ethical as well as material grounds. Workers were not the only class to suffer the injustices and dislocations of capitalism; peasants, farmers and elements of the middle classes did too. Social democrats could mobilize this cross-class constituency to take control of government. They could then institute a process of domesticating capitalism and expanding the scope of collective decision-making and cooperative production, as well as enhancing opportunities for citizens to augment their personal capabilities. In time, these incremental institutional changes would form subaltern classes and middle classes with the capabilities, sense of efficacy and solidarity to assume a self-determining role in political and economic life.

This model has informed the practice of several political movements. Eurocommunism, which made some headway in Italy, France and Spain prior to the neoliberal age, proposed essentially this route. Salvador Allende's Unidad Popular administration in Chile (1970–3) intended to follow the same path, though it was quickly engulfed by chaos and fell to a military coup. Two states in India led for various periods by the Communist Party of India (Marxist) – Kerala and West Bengal – also exemplify the model during their early decades. Obviously, implementing this strategy in the context of a neoliberal political and economic order introduces severe conflict and tension.

I explore the illustrative case of Kerala in Chapter 6. I selected this case because it is the purest expression of the model owing to this state's unusual circumstances. Kerala's status as a state within a federation has both constrained its Communist Party to adhere to India's democratic norms and buffered its experiment from external interference as long as the national government remained rhetorically committed to "socialism." In addition, this case nicely illustrates the tensions to which the strategy inevitably gives rise. The radical focus on eliminating historical inequities through class struggle and decommodifying labor precipitates an accumulation crisis. This crisis creates pressure to deradicalize the mobilizational model by shifting priority to accumulation. *Paradoxically, radical social democracy may become a victim of its own success.* By displacing the dominant class – landlords in Kerala's case – and fostering a comparatively well-educated and prosperous rural and urban middle class, the strategy creates beneficiaries who then embrace the consumer society and certain neoliberal policies. These elements reject the socialists who they hold responsible for the accumulation crisis. The radical party, with considerable intra-party dissension, responds by tacking toward moderate social democracy to retain its support base in competitive elections. But does this backtracking represent a failure of the model? That is a debatable proposition, considering the substantial degree of equal freedom attained through decades of class struggle in the case of Kerala.

Although moderate and radical social democrats may appear distinct, in reality they represent the poles of a continuum rather than mutually exclusive types. Moderate social democrats, such as the Workers Party (PT) in Brazil, assert the delimited social rights of citizens, including redistribution from growth, while avoiding antagonizing capital. Radical social democrats, in contrast, confront the dominant classes over issues of power and property, as in the case of Kerala from the 1950s to the 1980s. Even so, radical social democrats may, in the end, be driven by the accumulation imperative and the embourgeoisement of their followers to make their peace with capitalism (as eventually they did in West Bengal as well as Kerala), thus assuming a moderate social-democratic path. Moderate and radical ideological inclinations also overlap on certain important issues. Commonalities include a rejection of neoliberalism and imperialism, an acceptance, or at least tolerance, of (some) markets, a preference for a proactive and nationalist state role in economic life, a commitment to social development and rhetorical endorsement of participatory democracy. Not surprisingly, then, the leaders of the moderate and radical Left in Latin America usually see each other as allies (though the relationship is not without tension).

Where does populism fit? Populism is a slippery concept. Not only is it loosely used to cover a range of political phenomena, but also critics and politicians employ it as a derogatory label to discredit opponents. As a pejorative term, populism refers to demagogic leaders who allegedly manipulate the people within semi-democratic or authoritarian systems. Despite its tendentious and loose usage, the term refers to a very important tendency and cannot readily be abandoned. I distinguish in Figure 1.1 between *old-style populism* and *Left populism*. They both feature personalistic leadership, populist rhetoric and weakly institutionalized parties. But Left populism diverges from old-style populism in important ways.

Old-style populism, a common political model in Latin America and encountered widely elsewhere in the Global South, has four features.[13] The first is a political rhetoric that divides society into two antagonistic groups: the "people" and a supercilious/conniving/rapacious/venal "elite" or "oligarchy." Second, populism is characterized by a personalistic, charismatic leader, or a concerted attempt to portray a leader as charismatic; this leader cultivates a strong, emotional bond with his followers. Populist leaders are personalistic in the sense that loyalty to the leader, rather than commitment to a particular doctrine, is key. The leader manifests a distinct political style, involving, in addition to highly emotional rhetoric, a folksy manner and an accusatory moral tone in reference to enemies at home and abroad. Third, and following from the previous point, a populist party is loosely organized. The role of the party is to mobilize the people to carry out the leader's mission, to demonstrate through rallies the strength of the party and to reward followers through the distribution of patronage. The personalistic and clientelistic basis of populism means that the departure of the leader throws the movement into crisis.

Finally, old-style populism manifests a limited commitment to democratic checks and balances. The archetypal populists to whom many studies refer – President Juan Perón of Argentina (1946–55, 1973–4) and President Getúlio Vargas of Brazil (1930–45 and 1951–4) – only intermittently officiated in (semi-)democratic electoral systems. Perón resorted to violent and dictatorial measures from time to time, subverting the formal freedoms. Vargas served as a democratically elected president only in 1951–4. Democracy if necessary, but not necessarily democracy, is a phrase that aptly captures populist ambivalence.

In what sense, if any, is old-style populism a specifically leftist movement? Ernesto Laclau, who in several books has clarified the nature of populism, contends that populism is neither Right nor Left. Instead, it embraces diverse and contradictory political beliefs: "there is no *a priori* guarantee that the 'people' as a historical actor will be constituted around a progressive identity" (Laclau 2005: 246). Peronism in Argentina, it might be noted, has shifted ideologically between Right and Left, depending on circumstances and leaders. Carlos Menem, the Peronist president from 1989 to 1999, adopted a neoliberal populist discourse. In contrast, Néstor and Cristina Kirchner, Peronist presidents since 2003, moved sharply to the Left in opposition to neoliberalism. What remain constant, despite these shifts, are the challenge to the status quo and the commitment to building a new order. The leader and the party claim to act in the name of the sovereign people to depose or disempower the elite and rule on behalf of the people.

It is not surprising, in light of this ideological opaqueness, that various analysts have interpreted old-style populism in contrasting ways. In Latin American studies, for instance, analysts have offered two evaluations of the historical significance of populism (Motta 2011: 29–30). One interpretation understands populism as the inclusion of the popular classes, especially urban workers, in political life and in sharing the fruits of economic growth. In return for acquiescing to a class compromise engineered from above, urban workers in particular receive economic and social benefits. Thus, the focus is on redistribution, albeit to a limited group; we might therefore conclude that populism has been, or is often, part of the Left. But a contrary viewpoint is that populist governments construct a class coalition – involving principally the organized workers and the industrial bourgeoisie – in order to carry through a program of (import-substitution) industrialization. The regime ensures compliance with this project on the part of trade unions through a combination of co-optation of leaders, patronage and penalties. Here, the focus is on industrial development. But developmentalism may well reflect nationalist or right-wing agendas. Consistent with this latter viewpoint is the interpretation that populist parties co-opt leftist slogans and organized labor to hasten industrialization. In short, a welfare orientation vis-à-vis workers, in combination with a discourse of antagonism toward the oligarchy and popular empowerment, do not necessarily indicate a leftist orientation.

Left populism, in contrast, consistently and unambiguously aligns with the radical Left and opposes, not democracy as such, but *liberal* democracy. To this extent, it is innovative. Left populism dates from the early 2000s, with varying strains in Eastern and Central Europe, the Bolivarian Revolution of Hugo Chávez in Venezuela and somewhat similar regimes later in Ecuador and perhaps Bolivia (March 2007).

The context is important in understanding this phenomenon. Left populism emerges in countries with a history of populist or personalistic politics, a style of political life that is unlikely to disappear soon. Yet the collapse of Communism, coupled with public dissatisfaction with the volatility and inequality associated with the Washington Consensus in the 1990s, opened a search for new egalitarian and anti-capitalist formulas. Subsequently, "twenty-first-century socialism" abandoned the populist notion of a class pact in favor of a politics of confrontation. It also dropped the Marxist focus on the proletariat in order to position itself as the voice of the "people" vis-à-vis the oligarchy (March 2007: 66–9). And it avoided centralized planning in favor of a "socially oriented" (market) economy. Finally, in countries such as Venezuela, Ecuador and Bolivia with extensive hydrocarbon reserves, their enhanced leverage within the global economy provided them with a degree of freedom in articulating a counter-hegemonic position. The result has been a personalistic but consistently leftist populism.

I have suggested that Left populism has a less equivocal position on democracy than old-style populism. This statement will appear patently false to those who, explicitly or implicitly, identify democracy in general with liberal democracy. Left populists are certainly unsympathetic to the latter, on the grounds that it has perpetuated, or even deepened, vast inequalities in wealth, income and political power between the elite and the majority of citizens ("the people") (de la Torre 2007: 384–5). Moreover, liberal-democratic constitutions provide for limited expression of the popular will. On the basis of this critique, Left populists advocate an alternative form of democracy sometimes referred to as popular democracy. Rather than a set of procedural rules for choosing leaders, this alternative understands democracy as *a type of society* – one that is inclusive, egalitarian and permits forms of direct democracy. Left populists have experimented with different institutional arrangements, purportedly to arrive at workable models. Whether we should take these experiments seriously, or judge them as mere camouflage for a new authoritarianism, is an issue on which qualified observers strongly disagree. I broach this issue in Chapter 6.

The future of the diverse democratic Left is hard to predict, in light of the many uncertainties. It remains to be seen whether, in the longer term, the moderate social democrats can avoid co-optation by the elites yet maintain the conditions for sustained, broad-based prosperity. If the moderate Left falters while relative US power recedes, the radical Left may come to the fore. Left populism is a more likely alternative than radical social-democratic transitions, owing to the stringent conditions for the latter model to succeed. In articulating the disillusionment of people with both liberal capitalism and liberal democracy, it will probably take a less moderate form than one finds today. But can Left populism, if it proceeds far along the road to "socialism," avoid falling prey to the bureaucratic-collectivist trap?

Conclusion

Although the double movement identifies a universal and persistent tension within capitalism, the model needs modification when it is applied to the Global South in the neoliberal era. Consistent with the model, the neoliberal movement has championed the disembedding of economy from society, especially in Latin America and Africa. This intensified commodification of society and nature has energized disparate national counter-movements of societal protection of which the Left is often an element. The clash between the movement and the counter-movement, accumulation and redistribution, poses an acute dilemma with which the political organizations of the Left must grapple. That much remains the same. Circumstances have changed, however: the regions of the Global South not only differ markedly among themselves on many dimensions, but are also vastly different from Europe and North America during the first great transformation. Neoliberalism is not precisely the same as economic liberalism. The global market economy is today vastly more interconnected than in earlier centuries. The composition of the counter-movement differs from the earlier versions, with the labor movement no longer as prominent, and with communal identities often vying with class as a principle of political organization. These differences will receive attention in the next chapter and throughout the book. But Polanyi's preoccupation with how to limit the corrosive impact of unleashed market forces remains a powerful lens through which to understand the difficult choices facing the Left.

In the chapters that follow, I have generally utilized real-world cases instead of abstract models to derive lessons of broad import. Concrete experiences, as Denis Goulet (1979: 557) eloquently observes, "are the most important sources of wisdom about development strategies. It is from them that true alternative ... models of social reconstruction must come, not from purely cerebral model-building that has little regard for constraints, for human desires and limitations, and for the unpredictable vagaries of local conditions." What works reasonably well in one milieu may prove equally effective elsewhere, if the social and political conditions are similar. Where mass poverty, communal conflicts, weak states or warlord politics militate against the democratic Left at the national level, movements at the local level sometimes build on subnational solidarities to foster localized experiments in equitable cooperation. The contemporary reappearance of leftist alternatives in the Global South thus provides rich empirical materials for the study of historical possibilities.

Before examining these alternatives and the conditions for their emergence in chapters 4–7, I explore two broad themes to establish the context. Chapter 2 explores the nature and evolution of neoliberal development doctrine and the response of the Left as an element of the counter-movement. I contend that the Left offers a distinctive vision of development, despite the co-optation of its more popular concepts by the hegemonic neoliberal paradigm. Chapter 3 then argues that the effort to institute the self-regulating market has had some devastating socioeconomic and environmental effects, which has given impetus to the counter-movement to neoliberalism.

NOTES

1. Improved macroeconomic management, including the end of over-valued currencies, and enhanced accountability of politicians and administrators (where that occurred), certainly aided economic recovery.
2. The prominence of Latin America in the resurrection of the Left stems from its experiencing the longest and most doctrinaire application of neoliberal doctrine, its historical record of resistance to imperialism and capitalism, and the relatively advanced social and economic conditions in many countries. The Left in sub-Saharan Africa, which also has had a long experience of policies inspired by the Washington Consensus, is generally limited by mass poverty, weak states and limited class formation. South Africa is obviously an exception. In East Asia, effective developmental states were able to hold both

the Left and neoliberal restructuring at bay (until the 1990s in the latter case). These factors are explored further in Chapter 2.

3. President Barack Obama, a social liberal, acutely pinpointed the distinction in early 2013 when he pushed back against the Republican claim that he was some sort of a radical leftist. He pointed out that, a generation earlier, his reforms would have been considered mainstream proposals of moderate Republicans. It was the movement of the Republican Party to the far Right that made Obama's proposals appear leftist.

4. On the concept of "good" versus "bad" inequality, refer to the blog of two prominent economists, Gary Becker and Richard Posner, especially the post of January 30, 2011 at www.becker-posner-blog.com/2011/01/bad-and-good-inequality-becker.html

5. This section draws heavily on Polanyi (2001 [1944] and 1977). For an understanding of Polanyian concepts, Dale (2010a) is invaluable.

6. In Chapter 3, I elaborate why treating labor, land and money as commodities is so devastating.

7. This institutional viewpoint is nicely elaborated in Ebner (2011). I define decommodification in Chapter 5. Labor, in brief, is decommodified to the extent that workers are not dependent upon the sale of their labor power for their survival. In this sense, decommodification is equivalent to deproletarianization. "Fictitious commodities," for Polanyi, included land, labor and money.

8. For a discussion of the "hard" and "soft" Polanyi, refer to Dale (2010b).

9. For an Indian case study of the difficulties of organizing a Polanyian counter-movement, see Levien 2007.

10. A third imperative is pushing to the fore: ecological sustainability. This imperative receives attention in chapters 3 and 7.

11. Developmental states, by definition, engage in planning. However, they do not abolish markets, but rather employ market-friendly incentives to gain the cooperation of private firms in exploiting economic opportunities. See the classic study by Johnson (1987).

12. I refer to state developmentalism to distinguish it from a developmental state. The exceptional conditions for the latter – an effective, Weberian state bureaucracy and a developmentally oriented leadership that has close ties to the business elite, yet remains uncaptured by it – mean that developmental states are rare (Evans 1995). But less effective ("developmentalist") states can still play a positive role by establishing inclusionary growth as an urgent priority, by discouraging insider-elite rent-seeking, and by "nudging" enterprises to seek out promising opportunities by providing incentives and infrastructural investment. See Wade (2010).

13. See, for incisive critical reviews, March (2007), Comaroff (2011) and Jansen (2011).

2 Alternative visions: leftist versus neoliberal paradigms

Neoliberalism, the currently dominant policy framework and development ideology, supplanted the Keynesian order from the late 1970s on. Cracks appeared in the Keynesian consensus in 1971 when the United States withdrew its pledge to back its currency with gold at a set rate, the corner-stone of the Bretton Woods fixed exchange-rate regime. Further stresses flowed from a crisis of stagflation in the West and faltering state-directed import-substituting industrialization (ISI) and socialisms in the Global South and East. Neoliberal leaders emerged – most prominently General Augusto Pinochet in Chile, together with Margaret Thatcher and Ronald Reagan – who seized on the politico-economic malaise as signifying the failure of the state and Keynesian or socialist remedies, and the need for deregulation, liberalization, privatization and open economies to rejuvenate market forces.[1] At first, in the 1980s, this "Washington Consensus" was not widely contested.

But opposition mounted in the 1990s and thereafter. Probably the East Asian financial collapse of 1997 was the turning point, though other financial crises preceded and followed this catastrophe. The narrow, market-fundamentalist Washington Consensus gave way to an increasingly more complex, state-friendly and inclusive Post-Washington Consensus. The global financial crisis of 2008–9, how-ever, dealt a further, heavy blow to the dominant doctrine, even in its more complex and open-ended form. The Left, which had been humbled by the collapse of socialisms around the world, recovered its élan.

I contend that the Left's vision – what I will refer to as its *development paradigm* – remains distinct from the Post-Washington Consensus. The latter identifies an important role for the state in economic life and purveys a discourse of poverty alleviation, democracy, inclusiveness, participation and empowerment. But the leftist vision, with its focus on equal freedom, social solidarity and participatory democracy and its critique of liberal democracy and neoliberal capitalism, extends well beyond the Post-Washington Consensus.

A development paradigm is a meta-policy paradigm. A policy paradigm, as Peter Hall (1993: 279) explains, provides policy makers with an "interpretive framework" in selecting policies. "Policy makers customarily work within a framework of ideas and standards that specify not only the goals of policy and the kinds of instruments that can be used to attain them, but also the very nature of the problems they are meant to be addressing." The paradigm, therefore, sets the agenda for decision makers; once dominant, it excludes policies that are inconsistent with its assumptions about the world. A development paradigm covers a broader range of policy instruments than other policy paradigms, but serves the same purpose.

The Left's development vision, I argue, is not only distinctive but plausibly addresses the challenges of the Global South today.

The dialectics of development paradigms

Development paradigms are complex, diverse and fluid (Pieterse 1998). We must resist the temptation to treat the dominant paradigm as a homogeneous and more or less static set of notions and policies – as is implicit in such popular terms as *the* Washington Consensus and *the* Post-Washington Consensus. The ends and means of policy shift (within certain parameters) because circumstances change, policies fail and critics attack. Consequently, the mainstream practitioners respond by co-opting and adapting to their own use some of the popular concepts and approaches wielded by their critics, and by adjusting policy to shifting challenges. Normally, not one but several policy options (or, in the case of development paradigms, bundles of policies) are consistent with a paradigm's assumptions (Mehta 2011: 33). Although neoliberals in the World Bank, the International Monetary Fund (IMF) and the universities often vehemently disagree over policy,[2] their disagreements take place against the backdrop of many shared assumptions. Despite the policy shifts, decision makers remain clear as to what counts as "serious" proposals. Policy changes occur incrementally, within a broad consensus. It is the deeper, shared paradigmatic assumptions that bring coherence to the policy debate and provide the rationale for a new policy or strategy.

Equally important, the clash between, or among, development paradigms is highly political, raising issues of power as well as policy. Neoliberalism is not just an abstract worldview; its ascendancy has reflected and shaped power balances nationally and globally. The freeing of markets has restored, or established for the first time, the economic and political power of national elites composed of financiers, entrepreneurs, corporate leaders and professionals (Harvey 2005: 119). As one critic notes, "pro-business activism in the 1970s was built on, and further developed, a wide-ranging political and cultural project – the reconstruction of the everyday life of capitalism, in ways supportive of upward redistribution of a range of resources, and tolerant of widening inequalities of many kinds" (Duggan 2003: xi).

Rewards flow to those development professionals whose intellectual work systematically advances this reconstruction. In the World Bank, the most influential actor in shaping neoliberal development doctrine, one observer identifies the "art of paradigm maintenance" (Broad 2006). It involves a subtle process of orchestrating incentives to produce supportive studies within the research unit, and then widely publicizing such studies. Nonconformists cannot expect their careers to flourish.

A paradigm, to be lasting, must extend beyond the elite to engage the popular imagination. Neoliberalism is not just a technocratic theory. It popularizes and simplifies complex philosophical (liberal) and scientific (neoclassical) thought in order to motivate and guide political action. The doctrine evolves as its proponents expropriate popular ideas fielded by opponents and adapt to changing circumstances. Neoliberal "common sense" is propagated by business schools, economics departments, economic journalism, the international financial institutions, the World Trade Organization, the Organisation for Economic Co-operation and Development (OECD), the annual World Economic Forum, private foundations and think-tanks, the rhetoric of politicians, and popular culture, especially popular literature and film.[3] Although neoliberalism is most firmly rooted in the Anglo-American sphere, its adherents are found throughout the world's countries, in the business and middle classes and also as technocrats in economic ministries and central banks. By the early 1990s, neoliberal ideology had triumphed globally.

Neoliberalism's hegemony in the Global South – that is, its widespread acceptance as common sense – was not long-lasting, however. At some point, despite policy modifications, dominant paradigms fall into disrepute. Failed or poorly performing policies discredit paradigms. In the case of neoliberal doctrine, these failures include both lackluster economic performance in the 1980s and 1990s and major economic crises, especially the Great Recession of 2008–9. Exogenous events may also erode support, such as, in the case of neoliberalism, the rise of state-capitalist China, the association of neoliberalism with United States imperialism (especially in Latin America) and the allure of heterodox experiments (such as in Chávez's Venezuela or contemporary Uruguay). Whatever the circumstances, the declining influence of the dominant worldview introduces uncertainty and the search for a new paradigm. This is the era we have now entered.

A "paradigm shift" (Hall 1993: 279), amounting to an overthrow of the existing framework, may ensue. Eras of ideological flux generally involve a struggle between or among contending schools over the definition of the central policy problem and its solution. The ascendency of one paradigm is not, however, simply a matter of its winning a reasoned debate over its framework's theoretical and practical superiority. Power resources and normative issues also shape outcomes (Mehta 2011: 36–7). The proponents of the dominant paradigm deploy key resources. As mentioned, neoliberal governments, international organizations, transnational corporations and foundations have the power to advance the careers of neoliberalism's professional supporters (mainly economists), to direct loans, investment and aid to acquiescent governments in the developing world, and to nurture sympathetic non-governmental organizations and prestigious leaders from the Global South. On the other side, nonconforming governments, such as those in Venezuela and China, and anti-systemic movements may directly or indirectly assist opponents of the dominant paradigm and form regional alliances.

Each school tries to pull the uncommitted to its side by manipulating not only incentives, but also rhetorical themes; advocates will astutely frame the policy issue to make their framework more widely attractive. Neoliberal organizations, like critics on the Left, now officially endorse democratic governance, empowerment of the poor, the decentralization of power to regions and villages, the buttressing of civil society, participation, gender equity, sustainability, social safety nets, inclusiveness, and a more activist state. There is a dialectical interplay between the dominant paradigm and contending visions.

In effect, a hidden struggle over the meaning of key concepts ensues. As two analysts aptly note: "if words make worlds, struggles over meaning are not just about semantics: they gain a very real material dimension" (Cornwall and Brock 2005: 1,052). But the ascendancy of one camp – a paradigm shift – will be portrayed by the victors as the triumph of reason.

A paradigm shift has not yet occurred in international development, however. The evolving Post-Washington Consensus, which has replaced the market-fundamentalist Washington Consensus since 1997, remains dominant.[4] The dialectical relationship between neoliberalism and its challengers continues.

I turn now to explore the evolution of the neoliberal and progressive paradigms. It is relatively easier to identify the assumptions of the former than the latter. Neoliberalism is a well-established doctrine whereas the Left paradigm was thrown into disarray by the evident shortcomings of actually existing socialism and social democracy in the late twentieth century. The reconstruction of the latter paradigm is still under way, and its reconstruction is heavily contested.[5] What I present, here and in subsequent chapters, is an interpretation of an incipient Left paradigm that is (a) a counterpoint to the neoliberal paradigm and (b) plausible in its current assumptions, in light of the Left's past failures and present challenges.

Neoliberalism's paradigmatic assumptions

Five related assumptions underpin neoliberalism. They identify the nature of the *problems* that are likely to be encountered in achieving its *goals*, and the range of relevant *policy and institutional instruments* for dealing with them. These assumptions are not specific to the Global South; they apply universally.[6]

First, the foundational "Economic Man" assumption holds that *society is composed of individuals who have a propensity to act in a self-interested manner*. Individuals, unless constrained by external forces, act rationally in the sense that they calculate how to use scarce resources to their maximum advantage in exchanges of goods and services. Such an optimizing attitude is rational because scarcity dictates that not everyone can realize their material goals.

The rational-actor assumption takes hard and soft forms. The "hardest" version, common in the early neoliberal phase (1980–98), defines the utility that an economic agent seeks to maximize as monetary gain and the agent as persistently opportunistic and knowledgeable in calculating his/her strategic choices. This simplifying assumption – basically that economic agents act as "rational fools" (Sen 1977) – gained adherents with the post-1945 mathematical revolution in modern economics. It is far easier for economists to build mathematical models on the basis of a simplified notion of motivations than on the complexity of "real" agents, who mix emotions and normative commitments with material goals and possess limited information (Thaler 2000: 140). Milton Friedman's classic defense (1953) of the hard version of Economic Man – that theories should be assessed on their predictive powers, not on the realism of their assumptions – has worn thin for those unimpressed by neoclassical economics' predictive success.[7] Feminists, too, have criticized Economic Man as an inaccurate portrayal of the mind-set of the many women who engage in unpaid domestic or agricultural work. Women who are heavily involved in child-rearing and family care respond to motivations other than personal welfare, such as duty, love and altruism (Benería 1999). It appears that the simple utility-maximization model applies only under limited conditions: a market with multiple buyers and sellers in which anonymity prevails, and agents who enter transactions solely on the basis of price considerations. Prime examples include stock markets, foreign exchange markets and commodity futures markets (Gintis and Khurana 2008: 309; Block 1991: 88).

The softest version of the rational-actor model relaxes the notion of self-interest to include altruistic preferences (what Adam Smith termed sympathy) as well as mercenary ones. This version became more common in the 1990s and later when the rational-actor model came under heavy attack. Amartya Sen, whose assumptions identify him as a social liberal, adopts this expansive understanding of utility in order to argue that "reasoned social progress" is possible in developing countries. He contends that debate in liberal-democratic societies can lead the privileged elite to accept arguments based on social justice, even though this acquiescence works against the latter's material interests (Sen 1999: 123, 261–2, 279). Although this viewpoint is not problematical for an economist oriented to philosophical issues (such as Sen), it does strictly circumscribe the applicability of mathematical models based on the (necessarily) simplified understanding of preferences. Economists of the latter persuasion would need to stipulate that their models apply only to those limited situations where economic agents do act single-mindedly to maximize their material returns. This limitation is unlikely to be acceptable.

A broader criticism, articulated by Karl Polanyi (2001 [1994]) among others, is that liberals confuse *human nature* with *culture* in assuming that humans are naturally selfish. Rather than certain natural motivations (self-interest and individual competitiveness) molding institutions and practices, it is just as likely that institutions and cultural practices (markets in particular) nurture certain human propensities (self-interest and competitiveness) at the expense of others (cooperation and mutuality). Thus, a market mentality, far from being natural, may be just a self-fulfilling prophecy, given certain cultural changes.

Second, economic liberalism derives its ideological power from its allied root assumption that *markets are a natural feature of human society.* Adam Smith (1863 [1776]) famously declared in *The Wealth of Nations* that "the division of labour . . . is a necessary consequence of a certain propensity in human nature; the propensity to truck, barter and exchange one thing for another." Deepak Lal echoes this view in his defense of the contemporary relevance of classical liberalism: "archaeologists have . . . established that the instinct to 'truck and barter' . . . is of Stone Age vintage. It is also part of our basic human nature" (Lal 2008: 154). Even Amartya Sen adheres to this viewpoint, most clearly in his most popular book *Development as Freedom*, when he asserts that market exchange is as natural to humans as conversation:

The freedom to exchange words, or goods, or gifts does not need defensive justification in terms of their favorable but distant effects; they are part of the way human beings in society live and interact with each other (unless stopped by regulation or fiat). The contribution of the market mechanism to economic growth is ... important, but this comes only after the direct significance of the freedom to interchange – words, goods, gifts – has been acknowledged. (Sen 1999: 6)

Even if the consequences of market transactions are negative, Sen contends, "it can still be argued that there is some social loss involved in denying people the right to interact economically with each other" (1999: 26). This assumption apparently rules out any alternative to market economies as unnatural, and hence both undesirable and unviable.

The naturalness of markets and the focus on the sovereign individual exercising his liberty have led to the strong view that access to markets is both a basic right and essential for human progress. Deepak Lal claims that "what matters for development is not political but economic liberty" (Lal 2008: 233). Others claim that markets incline people to act in a moral manner (see the contributions to Zack 2008). Markets, it is claimed, are "important character development mechanisms," and "free exchange" is thus an important means for fostering and maintaining moral behavior (Casebeer 2008: 12). How is this benign effect achieved? The answer seems to be that market exchange requires, and hence fosters, honesty and cooperation among its participants. A similar line of argument leads one writer to conclude that the more developed the market economy, the more ethical it becomes (Sen 1999: 264). In contrast, Polanyi and his followers have sought to document that a market economy, far from being natural, is a recent creation, and that the competitive opportunism of market activity undermines moral values.

Third, the "invisible hand" metaphor, articulated by Adam Smith in 1776, plays a powerful role in justifying the operation of free markets. Smith's basic idea is that a multitude of individuals, each pursuing his/her own self-interest through market exchanges, inadvertently advance the common welfare by efficiently and optimally allocating resources and incomes. Therefore, economic liberals/neoliberals assume that *markets should be as self-regulating as possible.*[8]

Economic liberals/neoliberals, however, are more enthusiastic proponents of the "invisible hand" than even its progenitor. Important qualifications limit its applicability.[9] In the relevant passage in *The Wealth of Nations* (1863 [1776]), Smith notes that a profit-seeking business owner, "by pursuing his own interest ... frequently promotes that of the society more effectively than when he really intends to promote it." Smith uses the qualifier "frequently"; there are, in other words, circumstances in which self-interested market exchanges do not advance the common interest. In light of Smith's observations about the propensity of merchants to form cartels, we can assume that one of the conditions for the "invisible hand" to work is competitive markets. Conversely, in the many markets today that are dominated by oligopolies, the "invisible hand" does not apply, or applies only with limited effect. Also, Smith's concept arose from his benign religious convictions, and those today who do not share those convictions should be wary of wholeheartedly embracing the "invisible hand" (McKee 1992). For Smith, God's Divine Plan involved a natural harmony in which people would be guided, not by avarice, but by "sympathy" (empathy, in today's language) (McKee 1992; Folbre 2001; Finlayson et al. 2005; Sen 2009). If one could only remove external constraints (such as the detested mercantile state), a natural liberty would establish itself of its own accord. People would be governed by a natural sense of fairness. As Smith observed in *The Theory of Moral Sentiments* (2010 [1759]: viii):

However selfish soever man may be supposed, there are evidently some principles to his nature, which interest him in the fortunes of others, and render their happiness necessary to him, though he derives nothing from it except the pleasure of seeing it. Of this kind is pity or compassion, the emotion which we feel for the misery of others ... The greatest ruffian, the most hardened violator of the laws of society, is not altogether without it.

Thus, it is divinely inspired benevolence that moderates self-interest to serve the common welfare – an important nuance that rarely receives recognition by today's secular proponents of economic science.

Fourth, neoliberals assume (in accordance with the previous assumptions) that *the state should play a subsidiary role to markets*. If the market economy forms a separate system, obeying its own laws, then the state's role is only to facilitate market relations by maintaining order, protecting private property rights and contracts, ensuring the availability of the economic infrastructure, maintaining a sound currency and low price inflation, and (for some neoliberals) correcting market failures and constructing social safety nets. Beyond that, the state should not venture because politicians and bureaucrats are (a) likely to disrupt the market's logic and/or (b) engage in destructive rent-seeking. The latter is assumed to be an ever-present danger inasmuch as politicians, too, are rational actors oriented to self-interest.[10]

In the heyday of the Washington Consensus, market proponents held that state failures were more onerous than market failures. This judgment follows from the assumption that public officials have a propensity to use their power in a self-serving manner. Markets, on the other hand, are seen as impersonal mechanisms that, in the main, serve the public interest owing to the benign effect of the "invisible hand."

Finally, liberals and now neoliberals assume that *free markets and political freedom are mutually supportive*. In Milton Friedman's succinct words, "the kind of economic organization that provides economic freedom directly, namely competitive capitalism, also promotes political freedom because it separates economic power from political power and in this way enables the one to offset the other" (Friedman 1962: 9). Extending market relations and, concomitantly, limiting the state's economic role, in the liberal view, strengthens civil society as an autonomous sphere, thus fostering individual liberties and democratization.[11] As a US State Department official observed at a conference funded by his department in the early 1980s, "democracy and pluralism in Africa . . . will not thrive unless leaders seek truly open societies and free economies . . ." (Abrams 1986: 62–3). Similarly, three prominent liberal students of democracy concluded in 1988 that "the increasing movement away from statist economic policies and structures is among the most significant boosts to the democratic prospect in Africa" (Diamond, Linz and Lipset 1988: 27). Conversely, democracy is assumed to support a market economy. If the market's beneficial dispersal of economic power is indispensable to democracy, democracy's accountability and rule of law, in turn, provide markets with the needed predictability and security. Democracy and free enterprise, in this view, are conjoined.

The "governance" dimension of the Post-Washington Consensus focuses on the second relationship in contending that democratic institutions facilitate markets. By the late 1980s, statist and authoritarian developmental paths were discredited (except in East Asia) for their corruption and inefficiency. The antidote was democratization: a downsized liberal democratic state would foster market reform. Most of the assumptions of this benign relationship are present in a paper supported by the US Agency for International Development's Center for Democracy and Governance (Brinkerhoff 2000: 603):

Democratic governance creates a broad institutional framework that enables market-led economic growth to occur, for example, by creating a legal environment conducive to protection of property rights, enforcement of contracts, and predictability and stability of policies . . . [O]penness of policy dialogue, a free press, respect for human rights and the rule of law . . . strengthen the foundations on which sectoral reforms are built, and increase the likelihood of "virtuous circles" of improved, demand-driven performance and empowered citizens, and responsive and committed leadership.

Representative government, the rule of law, and a private realm of civil society are thus the institutional elements of an orderly, responsive and secure market economy.

These five underlying assumptions of the neoliberal development paradigm are abstract and broad in their implications, thus providing leeway for dissension among neoliberals in the identification of specific problems and their policy and institutional solutions. The neoliberal paradigm encompasses classical or orthodox liberals as well as proponents of social or inclusive neoliberalism. Despite this diversity, a significant distinction remains, as we shall see in Chapter 5, between the left wing of neoliberalism (social liberals) and the right wing of the Left (moderate social democrats).

The next section traces the evolution of the neoliberal development paradigm as it moved toward the center in response to challenges. I then defend the notion that a significant difference still obtains between the Post-Washington Consensus and the progressive paradigm.

Challenge and the adaptation of neoliberal doctrine

Whereas liberalism is a complex and variegated social philosophy that has evolved over more than three centuries, *neo*liberalism's roots are somewhat easier to summarize. The latter rose to prominence in the late 1970s and 1980s as a negation of Keynesian economics and state-directed development in general. In the Global South, both state-socialist and state-capitalist versions of import-substitution industrialization ran into crisis in this period. The reasons for the crisis were complex and varied, but one common explanation in the less-developed countries was the rent-seeking opportunities that highly protected national economies afforded an insider elite. Neoliberals, harking back to the classical liberal thinking of a century earlier, interpreted this tendency as validating its anti-state position. They were, moreover, well-placed to shape a paradigm shift as a result of Mexico's 1982 default on its external debt; this default ushered in a decade-long debt crisis in Latin America and Africa. The disappearance of private lending to Latin American and African governments compounded their economic crises. It also empowered the newly neoliberal IMF, the World Bank and bilateral donors to press their agenda via conditions attached to structural adjustment lending and technocratic advice to governments.

The Washington Consensus that held sway in the 1980s and most of the 1990s adhered closely to the first four neoliberal assumptions. The *goal* was to instigate sustained economic growth, on the assumption that such growth would overcome mass poverty and indebtedness. The neoliberal paradigm also suggested the *problems* that would need to be addressed in order to achieve the goal. Inefficiency and a lack of international competitiveness accounted for economic stagnation at the national level. These problems stemmed mainly from the market distortions introduced by excessive state intervention into economic life. In particular, ISI policies were a major source of these debilitating distortions.

Effective *policies* would remove these constraints on market forces. Eliminating fetters on economic rationality would allow markets to efficiently allocate resources and rewards, thus creating the conditions for economic recovery. Ten market-oriented measures became known as the Washington Consensus, a term coined by economist John Williamson (1990) to signify the common sense regarding development policy shared by Washington institutions such as the IMF, the World Bank, the Inter-American Development Bank and the US Treasury Department. Three measures sought to re-establish macroeconomic stability. Others redirected public expenditure*s* from subsidies and perhaps defense to education, health and infrastructure. To realize a country's comparative advantage and efficiently allocate resources, the Washington Consensus also advocated exchange-rate liberalization, trade liberalization, deregulation, and policies to attract direct foreign investment. The state, moreover, should shrink; privatization would allow the government to divest inefficient state-owned enterprises (SOEs). The state would, instead, refocus its attention on safeguarding property rights, rebuilding the rule of law, and providing high-quality public goods. This treatment would, it was expected, lead to the rapid recovery of moribund economies. Hence, the international financial institutions, along with bilateral donors such as the United States and Britain, provided loans to developing countries conditional upon their adoption of some or all of these remedies, and bilateral and multilateral trade agreements enshrined many of them.[12]

But, in practice, eliminating market distortions, privatizing SOEs and achieving low inflation did not suffice. By the late 1990s, even some members of the neoliberal establishment were expressing skepticism about the sufficiency of these remedies (Craig and Porter 2006: 2). The supplementation of the Washington Consensus began early, even before the East Asian financial collapse of 1997 that precipitated the Post-Washington Consensus.

Although 1997–8 marks a milestone, the backlash against neoliberalism had been building for several years. The collapse of the Thai baht in 1997 triggered a panicked outflow of footloose foreign capital not just from East Asia, but from other emerging markets as well. Russia in 1998 had to declare a moratorium on debt payments and devalue its currency. Brazil also experienced severe financial distress beginning in 1998. But this episode of extreme financial volatility, deriving from capital-account liberalization and the surfeit of speculative capital ("financialization"), was only the latest in a long string of financial disasters: Mexico in 1994,

Turkey in 1994, Argentina in 1995, Turkey in 2001, and Argentina's spectacular meltdown in 2001–2 (with severe repercussions in Uruguay). The disillusionment with free-market economics sprang not just from the volatility itself, but also from the dogged manner in which the IMF continued to prescribe the same liberalizing medicine that many believed was primarily responsible for the crises. This judgment was confirmed by a well-placed authority – Joseph Stiglitz, Chief Economist of the World Bank (1997–2001). Stiglitz claimed, in a caustic critique of the handling of the East Asian crisis, that the IMF and the US Treasury were forcing desperate governments to adopt market-fundamentalist policies that worsened conditions for ordinary people while benefiting transnational banks and corporations (Stiglitz 2002: ch. 4). Stiglitz (1998) was the first to refer to a Post-Washington Consensus.

Apart from the market volatility, the disappointing growth record of the Washington Consensus bred skepticism. On the one hand, the countries that had deviated from key free-market tenets, especially China, Vietnam, Korea and Taiwan, grew much faster in the 1980s and 1990s than those adhering more closely to them, such as Argentina, Ghana and Turkey before 2002. The fast-growth economies mixed selective liberalization and deregulation with heavy state direction – of cross-border capital flows, banking, the operations of national firms – and persistent, though diminishing, public ownership of productive assets and banks. On the other hand, many Latin American and African countries that adopted market-friendly reforms grew less rapidly in 1980–2000 than the heterodox countries or than they had during the preceding era of state-directed development (Easterly 2001; Milanovic 2003). And, in those countries undergoing neoliberal reform in the 1980s and 1990s that did achieve growth, the benefits accrued disproportionately to the wealthiest groups (as discussed in Chapter 3). Small farmers were particularly hard hit in countries whose governments yielded to demands to liberalize trade by abolishing marketing boards and restrictions on agricultural imports. Often, local farmers saw their livelihoods undermined by subsidized imports from the European Union, the United States and other Western producers (Stiglitz 2008; Mittal 2001). Consequently, such prominent mainstream economists as Paul Krugman and Jeffrey Sachs, in addition to Stiglitz, became vocal critics of neoliberal policies. Within the United Nations system, the more Keynesian-oriented or socially progressive agencies, such as the United Nations Conference on Trade and Development (UNCTAD) and the United Nations Development Programme (UNDP), continued to voice an alternative discourse to neoliberalism. As former World Bank economist Branco Milanovic aptly concluded in 2003, "something is clearly wrong."

Latin America experienced the most pronounced backlash against free-market prescriptions with the rise of a powerful counter-movement of societal protection. The region underwent a deep economic recession between 1998 and 2002, reinforcing the conviction that free-market remedies don't work (Luna 2007: 3; Panizza 2009: chaps. 6–9; Rovira Koltwasser 2010). In election campaigns, opposition parties of the Left contended that the Washington Consensus had failed and that it was time for a new direction. They were able to capitalize on popular resentment of the IMF, especially the belief that it is Western-dominated and unaccountable, intent on imposing US-style economic policies (Panizza 2009: 49). These tactics brought the democratic or quasi-democratic Left to power via elections in countries accounting for well over three-quarters of the region's population: Venezuela (since 1998), Chile (with the election of Socialist presidents in 2000 and 2006), Brazil (since 2003), Argentina (since 2003), Uruguay (since 2004), Bolivia (since 2005), Ecuador (since 2006), Nicaragua (since 2006), and Paraguay (2008–12). What unites these governments is not a common doctrine, but a commitment to tackling inequities, expanding popular participation (especially on the part of the indigenous population), and extending state power to achieve nationalist or social goals (Rénique 2005; Cameron 2009).[13]

In addition, revolts and mass protests against neoliberal reforms and privatizations occurred widely. They roiled Mexico (especially the Zapatistas [EZLN] in Chiapas since 1994), Venezuela (the Caracazo – heavy rioting – in 1989 and periodic clashes following the 1998 election of Hugo Chávez), Argentina (2001–2), Bolivia (periodically since 2003, with so-called water and gas "wars" over privatization, forcing the resignation of two presidents), Ecuador (in 2000, leading to the toppling of a government, and again in 2004–5 as erstwhile supporters forced a president to resign for betraying his radical promises), and Nicaragua (violent demonstrations in 2005 threatened to reduce the country to chaos). Further evidence of Latin American disillusionment includes the rejection of the US-backed Free Trade Area of the Americas in 2004, the establishment of regionally controlled economic and financial organizations to obviate recourse to Western-dominated institutions, and scattered reports of the alienated attitudes of people at the grassroots (e.g. Finn 2006).

In East and Southeast Asia, in contrast, most countries had belatedly and only reluctantly, embraced the free-market doctrine. Such rapidly industrializing countries as South Korea, Taiwan, China, Vietnam, Thailand and Malaysia had hewed more closely to the Japanese model of the developmental state. Only in the early and middle 1990s did some of these countries yield to pressures from the US government and the

World Trade Organization to undertake market liberalization, especially of financial and foreign exchange markets. The financial collapse of 1997–8 brought even such an economic powerhouse as South Korea to its knees. The subsequent misguided effort of the IMF to use its leverage with desperate governments to undertake yet further liberalization led to a backlash in the region (Stiglitz 2002: chap. 4). Massive demonstrations in South Korea, for instance, signaled a widespread anger (Lee, Wainwright and Kim 2010). Only those countries that had retained or reinstituted exchange controls – such as China and Malaysia – escaped largely unscathed in 1997, and again in 2008–2009.

In sub-Saharan Africa, the typically extreme dependence on Western trade, aid, loans and investment militated against outright rejection of neoliberal doctrine. As late as 1989, however, the Economic Commission for Africa and the Organization of African Unity (OAU), both with headquarters in Addis Ababa, adhered to a dependency analysis (see the ECA's *African Alternative Framework to Structural Adjustment Programmes for Socio-economic Recovery and Transformation*) that blamed the continent's economic woes primarily on external factors. Irrespective of these convictions, however, African governments from the early or middle 1980s had no choice but to seek loans and credits from the IMF, World Bank, and bilateral donors. However, liberalizing policies that reduced state powers rarely brought sustained development in Africa in the 1980s and 1990s. Resistance to these policies in this period took the form of half-hearted implementation, or even covert subversion, of conditions attached to loans. Such resistance, at the extreme, converted neoliberal policies into caricatures (Hibou 1999; Owusu 2003). African leaders officially endorsed neoliberal development doctrine only in 2001, with the promulgation of the OAU's New Partnership for Africa's Development (NEPAD). NEPAD deemed Africa's integration into the global economy to be beneficial, and agreed to foster the requisite improved governance through an Africa-based peer-review process. Although the more conciliatory language of the international financial institutions – poverty reduction, partnership, local ownership of reform programs – earned the rhetorical support of African leaders, it is not clear that much changed on the ground. Significantly, China's emergence since the early 2000s as a major trade partner, investor, aid donor and loan provider has sharply reduced the region's dependence on the international financial institutions and Western donors.

A major victim of the widespread disillusion with neoliberalism was the international financial institutions themselves, especially the IMF. The loan portfolios of the IMF and World Bank declined precipitously from 1999 as a result of two trends: a strongly performing global economy after

2002 that reduced demand for their loans, and an aversion to IMF conditions that induced developing countries to accelerate their repayment of loans and seek alternative sources for new loans. Between 1995 and 2005, World Bank lending to Middle-Income Developing Countries (MIDCs) fell by half, and even countries with massive loans, such as Argentina and Brazil, repaid their loans well ahead of schedule (World Bank 2007a). World Bank lending in 2008 was significantly lower than a decade earlier, even though concessionary lending via its International Development Association had grown (Guven 2012). The IMF's situation was even worse. One by one, the MIDCs accounting for the greater part of IMF lending repaid their loans and abstained from new ones. Outstanding loans declined tenfold in the period 2004 to 2007. By the latter year, the IMF's revenues fell short of even what it required to cover the organization's administrative costs (Guven 2012). Ironically, it was the Great Recession of 2008–9, instigated by the excess "animal spirits" of neoliberalism, which rejuvenated the two organizations by expanding their responsibilities and resources in dealing with the crisis.

Neoliberal reformers drew an important lesson from these extensive setbacks and criticisms. The lesson was not that the Washington Consensus was flawed and should be abandoned; rather, it was that market reforms must be undertaken as part of a much broader agenda of institutional and policy change. By 1999, this augmented agenda became known, misleadingly, as the *Post*-Washington Consensus.

Under President James Wolfensohn (1995–2005), the World Bank, as the foremost architect of mainstream development doctrine, shaped this augmented agenda into a holistic and multi-pronged strategy. This strategy includes the institutional programs that had already been added to the market-fundamentalist Washington Consensus before the East Asian crisis of 1997. Chief among them was institutional capacity-building in the sphere of governance, heralded by a landmark report on sub-Saharan Africa in 1989 (World Bank 1989). Overall, the Post-Washington Consensus is a major intellectual advance in locating economic development within a broad process of social change. It is, as well, a shrewd attempt to secure governmental and popular support for instituting a liberal market society (Fine 2001).[14]

The principal *goal* of the revamped neoliberal approach became poverty reduction or pro-poor growth, not economic growth *per se*. Proponents contended that the former focus on growth was inadequate because higher rates of growth did not necessarily translate into a significant reduction in poverty or an increase in the well-being of national populations (Wolfensohn 1999). Hence, it was better to concentrate directly on augmenting the well-being of people, especially those who were poor;

economic growth was just a means to achieving this goal. One immediate consequence was a renaming of World Bank and IMF loan programs – for instance, the IMF's Enhanced Structural Adjustment Facility became the Poverty Reduction and Growth Facility in 1999. Other goals, such as social and gender equity and sustainable development, came to the fore from time to time, but poverty reduction has generally taken pride of place in the Post-Washington Consensus.

The broader approach also expands the *problems* that need to be addressed in order to achieve poverty reduction and other goals. The Post-Washington Consensus implicitly acknowledges that freeing markets and shrinking states are insufficient to trigger economic growth (let alone pro-poor growth), but still holds that the best way forward lies in embracing markets and the private sector as the engine of development. However, to succeed, this embrace requires complementary programs, the number of which has progressively expanded. The "second-generation reforms," as they are often called, are heavily institutional in nature. Indeed, Dani Rodrik (2006: 980) suggests that, by the early 2000s, "institutional fundamentalism" had displaced the earlier market fundamentalism.

The central insight of the revamped approach is straightforward: markets can operate efficiently only within an appropriate institutional framework. This framework involves institutions that protect property and contracts, provide credit through a solvent and stable banking system, set the rules for fair competition, assure macroeconomic stability, peacefully resolve conflicts, supply reliable social and economic infrastructure, and prevent or correct egregious market failures (see, e.g., World Bank 1997; World Bank 2002). In addition, if the market system is to gain legitimacy, it must develop non-market institutions: safety nets to buffer the chronically poor and those who lose out in the move to flexible markets, accessible educational and perhaps health facilities, and political institutions through which people can hold their rulers to account. Civil society and social capital would also need to be nurtured, if the transformative goals of the Post-Washington Consensus were to be realized.[15] Capable and independent civil associations and social capital would buttress public accountability and participation and provide certain services that, hitherto, had been provided, if at all, by governmental agencies. Just to list the potential institutional and attitudinal issues – even without discussing the myriad of *policy and institutional innovations* that would be needed to resolve them – is to suggest the remarkably comprehensive and intrusive agenda that the Post-Washington Consensus represents.

Governance and specifically the state assumed more importance in the Post-Washington Consensus.[16] Although markets are still accorded primacy, states have an essential supporting role. Governments feature both as *subjects* – "partners" with the international financial institutions and donors in instituting efficient and legitimate market systems – and as the *objects* of capacity-building and institutional reorientation programs to mold capitalist states. As subjects, "market-friendly" states can, to the extent they possess the capacity, act as the "partner, catalyst and facilitator" of market-based development (World Bank 1997: 1–2). The World Bank's report *The State in a Changing World* offers a two-part strategy: to match a state's role to its capabilities in a particular country, and to upgrade that state's capabilities so that it can take on more complex tasks. If a state's capabilities are limited, it should leave more leeway to markets by concentrating on maintaining the macreconomic fundamentals. More capable states, in this technocratic view, would take on more difficult economic responsibilities. Yet, "capability is not destiny," in the sense that capacity building can work over the longer term (World Bank 1997: 7–11). Even the more effective states, however, should not yield to the temptation to "supplant market judgments with information and judgments generated in the public sector" or engage in "coordinating investment or picking winners" (World Bank 1997: 74, 75).

Additionally, the state has a major indirect role in forging a market-enhancing institutional framework. Karl Polanyi's pungent observation concerning the institutionalization of market systems in nineteenth-century Europe – that "laissez-faire was planned" (Polanyi 2001 [1944]) – applies equally to the Global South in the era of structural adjustment. States, in partnership with the international financial institutions, the World Trade Organization, bilateral donors or other external bodies, oversee (or acquiesce in) the market-enhancing restructuring and upgrading of their legal systems and an array of sectoral institutions, including the judiciary, the tax collection agency, the banking sector and financial regulations, oversight agencies, stock markets, think-tanks, collective-bargaining arrangements, education and social safety nets. The agenda is vast.

But it is one thing to acknowledge the need for effective governance and sectoral institutions; it is quite another to be able to create them. Programs usually fail when the political and bureaucratic elites sabotage accountability reforms, or when donors try to transfer unsuitable foreign institutional models, or when ethnic, religious or regional rivalries block efforts to enhance state effectiveness. More than two decades of capacity-building programs have brought home how difficult it is to create effective institutions (Rodrik 2006).

The period 2003–8, an era of sustained growth, seemed to vindicate the Post-Washington Consensus. However, an old-fashioned commodity boom, resulting from the insatiable demand for raw materials on the part of China and India, largely propelled this growth. Latin America's growth in the period 2002–8 reached an average of 3.5 percent, during an era of leftist governments in the region (Pearce 2009: 419). Africa experienced a commodity-based boom in 2003–8, with an average annual growth rate of 6 percent and with foreign investment and exports increasing fourfold during this period (Commission for Africa 2005: 3). This boom ended, but only temporarily, during the global financial crisis, a catastrophe that led many to question the future of neoliberal developmentalism.

The rise of inclusive neoliberalism

Even before 2008, the rise of China (and the relative decline of the United States) had the effect of loosening the ties binding governments to the Post-Washington Consensus. China's three decades of high growth – more than 10 percent per annum growth in per capita terms since 1980 – was achieved under the auspices of a directive and authoritarian one-party state, a trajectory that diverged from the neoliberal model. In 2010, China's displacement of Japan as the second-largest economy further underscored that country's economic prowess. Its massive commercial and concessional loans and grants to developing countries augmented its influence abroad, especially in Africa, the South Pacific and Latin America. Not only did China lend more money to these countries than the World Bank in 2008–10 ($US110 billion), but it was willing to fund each partner's own priorities and imposed few conditions (Gallagher 2011). Governments in Africa and Latin America thus gained greater independence in economic policy-making.

In 2004, some dissident voices in the Global South began to talk of a vaguely delineated "Beijing Consensus" as an alternative to the Post-Washington Consensus (Colley 2009). China's top-down "model" appealed to governments that favored not only greater state direction of their economies, but also an escape from the democratic governance requirements of the Post-Washington Consensus. But Beijing has not shown any enthusiasm for this so-called consensus. For one thing, it denies that it has a model that can be copied (de Haan 2010). China's development path was not mapped out in a grand plan. Instead, Deng Xiaoping, who launched China's economic reforms, spoke of "crossing the river by feeling the stones." Although the state has played a directive role in promoting certain economic sectors, it has done so by pragmatically adjusting to changing realities. Moreover, China's special conditions – its large size, the proximity of its industries to Hong Kong, its large diaspora of willing investors, and its relatively strong state and weak civil society – mean that China's path is unlikely to be widely replicated (Colley 2009).

Besides, it is doubtful that China is interested in breaking with the Post-Washington Consensus. Scholars of China note the extent to which the government has *adhered* to neoliberal tenets – including opening up its economy, selective privatization and selective liberalization (de Haan 2010). Neoliberalism provided a way for the Chinese leadership to deal with the crisis of state socialism in the late 1970s and 1980s. Centrally planned industrialization had reached its limits as factors of production lay idle without an internal market to spur growth. Although China today is not an exemplar of neoliberalism, it is undergoing a measured process of "neoliberalization" in which the state creates the conditions for a market economy (Fulong Wu 2008: 1,094–6). The rise of China does not portend the demise of neoliberalism.

Nevertheless, China's rise, in conjunction with the reduced influence of the international financial institutions, has led to a greater humility and openness to new approaches among the purveyors of neoliberal doctrine. As World Bank Vice-President Gobind Nankari observes in a 2005 report (World Bank 2005a: xiii) "there is no unique universal set of rules . . . We need to get away from formulae." The World Bank's prestigious "Growth Report" (World Bank 2008), written under the auspices of a stellar commission of experts, reinforces the message that no universal formula exists for promoting pro-poor growth, that context matters. The report thus rejected the "one-size-fits-all" approach to reform under the Washington Consensus and early Post-Washington Consensus, noting that the list of necessary reforms had grown steadily longer since the 1980s. Instead, economists should diagnose in each particular country the most significant constraints and search pragmatically for ways to alleviate them. The report is also more positive regarding a proactive role for the state – even to the point of accepting policies of industrial promotion (if they don't go on too long). The elevation of a Chinese national, Justin Yifu Lin, to the post of World Bank Chief Economist in 2008 was another indication of a shift in focus, especially since Lin stood solidly behind the Growth Report and a "new" structuralist economics according a strong role for the state in economic life (Lin and Monga 2010: 9, 15; Lin 2012). The Post-Washington Consensus had evolved toward a more pragmatic approach just as the Great Recession threatened its very foundations.

This global crisis led many authorities to question whether the dominant development paradigm could survive (McCulloch and Sumner 2009; Hugon 2010; Gore and Kozul-Wright 2011). Originating in the world's largest economies, the Great Recession wrought extensive, worldwide economic damage in 2009. The tribulations of the United States and the European Union are well known; unemployment, budget deficits and national debts exploded. China and India, however, experienced only a minor decline in their economic growth. Elsewhere in the Global South, the crisis led to major economic problems as commodity prices fell, foreign investment and remittances plummeted, stock markets collapsed and exchange rates oscillated. But most developing countries experienced a recovery in 2010 or 2011, until 2013 at least, spurred by renewed demand in China and India for primary commodities. The chief longer-term victims, for the first time since the rise of the Washington Consensus, were found in the Global North.

Whereas the Great Depression of the 1930s led to major ideological and policy shifts away from liberalism, the latest global crisis has not had the same effect. The Post-Washington Consensus remains largely intact, though market fundamentalism is discredited outside North America and Britain. A study of IMF and World Bank lending since the onset of the Great Recession notes a marked increase in loan disbursements *but no fundamental shift in priorities*. The policy and institutional reforms supported by the international financial institutions have continued to fall within the parameters of the Post-Washington Consensus, except for the IMF's acceptance of short-term fiscal and monetary stimulus and exchange controls as an emergency measure, and the World Bank's soaring support for "green" projects (Guven 2012; Van Waeyenberge and McKinley 2013). Indeed, the crisis augmented the IMF's influence on economic policy by handing that agency the task of disbursing emergency loans. It remains, by and large, the guardian of orthodox macroeconomic policy.

Yet some significant changes have occurred, portents of a multi-polar world. The G20 replaced the G7/8 in November 2008, acknowledging the rising economic clout of China, India, Brazil and South Africa. These countries have also demanded an enhanced presence in the executive bodies of the IMF, the World Bank and the United Nations. The Great Recession also accelerated several heterodox trends at the national level (McCulloch and Sumner 2009: 102–7; Birdsall and Fukuyama 2011: 46–50). One is a growing role for the state in economic development; deregulation is widely identified as the prime cause of the 2008 financial crisis in the US. Also, more extensive regulation of the financial sector and cross-border capital flows is now common. Even the IMF, as noted, has moved away from its campaign to promote capital-market liberalization under all circumstances. At its annual meeting in 2011, it endorsed the use of capital controls, though only as a last resort. Governments in various countries have also boldly moved toward orchestrating industrial strategies, intensifying a pre-existing trend.

Another trend is the buttressing of social protection, though usually in a way that is not inconsistent with the Post-Washington Consensus. China has set about forging a modern pension system. Latin American governments continued to consolidate their social programs, introduced since the region's leftward move, to reduce poverty and inequality. Of particular note is the conditional cash transfer schemes involving poor families successfully introduced in several countries (Birdsall and Fukuyama 2011: 49). In general, the Great Recession bred further skepticism of neoliberal remedies, yet it did not bury the now-chastened Post-Washington Consensus.

Why did the crisis not sweep away the neoliberal paradigm? For one thing, the rising powers of the Global South – China, India and Brazil – were more concerned to bolster their own international influence than transform the Post-Washington Consensus. For another, the consensus that poor governance and weak regulation caused the crisis seemed to vindicate the Post-Washington Consensus's focus on institutional strengthening and fiscal and monetary stability (Guven 2012). The key question remained unchanged: how to build effective state structures capable of correcting market failures? In addition, an alternative leftist paradigm was still inchoate in 2008. Leftist opinion-leaders generally agreed on what they were *against*, but differed on what should be done. And the setbacks of socialism in the twentieth century continued to limit its appeal.

Furthermore, the World Bank and other neoliberal think-tanks have nimbly defanged their critics by adopting and domesticating their attractive concepts. The line between the neoliberal and progressive paradigms has blurred as the World Bank appropriated the vocabulary of the Left. Some analysts have used the term "inclusive neoliberalism" or "social liberalism" to characterize the new rhetoric of bringing the poor and socially excluded into the mainstream (Craig and Porter 2006: 12; Ruckett 2010). But some common vocabulary obscures the divergent assumptions of what remain distinct development paradigms. Although this rhetorical shift in the Post-Washington Consensus did bring some concrete benefits to the poor,[17] it also represented an effort to reconstruct neoliberal hegemony.

The acme of inclusiveness, the World Bank's *World Development Report 2006: Equity and Development*, inadvertently acknowledges the clash of paradigms by inconsistently including elements of both within a single report. The report takes equal freedom as the goal: "individuals should have equal opportunities to pursue a life of their choosing and be spared from extreme deprivation in outcomes" (World Bank 2006: 2). However, "economic institutions and social arrangements . . . systematically favor the interests of those with more influence" in many countries (World

Bank 2006: 2). Where the wealthy dominate power structures, the report suggests, redistribution of assets, access to services and/or political power may be required. Otherwise, "[i]nequality traps can ... be rather stable, tending to persist over generations" (World Bank 2006: 10). But the inequality traps are left largely unaddressed. Instead of an assertion of the primacy of politics and the forging of a political challenge to the structures buttressing inequality, a faith in market solutions comes to the fore. The report advocates mainly uncontroversial measures: getting markets to function better, accessible and reasonably high-quality education, accessible health services, and targeted safety nets for the working poor and the vulnerable (World Bank 2006: 12). The radical diagnosis is not accompanied by radical remedies.

The process of co-opting radical terms, but retooling them to suit a depoliticized and technocratic agenda, has been a continuing feature of the Post-Washington Consensus. The World Bank has played a key role in this process.

Consider "poverty." In the Left's approach, poverty is a highly political concept. Material deprivation is the outcome of power relations – among or between classes, genders, castes or ethnic/racial groups – that perpetuate injustice, in the form of social exclusion and/or marked inequalities. A relational approach thus emphasizes the ability of certain groups to exploit others. The solution to poverty thus chiefly lies in reshaping unequal power relations. Consequently, empowerment of the poor through the creation of encompassing and independent organizations is essential. Overcoming poverty and inequality thus involves organization (trade unions, peasant associations, cooperatives, parties), appeals to solidarity, and political struggle.

But "poverty reduction" in the neoliberal sense denotes only a measurable decrease in the proportion of a national population earning incomes falling below a certain standard. It is a technical, apolitical issue divorced from the politically charged notions of social injustice and systemically based inequality. The solution to the poverty problem lies partly in targeting the "poor" in order for government to provide impoverished households and individuals with the resources they need to flourish (skills, education, credit, technology, nutrition). More generally, economic growth is needed, especially growth that benefits the poor. Growth, in turn, is seen as requiring market-oriented policy change, especially policies that allow the poor to participate effectively in market relations. Secondarily, safety nets targeted to the poor and conditional cash transfers will reduce poverty. Non-governmental organizations can help in providing services to the poor, but individual poor people are ultimately responsible for their own development. They must seize the new opportunities. *Divergent conceptions of poverty and its reduction/elimination reflect divergent paradigmatic assumptions.*

The story of the World Bank's controversial *World Development Report 2000/2001: Attacking Poverty* (2001) provides another illustration of paradigmatic conflict and the Bank's role in paradigm maintenance. This report, like the later one on equity, incoherently incorporates assumptions from both the neoliberal and the leftist paradigms in how to attack poverty.[18] The director of the team that wrote the first two drafts, the economist Ravi Kanbur, resigned from the World Bank when management, under pressure from the US Treasury, objected to the report's heavy emphasis on empowerment and social provision.[19] The report was hastily amended to ensure that open markets and economic growth feature centrally in the summary sections of chapters (Wade 2001: 1,439). Consequently, the published report is inconsistent in combining the neoliberals' faith in market-based solutions with the progressive view that empowerment is key to reducing poverty. It is hard to reconcile neoclassical market doctrine with the report's endorsement of (a) the importance of collective and not simply individual action, (b) the need for redistribution in many cases because the initial distribution of assets fosters inequality and poverty, and (c) the view that market forces may lead to long-term problems for the poor. This incoherence reflects a fundamental disagreement as to which road to follow.

Another example of clashing assumptions concerns "participation," a word that both neoliberals and progressives employ. For the latter, the word connotes political activism and the overthrow of old hierarchies. Participatory democracy involves the radical project of people participating directly in public decision-making, as for example in Participatory Budgeting (as originally championed by Brazil's Workers Party, most famously in Porto Alegre). But the word was appropriated and redefined in neoliberal discourse. In effect, the activist connotation was displaced by the idea of NGOs or communities managing development projects and providing services for the poor and of individuals playing a role in the running of such projects (Dagnino 2008: 61). Alternatively, "civil society" (usually civil society organizations/NGOs) "participate" in shaping anti-poverty programs through Poverty Reduction Strategy Papers (PRSPs), which are required in countries receiving concessional loans or debt relief. In reality, however, PRSPs from diverse countries read quite similarly, not diverging far from World Bank terminology (Cornwall and Brock 2005: 1,052). Again, neoliberal discourse depoliticized an originally highly political term.

Such terms as "democracy," "civil society" and "citizenship" could be deconstructed in the same manner to reveal divergent usages. The struggle over the meaning of words, I suggest, reflects contrasting development paradigms.

The distinctive Left vision

Bjorn Hettne (1994: 61–2) argues that development alternatives emerge as the "counterpoint" to the mainstream development strategy. They offer credible solutions to the contradictions and shortcomings of the conventional model in order to mobilize the discontent of those disadvantaged by it. Jan Nederveen Pieterse (1998) is skeptical, claiming that Hettne assumes that the mainstream model is more homogeneous and consistent than it actually is. How, he asks, can there be a counterpoint to a doctrine that is dynamic, diverse, complex and adaptable? Nevertheless, the dialectical movement does capture the evolution of ideas at a general level. The Left's "state-fundamentalist" strategies of the post-1945 era – various state socialisms and state capitalisms emphasizing import-substitution industrialization – fell into crisis in the 1970s and 1980s. Rejuvenated market-oriented neoliberal strategies superseded them, but later ran into trouble. After an extended period of rethinking, a new Left emerged in the 2000s with its egalitarian goals and state orientation intact, but with a new appreciation of the role of markets and democracy and a distrust of centralized planning. The policy bundles are diverse and shifting; however, *the counterpoint refers to paradigmatic assumptions, not to particular policies.*

Although the Left globally is even more fractious than the neoliberals, its adherents share common values and assumptions that constitute what we might call a development paradigm. This section merely sketches the shared values, such as equality (or better, equal freedom), the primacy of politics, solidarity, strong democracy, and shared prosperity.[20] These values and assumptions surface from time to time in the later chapters that focus on the diverse strategies within the democratic Left.

The global Left today shares, together with social liberals, the goal of "positive" or equal freedom. "Negative" freedom, as mentioned in Chapter 1, is the focus of classical liberalism. Individuals, to live lives of their own choosing, must be free of external constraints, especially state coercion, except in relation to any of their actions that limit the freedom of others. Government, therefore, has a strictly delimited role. In contrast, equal freedom involves not just the absence of external constraints, but also the equal opportunity of all persons to enjoy freedom, that is, to choose and live a meaningful life. A commitment to equal freedom thus involves broadening the control of all citizens over the direction of their lives: by eliminating discriminatory barriers that exclude certain groups (women, castes, lower classes, ethnic or religious minorities) from developing and exercising their capabilities; by ensuring the access of all citizens to the services, social protections and resources that provide everyone with the opportunity to develop their capabilities; and by instituting democratic and legal processes that allow individuals and groups to avoid domination. This commitment is consistent with the first article of the Universal Declaration of Human Rights, which states that "all human beings are born free and equal in dignity and rights." But where people are born to penury, illiteracy, poor health or malnutrition, social exclusion or the arbitrary power of others, they cannot lead lives of dignity and value. Equal freedom thus requires both the opportunity to enhance one's capabilities and the solidarity and instituted processes to protect oneself against domination.

That the Left has long subscribed to personal freedom as a prime value cannot be doubted, despite the oppressive record of state socialism in the past. This emancipatory message is scattered throughout Marx's writings, where the main criterion of a future socialist society is freedom of individuals (see, for precise references, Chattopadhyay 2010). In *The Communist Manifesto*, Marx and Engels succinctly enunciated the ideal of a society in which the freedom of each individual is the condition for the freedom of all. Engels later described socialism as an attempt "to organize society in such a way that every member of it can develop and use all his capabilities and powers in complete freedom and wisdom without thereby infringing the basic conditions of this society" (quoted in Lebowitz 2010: 13). Scholars of the Left have consistently noted the primacy of this value.[21]

Nor is it a value restricted to progressive in the Global North. This ideal is also reflected, for instance, in Venezuela's Bolivarian Constitution of 1999 (amended in 2009), written under the auspices of President Hugo Chávez and adopted by referendum. Article 20 states that "everyone has the right to the free development of his or her own personality, subject only to the limitations deriving from the rights of others and public and social order," while Article 62 declares that participation by citizens "in forming, carrying out and controlling the management of public affairs is a necessary way . . . to ensure their complete development, both individual and collective." Also, the progressive and Global South-oriented UNDP's *Human Development Reports*, founded in 1990 under the leadership of Dr Mahbub ul Haq of Pakistan, have championed what I term equal freedom. The *Human Development Report* of 2000, for instance, provides this simple yet compelling formulation:

[All individuals should enjoy] the basic freedoms of being able to meet bodily requirements, such as the ability to avoid starvation and undernourishment, to escape preventable morbidity or premature mortality. They [basic freedoms] also include the enabling opportunities given by schooling ... or the liberty and economic means to move freely and to choose one's abode. There are also important "social" freedoms, such as the capability to participate in the life of the community, to join in public discussion, to participate in political decision-making and even the elementary ability "to appear in public without shame."

The issue, of course, is how this vision is to be attained.

Essentially, the argument of the Left is that it, rather than the social liberals, adopts the cooperative means capable of realizing the radical end of equal freedom. What is at issue is not the sincerity of social liberals but the plausibility of their program. One of the most eloquent social liberals to focus on the developing world is Amartya Sen. Sen impressively presents his viewpoint in his influential *Development as Freedom* (1999), as well as in his more recent books (for example, Sen 2009: 228, 231–2). Sen has also had a formative influence on the *Human Development Reports*, which have countered the economistic bias of neoliberal development doctrine by introducing the notion of *human* development. But do social liberals offer the means to attain such a worthy goal in societies suffering from mass poverty, inequality and domination? Judging by *Development as Freedom*, to take one well-argued case, we are to suppose that liberal democracy, a limited state role recognizing the primacy of markets, and a focus on individual choice and action are a sufficient basis for moving toward a more just society.[22] Sadly, however, we know from long experience that liberal democracy, liberal capitalism and social safety nets are compatible with the perpetuation of mass poverty and inequality.

The goal of equalizing opportunities to enjoy freedom, if taken seriously, entails a truly radical project. It involves challenging elites at various levels because the goal requires a redistribution of power and resources to the poor and socially excluded. This end rarely can be won without solidarity and struggle, though, depending on circumstances, this struggle may be non-violent. Whereas the Left's assumptions regarding the primacy of participatory politics and the centrality of collective action are consonant with the goal, the social-liberal approach falls short.

The *primacy of politics* is thus the second assumption of a progressive development paradigm (see, for an extensive treatment, Berman 2006). Power is not exogenous to the market system, as neoclassical theory supposes, but endogenous. Karl Polanyi shows that the rise and spread of markets is not a natural and spontaneous process, as liberals suppose. Instead, states "institute" markets by – forcefully always and forcibly if necessary – reconstituting labor, land and money as commodities. What was true of capitalist development in Polanyi's European cases (misleadingly characterized as *laissez-faire*) remains true in the rise of market systems today in the formerly Communist and state-directed economies. Propelled by the IMF, the World Bank, regional development banks and bilateral aid donors, structural adjustment and poverty reduction programs require recipient governments to carry through domestic market liberalization, privatization, the opening up of national economies, and institutional capacity-building. Paradoxically, governments play a central role even in remaking economy and society in the free-market image.

Politics is primary not only in the unacknowledged instituting of market systems but also in the struggle for alternatives to market society. A Left alternative, in principle, involves democratically derived political forces guiding economic processes in the common good. This principle holds true for both socialists and social democrats. In liberal-democratic as well as authoritarian regimes, one commonly finds a mutually reinforcing relationship between wealth and power. The rich employ their wealth to gain political influence, and their political influence to gain further wealth.[23] The only way to combat this relationship is through collective organization and political action.

As Polanyi observes in his study of the initial great transformation (see Chapter 1), the "movement" toward a market economy inevitably incurs ecological and social damage, thus instigating a "counter-movement" of societal protection. The Left is initially part of the counter-movement. The movement and the counter-movement struggle for control of the national government in order to advance their divergent agendas. In the nineteenth and most of the twentieth centuries, counter-movements sought to counteract the deleterious effects of market forces through national and local political action, invoking reformist or revolutionary alternatives. The primacy of politics unavoidably places heavy responsibilities on the state, which explains why, in Chapter 4, I contend that effective states are critical to the success of leftist alternatives.

The global level figures more centrally in similar struggles today than a century ago. According to former World Bank Chief Economist and social liberal Joseph Stiglitz, global power structures have been biased in favor of the Global North:

> The international institutions . . . entrusted with writing the rules of the game and managing the global economy reflect the interests of the advanced industrial countries – or, more particularly, special interests within those countries . . . The end of the Cold War gave the United States . . . the opportunity to reshape the global system based on its own self-interest and that of its multinational corporations. Regrettably . . . it chose [this] course. (Stiglitz 2007: 276–7)

Global governance, global financial movements and globally negotiated economic rules impinge more deeply on domestic policy domains than ever before. But neoliberal globalization – especially the revolutions in information and telecommunications technologies – facilitates not only transnational production chains, international trade and worldwide financial markets, but also the organization and coordination of transnational counter-movements (especially via the internet). In short, both global and national market economies are inherently political in their provenance, evolution and pathways of transformation, and the Left recognizes this reality.

Solidarity, a third shared meta-norm, is as central to the Left as individualism is to the (neo)liberals. In the liberal/neoliberal tradition, individualism is both a normative and a methodological category. Normatively, the tradition assigns priority to individual liberties, including the right to participate in market exchange. Methodologically, the focus of neoclassical thinking is the individual decision maker, who with certain information and in a situation of scarcity, chooses the option that will maximize his/her utility. Solidarity for the Left is equally a normative and methodological category. It serves both as an end (the warmth of community) and an important means to other ends that cannot be won by individuals acting alone.

As a meta-norm, solidarity encompasses other, more specific norms – cooperation, trust and mutuality – that rein in individual opportunism and build community. Third World socialists, together with some of their Western and Eastern counterparts, have portrayed socialism as a "coming home" – a return to community. African socialism, for example, assumed that African societies before the colonial era were characterized by a significant degree of mutuality and equality.[24] Socialism, for Tanzania's Julius Nyerere and other African socialists, was the extension of mutuality beyond the kinship group to the nation as a whole. "Modern African socialism can draw from its traditional heritage the recognition of 'society' as an extension of the basic family unit" (Nyerere 1968: 12). Kwame Nkrumah of Ghana held a similar view before his overthrow in 1966 drove him toward a more conventional Marxist interpretation. Communalism, Nkrumah contended, is "the social-political ancestor of socialism" (Nkrumah 1970: 73). *Ubuntu* in Southern Africa today, though not specifically a socialist doctrine, is a philosophy that similarly draws on the (imagined) solidarity, cooperation and mutuality of village life to inspire a common identity and a basis for cooperation in the fragmented and anonymous urban areas (Van Binsberger 2001). The need for cooperation to overcome the social dislocations of the current era focuses attention on the possibilities of community solidarity (Andreasson 2010: 84–8).

Solidarity, the building of horizontal bonds among people who share common interests, also features as a major element of the Left's methodology. Progressives commonly think in terms of class solidarity, but not exclusively. Where caste, racial or ethnic categories overlap with class, progressives incorporate these existing solidarities into their struggles. Also, Left populists and moderate social democrats strive to cement trans-class solidarity: the "people" versus the oligarchy (Left populists), class alliances and class struggle (radical social democrats), or broad class compromises (moderate social democrats). Even community solidarity at the level of peasant villages or heterogeneous, poor city neighborhoods or shanty towns is valued as a potential resource. Equal freedom and solidarity are indeed mutually supportive. Organizational unity and cooperation in political struggle are key to winning equal freedom; conversely, positive freedom is central to forging a decent community life based on mutual respect.

But it is a dangerous mistake to regard individualism and solidarity as polar opposites. Normatively, individualism and solidarity are linked, as Marx understood when he noted that the free development of each is the condition for the free development of all. Also, group cooperation and individual competition for self-advancement are equally "natural" to human character. On the one hand, experimental research in behavioral economics, psychology and neuroscience suggest that people have a propensity to cooperate for the common good.[25] Evolutionary biology also supports the proposition that cooperation is a central motivation of human behavior. People are predisposed to cooperate because natural selection for human beings has operated at the group rather than the individual level. A large body of contemporary research supports the notion that a capacity to cooperate and feel empathy has given human groups a comparative evolutionary advantage (Faber, Pedersen and Schiller 2002: 326–8; Field 2004; Nowak and Highfield 2011; Brooks 2011). Natural selection favored groups that were cohesive and able to act collectively to achieve their goals. On the other hand, within groups, individuals have always competed with others for precedence. To acknowledge the biological basis of solidarity is thus not to deny the equal "naturalness" of individual competition and self-interest. *Dominant institutions shape what propensity is foremost.*

Deepening democracy is a fourth shared value of the Left today. The descent of Communism and state socialism into a caricature of socialism underlined the centrality of democracy to a progressive project. Democracy is an important means to achieving equal freedom, as well as an end in itself – a way of experiencing freedom. Liberal democracy, with its stress both on the procedures for mounting periodic elections that are free and fair and on protecting civil and political rights, is regarded as inadequate. Democracy should involve a greater degree of participation by people concerning the decisions that affect their lives, according to the Left. Disagreement arises on the scope of democratic decision-making: should it be limited to political life or include economic institutions as well?

Liberals/neoliberals do not have a monopoly on democracy. Indeed, there are reasons to doubt the benign relationship in the Global South between democracy and free enterprise as depicted by neoliberals. Fernando Henrique Cardoso (1986: 150) poses an important question: "Why . . . should we expect the private sector to be the harbinger of the good news of democratic society?" In Brazil, he argues, the relatively large and independent business class acceded to various forms of authoritarianism in the twentieth century, tepidly and conditionally opposing authoritarian rule only in the late 1970s. Big business has acquiesced in, or even supported, highly repressive authoritarian regimes, as in the generals' Argentina and General Pinochet's Chile. Furthermore, where liberal democracy has established itself in developing capitalist societies, it has often coexisted with vast poverty and inequality. The poor and near-poor classes tend not to be organized in their own autonomous movements, as earlier suggested, and are thus comparatively powerless. Modern capitalism tends to concentrate wealth, and hence power, rather than disperse it – contrary to much liberal theory.

As a means to equal freedom, democracy should be structured so as to prevent domination, according to the logic of the Left (Gould 1988: 78; Shapiro 2010: 15). Domination exists when one group or agency can arbitrarily limit or deny the opportunity of others to enjoy equal freedom. Domination often takes a political form, such as restrictions on civil and political rights and threats to the personal security of those who assert their rights. It may also involve the capacity to deny recalcitrant individuals the means to earn a family livelihood and to exclude or discriminate against stigmatized or marginalized groups. The case for extending democracy beyond the political sphere rests on the recognition that domination extends into the economic and social realms.

If countering domination is the pre-eminent instrumental grounds for deepening democracy, the degree of deepening depends on political realities in a particular country. Democratic institutional change varies widely among cases (as chapters 5 and 6 show). At a minimum, it involves complementing liberal democracy's constricted procedural view of democracy with institutions to decentralize power, foster participatory or consultative decision-making mechanisms, or introduce recall measures and referendums. People then obtain some direct control over the decisions affecting their everyday lives. Beyond that, democratic deepening entails extending democracy beyond the political sphere, into the social and economic realm. Worker-controlled enterprises and self-governed farmers' cooperatives are two examples in the economic sphere. The redistribution of social protections in the form of universal programs and the provision of accessible and high-quality public education, health services and housing advances a notion of democracy as a form of egalitarian society. Equal freedom and expansive notions of democracy are thus mutually reinforcing.

Some socialists have also emphasized the educative function of participating in democratic politics. Jean Jaurès (1859–1914), an early leader of France's Socialist Party, saw democratic practice as not only a framework within which to build a socialist movement but also an "apprenticeship" in living in a cooperative community (Kurtz 2013: 77–83). Jaurès believed that no single formula existed to guide socialists toward ending poverty, building community and securing peace. Instead, people would learn how to achieve these goals through democratic participation. A civic consciousness would emerge to support a socialist society. This idea continues to resonate on the Left in the Global South, as we shall see. For instance, the original conception of participatory budgeting was based precisely on this idea.

Finally, *economic prosperity* is obviously a valued goal in developing countries for the Left among others. For several decades, mainstream economists equated "development" with rapid economic growth. But high and rising inequality means that economic growth disproportionately benefits the rich and buttresses their domination of the poorer majority. Hence, on the Left (and indeed also in the Post-Washington Consensus), growth is now understood only as a necessary but not a sufficient condition of social advancement. Greater equality in income distribution is also needed. In the promotion of growth, the Left in the Global South has, for the most part, learned to live with markets. But socialists and social democrats implicitly assert the primacy of politics to ensure that markets remain useful servants, not overbearing masters. Needless to say, the productivist orientation of governments of the Left does not auger well for their combating climate change, a theme I take up in Chapter 7.

Before concluding this discussion, I should respond to a potential objection. How relevant is this vision – emphasizing in particular the equal freedom of all individuals – to the Global South, especially to Africa and East and South Asia where communal attachments remain strong?[26] It is still common in these regions for persons to define themselves in relation to primary communities: family, religious tradition, village, clan or ethnic group. For such people, exemplary fulfilment of their social obligations brings social esteem. Hence, justice or freedom – viewed as the equal opportunity of persons to realize their potential and shape their lives – may appear overly individualistic (Bell 2009: 9). Should progressive movements in such circumstances, then, aim only to revive social responsibility and to broaden a sense of community, not to maximize the equal freedom of persons?

In spite of communal attachments, the opportunity of persons to enjoy freedom remains crucial. *Communal ties may oppress as well as fortify people.* Traditional communities often enforce problematical norms and institutions, such as the subordination of women, lower castes and peasants, gender-based violence, female genital mutilation, slavery and autocracy. Where such problematical institutions hold sway, women, lower-caste individuals, slaves or commoners have a basic interest in questioning these features and, if need be, organizing to change them. It is unjust to foreclose the opportunity for persons to challenge these institutions and choose a different life than that ordained by prescriptive norms. In addition, communitarian values – "African socialism," "Asian values" – have provided a convenient pretext for some authoritarian leaders to suppress political and civil liberties in the name of preserving social harmony and collective rights (Hellsten 2004: 71–2). A pragmatic case can thus be made for assigning high priority to the equal freedom of individuals, even if one acknowledges the importance of social responsibility and communal relations.

Extending opportunities to enjoy freedom to the poor or lower classes is the essence of the Left's program. It requires reducing the unearned social advantages that shape the superior life chances of a minority. This project challenges not only national and local elites – insofar as it requires a redistribution of resources to groups that have hitherto been poor, marginalized and powerless – but also the global neoliberal order – insofar as the movement from below often questions property rights and foreign investments. In this world of conflicting interests, rights are more often seized than benignly granted by altruistic elites. Yet the liberal focus on individual choice and action deflects attention from the group dynamics of social change; the political structures that shape the distribution of resources and individual capabilities lie beyond the liberal's purview. In reality, disadvantaged groups and classes generally have their claims recognized only when they create encompassing political movements to challenge the existing dispensation. Abstracting equal freedom from power relations is fatal because, unfortunately, fairness does not rule the world.

Conclusion

I have suggested that we can discern the outlines of a new-Left development paradigm that is both distinct from the neoliberal paradigm and cognizant of the pitfalls of the Left in the twentieth century. The neoliberal development paradigm, under pressure from limited success in the 1980s and 1990s, socioeconomic crises and widespread criticism, has evolved from a market-fundamentalist Washington Consensus into a broader and more inclusive Post-Washington Consensus. Oriented primarily to poverty reduction rather than economic growth, the latter has moderated but not disowned the Washington Consensus. It recognizes that markets, to work properly, must be embedded in a nexus of facilitative institutions and policies, that such institutions must be constructed if they don't exist, that market-based development requires targeted social programs to build its legitimacy, and that the frustrating complexity of "development" demands that experts manifest humility and foster "partnerships" with recipient governments (and "civil society" too). In its evolution, the Post-Washington Consensus has defensively appropriated many popular concepts of the Left.

Yet the Left retains a distinctive development paradigm. The Post-Washington Consensus is concerned with incremental human betterment as achieved primarily through technically proficient agents who nurture well-functioning markets, responsible liberal-democratic states and safety nets. In contrast, the Left understands the goal as moving a society – local, national or global – closer to a model of social justice. This approach involves a critique of systemic injustice and an emphasis on political mobilization, political action and grassroots democracy to achieve the goal.

But if the Left is to avoid the pitfalls of its earlier strategies, it must reject not only the liberals' one-dimensional Economic Man, but also its own, equally one-dimensional, Social Man. The latter is the mythical "socialist man" who is enabled to realize his true, collectivist self when he is removed from corrupting capitalist influences. The starting point of any realistic development paradigm is the contradictory Socioeconomic Person (O'Boyle 2007): actually existing persons who are capable of extensive cooperation in the common good as well as intense individual competition for the available rewards. Egoistic drives are unlikely to be submerged for long, regardless of the social arrangements. Any Left alternative will thus continuously contend with the reality captured by Lord Acton's dictum that power corrupts and Robert Michels' "iron law" of oligarchy (Michels 1968 [1911]). To be realistic, a strategy must forge the conditions for augmenting cooperation, while acknowledging through institutional safeguards that individuals, regardless of the system, will also pursue their own interests. Only democratic institutions can serve the end of checking the entrenchment of a new class. Thus, struggling for equal freedom is more akin to embarking on an ongoing journey than arriving at a pre-selected destination.

A vision may or may not be utopian. The Left has certainly had its share of grand utopias. Utopias inspire enthusiasm in the short run, but disillusionment and worse follow in the longer term. This book focuses on practicable strategies deriving from actual practice. The outcomes, as we shall see, are far from ideal, though superior to the most likely alternatives. Before turning to the strategies, I offer a critique of neoliberalism that justifies the search for an alternative.

NOTES

1. For a concise history of neoliberalism, consult Harvey (2005).
2. Refer, for example, to the several books written by former World Bank Chief Economist Joseph Stiglitz since 2002. The neoliberal paradigm encompasses both classical or orthodox liberals and proponents of social or inclusive liberalism.
3. Neoliberalism is not the same thing as neoclassical economics, whose rigorous mathematical models have a limited relevance to real-world policy issues. However, neoliberalism derives much of its legitimacy from the purported status of neoclassical economics as a rigorous science and from the influence of neoclassical methodology in shaping the other social sciences. Neoliberals claim that their policies derive from objective knowledge (Finlayson et al. 2005). For an analysis of the impact on popular culture of Ayn Rand's novels and the films based on them, refer to Cotarelo (2005).
4. A massive 2007 survey carried out by the Pew Research Center (Washington, DC) as part of its Global Attitudes Project, involving 45,239 interviews in 47 countries worldwide, found widespread support for the main tenets of global neoliberalism, though correspondents registered concerns about inequality, threats to their cultures and ecological decline. See Stephen (2010: 222–4).
5. Some readers may object that the social-democratic and socialist approaches are so dissimilar as to constitute separate development paradigms. I suggest below that shared assumptions justify treating the Left as a distinctive viewpoint, in spite of the many disputes.
6. Post-development thinkers label the neoliberal paradigm a "false universalism," on the grounds that its conceptual categories are merely hidden means of maintaining hierarchy and control in the global system. Such a critique would presumably also apply to the leftist paradigm. But wide acceptance of the post-development viewpoint would cripple the oppositional movements of the Left. From this viewpoint, only spontaneous rebellions rooted in individual countries count as legitimate opposition to neoliberalism. Such isolated rebellions are usually contained and defeated.
7. For the critique mounted by behavioral economics, see Pesendorfer (2006). See also Hindmoor (2010: 194–6).
8. For an extended defense of the "invisible hand" in its original formulation, see Lal (2008).
9. Especially useful are the following secondary sources: Folbre (2001); Finlayson et al. (2005); Rist (2006).

10. A succinct statement of this view is the following: "political rights exercised by individuals in those democratic societies with relatively high levels of economic freedoms have been used less for providing edifying public goods and economic policies and more for pursuing rent seeking activities that benefit the few at the expense of the many" (Stroup 2007: 62). Lal (2008: 49) bluntly asserts that "most states are predatory – even democratic ones."

11. For one version of socialism, the compatibility of socialism and democracy accords with this liberal assumption. If a democracy requires a dispersal of power, and if this in turn requires a competitive economy and decentralized economic decision-making, market socialism would be as capable of supporting a democratic system as capitalism.

12. For an early statement of what became the Washington Consensus as it relates to Africa, see World Bank (1981). For a general survey of the evolution of this strategy into the 1990s, see Gore (2000).

13. Pearce (2009: 419) notes that Latin America exhibits "quite an eclectic range of interpretations of the meaning of progressive politics for a post-neoliberal age."

14. The new rhetoric of "partnership," the "ownership" of poverty reduction programs by recipient governments and the "participation" of civil society in these programs did not mean that Western donors and the international financial institutions surrendered their policy influence. Instead, the overt policy conditions attached to structural adjustment agreements gave way to process conditionality – only governments that performed well, by adhering to the correct policies and achieving results, received further loans and aid.

15. "Social capital" usually refers to the norms and networks that foster cooperation and trust, both of which are essential for well-functioning markets. As for civil society organizations, in reality many of them are better understood as elements of the counter-movement to *roll back* neoliberal measures, especially privatizations and ecologically unsound infrastructure and private investments. However, as long as neoliberal agencies controlled funding, many NGOs muted their criticism.

16. "[D]evelopment without an effective state is impossible" (World Bank 1997: 24).

17. Notably, support of conditional cash transfers to poor households, efforts to provide basic education and health care to the poor, and programs to encourage girls to attend schools (Hickey 2010: 1,149–52; Ruckett 2010).

18. One proposed element of an effective strategy – the governmental provision of effective safety nets before, or concurrent with, market-based reforms – is compatible with both neoliberal and progressive approaches, the distinction arising from the degree of universality, generosity and comprehensiveness of the social programs. See Chapter 5.

19. For the details of this story, see Wade (2001).

20. For a discussion of the commonalities and differences within the Latin American Left, see Arditi (2010).

21. For varying statements of this ideal, see Macpherson 1973: 109; Gould 1988: 40–64; Cunningham 2001: 276; Wright 2010: 18.

22. For a detailed critique with page references, refer to Sandbrook (2000a).

23. Some wealthy individuals act altruistically – for example Bill Gates and George Soros – but one cannot depend on altruism to forge equal freedom.

24. Prominent African socialists include Julius Nyerere, Kwame Nkrumah, Kenneth Kaunda, Sékou Touré and Leopold Senghor.
25. See Gintis (2000) and Rudd (2000), especially p. 133 where he lists sources in evolutionary psychology, experimental economics and evolutionary biology to support this conclusion. Greenfield (2009) concludes, on the basis of a review of the psychological literature, that human values and behavior adapt to the requirements of social change. Individualism, she suggests, is an adaptation to certain patterns of institutional development and socialization.
26. See, for example, Wiredu (2008) for this criticism.

3   How neoliberalism fails

Free markets, as Karl Polanyi memorably argues in *The Great Transformation* (2001 [1944]), tend to become tyrannical and destructive masters. The "great transformation" signifies the rise of a market system as the economy not only detaches itself from confining social norms and regulations, but also subordinates social institutions to economic imperatives (efficiency, commodification, profitability) and the instrumental drives of opportunistic actors. However, the liberal movement never actually realizes the ideal of a self-regulating market system owing to the destructiveness of unleashed market forces. A dialectical "double movement" arises in which the movement toward a liberal-market economy creates such damage to society and nature that a counter-movement of societal protection spontaneously arises, according to Polanyi.

Of particular importance is the continuous commodification of labor, land and money – the "fictitious commodities" – that is driven by the logic of profitability. Liberals believe that all markets, including those for labor, land and money, must operate according to the same principle of market-determined prices, if an efficient and productive market economy is to develop. But these three factors of production differ qualitatively from other markets, Polanyi aptly notes (2001 [1944], chaps. 11–18). They are either not produced at all or, if produced, not for sale on the market. To treat labor, land and money as if they were commodities like the others leads to disaster. Labor markets are unique in involving the sale of labor power, which is embodied in human beings. Human beings are ends in themselves; to treat them as disposable commodities subject to the whim of self-interested actors would ultimately undermine social solidarities and subject people to abject insecurity. Land and other natural phenomena, such as water and forests, are distinctive inasmuch as they are in finite supply and easily degraded, yet are crucial to human existence. Money, when treated as a commodity rather than a medium of exchange, a store of value and a means of productive investment, turns predatory – breeding speculation that starves productive enterprises of capital while feeding inflationary bubbles. Hence, the attempt to create a self-adjusting market system, as is the intent of the Washington Consensus in the developing world, is "utopian" in the sense of impossible. A counter-movement emerges to rein in market forces, though the result may be a stultifying deadlock.

What Polanyi identifies in the double movement is, as I suggest in Chapter 1, actually a persistent and unstable tension in capitalism rather than an irreconcilable contradiction. If this is so, we cannot conclude from finding that neoliberal policies have had detrimental consequences that socialist transformation is the only solution. It may be possible for a left-of-center government to work out a (provisionally) viable modus vivendi between the movement and the counter-movement, commodification and decommodification. In other words, what may be at issue is not the replacement of capitalism with another system, but the displacement of neoliberalism by a more benign *variety* of capitalism. But this part of the story must await later chapters. I turn now to catalogue the unintended consequences of the second great transformation in the Global South.

This chapter probes the destructive dimensions of neoliberal development doctrine in the regions of its greatest influence: Latin America and Africa. I am not suggesting that neoliberalism has provided no benefits to the Global South. It is important, as the neoliberals propose, to bring inflation under control, to rebuild decayed and decrepit political, bureaucratic, judicial, banking, tax collection and oversight institutions, to reduce rent-seeking, and to construct safety nets. But the approach exacted too great a cost. These costs include the following:

- Liberalized capital markets are prone to boom-and-bust cycles. Speculative bubbles burst or investor panic suddenly escalates, leading to financial collapses and major recessions with high unemployment, impoverishment and new sources of insecurity.
- Free-market forces, including globalization, tend to augment inequalities of income, wealth and opportunities. High inequality has a number of unfortunate consequences: it undermines genuine democracy, impedes the reduction of absolute poverty, generates the conditions for poor health statistics, high criminality and low social cohesion, and increases personal insecurity and the propensity for political violence.
- Free markets treat nature as a store of commodities to be exploited for privately appropriated profit. This orientation, combined with the negative externalities of waste disposal into the air, land and waterways and excessive greenhouse gas emissions, threatens to undermine a society's ecological foundations. Yet the logic of market profitability motivates firms to externalize their costs of production and distribution in these ways, while internalizing the benefits.

- The combination of market volatility and recession, high inequalities and environmental decline set the stage, in countries with already weak institutions, for violent conflict and even state collapse.

Although liberal market systems breed these destructive tendencies, I argue in later chapters that democratically controlled markets have provisionally built defenses against them.

The socioeconomic record

Between 1980 and 2002, market reform did not fulfill its promise in narrow growth terms. A former World Bank economist, in an article tellingly entitled "The Lost Decades," makes this point. One statistic dramatically illustrates the lack of success: whereas the median per capita income growth in developing countries in the era of state interventionism (1960–79) reached 2.5 percent, it was a disastrous 0.0 percent in 1980–99 (Easterly 2001: 135). Table 3.1, which uses purchasing power parity (PPP) exchange rates to reflect comparative living standards, shows that the growth rate of per capita gross domestic product declined in every region of the developing world in 1980–99 compared to the preceding two decades.

Branko Milanovic (2003) similarly proposes that the development record of 1960–78 is superior on all measures to that of 1978–98. He also notes that the best performers in the second period – especially China and India – were far from paragons of free-market policies. Since 1997, Latin America, East Asia, Russia and Turkey have suffered devastating financial crises. Latin America recovered in the first half of the 1990s but

Table 3.1 *Average percentage growth in per capita GDP (1990 Int$)*

	1960–1979	1980–1999	2000–2008
Total former USSR	3.7	–2.1	7.8
Total Latin America	3.8	0.47	2.1
Total 30 East Asian countries	2.6	0.93	5.2
Total 15 West Asian countries	6.3	–0.09	3.0
Total Africa	2.5	–0.19	2.4
World average	3.2	1.3	3.1

Source: Maddison Project, *Statistics on World Population, GDP, Per Capita GDP, 1–2008 AD*. www.ggdc.net/maddison/Historial_Statistics/horizontal-file_02–2010.xls
Note: An international dollar (Int$) in 1990 would buy in the cited region an equivalent bundle of goods and services as a US dollar would buy in the United States in that year.

then foundered. Argentina and Uruguay underwent a severe economic crisis in 2001. Growth continued to stagnate in sub-Saharan Africa, despite policy and institutional reforms and high levels of foreign aid since the early 1980s. There were a few African success stories: Mauritius, Botswana, Mozambique and Tanzania are often mentioned. Many of the formerly communist countries that undertook market reform in the 1990s suffered economic collapse. Neoliberal programs were not turning out as expected.

Leaving aside the recession years (in the Global South) of 2009–10, the period 2003–13 was an era of economic boom in most developing countries. The high demand for commodities, especially on the part of rapidly industrializing China and India, provided the main impetus. Emerging markets generally recovered in 2010, though the earlier front-runners (China, India, Brazil and Russia) did not resume the elevated growth trajectories of the prior era. Table 3.1 does not fully reflect the high growth rate since it includes the troubled first two years of the new century in the third column. Nonetheless, the extent of the recovery is clear. Latin American and African countries have experienced high, and in some cases unprecedented, rates of growth for an extended period. Whether an old-fashioned commodity boom should vindicate neoliberalism is a moot point, however, for the demand mainly originated in countries pursuing the *least* doctrinaire economic policies.

Poverty trends during the neoliberal era have been largely positive. The *Rural Poverty Report, 2011* (International Fund for Agricultural Development [IFAD] 2011) records a major decline in both "poverty" (those living on less than $US2/day) and "extreme poverty" (those subsisting on less than $US1.25/day) between 1988 and 2008. Whereas 69 percent of the people in the Global South lived in poverty in 1988, only 51 percent did by 2008. Similarly, extreme poverty dropped from 45 percent of the population in 1988 to 27 percent in 2008. That is, roughly 1.4 billion people in 2008 struggled to survive on under $US1.25/day in the developing world.

The trends vary markedly by region, however (IFAD 2011). On the one hand, East Asia (mainly China) has led the world in poverty reduction. For instance, rural poverty has fallen from 98 percent to 35 percent in two decades (1988–2008). On the other hand, sub-Saharan Africa is the only region in which the number of extremely poor people continues to rise. In addition, the incidence of both poverty and extreme poverty has grown marginally there over the twenty years to 2008. Most African countries will not meet the Millennium Development Goal of halving their poverty rates by 2015. Latin America and the Caribbean ranks between East Asia and Africa in poverty reduction. The incidence of both poverty and extreme poverty has fallen significantly over the two decades, though the poverty rates for indigenous peoples is as much as eight times higher than the rate for the non-indigenous. The distribution of the world's poor has thus shifted significantly since the early 1980s, especially from East Asia to Africa. The overall trends may appear less favorable if different time periods and data sets are employed, however (see, for example, Chen and Ravallion 2007).

Whether we can attribute the successes to neoliberal policies is more controversial. East Asia, apparently the most successful region, has also been the most resistant to free-market prescriptions. Sub-Saharan Africa, the least successful in reducing poverty, has been the region most dependent on the neoliberal international financial institutions and aid donors – until the 2000s when China emerged as a major dispenser of loans and aid to Africa. The Latin American poor, as we shall see later, have benefited not just from the trickle-down effect of the commodity boom, but also from the social programs of the many leftist governments since 2000. The link between the Washington and Post-Washington Consensuses and poverty reduction is far from self-evident.

In addition, several destructive tendencies associated with neoliberal policies have revealed themselves during the past three decades. The remainder of the chapter probes this part of the record.

Market volatility and recession

Deregulated financial markets, advocated by neoliberals since the 1970s, have bred destructive market volatility and restricted national autonomy in designing monetary, fiscal and even social policy. For these reasons, the Bretton Woods system, established at the end of World War II, combined a commitment to free trade with national controls on cross-border capital flows and pegged currencies. The Great Depression had discredited the notion of free capital flows. Speculative capital movements and unstable exchange rates had fostered beggar-thy-neighbor protectionism, exacerbating the economic depression of the 1930s. Furthermore, Keynes and his supporters advocated capital controls in order to insulate counter-cyclical government policies and incipient welfare programs from the financial power of capital. The threat of investors fleeing a country's currency, bonds and equities would constrain governments to preserve conservative monetary and fiscal policies; yet these policies are counterproductive in times of recession. Thus, in the period from the end of World War II until the 1970s, exchange controls and the close monitoring of pegged exchange rates by the central banks and the IMF moderated financial instability and enhanced national policy-making autonomy. But treating money as a commodity and accepting the resultant financialization of economies have been prominent features of neoliberalism.

Beginning in the early 1970s, industrial countries removed capital controls, floated their currencies,[1] and, since the early 1980s, put pressure on developing countries to follow suit. The crisis of stagflation in the 1970s and early 1980s gave Milton Friedman and others of the Chicago School an opening to argue that the unfettered, self-regulating market was the best vehicle for attaining prosperity. The state, especially regulation, was the problem, and the deregulated market was the solution.[2] This advice met with a receptive hearing. The revolutions in telecommunications and information processing facilitated global market activities, and the expanding transnational corporations and the powerful Anglo-American states pushed financial and capital market liberalization forward. A liberal financial order would allow the United States to finance its growing deficits, as free capital movements would encourage investors and central banks to build their reserves of US dollars. It would also open new global opportunities for the already well-developed US (and British) financial institutions. The shift in ascendency from Keynesian to neoliberal policies, the conversion of the IMF and the World Bank to the ascendant doctrine, and the debt crisis of the 1980s universalized the move to liberalized financial markets. By the mid 1990s, few holdouts remained.

The shift had a theoretical justification. Liberalized capital markets, so it is argued, would bolster the stability of the global financial system. Ease of cross-border financial flows would allow countries lacking sufficient investment or facing financial shortfalls to borrow from the rest the world. Not only would capital flow to where it was scarce, but also the risk of financial disaster in any one country or region would be minimized.

The reality, however, has diverged from neoclassical economic precepts. Deregulation of financial markets and the floating of currencies ushered in "financialization," where the financial sector came to dominate the real economy and generate a rising share of profits. This trend was unhealthy for two reasons. Speculation in foreign currencies, bond markets and exotic derivatives not only threatened to starve productive enterprises of long-term investment finance, but also encouraged these enterprises to emulate the stars of the financial world in seeking short-term speculative profits. Furthermore, as financial speculation grew, market volatility increased in the form of "bubbles" and "busts." Speculators, institutional and individual, flooded financial markets, making profits from minor shifts in the value of currencies, bond and equity markets, and interest-rate differentials, and from selling exotic financial "instruments." By 2010, the daily turnover in foreign exchange markets was $4 trillion, only about 5 percent of which resulted from commercial transactions in goods and services (Jacque 2010: 1). Speculative movements eventually became too massive for a central bank to control by buying or selling its own currency. Worse, capital flows to and from developing countries have been pro-cyclical, not anti-cyclical as theory assumed; lenders have reduced their lending to countries suffering financial shortfalls (Stiglitz 2010: 1). Moreover, the growing integration of financial markets fomented contagion: a financial crisis in one or several countries quickly spread to others.[3] Disaster ensued when speculators, succumbing to panic at the hint of financial problems afflicting a country or region, hastily withdrew their money.

A series of devastating financial crises accompanied financialization, eventually engulfing even the United States, Britain and the euro zone. Financial and/or currency crises have afflicted Mexico (1994), Thailand, Indonesia, South Korea and the Philippines (1997–8), Russia (1998), Brazil (1999), Turkey (2000), Argentina and Uruguay (2001–2), and the US and the world (2008–9). Contagion has spread the effects of volatility more widely than hitherto. Collapse in the value of national currencies, insolvency of banks, reversal of growth rates and sudden increases in unemployment and poverty are the main symptoms of crisis. According to one expert's estimate, the financial crises of 1994–2002 raised the incidence of poverty 7 percent above what it would otherwise have been in the affected countries (Cline 2002).

In East Asia's financial crisis in 1997–8, a net private inflow of $93 billion in 1996 was followed by a net outflow of $12 billion in 1997. This incredible swing of $105 billion in the supply of private capital in one year represented 10 percent of the combined GDP of Thailand, South Korea, Indonesia, the Philippines and Malaysia (Wolf 1998). Were these five economies in such dire shape that they deserved such brutal treatment from portfolio investors and commercial banks? The IMF and other neo-liberals answered in the affirmative, citing lax financial regulation and "crony capitalism."

But others were skeptical of this convenient explanation. After all, IMF experts had praised East Asia in annual economic surveys, and the World Bank had issued its *East Asian Miracle* report in 1994 lauding the region's "economic fundamentals" (Hoaglan 1998). Credit-rating agencies had encouraged fund managers to invest heavily in East Asian equities and bonds. Critics pointed out that it had been the recent capital-account liberalizations in East Asia, pressed by the United States Treasury and the IMF, which permitted an investors' panic occasioned by short-term liquidity problems to wreak havoc. Tellingly, those countries that had retained capital controls, such as China and Vietnam, emerged relatively unscathed.

Even such an economic powerhouse as South Korea was brought to its knees. Its vulnerability arose in large part because its mammoth integrated *chaebols* (conglomerates) had taken advantage of financial liberalization to borrow heavily from foreign banks. The hasty exit of foreign capital in 1997 led to economic disaster: a 9 percent decline in per capita GDP, a threefold increase in the poverty rate, and the collapse of 10 banks and 284 financial institutions (Kim and Park 2006: 439). Furthermore, an IMF agreement required even further liberalization, especially of South Korea's labor markets. Although the county's economy had recovered by 2002–3, income inequality had also grown.

Following the East Asian crisis, many experts called for reform of the international financial architecture to enhance stability (for example, Stiglitz 2002: chap. 4). Only strict regulation of financial markets can reduce the risks of financial disasters. But another deleterious effect of financialization is to augment the political influence of financiers. Instead of stricter regulation, the IMF and US Treasury attached conditions to their massive loans requiring even further liberalization in East Asia.

In 2008–9, the worst global financial crisis since the 1930s struck, further illustrating how unregulated capital markets breed periodic melt-downs with widely ramifying effects.[4] The havoc began with the meltdown of the sub-prime mortgage market in the United States. Stock markets crashed, first in the United States and Europe, and then in most developing and emerging markets. International trade fell dramatically. Volatile capital flows had dire consequences in developing countries, even though these countries bore no responsibility for the disaster. Consumers, in developing countries as elsewhere, faced rising food prices, while economic growth and employment plummeted. In February 2010, thirty-two countries were experiencing food emergencies, according to the Food and Agricultural Organization. In 2008–9, 34 million people lost their jobs (UNDP 2010). Redundant workers moved into self-employment in the informal sector where incomes were already low. Poverty reduction went into reverse in 2009–10; the UNDP reported that an additional 64 million people in the Global South fell below the internationally established poverty line of $US1.25/day (UNDP 2010). The World Bank estimated that the crisis would consign 46 million more people to "severe" poverty and another 53 million to poverty, while between 200,000 and 400,000 extra children would die annually during the crisis (World Bank 2009: 11). Overall, the World Bank concluded that the global recession set back the fight against poverty by seven years.

Africa was particularly hard hit. It suffered a triple blow: a major drop in demand for its commodity exports together with a decrease in revenues from tourism; a decline in foreign direct investment; and the shrinking of remittances from family members working abroad who lost their jobs. The loss of foreign earnings led to a decline in the value of many currencies, leading to higher rates of inflation and soaring food prices. One consequence was growing malnutrition that, in the case of millions of young children, may have involved permanent physical or mental impairment (York 2009). The severe downturn lasted for at least a year.

This catastrophe undercut neoliberalism as a development paradigm. It vividly refuted three neoliberal assumptions (Nesvetailova and Palan 2010: 798–9). First, deregulation found justification in the precept that markets efficiently allocate resources; in reality, however, open financial markets proved efficient at allocating resources to the *bankers* rather than to productive firms. Financiers acted more like rent-seekers than entrepreneurs in bringing ruin to economies around the world. Second, neoliberals assume that the individual pursuit of self-interest is the best guarantor of market stability and the public interest (the vaunted "invisible hand"). In reality, avidity produced market instability and devastating declines in the living standards of workers, farmers, the poor and the middle class. Even the libertarian former head of the US Federal Reserve Board, Alan Greenspan, admitted, in his October 2008 Congressional testimony, that "[t]hose of us who have looked to the self-interest of lending institutions to protect shareholders' equity . . . are in a state of shocked disbelief." "I have," he confessed, "found a flaw." Third, it is assumed that a minimal role for government is best to avoid rent-seeking and distortions of market signals. In reality, proactive governments in the US, Europe and elsewhere first forced through global capital-market liberalization, mainly through the IMF, and then massively intervened to rescue the financial elite from its folly through schemes producing massive sovereign debts.

Despite the debacle, little has yet been done to rein in the financial elites and their destructive practices. Leaders within the G8 proposed a currency transaction tax and other constraints on speculative financial movements, but little changed. Financial capital remained politically powerful; indeed, it retained a virtual veto power over economic policy in the US and the UK, its power abetted by right-wing populism and the decline of organized labor. The financial oligarchies have wielded the political and ideological resources to block stringent regulation of financial markets in the OECD countries.

This absence of international agreement meant that individual developing countries had to introduce their own financial controls. An influx of foreign funds into "emerging markets" in 2010–12 in search of high returns raised the value of their currencies.[5] This rise undermined competitiveness in export markets in the relevant countries, and raised the specter of asset bubbles. Consequently, by early 2011, at least a dozen major developing countries had introduced withholding taxes on incoming investment capital, time restrictions on selling bonds and bills, and interventions in foreign-exchange markets to quell volatility and currency revaluations. Conditional support for such measures derived from an unexpected source – the IMF. An IMF staff paper released in 2010 found that capital controls were advisable under certain conditions (Ostry et al. 2010). The next year, the IMF officially recognized that capital inflows can be destabilizing by feeding asset bubbles, currency appreciation and volatile markets. It called for "capital flow management measures," though only as a last resort (IMF 2011). An old free-market orthodoxy was thus overturned, though the principal neoliberal powers continued to demand capital-account liberalization in bilateral trade agreements.

Regardless of its shortcomings, neoliberalism remains dominant in policy discourse for now. In 2008, a revived IMF imposed 224 economic conditions in agreements with fifteen governments that desperately needed its loans. Fiscal reform was the most common condition, followed by financial liberalization, privatization, trade reform, exchange-rate adjustments and the liberalization of prices (Hailu 2009). Nevertheless, some developing countries, such as China, India, Brazil, Russia, Thailand, Turkey, Malaysia and South Africa, have retained or imposed their own national controls on capital movements. In the longer run, the massive deficits run by US presidents George W. Bush and Barack Obama, together with the emergence of China as the largest holder of US debt, erode the capacity of US governments to shape the global economy in its own image.

Growing inequality

Although inequality is a complex and controversial subject, a few truths can be simply stated. First, it is not only absolute poverty that causes major human suffering; inequality does too. Second, inequality, both among the global population as a whole and intra-nationally, is high and has grown markedly since the advent of neoliberalism. Finally, the correlation between neoliberal policies and rising income and wealth inequalities is not spurious. Dynamic features of neoliberalism accelerate regional, national and global inequalities. Consider each of these points in turn.

First, pronounced inequality is oppressive, in many ways as oppressive as poverty. Inequality is usually measured in income terms, but it also includes disparities in wealth and access to basic services such as education, health care and sanitation. High and persistent inequality leads to a number of social pathologies and unfortunate consequences, according to many studies:

- High and especially growing inequality lowers the poverty-reducing effect of economic growth.
- The higher the inequality of societies, the lower their social cohesion. The more unequal the society, the higher the incidence of mutual distrust, homicides and violent crime, mental illness, obesity, illegal drug use and persistent poverty (Wilkinson and Pickett 2010). "If you fail to avoid high inequality, you will need more prisons and more police" (Wilkinson and Pickett 2010: 246). Inequality lowers moral constraints on robbery and violence owing to envy of the rich or anger at social injustice (Thorbecke and Charumilund 2002: 1,492; Wilkinson 2004: 3; Demombynes and Ozler 2006: 311–12).
- Being born into a lower-class family in an inegalitarian society is a major determinant of a person's life chances. The less well-off tend to have less education, poorer job prospects and shorter and less healthy lives than the better-off (Wilkinson and Pickett 2010).
- Democracy, if it exists, will lack substance in highly inegalitarian societies. The wealthy can use their rapidly accruing riches to "invest" in the political process, in licit or illicit ways. The return on such investments is political influence, which translates into policies that further enrich the wealthy and shield them from paying their fair share of taxes. Pseudo-democracy masks the reality of oligarchy. (Nel 2006: 699–700; Huber 2009: 654).
- Finally, high inequality in certain circumstances breeds deadly conflict. Inequality accentuates struggles for state power because the state is seen as the mainstay of the existing system. Perceived *horizontal* inequalities among ethnic, religious, racial, or regional groups, if unresolved, can lead to civil war or ethnic cleansing. *Vertical* inequalities, on the other hand, divide the population on a class or quasi-class basis, leading to populist outbursts (peasant wars, urban riots, millenarian movements or tax revolts), or even revolutions.

Overall, high inequality is divisive and counterproductive for all but the elite, who can insulate themselves from harsh realities by accessing private services and secluding themselves behind the walls of gated communities.

To avoid misunderstanding, I am not suggesting that equal freedom demands an equality of outcomes. Moderate income and asset inequality is justifiable, provided a genuine equality of opportunity exists. Individuals who diligently hone their capabilities, work harder than most people, or make an outsized contribution to society deserve their moderately high incomes. Motivation and contributions to the common welfare vary among individuals, and so should material rewards. What is unacceptable, however, is to treat labor as a mere commodity whose fate depends on nothing else than the profit calculations of corporate executives.

At some hazy level, inequality becomes intolerable. As Albert Hirschman points out, the public's tolerance for disparities of income and wealth tends to be substantial in the early stages of economic development. People believe that, in the long run, they or their children will benefit from development. "But this tolerance is like a credit that falls due at a certain date. It is extended in the expectation that eventually the disparities will narrow again. If this does not happen, there is bound to be trouble and, perhaps, disaster" (Hirschman 1973: 545). The repudiation of popular expectations, often aggravated by the arrogance and venality of the rich, spurs widespread anger at social injustice. The elite's traditional justification for inequality – that they have earned their rewards through hard work, superior education or virtue, and that poor people are poor for personal or cultural reasons – rings false.

Although statistical analysis cannot establish the degree of inequality that people regard as tolerable, inequality is high and has grown since the advent of neoliberalism. I focus on three dimensions: inequality among individuals in the global population, the development gap between the poorest countries and the high-income countries, and inequality within countries.

Inequality within the world's population as a whole is extremely high. China and India, accounting for one-third of the world's population, underwent rapid economic expansion during the past two or three decades. This trend would have reduced world inequality. However, growing inequality, especially within China with its initially high "socialist" equality, has offset this trend. A large-scale study by the World Bank (Milanovic 2002) found that world inequality is not only very high but also increased in recent years: between 1988 and 1993, the Gini coefficient of income distribution rose from 62.8 to 66.0 (p. 88).[6] Furthermore, the bottom 5 percent of the world's people grew poorer, as their real incomes fell by one-quarter during this period, whereas the richest quintile grew richer – by 12 percent in real terms (p. 88). Remarkably, the richest 1 percent of the world's population received as much income as the bottom 57 percent (p. 88). By 2002, the Gini coefficient for global inequality, based on purchasing power parity (PPP) exchange rates, reached 70 (Ferreira and Milanovic 2009). Another massive data analysis carried out by the World Institute for Economic Development Research found that, in the year 2000, the richest 2 percent of the world's adults owned more than half of the wealth of the globe's households (United Nations University 2007; see also Edward 2005; Kai and Hamori 2009). On a global basis, therefore, the rich have become spectacularly richer in the neoliberal era.

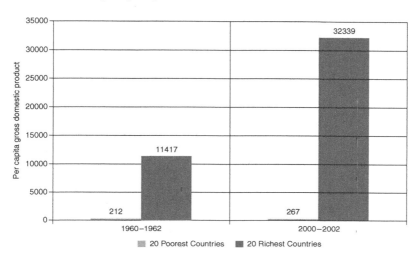

Figure 3.1 Development Gap between the Poorest and Richest Countries, 1960–1962 and 2000–2002 (per capita GDP in constant 1995 US$, simple average)
Source: World Commission on the Social Dimensions of Development 2004: 37.

In addition, the development gap between the low-income and the high-income countries has grown. The size of the gap depends on whether one measures the mean income of countries at official exchange rates or purchasing power parity, and whether or not one presents an average weighted by size of population. However, these methodological issues are too complex to enter into here. Suffice it to say that the prestigious World Commission on the Social Dimensions of Development, appointed by the International Labour Organization, chose to compute the development gap using unweighted averages of the GDP per capita for the 20 poorest and 20 richest countries at the current exchange rate in US dollars. As Figure 3.1 shows, the income gap between the richest and poorest countries increased significantly over forty years. Whereas the richest countries had average incomes 54 times as great as those in the poorest countries in 1960–2, this gap had widened by 2000–2 to 121 times as great.

A third measure of inequality is that found within countries. In general, inequality has grown since the 1970s within most countries and regions of the Global South. One massive study (Cornia, Addison and Kushi 2004) concluded that, during the first two decades of neoliberal hegemony, inequality had risen, often sharply, in most countries. Income inequality increased in 48 of the 73 countries for which high-quality data was

Table 3.2 *Gini coefficient: averages by region and decade*

Region	1970s	1980s	1990s	2005
Levels				
Latin America and the Caribbean	48.8	51.2	52.5	52.1
Asia	39.0	39.3	40.1	44.2
Developed countries	28.2	28.4	29.8	30.3
Eastern Europe	25.6	26.5	29.7	34.1
Changes		*1970s–80s*	*1980s–90s*	*1990s–00s*
Latin America and the Caribbean		2.4	1.3	−0.5
Asia		0.2	0.8	4.1
Developed countries		0.2	1.4	0.4
Eastern Europe		0.9	3.2	4.4
Difference in Gini points: Latin	*1970s*	*1980s*	*1990s*	*2005*
America and the Caribbean vs.				
Asia	9.8	11.9	12.5	7.9
Developed countries	20.6	22.8	22.7	21.8
Eastern Europe	23.2	24.7	22.9	18.0

Source: Gasparini, Cruces, Tornarolli and Marchionni 2009

available, whereas it remained constant in 16 countries (including such large ones as India and Brazil) and fell in only 9 of the sample countries (accounting for only 5 percent of the sample's total population).

Consider the regional trends. Table 3.2 reveals that income distribution has become more unequal in each decade since the 1970s in Asia, the former Communist countries of Eastern Europe, and the developed world. In Latin America and the Caribbean (LAC), where income inequality was already relatively high in 1970, it increased in each successive decade until 2000. Since then, 12 of the 17 Latin American countries registered a gradual decline in their Gini indexes (Economic Commission for Latin America and the Caribbean 2011: 52). Cash transfer schemes to the poorest households, coupled with improvements in social protection and in the quality and accessibility of educational, health and other services, turned the tide. In Venezuela, for example, inequality rose sharply in the decade prior to Hugo Chávez's election victory in 1998 (the Gini moving from 42.6 in 1989 to 47.2 in 1998). A series of egalitarian reforms followed (see Chapter 6). By 2006, Venezuela ranked as the most egalitarian Latin American country (with a Gini index of 44.7) (Gasparini et al. 2009), with further improvement in the Gini in subsequent years. The next most equal country was Uruguay, a moderate social democracy. Declining inequality in Latin America thus followed governmental shifts to the left from 1998 onwards.

Eastern Europe and Russia experienced a rapid rise of inequality following "shock therapy" in the late 1980s and early 1990s, as Table 3.2 confirms. The sudden dismantling of controls and subsidies, together with the privatization of state-owned enterprises into the hands of opportunistic former bureaucrats, was disastrous in Russia and several other countries. The economies initially contracted, millions of people were reduced to poverty, the birth rates declined, alcoholism rose, and inequality increased sharply as the countries underwent a form of "gangster capitalism" (Holmstrom and Smith 2000).

China, which avoided the worst excesses of gangster capitalism through a policy of gradual neoliberalization, achieved rapid growth that raised 627 million people above the poverty line between 1978 and 2004 (Valli 2009; see also Wan 2008). Inequality, however, rose rapidly. China's Gini coefficient of 39.6 in 1978 had increased to 46.9 by 2004 (Valli 2009). Inequality emerged on a regional basis (the coastal regions did particularly well) and an urban–rural basis (with the urban areas pulling ahead of the rural areas), as well as on a vertical or societal basis (Riskin, Renwei and Li 2001). By the mid 2000s, inequality had become a volatile political issue.

In India as well, a rise in inequality accompanied neoliberal reforms and economic growth. In the twenty years ending in 2003, India's Gini index rose 15 percent to 36.0 while its accelerated economic growth lifted some 21 million Indians above the poverty line (Wagle 2007) Growing inequality also produced political tensions.

Inequality in Africa apparently remained high from the onset of the neoliberal period.[7] A report on the "inequality predicament" by the United Nations Economic and Social Affairs Department (2005) claims that inequality in sub-Saharan Africa is the highest in the world, whether measured by income, education, health statistics or access to power. An IMF study tentatively confirms the high income inequality while noting a study that arrived at different conclusions (Lopes 2005: 6–7). Urban–rural inequalities are marked, whether measured by asset ownership, educational attainment, health indicators or amenities (Sahn and Stifel 2003). Regional disparities have also increased, as a result of the tendency for investment and infrastructure to concentrate in economically dynamic regions or cities. Where these regional disparities overlap with ethnic or religious boundaries, inequalities often generate political divisions (Kanbur and Venables 2005: 8–11).

The relatively high inequality in African countries masks a lot of variation. On the high side are South Africa (with a Gini of 66), Zimbabwe (60) and Nigeria (48); at the other extreme are Ghana (39) and Uganda (38) (Christiaensen, Demery and Paternostro 2002: 6–7; on South Africa, see May and Meth 2007: 277). In Nigeria, in spite of the billions of dollars in oil revenues that flow annually to the government, nearly 70 percent of the population live in poverty. Since the end of apartheid in South Africa (Africa's largest or second-largest economy), interracial income inequality has diminished while intraracial disparities have grown. (South Africa, Republic of 2007: 22). Poverty, too, has increased – to almost 20 percent of the population in 2000 at the PPP $US1.00/day level (May and Meth 2007: 274). Overall, there has been a slight growth in income inequality. However, the major growth of spending on social services somewhat mitigates the income inequality (May and Meth 2007: 276). With some exceptions, inequality in African countries in high and growing.

Although the trends in income distribution are clear, the link between global neoliberalism and these trends is contested. Advocates of globalization are convinced that its benefits far outweigh any costs. It is true that high inequality preceded the neoliberal era in many countries of Latin America and Africa, though typically distributional trends worsened further after 1980. Such factors as land concentration, the urban bias of public and private investment, regional and class disparities in education, and differential political influence had underpinned inequality long before neoliberalism. Yet these "traditional" causes of national inequality do not adequately account for the worsening income distribution since 1980 (Cornia and Court 2001: 14–15). The judicious judgment of development economist Albert Berry (2014), who has studied income distribution for decades, aptly sums up the available evidence: global neoliberalism "has probably been one of the significant contributors to the general trend toward increasing inequality over the last couple of decades."

Although many factors shape distributional outcomes, certain dynamics in global neoliberalism exacerbate inequality nationally and globally. First, markets reward those who possess scarce assets while penalizing those who don't, unless governments intervene. A technological revolution in information processing and communications, together with the liberalization of global markets, has empowered owners of such scarce assets as financial capital, human capital relevant to the knowledge economy, and intellectual property to capture more of the gains from economic activity. Second, concentrated income and wealth, in turn, translate into disproportionate political influence, which allows the wealthy to manipulate tax and other policies to advance their interests. A vicious circle thus perpetuates itself.

The liberalization of domestic banking and cross-border capital flows has been a major contributor to global inequality. Such liberalization permits financiers to speculate on a global scale, thus magnifying their profits while often socializing their losses via government bailouts in the event of a speculation-induced recession. Furthermore, financial crises exacerbated by the panic-induced rapid exit of "hot" money have had major impacts on income distribution. Unmanageable external debts, declining currencies, and deficit reduction prod governments to cut social expenditures that help the poor and middle class, such as food subsidies, educational and health services, safety nets and public employment. Also, high domestic interest rates to stem financial outflows and inflation choke investment, resulting in high unemployment. A rise in inequality and poverty that lasts several years is a common outcome (Cornia and Court 2001: 17–18).

Meanwhile, the global surplus of unskilled and semi-skilled labor exerts a downward pressure on wages in open economies. Domestic workers must compete for jobs with workers in other countries who are willing to settle for lower wages. In theory, enhancing labor "flexibility" reduces poverty and inequality by augmenting efficiency and encouraging further investment, thus fostering lower unemployment. In practice, just the opposite is often the case. When deregulation of labor markets is combined with deregulated financial markets, trade liberalization and openness to foreign investment, workers tend to suffer. Flexibility generally means lower minimum wages, a decline of employment protections and union rights, and often a fall in public employment – a recipe for lower wage rates and higher income inequality (Cornia and Court 2001: 19). In Latin America in the 1990s, for example, labor flexibility actually left workers with stagnant incomes, higher unemployment and heightened job insecurity (Leiva 2006). Of course, workers in developing countries should benefit from the exodus of manufacturing and service jobs from the high-income countries. However, this benefit is tempered by two tendencies: for large firms to sub-contract labor-intensive processes to the low-wage informal sector, and to seek out even lower-cost platforms in other jurisdictions. Only decisive governmental interventions can, to some degree, shield workers from these pressures.

Neoliberal reforms of the tax system and user fees for public services have also detrimentally affected lower income earners. On the one hand, the common shifting of the revenue burden from hard-to-collect income taxes to consumption in the form of value-added taxes benefits the richest people. Because the rich spend a smaller share of their income on consumption than the poor, this shift is inherently inegalitarian. To compound the inequity, ordinary citizens must shoulder a larger share of public expenditures from which they derive no benefit – such as public-sector pensions and university education. On the other hand, user fees for health care and other services were, in many countries, a new financial burden for the less well-off in the 1980s and 1990s. The recent trend in the Post-Washington Consensus toward universal, free primary education provides some relief, though educational budgets and thus the quality of instruction are usually inadequate (Cornia and Court 2001: 20).

The impact of neoliberal policies is sometimes dramatic. Consider the case of South Korea. Resistant to neoliberal reform as a developmental state until the early 1990s, Korea retained an egalitarian income distribution until the onset of the financial crisis in 1997 (with a Gini of 27). Thereafter, major reductions in corporate tax rates, heightened flexibility in labor markets, increased openness to foreign direct investment and financialization led to rising income inequality or, more precisely, a "bipolarization" of income shares (Park and Mah 2011). Another dramatic instance concerns "shock therapy" in many of the former Communist countries that undertook a rapid transition to a market economy. Hasty privatization of state-owned corporations usually concentrated the ownership of formerly public assets in the hands of political insiders, at bargain prices. To compound the negative distributional effects, lay-offs of employees by the new owners contributed to unemployment and poverty. No wonder that people use the term "gangster capitalism" to refer to these cases (Hellman 1998; Holmstrom and Smith 2000).

It is no accident that only where the Left came to power in Latin America did inequality wane. One study of income distribution concludes that moderate social-democratic regimes (Brazil, Uruguay, Chile) and Left-populist regimes (Bolivia, Ecuador, Venezuela) have a better record of lessening inequality than neoliberal regimes (such as Colombia, Peru and Mexico) (Birdsall, Lustig and McLeod 2010). Although economic factors such as technological change have an impact on income distribution, hierarchical power relations cement inequality by transmitting it from one generation to the next. Tackling inequality will thus require more than fine-tuning markets and mounting targeted social safety nets. It will usually need to involve social-movement activism and collective political action.

Power relations also matter in reducing the North–South development gap. The enormous market power of the United States, the European Union and Japan has allowed them to negotiate favorable trade and investment agreements on multilateral and bilateral bases. These agreements have skewed the rules to their benefit in trade, intellectual property rights, and investment.

Although the dispute between economistic and political interpretations of inequality cannot be satisfactorily resolved in a few brief paragraphs, we may at least agree that the policies of the Washington Consensus have accentuated inequalities and that the Post-Washington Consensus has failed to reverse this trend.

Ecological degradation

The promise of modernity – of growing material prosperity on the basis of appropriating nature – captivates the people of China, India and Brazil today as it earlier entranced the West and Japan. But an expanding global population, rising per capita consumption and the deeper commodification of nature are producing predictable consequences: most of the earth's ecosystems are under severe or moderate stress.[8] Certain neoliberal policies bear some responsibility for these worsening trends.

To summarize the ecological threats facing humankind is a daunting challenge. Ecological degradation takes the form of: global warming linked to the burning of fossil fuels; looming scarcities of accessible energy reserves, fresh water and food; rising pollution of air, water and land; and escalating rates of extinctions of flora and fauna, tied in particular to deforestation.[9] These trends portend several major dangers, especially for the Global South:

- the prospect of catastrophic climate change if average world temperatures rise more than two degrees Celsius over preindustrial levels, leading to crop failures, desertification, erratic and extreme weather episodes, acidification of the oceans, and rising sea levels that put people on islands and in coastal areas at risk;
- resource wars, both civil wars and interstate conflicts, resulting from disputes over shrinking water supplies, arable land and lucrative oil supplies;
- rising tensions and conflicts in areas in which environmental refugees congregate, in both the Global South and North; and
- pandemics as rising temperatures, global population movements, violent conflicts and persistent mass poverty provide optimal conditions for the transmission of diseases and parasites.

Although these threats are well documented, the allure of consumer societies and the complexity and cost of solutions forestall effective solutions.

Climate change is wreaking its most detrimental effects on the poor in the poorest countries of the Global South, despite the fact that they bear the least responsibility for greenhouse gas emissions. Island countries and massive coastal cities in the developing world are most at risk as ocean levels rise.[10] Flooding represents a major threat to the concentrated populations that reside in low-lying areas with marshy soil and poor water drainage, as for example in Bangladesh. The vast semi-arid areas of sub-Saharan Africa and the tropical region of Latin America are undergoing exceptionally high rates of warming and drying (Robert 2001). To compound the tragedy, the low-income countries have a limited fiscal

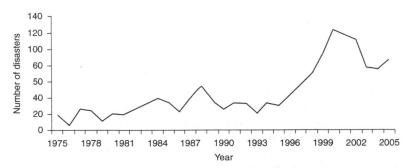

Figure 3.2 Number of Natural Disasters in Sub-Saharan Africa since 1975
Source: World Bank (2007c)

capacity to adapt to a changing climate. And the wealthy countries of the Global North are reluctant to provide the financial and technological resources to deal with the problems. The World Bank (2010) estimates that, by 2030, the cost of mitigating climate change in developing countries will be $US140–175 billion per year (in today's dollars). However, in recent years, the financial resources allocated for this purpose by donors and donor agencies averaged only $US8 billion.

Sub-Saharan Africa is the region most vulnerable to climate change. It has experienced an escalation of "natural" disasters since 1975 (see Figure 3.2), in the form of unusual floods, prolonged droughts, and erratic changes in seasons. Drought, always a menace in the semi-arid regions, has become more frequent. The Sahel region of West Africa (just south of the Sahara Desert) has experienced a substantial decline in rainfall, leading to recurrent droughts in Burkina Faso, Mali and Niger and a decline in river discharge by 40 percent since 1970 (UNDP 2006). One visible effect of climate change (compounded by mismanagement) is the shrinkage of Lake Chad, where water levels have dropped by a stunning 95 percent over four decades (United Nations Environmental Programme 2006).

The future looks bleak. Farmers involved in rain-fed agriculture can expect a decline in yields of up to 50 percent in some countries (Intergovernmental Panel on Climate Change 2007). A 2010 report by the Hadley Centre for Climate Prediction and Research in the UK (Leahy 2010) notes that, when global temperatures rise an average of 2.0 degrees Celsius, southern Africa will warm an additional 1.5–3.5 degrees above the norm. This region should therefore expect to become much warmer and drier. Maize, currently the main food crop, will not grow under the projected conditions. In the Sahel, it will also be difficult to grow food; an expert study predicts that crop yields will fall by 18 percent. Throughout West Africa, the median loss will be 11 percent (Rondier et al. 2011). Elsewhere, longer dry periods and fewer, but heavier, episodes of rainfall will periodically wreak havoc on crop production, reducing output and raising poverty.[11] Projected declines in annual rainfall portend a drastic lowering of flows in the Nile, which are being further reduced by new upstream irrigation and hydroelectric projects. The diminished flows will have negative repercussions for 300 million people living in seven countries (Taye and Willems 2011). The Millennium Development Goals of halving malnutrition and poverty in sub-Saharan Africa by 2015 are unlikely to be reached under these emerging conditions.

What role does neoliberalism, or capitalism more generally, play in this ecological decline? A definitive answer is hard to arrive at, despite the confident assertions of contending schools. Three viewpoints predominate. *Neoliberal environmentalism* holds that neoliberalism is not just compatible with environmental sustainability: it is essential to achieving this goal. Limited regulation, market incentives, private ownership of resources, and technological innovation can deal with the environmental challenges. *Marxist/radical environmentalism* or *eco-socialism*, in contrast, contends that capitalism's inner logic – its ceaseless drive to accumulate capital – is incompatible with ecological sustainability. Capitalism will thus need to be transformed for the economy to incorporate a new logic of community and sufficiency. A third viewpoint, *social-democratic environmentalism*, assumes that not an ineluctable capitalist logic, but rather the political and cultural power of capital, ultimately impedes an ecologically sustainable capitalism. Sustainability is incompatible with neoliberalism, dominated as it is by a business class committed to market freedom. But it is compatible, according to this view, with a "green" social-democratic variety of capitalism, which asserts the primacy of politics vis-à-vis markets. Consider each viewpoint in turn.

For neoliberal environmentalists, well-functioning markets rather than detailed environmental regulations are regarded as the best means of protecting natural resources. Extending private ownership to unowned, state-owned or common-property resources is beneficial because private ownership promotes, it is believed, not only innovation and entrepreneurship but also a means to price and thereby ration scarce resources. Privatization avoids what Hardin famously refers to as the "tragedy of the commons," whereby resources held in common are allegedly overused.[12] Thus, forests, fresh water, land governed by communal arrangements, fish (in fish farms using public water), genetic material and even carbon dioxide (as in "cap-and-trade" systems) have been, or are being, converted into saleable commodities.[13] A controversial example is the sale or leasing by (mainly) African governments of land to foreign corporations and individuals for export-oriented food and biofuel production – "land grabs" that totaled an estimated 50 million hectares of fertile land by 2010 (Vidal 2010). (Not only is hunger already widespread in several of the twenty countries involved, but also much of the alienated land had formerly been governed by communal land regulations.) An instrumental view of nature as a storehouse of commodities and a "sink" for waste disposal underpins this approach.

Neoliberals, though agreeing on the feasibility of a green neoliberalism, disagree on the degree of governmental regulation that will be needed. The division mirrors that between the market-fundamentalist Washington Consensus and the more nuanced market perspective of the Post-Washington Consensus (see Chapter 2).

Market-fundamentalists hew to the view that free markets, assisted by technological development, can solve environmental problems generated by economic growth. The economist Wilfred Beckerman (1995) typically argues that what is needed, especially in the developing countries, is rapid economic development. High rates of growth will generate not only the *resources* for cleaner technologies, sanitation and poverty amelioration, but also the *demand* on the part of the expanding middle classes for a cleaner environment (Beckerman 1995: 40). Moreover, scarcity of energy or raw materials will not pose a problem. The increase in prices of scarce resources will raise demand for more efficient technologies and the substitution of a plentiful input for a scarce one. Hence, market-based economic development as promoted by neoliberal globalization is the *solution* to ecological decline, not the problem. Governments have, at most, only a small part to play in this drama. Moreover, policy should be designed "to enable market forces to operate in the environmental sphere, or to mimic the operation of the market," perhaps by the careful application of pollution charges (Beckerman 1995: 3; see also Jacobs 1997). In short, the market will send the proper price signals to rectify ecological problems.

"Ecological modernization" theorists reject this market fundamentalism in favor of more prominent roles for governments and environmental movements. Ecological Modernization Theory (EMT) emerged in the 1980s, mainly in relation to high-income countries, to counter neo-Marxist and other radical critics who located ecological decline in the inner logic of capitalism.[14] For EMT, capitalist industrialization creates ecological damage, but repairing this damage requires more, not less, modernization! A faith in technological innovation suffuses EMT. The state can facilitate innovation and ecologically sustainable practices by generating the appropriate incentives. The role of the state should move, according to A. P. J. Mol, "from domineering, over-regulated environmental policy to a policy which creates favorable conditions and contexts for environmentally sound practices and behavior on the part of producers and consumers." The state should focus on "steering via economic mechanisms" (quoted in Buttel 2000: 61). Yet EMT theorists recognize that "economic mechanisms, institutions and dynamics will always fall short in fully articulating environmental interests and pushing environmental reforms, if they are not constantly ... propelled by environmental institutions and environmental movements. Neo-liberals who would have us believe that we can leave the environment to the economic institutions and actors are wrong" (Mol 2001: 211).

Recognizing that globalization has shifted environmental problems to the supra-national level, ecological modernizers have moved from their initial national focus to consider global relationships. But the approach has remained largely the same (Mol 2001). The state–market relationship it proposes is congruent with the complex neoliberalism of the Post-Washington Consensus.

Consider the green developmentalism of the World Bank, the main shaper of the latter "consensus." In the late 1980s and early 1990s, the World Bank was under attack by a coalition of environmental non-governmental organizations. They denounced the World Bank for financing environmentally destructive infrastructural projects, especially dams and highways through tropical rainforests. In 1987, the World Bank adopted environmental protection as a criterion for funding projects, but "the shift ... was largely tactical, a response to the need to reduce the threat to its lending resources" (Wade 2004: 83). With the publication of its *World Development Report 1992* on *Development and the Environment,* the World Bank (1992) declared environmental sustainability to be a central goal of its lending policies – but even then it remained unclear whether this formal commitment materially modified the World Bank's actual practice (Wade 2004: 93; Goldman 2004: 167). This report is exceptionally optimistic in espousing a green developmentalism, concluding that the world could achieve ecological sustainability while global output grew by 350 percent over four decades. This feat depends on market forces and policies providing appropriate incentives (for abatement technologies) and regulations (of pollution levels) that would together promote the substitution of abundant for scarce inputs, technical progress, and unspecified "structural change." The report promotes the view that technological innovation can generate the needed efficient use of energy and resources and clean production techniques.[15]

The *World Development Report 2010: Development and Climate Change* (World Bank 2010) manifests the same optimism. Economic development is compatible with the needed reduction in greenhouse gas emissions. The World Bank continues to place its faith primarily in the magic of markets: provided that carbon is priced appropriately via a tax or a cap-and-trade system, market forces will impel innovation to increase the energy efficiency of known technologies while developing new low-carbon processes and carbon-capture technologies. It will also be necessary, according to the report, to improve the management of water resources, to foster higher-yield yet sustainable agriculture in the context of a worsening climate, to remove perverse incentives that encourage energy use, and to vastly augment the transfer of funds to allow developing countries to adapt to climate change. The message is unambiguous. Neoliberal capitalism can secure the well-being of current and future generations, in the Global North as well as the South, through a process of incremental change.

We have reason to be skeptical of this sanguine outlook. Although I cannot develop the critique, the following challenges to the conventional view bear consideration.

- How realistic is the benign thesis that economic growth, at a certain point, instills in national governments both the will (owing to growing popular demand) and the (fiscal) capacity to act to preserve the environment? First, highly polluting firms have relocated their facilities from well-regulated developed countries to developing countries with low environmental standards (OECD 1997; White and Whitney 2014: 13). In this case, ecological improvements in one society are offset by deterioration in others. Additionally, certain grave environmental problems typically worsen with growing affluence: rising per capita emissions of carbon dioxide, increasing resource usage, water shortages, mounting volumes of solid waste, and the extinction of species (York and Rosa 2003: 276; see also Harper 2000). Furthermore, can we rely on the middle class to press the case for environmental protection? All the polls suggest that, in the United States, a lower proportion of the population today accepts the global warming thesis than a decade ago.

- The faith in technological fixes and market solutions is comforting, but is it persuasive? We're experiencing a rapid depletion and contamination of natural capital, trends that will only worsen as China, India and Brazil further industrialize. Increasing efficiency does not solve the problem because any improvements in the resource intensity of products are overtaken by the exponential growth in their consumption (York and Rosa 2003: 281). Furthermore, the law of entropy suggests that one cannot indefinitely increase the productivity of a unit of natural capital or the rate of recycling of energy and other resources. It will, in short, be necessary for governmental authorities at the national and global levels to impose *quantitative constraints* on the resource flows entering national economies. Markets respond only to relative scarcities; if the price of oil rises, for example, consumers will shift to coal. But we confront not relative but *absolute* limits insofar as, even by the early 2000s, many national economies had already exceeded their maximum sustainable scale. We needed 1.3 planet earths then to sustain our level of consumption of resources and waste assimilation. "No amount of relative scarcity information can render the market effective at ensuring the sustainable rate of natural resource use."[16]

- The proliferation of free-trade agreements (multilateral, regional and bilateral) has stacked the deck against the environment. Free-trade agreements typically accord priority to freer trade, construing many environmental regulations as unwarranted constraints on trade. Even the North American Free Trade Agreement (NAFTA), which includes a side agreement on environmental cooperation, has had this effect (Swenarchuk and Sinclair 2014; Gallagher 2009: 62). In addition, freer multilateral trade has negatively impacted the environment insofar as the transport of goods over long distances consumes massive volumes of fossil fuels.

- Is it rational to promote ever-higher consumption in the industrial world when it is clear that growing consumption not only incurs environmental damage but also, beyond a certain point, fails to increase our happiness or well-being (Myers 2006)?

As much of the damage inflicted on the world's ecosystems is irreversible in the short term, it is dangerous to entrust our future to the supposedly benign tendencies of minimally regulated market forces.[17]

If the neoliberal position is unconvincing, does the Marxist-radical or the social-democratic Left offer a more plausible approach? At issue on the Left is the adaptability of capitalism. Capitalists have demonstrated a remarkable capacity to adjust to government-imposed constraints (for example, the welfare state and labor rights), but will they be able to adapt to the tough ecological limits that our survival seems to demand? Or will an immutable capitalist logic block the transition to a sustainable economy? We cannot, with certainty, know the answer to this fundamental question.

Marxists and other radical analysts claim that sustainability requires the end of capitalism. Eco-socialism "locates the causes of contemporary environmental abuse in the workings of the economic mode of production of capitalism, and the institutions and world view necessary to its functioning" (Pepper 2010: 34). Consequently, asserts David Harvey, "nothing short of a radical replacement of the capitalist mode of production will suffice to institute a new and saner regime of socio-ecological relations" (1998: 30). The subtitle of another work bluntly states the options: *The End of Capitalism or the End of the World* (Kovel 2002). The reason is an alleged inner logic of capitalism – grow or die. James O'Connor, in a widely cited book, captures this logic in what he calls the "second contradiction" of capitalism. For O'Connor, capitalism is caught in a terminal conflict: the necessarily unending quest of capitalists to accumulate capital eventually undermines the ecological (and other) conditions of production, leading to disaster (O'Connor 1998: 10, 247).

Why might capitalist economies be driven to ever greater production and consumption, and hence to ecological catastrophe? Analysts canvass several possibilities.

- Where advertising media and popular culture equate wealth and consumption with well-being, the wants of people are insatiable.
- Firms that fail to expand their earnings, quarter after quarter, fall into crisis. Stockholders dump their stocks. Firms cannot repay their loans. Executives fail to earn bonuses and may lose their jobs. Competitors contemplate takeovers. Hence, corporate management is fixated on profitability and expansion.
- Competition drives firms to augment their profits by shifting some of their costs of production and distribution onto third parties. Such "negative externalities" include pollution, greenhouse gas emissions and the overuse of scarce natural resources such as fresh water or natural gas. If firms had to internalize the costs of these socially harmful practices, many would be unprofitable (Wallerstein 1999: 6–7).[18] In any case, a power imbalance protects the externalizers from being held to account; those who experience the externalities are numerous and unorganized whereas the externalizers are usually politically influential large corporations (Hahnel 2007: 1,142). Governments cannot cover the costs of rehabilitation either, because to do so would lead to major tax hikes and a storm of protest. Consequently, little is done. There is "no exit" from this dilemma within capitalism, according to Immanuel Wallerstein (1999).
- When economic growth ceases, an economic and political crisis ensues. "A negative profit rate spells economic trouble; at the least, a recession, at the most, a general crisis, a deflation of capital values, and depression" (O'Connor 1998: 240). Thus, a government that restrains profits or new investments to achieve ecological objectives threatens the health of the capitalist system (as well as the government's re-election prospects). Conversely, most politicians and citizens see economic growth

as a universal panacea, solving problems of unemployment, poverty, inequality and budgetary deficits.

That these are salient factors in contemporary capitalism can hardly be disputed; the issue is whether these "contradictions" are mutable or immutable.

The "treadmill of production" theory has much in common with the Marxist position (Gould, Pellow and Schnaiberg 2008). Although the theory is complex, it adheres to a deterministic view that a particular capitalist logic of unending expansion spreads ecological destruction throughout the world. The search for profits inevitably leads to increasing levels of resource usage and pollution, as one round of labor-saving but energy-intensive investment follows another. Each round of investment creates profits that have to be plowed back into further research and production. The "treadmill" metaphor conveys the idea of a national, and ultimately a global, population jogging in place, unable to contain growing ecological problems even while technologies become ever more efficient. The conclusion follows that environmentalists must challenge the production logic, though the authors leave it to the anti-corporate global movement and local initiative to find sustainable alternatives.

Is it then realistic to hope to realign capitalist economies so that they become ecologically sustainable? If unending growth were a capitalist imperative, the answer would be no. But the "logic" of capitalism is rather one of profitability, and *profits can be made under diverse circumstances*.

Profitability is theoretically compatible with nationally prescribed limits on throughputs, which are required to foster sustainable economies. To assert this compatibility in principle, however, is not to suggest that the transition to sustainability will be easy. It will be very difficult; but *the difficulties arise from contingent political and cultural obstacles, not from immutable contradictions*. Ecologically unsustainable neoliberal capitalism persists for three reasons. First, powerful classes benefit from the existing order and resist the notion that the state should impose ecological limits. Second, a pervasive culture of possessive individualism portrays economic growth as a panacea for various social problems and personal affluence and choice as the primary values. People desire sustainability in theory, but not in practice if it requires material sacrifice. Thus, a major hurdle in instituting a sustainable or "green" capitalism is arriving at a new social contract that equitably allocates the burdens and rewards of transition. A new pact either has to be imposed from above (as might happen in China) or negotiated, most likely by a proactive social-democratic government. Finally, unsustainable neoliberal policies persist because national accounts fail to factor in the environmental costs of growth. If they included the costs of depleting natural capital, it would be clear that economic "growth" under current conditions actually makes us poorer (Daly 2007: 12). Ecological sustainability is thus primarily a political rather than economic problem; it involves confronting the vested interests in neoliberalism while shifting toward another, more regulated and equitable, variety of capitalism.

Sustainability, in effect, requires conceptualizing the economy as a subsystem of the natural environment (Daly 1991). An upper, biophysical limit on growth exists, in both the natural resource inputs into production processes and the pollution-sinks for waste products. Consequently, governments will need to impose quantitative limits on the resources flowing through national economies. To exceed these limits, as many national economies have already done, is to deplete natural capital and court disaster. Hence, the goal must be for all countries to move toward constant populations and the "steady-state economy" that Herman Daly and others have long championed (Daly 1991; Daly 2007).

A steady-state economy is not a static economy, contrary to a common belief. True, the latter demands a constant level of resource *inflows*, consonant with the regenerative capacity of the natural environment. Governments might manage the inflows through a system of tradable resource-use permits. They would auction off these permits to the highest bidders, the number of permits being determined by the estimated sustainable use of resource throughputs for a particular population. The revenues earned by the governments could then offset reductions in less socially desirable taxes, such as payroll taxes. But a steady-state economy does not assume a static *outflow* of products and services. Despite constant resource volumes, firms would still compete on the basis of improvements in the quality of goods produced and the lower prices that more efficient technologies permit. Thus, firms could continue to make healthy profits and new investment; these investments would augment employment; incentives would still reward entrepreneurship, effort, innovation and thrift; and people would retain the ethos of economic advancement, which is central to capitalism.[19] Treating the economy as a subsystem of the natural environment could re-embed the economy in nature without destroying either. Of course, what I am proposing is, as yet, only a theoretical possibility.

A transition to an eventual steady-state economy requires developmentalist states (as defined in chapters 1 and 5), whether democratic or authoritarian. "Free" markets are incapable of dealing with the situation of absolute scarcity; the state must thus govern markets in a manner that regenerates the ecosystem. Clearly, the steady-state economy assumes an effective state that is capable of enforcing limits opposed by powerful groups. Many states in the Global South lack this strength, especially the fragile states of the low-income countries. But the latter's participation is not essential because they contribute little to destructive global ecological trends. Progress toward sustainable economies does require a transition to steady-state economies in the high-income countries and the emerging economic powerhouses of Russia, China, India and Brazil. Indeed, China has already begun the transition with enormous investments in sustainable energy and green technologies. Imposing quantitative limits on resource inputs presupposes the primacy of politics, not markets.

Many readers will regard a steady-state economy as utopian. Granted, there are many obstacles to overcome. Looming ecological limits may lead to international conflict as some national governments contemplate appropriating the remaining stocks of natural resources through force of arms. National debates over how to share the costs of sustainability may deteriorate into class warfare as issues of distribution rise to the fore. Facing such a divisive and complex issue, political leaders and citizens will prefer the comforting prospect of technological fixes for their ecological problems. But this easy solution is illusory because of the vast scope of the challenge – a growing world population, rising per capita consumption and collapsing ecosystems – and the tendency for technological solutions to give rise to new problems. (A case in point is nuclear energy, which releases no harmful emissions after the facilities are completed, but is both enormously expensive and highly dangerous.). The obstacles to a steady-state capitalist economy are admittedly formidable, but they pale in comparison to the uncertainty unleashed by the worldwide socialist transformation proposed by those who contend that capitalist logic inherently leads to ecological disaster. And it is still unclear what transcending capitalism precisely entails, if we rule out Stalinist central planning.

Developmentalist states guided by democratic leftist regimes probably hold out the best hope for dealing with ecological challenges. Significantly, such regimes in the Global South as well as the North have *already demonstrated a superior environmental record than other regimes.* I will take up the issue of green social democracy in the concluding chapter.

This section has sketched the scope of the environmental challenges and the main approaches to dealing with them. The neoliberal era has been one of a deepening environmental crisis, together with proposals for rather implausible market-based solutions. Marxist/radical approaches identify real tendencies within capitalism that aggravate ecological problems. They claim that there is no escape from these tendencies within capitalism. But such theories are rather too emphatic in their structural determinism, as well as too vague as to what ecologically sustainable system might replace capitalism, and how. In fact, capitalism has proven to be a protean system, remarkably adaptive to various sorts of constraints. The most promising approach bets on the adaptability of capitalism through movement toward a social-market variety that is also a steady-state economy. Although no easy escape beckons, green social democracy offers some hope for a sustainable and democratic future.

In addition to the dimensions of environmental crisis already adduced, the propensity of ecological decline to combine with inequality and poverty in breeding deadly conflict is a further devastating tendency of the movement toward a self-regulating market.

Deadly conflict

The neoliberal era has not been a peaceful one. Although the causes of instability and violence are complex, market liberalization can create conditions conducive to these outcomes.

Civil wars and insurrections, ethnic/religious strife, rampant urban criminality and the chaos associated with failing or failed states have marked the post-Cold War era, especially in sub-Saharan Africa, Latin America and the Caribbean, and South Asia. *Armed conflicts* (including interstate and intrastate violent conflicts), which began to rise in number in 1974, peaked in 1992 at 54 events – nearly all involving intrastate hostilities. The number then tapered off to 29 in 2003, after which armed conflicts again rose. Some 36 active conflicts existed in 2008, an increase of nearly one-quarter since 2003 but fewer than those recorded in 1992 (Harbom and Wallensteen 2009: Fig. 1, p. 579). Africa experienced the highest increase in the latest period, moving from 7 such conflicts in 2005 to 12 in 2008, though the number has since declined. The bulk of these 12 conflicts took place within states, with a quarter of the conflicts involving more than one rebel group challenging the government (Harbom and Wallensteen 2009: 578).

In the early 2000s there was also an upsurge of *communal violence* not directly involving government forces. Of 123 such episodes that produced at least 25 deaths in 2002–5, Africa accounted for 90 of them (Uppsala Conflict Data Program). Nigeria alone recorded 17 episodes in this period, mostly interethnic conflicts.[20] Land rights have been a particularly contentious issue, pitting one ethnic group against another. Motivated to flee primarily by generalized violence, *internal displaced persons* (IDPs) numbered 26 million in 2008 (Internal Displacement Monitoring Centre 2009: 13). Nineteen African countries accounted for 11.6 million IDPs; Sudan alone had an estimated 4.9 million displaced persons. The Americas followed Africa in total numbers.

Finally, *criminality*, endemic in many cities, takes on the character of a primitive rebellion (Gillespie 2006: 35). Weak law enforcement, together with the demographic predominance of young people, widespread poverty, high inequality and family breakdown, breed powerful gangs that dominate the sprawling slums.[21] In Brazil, for example, both São Paulo and Rio de Janeiro suffered mini-insurrections in 2006, spearheaded by gang members who attacked police stations. The country's president had to deploy the army in Rio de Janeiro to ward off the criminal gangs. Violence has become a virulent force in the less developed regions of the world.

Fragile states are the site of many of these deadly conflicts. The Fund for Peace has developed a "Failed State Index" based on twelve indicators. Its ranking reveals that ten of the fifteen countries that most closely fit the profile of a failed state are located in sub-Saharan Africa (Fund for Peace 2010). Declining states raise the probability of insurgencies or civil wars owing to the opportunity that such weakness signals to potential insurgents. Failing states also augment human suffering (especially poverty and despair) by subjecting their citizens to predatory state officials, brutal warlords and criminals.[22] Ecological decline often further weakens failing states; opportunists take advantage of, and further undermine, weak states by plundering natural resources and fomenting rebellion among the disaffected. Fragile states also provide havens for national and transnational crime syndicates, especially those engaged in the illegal drug trade.

That this record of instability and violence is dismal is beyond question, but what is contested is whether market liberalization is implicated in the genesis of these pathologies or, instead, is part of the solution.

For some social scientists, neoliberalism's triumph has ushered in a more peaceful and prosperous world. Free markets, free trade and liberal democracy, it is thought, together represent the final stage of societal evolution (Fukuyama 1992). With the collapse of state socialism in the 1980s, all countries could adopt a market orientation and open economies. Free global markets, it was believed, facilitate the free movement of ideas as well as products, thereby opening closed states to the outside world. Free trade and investment, furthermore, foster the prosperity needed to reduce poverty and defuse conflicts (see e.g., Li and Schaub 2004: 254). Democratization and the development of civil societies would, in time, accompany economic liberalism. All these changes would facilitate a more peaceful world.

But a darker view competes with this sanguine perspective: that liberated market forces, by introducing new forms of insecurity and dislocation, forge conditions conducive to deadly conflict. This is not just the view of radical critics. The US Central Intelligence Agency also predicts a tumultuous era (in its *Global Trends, 2015,* issued in 2000): "[Globalization's] evolution will be rocky, marked by chronic financial volatility and a widening economic divide. Regions, countries, and groups feeling left behind will face deepening economic stagnation, political instability, and cultural alienation. They will foster political, ethnic, ideological, and religious extremism, along with the violence that often accompanies it." *Global Trends 2025* arrived at a similar prognosis, though emphasizing the destabilizing effect of climate change and the competition for scarce resources (as cited in Klare 2008). This darker view is more in tune with the realities of the epoch than the benign neoliberal prognosis.

Market liberalization has actually been associated with diverse political conditions. In many cases, the outcome approximates the darker scenario: sporadic growth, volatility, inequality and violent conflict. Sierra Leone in the 1990s is a case in point. In other countries, the liberalization of statist economies seems to have had the benign impact that the optimistic neoliberal perspective forecasts. The case of Mauritius since the mid 1980s is a good illustration. How can we explain this divergence?

As a general tendency, I suggest, external and internal liberalization generates conditions conducive to instability and conflict. Virtually the entire human population has been drawn into a growing dependence on markets that, when ineffectively regulated, subject people to rapid and sometimes devastating changes in fortune. Market liberalization not only heightens the economic insecurity of certain groups, but also often deepens social cleavages – by shifting opportunities on a communal, regional or class basis – and vitiates a state's capacity to deliver order, valued services and patronage. The rise in insecurity and sense of injustice, if coupled with an increasingly ineffective and unpopular regime, provides an opening for anti-systemic movements. Demographic trends magnify the probability of political unrest. Young men – the potential shock troops of rebellion – form a growing proportion of populations in countries with rapid population growth; in Middle Eastern countries, for instance, half the population or more is under 25 years of age. Young men without prospects, the contemporary embodiment of Marx's "dangerous classes," are disproportionately represented among those adversely affected by market conditions. Yet grievances do not necessarily generate anti-state mobilization and rebellion.

Neoliberal policies have the effect of accelerating existing tendencies toward state fragmentation and conflict. These policies are not, in themselves, a sufficient condition for deadly violence; many countries have liberalized their markets while enjoying peace and growing prosperity. Botswana and Mauritius are two examples in a region (sub-Saharan Africa) beset with political disorder. Nonetheless, global neoliberalism is a remote or underlying cause of deadly conflict in many other cases.

The low-income countries are most vulnerable to political violence. At least one-third of their populations fall below the international poverty line; their governments have limited institutional resources to counteract disorder through mounting safety nets, resolving conflicts and applying force; their economic and social infrastructure is limited and dilapidated; and they typically suffer from localized unrest or incipient armed conflicts. Neoliberal policies, when refracted through weak political institutions, foment serious challenges to governments.

The trends I discussed earlier – market volatility and periodic financial crashes, growing inequalities, and climate change, desertification and resource shortages – have the cumulative effect of deepening incipient divisions and undermining state power. First, *market volatility* resulting from trade and capital-account liberalization raises the likelihood of violent conflict because some groups lose out while others gain (Bussmann, Schneider and Wiesehomeier 2005: 560–1). Typically, trade liberalization involves a reduction or elimination of price controls and subsidies to producers, in addition to incentives for export orientation and low tariffs. These policies in agriculture can wreak havoc in the livelihoods of smallholders, as cheap (and often subsidized) imports undercut local production. When India liberalized the import of soybean and soy oil products in 1999, subsidized imports from Western countries rose by 60 percent in the first year. "[P]rices crashed by more than two-thirds, and millions of oilseed-producing farmers had lost their market, unable even to recover what they had spent on cultivation. The entire edible oil production and processing industry was also destroyed. Millions of small mills have closed down" (Mittal 2001). The phasing-out of fertilizer subsidies, often required under IMF conditionality, raises production costs, and helps drive many small farmers into insolvency. As these policies drive smallholders to the wall, export-oriented foreign companies buy them out or lease large tracts of land from governments. Young men and former farmers head for the burgeoning urban slums. Export receipts may increase and subsidized wheat and rice imports from the European Union and the United States may lower food prices, but at the expense of declining food self-sufficiency, growing insecurity and inequality, and bitterness.

Trade liberalization in industry also produces many losers, along with winners. Even if the freer trade maintains or increases overall output and labor productivity, it will lead to the failure of some firms and to retrenchment of workers. Chronic insecurity grows, as industries wax and wane, better-paid permanent jobs vanish, and unskilled and even skilled workers see their real wages fall (Luttwak 1999). This insecurity naturally fosters anger and protest.

Market volatility also arises with the liberalization of banking and cross-border financial movements. These policies, as I discussed earlier, create the conditions for periodic financial crises as "hot" money flows into emerging markets and then, suddenly, flees in panic, dramatically raising unemployment and poverty levels. IMF-style stabilization programs, designed to remedy financial disequilibria, have also raised societal tensions and fostered conflict (FitzGerald 2002: 79). Slashing public spending entails a reduction or elimination of popular subsidies; job losses; and a reduction of public investment and services. Raising the real interest rate harms small producers. The falling value of the local currency and cuts in subsidies lead to higher food and energy prices. These shifts are tantamount to reneging on an implicit social contract or informal patron–client arrangements. Not only will these sudden losses alienate strategically located public employees, but they will also weaken the government's support in other key constituencies as services deteriorate, prices rise and patronage resources shrink (Tirman 2005: 36). Even in a middle-income country, Argentina, a financial collapse in 2001 pushed 16 million below the poverty line, left nearly half the labor force unemployed or underemployed, and reduced one-quarter of the population to hunger. Spontaneous protests beginning in December 2001 led to a declaration of a state of siege. But political unrest sporadically continued, while five successive presidents resigned (López Levy 2004: 2–3, 10; Giarracca and Teubal 2004). The turbulence ceased only with the election of Néstor Kirchner as president in April 2003. Rising tensions and popular protests accompanied by falling state capacity are a recipe for political disaster in liberalizing economies.

Second, the *new inequalities* spawned by liberalization are destabilizing. Relative deprivation is a powerful motivator of intergroup violence. A large-scale quantitative study concludes: "The risk of political disintegration increases with a surge of income disparities by class, region and community" (Nafziger and Auvinen 2002: 156). In stratified class societies, growing inequality will deepen class tensions and augment the appeal of left-wing and populist movements. This pattern characterized much of Latin America from the late 1990s onward. Particularly explosive are the liberalization of agricultural markets and the creation of private property in land where smallholders had hitherto held only communal rights to land use. The enhanced vulnerability and insecurity of rural populations have fomented conflicts along class or ethnic lines.[23] In African and Asian countries where communal cleavages had already emerged, growing disparities have exacerbated regional, ethnic and religious divisions. People develop a notion of what constitutes a "fair" sharing of public resources and wealth among ethnic groups, both at the elite and the rank-and-file levels. Any major divergence from this distributional pattern evokes protest and possibly insurrection (Crawford 1998: 35; Azam 2001: 430–1). Secessionist movements, civil wars, pogroms, warlord conflicts, or low-intensity insurrections have been the unfortunate outcome.[24]

The same level of vertical or horizontal inequality that leads to armed conflict in one country, however, may not do so in others. Contextual factors clearly shape outcomes. People construct their ethnic, racial and religious identities on the basis of past disputes and differences. The history of ethnic/religious relations, the existence of inclusive or exclusive ideologies, and the regional distribution of public services and infrastructure are thus important contingent factors (Thorbecke and Charumilund 2002: 1,485–6; Ostby, Nordast and Rod 2009). The strength or weakness of the national state is particularly significant. Grievances are more likely to result in insurrection if the aggrieved groups confront a corrupt state with a weak repressive capacity and no hegemonic ideology. Organizational factors are also important. Do the potential rebels have access to an external sponsor? To a lucrative and portable resource such as diamonds, gold or oil? To weapons? To a sanctuary? If the answer to these questions is yes, counter-elites are more likely to mobilize followers and undertake an insurrection than if the answer is negative. Listing these contingent conditions reinforces the notion that neoliberal influences on conflict via inequality are indeed remote and mediated.

Third, *ecological decline and climatic disasters* constitute another indirect influence on armed conflicts and interethnic violence. Climate change, together with shortages of water, food and energy, constitutes a grave threat to the peace and future prosperity of fragile states (as suggested earlier). Water and food insecurity – resulting from severe droughts, desertification and extreme temperatures – leads to persistent, even worsening, poverty and hunger, the spread of disease, and heightened mortality rates. These conditions spawn interethnic conflict, as pastoralists trespass on the land cultivated by agriculturalists or the supposedly indigenous inhabitants of a region attack the "strangers" who currently till the contested soil. "Climate wars," the prototype being Darfur's civil war in Sudan, are likely to become more common. A pioneering study found a significant positive relationship between hotter years in Africa and the incidence of armed conflict. Extrapolating from temperature trends, it predicts a 54 percent increase in wars by 2030 in Africa, involving an additional 393,000 battle deaths (Burke et al. 2009). Another study confirms this prognosis, contending that "the effects of climate change threaten peace and stability in many parts of the world, especially in those which are experiencing national instability, weak government, economic problems, and instability" (González Bustelo 2008: 2; see also Goering 2011).

Resource wars on an interstate basis are also likely to become more frequent. Countries that lack adequate supplies of fresh water, energy or productive soils will be tempted to wage war on weak neighboring states with plentiful supplies, or which allegedly overuse a shared resource such as a river (Schwartz and Randall 2003). For instance, Ethiopia's building of the Millennium Dam on its Blue Nile – destined to be the largest hydroelectric project in Africa – has raised tensions with downstream Egypt. Climate change together with the growth of both populations and economies make resource wars more likely.

Whether these various distributional shifts, new insecurities and external shocks actually engender deadly violence depends centrally on the capacity of the central state to mediate or repress conflict and the effectiveness of the protest movements. Although an exploration of the second factor would take us too far afield, I should comment on the first. If states had begun to disintegrate before the initiation of macroeconomic stabilization, liberalization and democratization, then the new inequalities, uncertainties and dislocations hastened that process. Two trends undermine state effectiveness. First, the legitimacy and mediatory capacity of a state depends heavily on its provision of basic services – education, health, clean water, roads – together with the mounting of safety nets and, in many cases, the servicing of patron–client networks. However, external shocks – reduction of aid channeled through official channels, declines in the terms of trade, outflows of foreign capital, IMF-sponsored austerity programs – curtail a government's resources just as political tensions are rising. Central governments will then be less able to manage conflict by compensating the regions, classes, and young men who bear the brunt of the adjustments. Indeed, they may be unable even to maintain order, as emboldened regional leaders defy central authority. Emergent warlords may capture lucrative local resources – gold, diamonds, oil or timber – in order to build their own patronage networks.[25] Second, the authority of the government will suffer if it is seen as the puppet of external forces, such as the IMF or the US government. If national elites buy into the Washington or Post-Washington Consensus, this "consensus" risks alienating those domestic groups that clamor for protection from unleashed market forces. The consequent political turbulence, in turn, motivates threatened political leaders to move toward more centralized and authoritarian governance, despite democratic constitutions. National disintegration is then manifest in growing regional, communal, or class challenges to autocratic state authority.

When democratization accompanies economic liberalization in fragile states, the new party-based competition for power often sharpens divisions and raises social tensions (Snyder 2000; Sandbrook 2000b: chap. 4). Although established democracies provide institutional mechanisms for managing and resolving conflicts, *democratization*, the process of establishing such democracies, is fraught with mutual suspicions and anxiety. It is tempting for aspiring leaders to exploit existing ethnic grievances and identities to build voting blocs. In this event, out-groups may come to regard elections as zero-sum games, thus dangerously raising the stakes.

Development, in short, is a more knotty challenge than the early liberalizers imagined.

Conclusion

Neoliberal policies, though portrayed as the solution to developmental problems, are often part of the problems instead. These policies seek to propel growth and poverty reduction by the liberalization of domestic markets, opening up domestic economies to global market forces, the improvement of governance and collateral institutions, and the fostering of civil societies, decentralisation and social capital. But the deeper commodification of nature and social relations that this program entails has the effect of subjecting the essences of life to the opportunistic side of human personality. The detrimental consequences, this chapter suggests, are market volatility wreaking periodic havoc, growing inequalities that alienate many, ecological devastation, and the risk of deadly conflict. The danger is that the various dimensions of this multiple crisis will become mutually reinforcing, forming a downward spiral of human misery.

This mutually reinforcing effect is most pronounced in the least developed countries. Here, states are often fragile, mass poverty exists alongside high social and regional inequalities, and climate change, induced by global warming, already wreaks unprecedented droughts, desertification, floods and violent storms. High poverty and inequality, exacerbated by climate change and water and energy shortages, can instigate various forms of political violence in countries where state structures and legitimacy are weak. Although liberalism's vaunted "creative destruction" may augment global efficiency in the long run, the immediate costs are uncertainty and upheaval.

This damage instigates a disparate counter-movement of societal protection of which the Left is sometimes a part. But the vast regions of the Global South harbor a great diversity of conditions, and these circumstances delimit historical possibilities. Before discussing the strategies and dilemmas of the Left, we need to consider the hard realities shaping the practicability and nature of alternatives both within and beyond capitalism.

NOTES

1. In 1971, President Richard Nixon renounced the US government's promise to redeem US currency at a rate of $32 per ounce of gold. Most other currencies had been pegged to the US dollar.
2. Many governments in the Global South abused their policy autonomy to build highly protected economies with over-valued national currencies, thus lending credence to neoliberal prescriptions of rolling back the state.
3. Crises inevitably followed because the textbook theory that "self-interested behavior of sellers and buyers leads to equilibrating price adjustments whenever there is excess supply or demand" is often wrong. Instead, the "disequilibrating forces that are also the product of self-interested behavior" frequently overwhelm the equilibrating forces (Hahnel 2007: 1,145–6).
4. The statistics in this paragraph derive from Ghosh (2010: 213–20).
5. Exceptionally low interest rates in high-income countries impelled fund managers and traders in the latter countries to seek higher returns in emerging markets.
6. The Gini measures a range from 0, which indicates perfect equality of distribution, to 100, which represents perfect inequality. A Gini of more than 40 is high.
7. Firm trends cannot be drawn owing to unreliable, missing or non-comparable data.
8. The United Nations' Millennium Ecosystem Assessment, involving the collaboration of ten thousand scientists, concluded that 60 percent of "ecosystem services" – including the water cycle, the regulation of climate, pollination, global fisheries and natural waste treatment – were being used unsustainably, and were thus degrading (Ellwood 2010: 20).
9. Concise summaries of these trends can be found in Brown (2009), Morgan (2009), and Seidel (2011).
10. Ocean levels are projected to rise by about 1.8 meters by the end of the twenty-first century (UNDP 2006).
11. For evidence on how climate change impoverishes peasants, see Mideksa (2010).
12. The work of Elinor Ostrom (1990) showed, to the contrary, that natural resources held in common by a community (that excludes outsiders) were well protected by social norms and institutions.
13. This commodification sometimes provokes mass protests, as in the famous "water war" of Cochabamba, Bolivia in 1999–2000 that reversed the privatization of water delivery.
14. For a list of the major writers on Ecological Modernization Theory, refer to York and Rosa (2003).

15. Refer to Hawken, Lovine and Lovine (1999) for an example of this technocratic-managerial approach in which business solves environmental problems in its quest for higher productivity. But the assumption that the most efficient techniques inevitably win out is naïve – an unwarranted green technological determinism.

16. This bullet draws heavily on Lawn (2005: 219–21). The quote appears on p. 221.

17. By 2050, the world's population will have grown to 9 billion. For this population to live at the living standard of the top billion in 2004, we would need the resources and natural services of at least three, and probably five, planet earths (Porritt 2005: 285). See also Harper (2000: 373).

18. Consider the price charged for gasoline. The pump price of $3.00 per gallon in the United States in mid 2009 reflected only the cost of finding the oil, pumping it to the surface, refining it, and distributing gasoline to service centers, together with profits. But oil companies could only remain profitable by receiving tax subsidies and externalizing other major costs of production, including the costs of compensating societies for the damage inflicted by climate change, the health care costs of treating respiratory illnesses, and the military costs of protecting US access to oil reserves in the Middle East. Earth Policy President Lester Brown estimates that the price per gallon of gasoline, if one internalizes these externalities and removes subsidies, would be $15. At this price, demand would collapse, along with the US economy (Brown 2009).

19. This paragraph draws heavily on Lawn (2005: 210–24). See also Jackson (2009: chaps. 8 and 9).

20. For analysis of the latest incidents of deadly violence, refer to the website of the International Crisis Group, www.crisisgroup.org/.

21. For the massive dimensions of crime in Latin America and its causes, see Kliksberg (2006).

22. Consider the case of Guinea, which has suffered under authoritarian regimes and a gradually disintegrating state for more than fifty years. A majority of the population is both illiterate and poor; Guinea typically ranks near the bottom of the Human Development Index. Much of its wealth, derived from the export of gold, uranium and lumber, is stolen (Rowe 2010). The country is 173rd of 180 countries on Transparency International's Corruption Index. The Guinean state barely functions. The army and police act with impunity. Only the army's massacre of unarmed civilians and rape of scores of women in Conakry in September 2009 brought an international outcry and the promise of future elections.

23. See, e.g., the insightful analysis of Mexico's Chiapas rebellion in Tschirgi (1999). On the role of land in class formation and conflict in Africa, see Peters (2004).

24. Most of the fifty or so armed conflicts that raged within countries of what were formerly known as the Second and Third Worlds in the early 1990s had a communal basis (Harbom and Wallensteen 2009).

25. For the general process, see Reno (1998) and Putzell (2005). For an analysis of the textbook case of Sierra Leone, see Keen (2005).

4 Making history: agency, constraints and realities

In the Global South, the restrictive realities with which the Left contends are typically more numerous and onerous than those encountered by European socialists in the late nineteenth and twentieth centuries. For instance, in *The Great Transformation*, with its European and specifically British focus, Karl Polanyi could take for granted certain societal features and potential remedies that his counterparts in the Global South must treat as problematical. Polanyi could assume effective states able to maintain order and implement complex policies, class-divided but fairly cohesive societies, strong and autonomous organizations of the subaltern classes (especially labor), a lengthy democratic tradition, the rule of law, and national economies that not only would be shielded from volatile capital flows but also yielded sizable fiscal resources for redistribution. Some or all of these conditions do not obtain in the developing world, depending on the country.

In addition, Polanyi might retain confidence until his death in 1964 that a form of democratic planning could replace market societies and maximize freedom. But we are much more aware today of the limitations and dangers of central planning. Even modern notions of "participatory" and decentralized planning are probably doomed to failure (except at the local level). But this recognition presents yet another dilemma. On the one hand, markets now appear indispensable in complex, globally integrated economies. On the other hand, markets are cultural as well as economic institutions. The market's ever deeper penetration of societies breeds an individualistic, consumerist mentality that is inimical to the solidarity principles associated with the Left. Dealing with this contradictory reality involves difficult choices.

It is the task of political leadership to find ways of taming, adapting to, or circumventing structural constraints and recalcitrant realities. Adept leaders at the head of coherent organizations can redefine possibilities. leftist movements still make history, though never in circumstances of their own choosing.

The politics of the Left

Although movements of the Left cannot control the historical/structural conditions they encounter when they seek or attain power, they can make strategic and organizational choices that enhance their possibility of success. Here I refer specifically to the success of a Left that respects democracy as a means of struggle as well as an important end in any society it spawns. The politics of the Left concerns the construction of a progressive party or coalition and its interactions with social movements and the mainly class constituencies to which the Left appeals. Parties are important to the success of the Left, but strong parties cannot be conjured out of thin air. All the constraints considered in the next section shape what is possible. In addition, the typical single-issue focus of social movements (whether of workers, peasants, cooperatives, the landless, women, aboriginal communities, castes or others) presents progressive parties with major challenges in framing their programs. The party may want to form a mutually supportive, synergistic relationship with social movements, but such a relationship is hard to maintain in light of the societal conflicts. Finally, building redistributive coalitions also presents knotty issues owing to the typically fragmented class structure, not to mention communal loyalties.

Concerning the party, Atul Kohli's comparative study of India's states (1987) demonstrates the critically important role of left-of-center parties in explaining the divergent distributive outcomes. Regimes featuring an effective left-of-center party have superior distributive results – a conclusion that is doubtless applicable beyond the Indian cases. Effective leftist parties are characterized by cohesive leadership, programmatic appeal based on a coherent ideology, and organizational strength, according to Kohli. A party has organizational strength when it is able to penetrate society and mobilize potential constituencies. These constituencies vary with the level of economic development, but typically include some combination of organized workers, rural laborers, tenants, poor and middle peasants, informal-sector workers, and elements of the middle class. Competitive-party regimes featuring a leftist party with the traits just described will achieve more in the way of redistribution than regimes lacking them.

It is clear why regime type matters. Governments led by cohesive, programmatic parties with strongly organized popular support can maximize their autonomy from the dominant classes, whether landlords or corporations. This enhanced autonomy provides some leeway to progressive governments in changing the rules of economic life to promote social equity. The party's organizational power also allows it, and the state agencies its leaders direct, to restructure norms and institutions within civil society that hitherto perpetuated domination or intolerance, on a class, gender, caste, ethnic, religious or factional basis. Existing hegemonies, whether within constituent communities or within society as a whole, challenge the values espoused by the Left.

The "primacy of politics" refers precisely to the ways in which a state, democratically directed by a well-organized leftist party/coalition and uneasily responsive to autonomous organizations of civil society, actively promotes in the economy and civil society the common interest in equal freedom.

Left populism and social democracy, especially the radical variant, represent a rupture in hegemony. They aim to redistribute power, income, services, respect and sometimes assets to the many who may have acquiesced in the existing inegalitarian order. This rupture is unlikely to occur without the self-organization of various subordinate classes, strata and interests (Rueschemeyer 2004). They form social movements and civil associations dedicated to emancipation and improvement in their various guises. Such organizations may aim to achieve national liberation, labor rights and protection, caste uplift, the peasantry's right to land held by predatory landlords, human rights and democratization, equal rights for women, environmental preservation, aboriginal rights, the recognition of religious communities, and land rights of squatters in spontaneous urban settlements. Their activities may include demonstrations, protests, campaigns to influence public opinion, and civil disobedience. It is the difficult task of the leftist party to weld together several single-issue movements into a coalition, under the rubric of fairness and social change.

Radical parties, such as the Communist Party of India (Marxist) in Kerala and West Bengal, may play a role in instituting social movements (see Chapter 6). But social movements, for example labor movements or associations of indigenous people, may also develop autonomously and then cooperate to establish a socialist/social-democratic party (as in Brazil and Bolivia). Regardless of their origin, modern social movements and civil associations not only provide impetus for social change, but also may check oligarchical tendencies when radical parties assume political office.

It may take decades for social-movement activism to reignite following periods of harsh repression. Chile is a case in point. The brutal dictatorship of Augusto Pinochet eviscerated leftist associations after 1973. Only in the mid 1980s did civil society demonstrate its opposition to the dictatorship through the famous "banging of the pots" protests in middle-class and poor neighborhoods. But the major parties of the Concertación, when this coalition came to power in 1990, fostered neither participatory institutions nor linkages with social movements. The rebirth of civil-society activism dates only from 2006, during the presidency of the

Socialist Michelle Bachelet, and peaked in 2011 during the presidency of center-Right Sebastián Piñera. Massive protests emerged concerning increased gas prices, the building of mega-dams in Patagonia without public consultation, the rights of the indigenous people and, above all, an educational system perpetuating Chile's immense inequalities. The last grievance provoked a long series of public protests in 2011 and 2012, spearheaded by secondary and university students but later joined by trade unionists, the middle class and people from the *barrios*. Secondary students, who boycotted classes for so long in 2011 that many of them had to repeat their grades, demanded decommodification of education under the rubric "education can never be a business." Yet the proliferation of demands that accompanied the broadening of the protests in 2012 led to an incoherence that weakened the protest movement. Nevertheless, this evident rebirth of civil society portends a reinvigorated struggle in Chile around issues of equality and fairness.

Given the typically fragmented class structure of developing countries, the constituencies and social movements to which the Left appeals are highly diverse. It is difficult to design platforms and programs that knit together heterogeneous redistributive coalitions. The Left thus faces more onerous organizational challenges than those that confronted the Left in the more ethnically homogeneous and class-structured societies of nineteenth- and twentieth-century European countries. But, it must also be stated, the contrast between the Global South and the Global North is becoming less distinct in the twenty-first century. In the North, high rates of immigration are creating more heterogeneous societies. Globalization and deindustrialization have fragmented and depleted the working class. Technological change, outsourcing and growing inequality are stratifying the middle class. Resurgent religious attachments are also evident. In short, leftist parties throughout the world are facing increasingly similar challenges.

In the Global South today, labor movements rarely play as prominent a role in the Left as they did in the West in the initial era of economic liberalism (1830–1940). This diminished role is partly an outcome of a colonial international division of labor that characterized the late nineteenth and early to mid twentieth centuries. In this imperial arrangement, the "Third World" exported raw materials in exchange for imports of manufactured goods from the Western countries and Japan. This pattern of trade restricted the growth of an industrial working class. From the 1950s to the 1970s, import-substitution industrialization in the developing world allowed for the limited development of this class. Unions and workers then played a more important political role, as for example in Latin America's populist politics, prominently in Mexico, Argentina and Brazil. Export-oriented manufacturing since the 1960s in a few East and

Southeast Asian "tigers" and highly urbanized Latin American countries has boosted the size and importance of industrial workers. But neoliberal policies since the 1980s have undercut the influence of trade-union movements in typical ways.

Consider the impact of these policies. Except in East Asia, formal-sector employment declined or held steady while precarious employment and self-employment in the informal sector expanded.[1] In Latin America, for instance, just over half of non-agricultural workers labored in the non-unionized informal sector in the mid 2000s (Tokman 2007: 81). Privatization of overstaffed state corporations, cutbacks in the civil service, and trade liberalization that bankrupted many import-substitution firms have contributed to this trend. Formal-sector corporations that commonly sub-contract their labor-intensive processes to low-cost informal-sector firms also diminish formal-sector employment and limit the power of industrial unions. Moreover, trade liberalization, when accompanied by capital-account liberalization and openness to foreign investment, weakened trade unions by pitting workers in one country against workers in other countries with lower costs. In addition, pressure on governments from employers and the IMF to foster "flexible" labor markets led to more restrictive labor codes in many countries. They curtailed union and collective bargaining rights and transferred more power to employers. In certain cases, notably General Pinochet's Chile and South Korea, governments engaged in outright repression of organized labor in the 1970s and 1980s. Finally, the typically large "industrial reserve army" of the unemployed and semi-employed, together with governmental controls on unions, allow employers to hire workers at low wages and few benefits (Akhtar 2005: 136).

A growing number of employees, according to Guy Standing (2011), were thus pushed into a "precariat." The precariat lacks not only job security and adequate incomes, but also working-class identities. These conditions, which widely exist, are not conducive to the development of a powerful working class.

Nevertheless, organized labor is rarely quiescent. Organized workers in the more dynamic countries not only grew in number in the 2003–8 economic boom, but also suffered similarly wretched conditions as Western workers faced in the early twentieth century. In India, South Korea, the southern cone of Latin America, Brazil and South Africa, for example, the union movements are both well organized and politically engaged. Also, transnational union networks are emerging to challenge transnational corporations wherever they do business (Anner 2011). SIGTUR (Southern Initiative on Globalization and Trade Union Rights), a progressive alliance of trade unions from South Africa,

Australia, Singapore, Pakistan, India, Indonesia, East Timor, Thailand, Brazil and Argentina, is a case in point (see Lambert and Webster 2014). As for the political orientation of the world's largest working class – in the People's Republic of China – it remains unclear, owing to the party-state's co-optation of unions and the workers' unique experience of mistreatment under both state-socialist and state-capitalist auspices. But even where workers' organizations are state-controlled, wildcat strikes and boycotts often prove effective. Most workers, after all, work in vast cities where burgeoning squatter settlements house a multitude of self-employed and casually employed poor people. Working-class actions sometimes ignite more broadly based protests. Thus, trade unions, though not as central to the Left as in the earlier Western cases, usually play a part in counter-movements to neoliberalism.

Living close to the workers in the cities are the mainly poor people eking out an existence in the informal sector. The number involved in the informal sector is huge and growing, especially in the lower-income countries. According to estimates of the International Labour Organization (Schlyter 2003: 1) the informal sector in many developing countries accounts for up to 90 percent of the workforce and the vast majority of new jobs. In South Asia, formal-sector employment apparently accounts for only about 20 percent of the total labor force. This informal – largely unrecorded, unregulated, small-scale – sector encompasses a variety of activities including illegal or semi-legal services, artisanal work, small-scale capitalist enterprises and contractors, hawking and peddling and day labor. To complicate class identities further, some individuals work in both the formal sector as employees and the informal sector as self-employed individuals.

Are the burgeoning urban poor of the informal sector capable of concerted collective organization and action, or do they act more as mobs or crowds prone to occasional outbursts? Successful associations have developed in the informal sector. The Self-Employed Women's Association in India (SEWA) is often held up as a worthy example (Kapoor 2007). It represents three hundred thousand self-employed women, advancing their legal rights and access to health care and childcare. SEWA has inspired similar initiatives in South Africa and elsewhere. Unionlike associations for informal laborers have also emerged in Latin America. And Kerala's Left has succeeded in organizing various informal-sector groups and winning social protection and other benefits for them. But many obstacles impede the organization of the informal sector by the Left.

For instance, the urban poor are often internally divided by race, ethnicity or religion. Negative stereotypes abound. It is not unusual for Brazil's unionized workers, for example, to associate *favelados* (slum dwellers) with criminals (Gledhill 2006: 332). Furthermore, many poor and vulnerable people search for community and an outlet for their frustration, not in secular movements or leftist politics, but in fundamentalist religions: Islamism in the slums of North Africa, for instance, and Pentecostal churches in Latin American and many African cities.[2] One expert refers to Pentecostal Christianity as the "largest self-organized movement of urban poor people on the planet," with 40 million converts in Latin America alone (Davis 2006). Criminal gangs are another outlet for the alienation of young unemployed men, as well as an avenue for acquiring material goods. Some elements of the informal sector thus embody what Marx and Engels called the "dangerous classes" – individuals who are susceptible to populist appeals and clientelistic enticements and periodically engage in rioting and looting. Union and party organizing in the slums is challenging.

Rural groups play a diminishing role in the politics of the Left in our rapidly urbanizing world. In many middle-income developing countries of Latin America and East Asia, rural populations already form a small and falling share of national populations. In Africa and South Asia, however, the majority still live on the land.

Commodification of nature under neoliberal auspices has spawned a variety of rural and agricultural grievances that progressive parties have taken up. Neoliberal policies of privatizing land formerly governed by communal tenure arrangements have created many losers, as well as some winners. The building of dams, the installation of large, polluting mines and oil wells, the leasing and sale of vast tracts of agricultural land to foreigners ("land grabs") and the opening up of virgin forests to timber companies have alienated rural inhabitants (as well as environmentalists). Trade liberalization has allowed imports to undercut local agricultural producers, while the end of subsidies for fertilizers and other inputs places farmers in a more insecure position. Consequently, agrarian-based associations organize to demand price protection, subsidies, cheap credit, secure land rights, and the redistribution of concentrated landholdings.

Where instances of dispossession occur in regions dominated by indigenous communities, as for example in Bolivia and Ecuador, the economic demands of peasants interlink with ethnic/cultural demands for greater respect and territorial autonomy.[3] The resultant social movements tend to be powerful nationally, if the indigenous groups comprise a large part of the population. But the leftist parties who champion these cultural and economic grievances will be confronted with difficult choices when they form governments. The drive for economic growth by exploiting natural resources will often conflict with demands by indigenous people for the preservation of their lands and way of life and for local control of strategic natural resources.

National associations of peasants and small farmers have increasingly coordinated their protests and advocacy through transnational movements. A well-known example is La Via Campesina, which emerged in 1993 to represent small and medium farmers, rural women and indigenous communities, especially in Brazil. It has opposed neoliberal policies affecting its members and advocated family-farm-based sustainable agriculture and "food sovereignty" (the local production of a country's food requirements). It now boasts 150 local and national organizations as members, located in 70 countries in the Americas, Asia, Africa and Europe. Its advocacy has placed the organization in opposition to transnational agribusiness, prodding left-of-center governments to take action.

What of the amorphous "middle class"? Can the Left hope to appeal to the diverse groups aggregated under this rubric? To pose this question is to run up against the definitional issue. Although analysts talk about the proclivities and attitudes of the middle class, they use the term to apply to varying segments of national populations. Either a relative or an absolute standard is applied; the choice determines the purported size of the middle class and the likelihood that it constitutes a sociological reality rather than just a statistical category. Relative standards vary, though they all equate middle-income strata with the middle class. A common approach is to define the latter as comprising those who earn between 50 percent and 150 percent of the median income. The absolute measures, though also somewhat arbitrary, reflect an estimate of the income required by a family to support a "middle-class" lifestyle. Obviously, this measure is more likely to encompass a group with common interests and outlook than the relative standard. But the two measures often diverge in the proportion of the population deemed to be middle class. A recent South African study reports that the relative standard produced a category that encompassed 31.6 percent of the population, including a high percentage of African households in addition to white households. The absolute measure selected only 20.4 percent of households, with whites over-represented and Africans under-represented (Visagie and Posel 2013). Two reviews of studies of the middle class in Latin America also illustrate the variation in the proportions considered middle class. One paper concludes that this class comprises between one-third to three-fifths of the total, depending on whether an absolute or relative standard is used (Cruces and Diego Battistón 2011), whereas the other estimates the size of the middle class as falling between 35 percent and 55 percent, depending on the country and measure (Castellani and Parent 2010). It is also estimated that Asia alone will account for two-thirds of the world's middle class by 2030 (up from a 28 percent share in 2012) (Sanyal 2012). Whatever the precise numbers, the middle class has certainly expanded rapidly since 2002, especially in China and India, and now represents a substantial portion of electorates in the Global South.

Leftist parties cannot usually achieve electoral victories without claiming a substantial portion of the middle-class vote. There are reasons why the Left, even the radical Left, is able to do so. It is not only the smallholders, indigenous people, the informal-sector poor and the workers who experience economic insecurity as a result of neoliberal policies; members of the vaguely delineated "middle class" do as well. The precariousness of their employment, together with the insecurity deriving from inadequate social protection and expensive private services, dispose them to favor a strong state role in economic and social life (Tokman 2007; Riesco 2009: S33–4). White-collar employees, managers and professionals who lose their jobs, farmers who see prices for their produce undercut by cheap imports, public servants who are laid off through privatization or retrenchment, teachers who are not paid, and educated youth who cannot find satisfactory work – all these groups grapple with insecurity. Periodic financial crises fueled by speculative currency flows impoverish large segments of national populations, including the middle class (see Chapter 3). A longitudinal study of middle-class families in Mexico and Chile during a five-year period found that about one-sixth of the households fell into poverty during the years before 2006 (Torche and Lopez-Calva 2013: 425). Moreover, the poor quality of public education and health services, together with inadequate public pensions, frustrate middle-class families who cannot afford superior privatized services and pension plans. Meanwhile, pollution of air, water and soil as a result of the headlong rush to develop precipitates the emergence of environmental movements and protests, with considerable middle-class support. Corruption, abuses of authority, and the impunity enjoyed by the wealthy repulse middle-class as well as other voters. Consequently, Left populist and social-democratic parties have been able to construct cross-class coalitions in which the middle class has been a substantial element (for Europe, see Baldwin 1990: 9, 28; for the developing world, see Deacon and Cohen 2011: 242–3; Teichman 2012: 175–9).

Leftist parties may be able to frame issues in a way that appeals to the more economically vulnerable middle-class voters, but how firm is this support? The latter may respond positively to proposals for universal social protections, good public services and the protection of human rights and the environment. With neoliberal policies associated in the popular mind with the IMF, Western governments and transnational corporations, a nationalist appeal to reclaim economic and social policy may also resonate, especially in Latin America (Silva 2012: 22–3). Another widely popular theme is a renewed role for the state in economic life; the Left attracts support by promising to halt privatizations, create jobs, assist the unemployed and support farmers. Campaigns against corruption and extending participatory democracy will appeal to the middle-class along with other voters. But a newly prosperous, emergent middle class may desert the leftist coalition in the event of hard economic times or the party's move to a more radical position. Middle-class voters will tend to be pro-growth, and little interested in tackling deep-seated inequalities. Although research does not yet support an unequivocal conclusion, it is likely that the middle class is a volatile and unreliable ally of the Left.

Consider finally the role of social movements. Ideally, synergy develops between the progressive party/coalition and autonomous social movements of civil society (union federations, peasant and farmer organizations, human rights groups, justice movements, indigenous peoples associations, and so on). Synergy is important because it means that the limitations of each are balanced by the strength of the other. Parties play an indispensable role in bringing the Left to power – by means of good leadership, the unity of the party or coalition, and astute framing of the issues. Competition among parties in a democratic system impels parties of the Left to seek the support of social movements and voters with a programmatic appeal featuring enhanced fairness, democracy, national control and social citizenship. But the wealthy elites have long used the state and the legal system to protect their privileges. If the progressive party or coalition wins power, its leaders may well be co-opted by the oligarchy. Scrutiny on the part of the press and autonomous social movements is the best way to keep the new government attuned to its commitments.

Conversely, the progressive government has an important role to play in civil society. Many retrogressive practices survive in the private sphere. It is the role of the government in this situation to intervene in civil society to weaken or eliminate patriarchal, exclusionary, discriminatory and autocratic practices. The complementarity of civil and political society will, in the best-case scenario, drive forward the goal of equal freedom.

Commonly, however, a positive synergy does not develop because the circumstances are highly unpropitious. For one thing, the state apparatus may be ineffectual and riddled with corruption. In this case, it will be very difficult for the left-of-center government to deliver the public goods and democratic order it promised. Or dominant elites may prevail in the countryside. Or the poor may have become accustomed to receiving the material rewards of clientelistic politics. Or divided, parochial loyalties may sap the strength of both social movements and party. It is time now to consider the structural constraints and obdurate realities that constrain movements of the Left in achieving their goals.

Historical and structural constraints

"Opportunity structure," a concept developed by Fred Block and Margaret Somers, is a tool for understanding the national variations in constraints on political action. It focuses our attention on the relationships among international factors, national states, and contending national social forces in political-economic change. "Particular moments in the organization of the international economic regime provide particular kinds of opportunities for states to act, and this degree of freedom or unfreedom, in turn, shapes what is possible for class [and other group] struggle" (Block and Somers 1984: 73). The global opportunity structure thus constrains what national states can achieve; but domestic factors are also important in understanding outcomes – such factors as the level of economic development, class structure, ethnic or regional cleavages, the existence of autonomous civil-society organizations, cultural norms, the strength of state institutions and democratic or authoritarian status. The global and national opportunity structures together shape how effective political movements can be in instituting leftist alternatives.[4]

The global opportunity structure

Neoliberal globalization restricts the policy autonomy of national states through a variety of pressures that "discipline" governments implementing measures deemed hostile to free markets. The most significant of the pressures weighing on seemingly recalcitrant governments include the denial of private investment and capital flight, the rejection of loans and credit by the international financial institutions and donors, and the new imperialism of free trade as practiced principally by the United States. Although leftist movements may hope eventually to transform or reform this neoliberal global order, they must currently achieve their national goals within its limits. Yet too complete an adaptation to this reality by the adoption of neoliberal measures undercuts the Left's distinctive vision, lending credence to critics who claim that movements have sold out. Sometimes, a leftist government seems to have only two unpalatable choices: retaining its militancy, with the risk of capital flight and economic chaos, or diluting its program, with the risk of losing popular support.

A brief historical tour indicates the fluctuations in the global opportunity structure, leading to today's conjuncture. The first phase of global capitalism (1830–1940) was an era of imperialism, in which most of the non-Western world fell under the direct or indirect control of Europe, the United States and Japan. This era of colonialism and the "imperialism of free trade" in Latin America gave way to a post-World War II "golden age" of capitalism (1948–75). Keynesian economics in the West, Communism in the East, and state-directed development in the decolonized South provided some insulation of national economies from global influences. Governments sufficiently restricted the mobility of capital that firms saw their interests as linked to the development of national markets.

Since the late 1970s, however, global economic and geopolitical trends have dissolved this link. Capital counter-attacked, first in a West afflicted by stagflation, demanding among other policies a roll-back of capital controls and a dilution of monetary controls. Neoliberal dominance is manifest in the ensuing worldwide weakening of governmental powers to regulate the flow of goods, services, capital and skills across national boundaries. Technological revolutions in information processing, tele-communications and transport facilitated trends toward transnational production chains, worldwide financial markets and growing international trade. But politics and power remain key: lying behind global neo-liberalism is the augmented power of transnational capital and the new imperialism of free trade. The effect of these trends was to reduce the decision-making autonomy of national states, posing major challenges for national movements pursuing alternative to neoliberalism. Global governance, global financial movements and globally negotiated economic rules came to impinge more deeply on domestic policy domains than ever before.

Globalization constrains the capacity of leftist governments to undertake redistributive policies. First, the Global North's self-serving version of free trade – that perpetuates subsidies and trade barriers to protect their uncompetitive agricultural products and that outlaws infant-industry subsidization as "protectionist" – has reduced job-creating growth in many countries below the level it might be with a more level playing field.[5] Second, cross-border capital mobility, fostered by banking deregulation, capital-account liberalization and trade agreements, not only leads to periodic financial instability but also threatens with financial ruin countries deemed inhospitable to investors. As of 2012, an advisor to the World Trade Organization estimated that $3.7 trillion crossed national borders each day, equivalent to 5 percent of total global economic output (Hancock 2011: 6). This capital mobility has augmented the power of transnational capital to punish governments adopting measures deemed hostile to investors. Governments must compete for scarce foreign investment, and those that stray from conservative monetary and fiscal policies or nationalize local assets risk capital flight, speculative attacks on their currencies, high unemployment and a jump in poverty. This threat attunes even leftist governments to the demands of foreign investors for restrictive monetary and fiscal policies, often trumping the demands of their supporters for progressive tax reform, social protection schemes and accessible and high-quality services.

Third, the numerous multilateral and bilateral trade and investment agreements play an important role in restricting the policy autonomy of the signatories. Many governments feel they have no choice but to sign such treaties for fear of exclusion from lucrative markets or from coveted investment inflows. Signatories usually cannot impose special conditions on foreign investors and must permit foreign investors to sue the government for laws, regulations or practices that lower investors' profits for unacceptable reasons or infringe their intellectual property rights. Treaties administered by the World Trade Organization, especially the General Agreement on Trade in Services, the Trade Related Investment Measures Agreement, and the Trade Related Intellectual Property Rights Agreement, have expanded the legal rights of foreign corporations. Regional agreements, such as the North American Free Trade Agreement and the Central American Free Trade Agreement, and bilateral treaties have had the same effect. Remarkably, UNCTAD (2012) reports that an estimated 3,000 bilateral investment treaties were in force in 2011, up from only 385 in 1989. Moreover, investment rules are often included in preferential trade agreements. Tribunals have ruled that even environmental and health and safety regulations involve the "taking" of private property because they impose unjustifiable costs on the owners.[6] Finally, changes in the rules governing the international financial institutions since 1980 have empowered them to require neoliberal policy changes in exchange for certain types of loans and debt relief. In short, the global economic order has not been friendly to progressive governments in the Global South that wish to follow heterodox policies or exercise control over firms operating within their boundaries.

This outcome is not just the result of spontaneous economic forces. In effect, the United States government has used its powerful position to project globally its neoliberal agenda and discourage counter-hegemonic projects. It could undertake such an ambitious project for several reasons: the US's geopolitical position as the world's only superpower following the collapse of the Soviet Union in 1991, its economic power as the world's largest economy, its influence over the Washington-based international financial institutions and its cultural clout as exercised through its globally acclaimed universities, business schools and popular culture. Although President George W. Bush (2000–8) did not originate the US imperial system, he did expand it both by proclaiming a unilateralist approach and by projecting military power into the Arabian Gulf, Central Asia and Africa. For example, AFRICOM (the US Military Command in Africa) has, since its inauguration in 2008, allowed the

US and NATO to project military power into Africa, though working usually through African armed forces. The US's massive relative power has begun to wane recently, however, owing to several factors, especially the growing power of the BRIC group of countries – Brazil, Russia, India and especially China.

The "imperialism of free trade" (Gallagher and Robinson 1953) or "Open Door Imperialism" (Williams 1972) has a long history. Imperialism, of course, is a highly contested term. Not only do analysts mean different things by imperialism, but also its roots have been traced to both geopolitical pressures and economic imperatives associated with capitalism.[7] As I do not have the space to enter into this complex debate, I make only a limited argument. Whatever else imperialism may be in the neoliberal era, and whatever other motivations might impel US imperialism, it is given impetus from pressures arising from the neoliberal project spearheaded by the United States.

When major powers pursue a liberal or neoliberal policy of opening or keeping open foreign doors to their trade and investment, the result is often formal or informal empire. In the case of nineteenth-century Britain, imperialism was largely a function – directly or indirectly – of its economic expansion (Gallagher and Robinson 1953). The same can largely be said of the United States beginning in the 1890s, though in this case the material interest of the business elite and other citizens in expanding capitalism was intertwined with the idealist goal of extending democracy and individual rights to benighted foreigners (Williams 1972: 9). The rise of neoliberalism in the late 1970s gave a similar impetus to an expansionist foreign policy.

A liberal/neoliberal foreign economic policy on the part of a hegemonic power fosters the extension of formal or informal empire in three ways.[8] First, a free-market domestic and foreign agenda buttresses the economic power of the dominant country's corporate elite, thus enhancing its influence on public policy. There is a consolidation of economic power in fewer hands, as corporations merge and as coordination among giant corporations grows via policy networks (Carroll and Sapinski 2010). Today, 51 of the world's 100 largest economies are transnational corporations. Large nationally based corporations and financial services firms augment their leverage over government policy as they convert their economic power into political power through generous contributions to electoral campaigns, well-connected lobbyists, the funding of think-tanks, foundations and advertising campaigns, the threat of capital strikes if their interests are threatened, and the appointment of top government officials from the ranks of the corporate elite. The reduced autonomy of the US state from its corporate elite disposes it to intervene abroad to advance the interests of its transnational corporations, especially by opening doors to US trade, investment and capital inflows and safeguarding energy supplies and intellectual property rights. Such interventions may range from gunboat diplomacy to sending in teams from the IMF. The US government has come under intense pressure from corporations owing to the rise of industrial competitors, especially China, and the expansion of globally mobile financial capital based on Wall Street.

Second, free markets do not work effectively in the absence of supportive institutions. In peripheral economies where these institutions do not exist, powerful liberal/neoliberal governments are under pressure to oversee the installation of a functional institutional framework. The most important institutions are private property, predictable and competent government, the rule of law, and a well-functioning financial sector. In the neoliberal era, the intrusive role of institutional facilitators has been played by the IMF, World Bank, regional development banks and aid donors. The United States and its allies have been highly influential in the international financial institutions owing to their significant funding of these organizations, the location of these agencies in Washington, and the predominance of economists educated in US and British universities (Peet 2009). Periodic economic crises in the Global South, beginning with the debt crisis in the 1980s, provided the international financial institutions (and the US Treasury) with considerable policy leverage as lenders of last resort. Structural adjustment programs and, later, Poverty Reduction Strategy Papers committed governments to a range of policy and institutional conditions in exchange for loans and debt cancellation.

Third, hegemonic powers are also drawn into the internal affairs of foreign countries to quell unrest (political violence, "extremist" movements, terrorism), which often accompanies the dislocations associated with economic liberalism. Markets cannot operate in the absence of order: yet free markets are destabilizing because they introduce or reinforce inequalities, create new economic insecurities, and are prone to devastating fluctuations (see Chapter 3). In the post-9/11 world, threats both to the US's strategic position and the global market economy have centered on radical Islamism and fragile or failed states, which provide havens for terrorists, pirates and drug traffickers. The quest for order in fragile states gives impetus to the state-building conducted by the international financial institutions and donors in the form of governance and democracy programs. Where these programs do not suffice in restoring order, military assistance, covert action by special operations forces or even US and allied troops may be needed to bolster (or change) regimes and defeat extremism and terrorism.[9] The shock of 9/11 strengthened the predisposition of the George W. Bush administration to intervene unilaterally, under the rubric of a global war against terrorism (Dumbrell 2010: 18). Obama wished to resist this trend, but found himself drawn in regardless.

Although neoliberalism (and United States power) is still dominant, the global opportunity structure has shifted in the new millennium to accord greater national autonomy to Asian, African and Latin American states, especially the larger ones. On the one hand, America's relative power has declined, owing to the country's massive fiscal and trade deficits, its distraction by wars in the Middle East, its increasingly dysfunctional political system, and the rise of the BRIC powers. The US has become a major debtor nation, a fiscal situation exacerbated by major tax cuts and the cost of foreign wars. China's remarkable economic growth since 1980 has fueled its military power and rising influence in the world. Russia, buoyed by oil and gas revenues, started to recover from the collapse of the Soviet Union in the late 1990s. Its invasion of Georgia in August 2008 demonstrated its newfound assertiveness and the inability of the West to counter its move. The replacement of the G8 by the G20 in 2009 reflected the growing influence of the larger and more prosperous countries of the Global South, especially in Asia (see Cammack 2012; Pieterse 2014).

On the other hand, the formerly dependent states of sub-Saharan Africa and Latin America have gained greater autonomy from the West as a result of a commodity boom, cheap credit and the availability of China and India as alternative sources of investment, aid, loans and trade.[10] The influence of the internatonal financial institutions fell (2000–9), along with their loan portfolios. It is not coincidental that the rise of the Left in Latin America dates from the early 2000s.

The global financial collapse of 2008–9 gave further impetus to heterodox development strategies. This catastrophe threw tens of millions out of work and dramatically increased debt burdens at all levels. That the worst effects were felt in the heartlands of neoliberalism in the United States and Western Europe contributed to a more skeptical view of neoliberal doctrine and American economic leadership. Following this crisis, the United States was unable to persuade China to revalue its currency significantly in order to reduce the American trade deficit or to sway the G20 (in November 2010) to establish rules to deal with gross trade imbalances. Emblematic of a shifting global power balance was the appointment in mid 2008 of a Chinese national as chief economist of the World Bank, one moreover who espoused a "new structuralist economics" that assigned an important role in economic development to a proactive state (Lin 2012). Moreover, a number of governments in the Global South in 2010–11 emulated the Malaysian and Chinese examples of capital controls. Changing global circumstances presented new opportunities to anti-neoliberal forces.

Yet none of the new economic powers championed more than a moderation of neoliberal doctrine. China and India, having learned how to exploit the opportunities associated with the US-protected world order, were reluctant to press for an alternative. Influential segments of national business classes worldwide have gained a vested interest in neoliberalism, which has buttressed their power and privilege. Furthermore, capitalism's culture of possessive individualism has expanded far beyond national business elites. High annual rates of economic growth in China, India, Latin America and sub-Saharan Africa in the 2000s (and earlier in the first two countries) have forged numerically large middle classes of avid consumers. About one-quarter of the populations of China and India (300 million people in each case) and perhaps 60 million Africans participate (Sengupta 2011: 1–2; "Africa's Hopeful Economies" 2011: 82). The neoliberal era is far from over.

Thus, the global opportunity structure, though now more favorable to heterodox economic strategies, still constrains left-wing movements. Leftist development alternatives, as I show in chapters 5 and 6, have had to learn to live with an unpropitious neoliberal globalization and geopolitical configuration, even while working to augment national protection and change the global order. Social-democratic regimes have adapted to global realities by selectively adopting neoliberal policies. This tactic allows such regimes to survive, though by blurring the distinctiveness of their programs relative to the Post-Washington Consensus. Socialisms for their part, whether old-style as in the case of Cuba or new-style as in the case of Venezuela, persist by rallying regional support in opposition to American imperialism and by making accommodations with the market. Meanwhile, locally based experiments in equitable cooperation (Chapter 7) usually need the support of regional or national government to survive. Despite the continuing global-level constraints, however, a new Left has won some significant gains. In these cases, leftist movements have taken advantage of relatively favorable national opportunity structures.

National opportunity structures

Certain conditions are more conducive to the success of left-wing alternatives than others: a relatively advanced level of capitalist development, a class-structured society in which communal divisions are secondary, well-organized and autonomous social movements, a history of democratic governance, an effective state, and a level of social solidarity that holds an individualistic market mentality in check. Obviously, very few countries in the Global South exhibit many of these facilitative circumstances.

Socioeconomic conditions   Paul Baran aptly observed that "socialism in backward and underdeveloped countries has a powerful tendency to become a backward and underdeveloped socialism."[11] The same observation applies equally to social democracy. Both socialism and social democracy depend upon a programmatic appeal for popular support that is most persuasive in societies with class identities, traditions of independent political and social organizations on a non-parochial basis, and a civic culture.

Yet many countries in the Global South, especially those classified as low-income or "fragile states," lack these features. Instead, one finds countries featuring some combination of mass poverty, insular peasant societies, horizontal cleavages of ethnicity, religion or region that overshadow national class identities, authoritarian tendencies, and the prevalence of clientelist and populist politics. These countries are found primarily in sub-Saharan Africa, South Asia and the Caribbean/Central America. The common illiteracy and physical isolation of peasant households, together with parochial identities, endemic diseases and preoccupation with day-to-day survival, sap popular capacity to hold elites accountable. Peasant-based revolutions have occurred, of course – in China, Vietnam and elsewhere – but the outcome has been bureaucratic collectivism rather than socialism. Mass poverty, furthermore, diminishes the resource base with which to finance an effective state and universal, redistributive policies. And widespread poverty, especially when combined with a history of clientelism and corruption, erodes the probity of socialist/social-democratic cadres when they are faced with the temptations of office. "Peasants and workers coming out of poverty are not as a rule . . . interested in public office unless they can use it to cease being a peasant or worker, i.e. to cease being poor" (Kitching 1983: 53). Ideological fervor rapidly dissipates, and bureaucracies decline into neopatrimonial administrations.

In addition, commonly encountered personalistic and clientelistic politics undercut the national class identities on which leftist movements depend. Patron–clientship is a common informal institution; it denotes hierarchical relationships of selective incorporation that subordinate and divide the poor, thereby inhibiting lower-class solidarity and political mobilization. Instead of united class action, these conditions incline the poor and the exploited to seek individual remedies for generic problems such as unemployment, poor services, predatory officials, and lack of money to pay school fees or bribes. Additionally, a typically small organized working class, together with a large and unorganized informal sector in both rural and urban areas, deprives radical movements of the organized mass base and independent power centers to hold leaders accountable. Class is the predominant political identity in only a minority of developing countries, largely middle-income, more industrialized countries. The counter-movement to market liberalism is usually highly heterogeneous, with disparate interests and goals.

Finally, authoritarian tendencies in societies, whether manifest in outright dictatorship or pseudo-democracy, lead to the suppression of independent political and social movements. The absence of a democratic tradition also conduces to the degeneration into tyranny of any popular movement that attains power. Although none of these tendencies is inevitable, they are common and explain why socialism and social democracy in poor and underdeveloped countries so often deteriorate into caricature. Social conditions often form an opportunity structure that is unsupportive of class-based political movements seeking social redress.

The challenge to progressive parties, therefore, is to counter the divisiveness of civil society and promote a civic public of engaged citizens, primarily through a programmatic rather than a populist/clientelist appeal. The inclusiveness of such parties, their willingness to enter into coalitions and their programmatic politics are designed to allay mutual mistrust among particularistic groups. The leftist party/coalition, and the government to which it may give birth, must also counter the retrogressive aspects of "traditional" communities, such as patriarchy, intolerance, inequality and autocratic decision-making. To the extent that the movement and left-of-center government succeed, a civic community emerges – that is, the party/movement, in the words of one theorist, "rescues" civil society (Walzer 1999). A mobilized, rights-conscious civic public can then, in turn, counter opportunism, corruption and authoritarian tendencies in the national movement and state bureaucracy. This mutually supportive relationship reflects the positive synergy to which I earlier alluded.

Political conditions   The state – the continuous administrative, legal and coercive system that holds sway in a delimited territory – poses two challenges to the Left. First, a reasonably effective, developmentally oriented state is essential to any progressive alternative. Left populism and the radical and moderate varieties of social democracy all depend for their success on the probity, commitment and skills of the state apparatus. Yet, needless to say, strong states are rare. Second, the state must exercise enough autonomy from big business and its allies to permit a progressive government to undertake redistributive and other measures favoring the lower classes. As markets and much private property remain, the government faces some difficult choices. It must either bring a section of the dominant class on side through a class compromise or undertake social mobilization and class struggle. Each choice is fraught with danger.

Effective states are required by the Left even after the era of state socialism and centralized planning. The state is called upon to restrain and channel market forces so as to protect society and nature, to orchestrate incentives and regulations in order to foster job-creating economic growth, to administer the redistribution of services and social protections, and to augment inclusiveness by generating new opportunities for the poor and excluded. Equally important, the left-of-center government uses the state apparatus to reshape relations between the civil and political spheres in order to deepen democracy, especially by means of decentralizing decision-making powers and transferring revenues. To achieve such far-reaching goals, states need to be relatively effective and autonomous from the dominant economic class.

Yet the norm is varying degrees of ineffectiveness. Peter Evans (1995), in a wide-ranging exploration of the "secret" of the (authoritarian) developmental state, observes that such states were few in the Global South (in the mid 1990s). Rather, "predatory states" and "intermediate states" constituted the majority of cases (Evans 1995: 12, 45–7, 60). The former manifests self-aggrandizing leaderships, personalistic governments, the predominance of ethnic or other parochial identities, and the mercenary linkages of clientelism and corruption. The intermediate type features a modicum of bureaucratic organization and/or limited bureaucratic autonomy; nevertheless, clientelism, populism and rent-seeking remain common tendencies. Consequently, inconsistencies in industrial strategy abound and few state-sponsored collaborative projects with the industrial elite succeed. Atul Kohli (2004), in an impressive examination of the historical circumstances that produce economically effective "cohesive-capitalist states," also arrives at a tripartite classification of developing-world states. Kohli concludes that the "neopatrimonial states" (akin to Evans's predatory category) and "fragmented-multiclass states" (similar to intermediate states) together account for the bulk of the developing-world cases (2004: 9–10). Clearly, socialist and social-democratic prospects are bleak where predatory or neopatrimonial states prevail, but somewhat more promising in the context of intermediate states.

But that is not the end of the story. Some states that became effective states did not initially appear to be so. Syngman Rhee's government in South Korea in the early 1960s, for example, did not wield an efficient and disciplined bureaucracy, nor did the leadership abjure clientelism and corruption. However, committed cadres after 1965 were able to build a strong (authoritarian) state capacity. Granted, General Park as Korea's president had unusual advantages in this quest, especially the Japanese model as installed in Korea during its status as a Japanese colony (1910–45), a homogeneous population, a long history of central-ized rule, the evisceration of the landed oligarchy during the Korean War, the threat of Communism to act as a spur, a cohesive elite, and the support of the USA. Few aspiring developmental states will enjoy similarly advantageous conditions. Nor is the developmental state on the Korean model one to be emulated by the Left, for this model included repression of the working class and the goal of forging a modern capital-ist class. What is optimally needed is a *democratic* developmental state, which adds yet another level of complexity. But even if democratic developmental states are exceedingly rare, less disciplined and effective "developmentalist" states (as defined in Chapter 1, and elaborated in Chapter 5) may still emerge out of intermediate states to advance the Left's agenda.

The key point is that existing state capacity is not immutable (see UNRISD 2010: 65, 259–60). Committed leaderships can build states: they can find ways to *augment state revenues*, cultivate *generalized support of the public* – through nationalist and anti-corruption appeals, good governance, and the expansion of employment and social protections – and bolster *administrative capacity* through reforms aimed at enhancing meritocracy. Mauritius and Kerala (a state of India), though both fea-turing heterogeneous populations and initially low incomes, have forged "good-enough" states to support their equitable development paths (see chapters 5 and 6 respectively). Even countries that have experienced devastating civil wars, such as Rwanda, have clawed their way back to relative prosperity, owing to the determination of a ruling elite to avoid the pitfalls of neopatrimonial rule and the willingness of external donors to help. Rwanda and other sub-Saharan cases are cited as cases of "developmental patrimonialism" (Booth and Golooba-Mutebi 2011; Booth 2011). Determined human agency can make a difference in forg-ing developmentally oriented and socially inclusive states even in unpro-pitious circumstances.

The second requirement – that the state exercise autonomy from big business and its allies to advance the Left's goals – is equally demanding. On the dawn of its electoral success, a progressive government confronts the "structural power" of capital.

Structural power refers to the direct and indirect ways that corporations and their allies influence a regime's policy agenda. Neoliberal globalization accentuates the power of business because governments, to survive, are constantly under pressure to enhance their country's "competitiveness" in international markets and attract foreign investment and credit. To make matters more difficult, negotiated agreements have shifted decision-making power from the national level to supranational institutions such as the

IMF, the World Bank and the World Trade Organization. Insofar as these institutions reflect a neoliberal worldview, leftist governments must tread warily in dealing with them.

Domestically, structural power is magnified when an economy is dominated by concentrated economic power in the form of local and transnational corporations, when a few large media empires control newspapers, television and radio, and when well-organized employers' associations and corporations employ lobbyists, think-tanks and public opinion campaigns and provide campaign finance. If the Left in power challenges the role of the private sector, the private media and other mediators of public opinion undertake a prolonged campaign to discredit the government. Progressive governments in Brazil, Chile, Ecuador and Venezuela, for example, have suffered this onslaught.[12] The more of these conditions that obtain, the greater the capacity of the corporate elite to shape policy discourses – whether concerning taxes on business, deregulation, flexible labor markets, subsidies, a favorable investment climate, or lenient environmental standards or enforcement. However, where a country, such as Venezuela, boasts large reserves of a relatively scarce and essential commodity (oil), its government enjoys more independence on policy matters.

As long as a market economy based on private property exists, the Left will have to deal with the tension between economic power and political power. It is widely accepted that the state in a capitalist society exercises only "relative" autonomy.[13] The state's independence is limited by its perpetual need to extract revenues, which are generated (or not) by productive enterprises. For this reason, as well as concern that economic decline will undercut their popular following, progressive governments are constantly drawn back to the requirements of capital accumulation. Still, the state is rarely a mere instrument of the ruling class. Business's structural power varies from country to country. Moreover, the party/ coalition disposes of its own source of countervailing power: a cohesive, ideologically coherent, well-led and widely supported left-of-center party/coalition represents a counter-weight to the structural power of capital. The better organized and the broader this movement, the greater is the pressure on the government to remain firm in, its egalitarian, developmentalist orientation and resist unpalatable compromises. These conflicting pressures shape whether a leftist party follows a moderate path, negotiating a class compromise with capital, or adopts the path of class struggle in a radical-democratic strategy of transition to some version of socialism. In reality, however, moderate social democracy represents the left wing of the possible in most cases, owing to the power of national and transnational capital.

If centralized, top-down planning or even participatory planning could work to advance development and freedom, a revolutionary rupture would make sense. But the impracticability and oligarchical tendency of planning – and consequently the indispensability of markets – constitutes an obdurate reality that the Left ignores at its peril.

The indispensable market

Socialist experiments faltered in the twentieth century, lapsing into a centralized and authoritarian bureaucratic collectivism. Bureaucratic collectivism involved a merging of political society with the state apparatus, forming a party-state. This party-state then eliminated, or severely reduced, the autonomy of civil society and private property rights, subjecting the economy to centralized control. At the extreme, this control entailed the replacement of markets by a central plan and a command economy. Centralized planning failed, however, devastating society and nature. Cuba and North Korea are the only surviving exemplars, and Cuba under President Raúl Castro is gradually introducing market reforms.

The limitations of central planning are widely understood (see Bauman 1967; Roemer 1996: 15–16; Folbre 2001: 215; Malleson 2012: 328–9). Severe technical obstacles impede command planning in complex, rapidly changing national economies, especially in cases where the economy is entangled in foreign trade and investment. "The multiplicity, diversity and unpredictable changeability of wants, resources and technologies in modern economies ... defies the information processing and resource allocating capabilities of centrally planned and controlled systems" (Nelson 2003: 700). And the lack of competition removes a major impetus for efficiency-enhancing or product-improving innovations. In addition, missing or perverse incentives undermine efficiency. Workers have little incentive to work hard because they are rarely fired. In any case, the consumer goods on which they might spend their wages are unavailable or are of poor quality. Equally devastating, managers of enterprises and regional state officials generate misleading economic data in order to advance their own careers by presenting a positive record of local achievement. Poor data lead inevitably to faulty plans.

Finally, the planners tend not to be accountable to the people. Consequently, powerful bureaucrats are tempted to collude with others to misuse their positions for personal gain. (A genuinely democratic planning system would, in principle, obviate this problem.) Planning thus fails economically (at least beyond the early stage of industrialization), in addition to spawning a new bureaucratic and oppressive class society.

Can participatory or libertarian socialism, which has committed advocates, work more effectively? This model rejects centralized, authoritarian planning in favor of a decentralized, bottom-up planning system; in principle, the latter empowers ordinary producers and consumers to jointly plan the economy through a complex system of decision making.[14] "The linchpin of all libertarian socialist thinking," observes Chris Hahnel (2005: 140), is "the conviction that workers and consumers are quite capable of managing themselves and their own division of labor efficiently and equitably." Private property, along with markets, disappears, replaced by some form of collective or cooperative ownership. People jointly make decisions regarding production and consumption by means of a complex and decentralized set of institutions. Workers' councils within each enterprise and consumers' councils organized at the neighborhood level constitute the base of participatory planning. More inclusive regional and national councils and confederations receive plans concerning production and consumption from their lower units and communicate with each other to coordinate a final plan. Planning boards, established by the state, play a critical role in channeling data to the various councils.

In this scheme, the state would be required not only to provide vast amounts of accurate data, but also to devise procedures ensuring that the various councils and committees arrive, in a timely fashion, at negotiated agreements concerning production and consumption. It would need to develop procedures for melding the multitude of plans, negotiated at various levels, into a coherent and realistic plan for the economy as a whole, and coordinate the plan's implementation through a variety of decentralized production and distribution enterprises. Finally, workers' councils within their enterprises would decide who will manage the firms, how the different tasks will be allocated, and who will receive what material incentives according to the effort and sacrifice that each worker has expended.

Even among socialists, critics have questioned whether such a complex system could ever work (Weisskopf 1992: 15). Champions of participatory socialism themselves acknowledge that this strategy can be achieved only in the long run (Hahnel 2005: 253). Propelled by a popular movement, the socialist party leadership would socialize private property and replace markets with a complex and hierarchical set of participatory institutions of workers and consumers. The abolition of private property, not to mention the necessary transformation of the culture of possessive individualism, would require a revolution. *Homo socialis* would have to replace *homo economicus*, with the introduction of a new system of non-market incentives and cooperative decision-making.

Even then, the feasibility of the system is doubtful (see Malleson 2012: 331–2). How accurately can consumers predict what they will wish to consume in the following year? How can producers forecast what they can produce, in light of uncertainties concerning the availability and cost of raw materials and changing technologies? How will demand actually be coordinated with supply, given the shifts in demand for goods that will inevitably occur? Will people willingly participate on a continuing basis in numerous, demanding meetings and negotiations that require considerable technical knowledge? The short answer is that national economies are too complex to plan, even on a participatory basis.

But this conclusion does not rule out the practicability of planning at lower levels and with respect to narrower tasks. Democratic planning at the local level can work quite effectively, especially if it is restricted to infrastructural and services provision. Instances of this approach in the form of participatory budgeting and decentralized planning (in Kerala, for example) receive attention in the chapters that follow. Such experiments not only provide public facilities and services that ordinary people identify through participatory procedures, but also empower groups that formerly played no part in public life.

At the national (and international) level, the case for markets rests on the likelihood of realizing the practical advantages of markets while controlling their destructive social and ecological effects. Markets and their associated material incentives offer several well-known advantages in complex national economies operating within a global system. Market competition engenders strong incentives for firms to provide goods and services that "customers want or can be persuaded they want," and to do so in a "moderately efficient" manner (Nelson 2003: 700). Competition also stimulates technical and scientific innovation – Josef Schumpeter's vaunted "creative destruction."[15] In addition, the rise of market economies has, for some groups, been a *liberating* rather than a confining force. Marshall Berman speaks of "development" as a Faustian bargain in which the quest for prosperity through the market destroys valued traditional institutions in the name of increased efficiency (Berman 1982). Yet some traditional norms and institutions that market forces undermine have perpetuated hierarchy, patriarchy, domination and exclusion. Their demise, though a loss to the dominant elites, may be experienced as *emancipation* by the dominated.

Emergent markets have variously fostered new opportunities for subordinated women, slaves, serfs, ethnic minorities and castes subject to social exclusion.[16] In addition, liberalism's discourses on "development" and "democracy" have furnished the wretched of the earth with normative themes – freedom, justice, human rights, participation – that they have used to gain greater voice and opportunity in currently patriarchal, status-ridden and autocratic societies. Emancipation does not therefore neatly align with Polanyi's "counter-movement" of societal protection; his "double movement" might better be reconceived as a triple movement, with emancipation as a separate movement with a variable relationship to the other two (Fraser 2011). Awareness of the dangers posed by markets should not blind us to their potential benefits.

If the market is indispensable at the national level, the models of the Left range from market socialism at one end of the spectrum to the social market at the other. Market socialism, in principle, takes advantage of the efficiency gains of markets while ensuring a more egalitarian distribution of assets and power than capitalist alternatives.[17] All productive enterprises in this system are either workers' cooperatives or managed by a democratic state that distributes the profits to the people. But this alternative exists only at the theoretical level. The "social economy" is closer to the reality of actual experiments in the Global South.

The social economy is based on the assumption that the disutilities of markets escalate when markets are extended to the "fictitious commodities" – labor, nature and money. Polanyi suggests that we should reject *market society* or a self-regulating market system, but not necessarily *a society with markets*.[18] To build an economic system on the "commodity fiction" is to induce severe social dislocations, inequalities and environmental degradation (see Chapter 3). Markets for machinery, consumer goods and services, and stocks (real commodities) are actually distinct from markets for the factors of production. Markets for the former usefully adjust supply to demand and fulfill human needs; they should be as self-regulating as possible. But the same logic does not apply to labor, land and money. These considerations suggest that the (re-)embedding of markets for the fictitious commodities – in protective state legislation, regulation and social norms – is of special importance to leftist programs. The re-embedding of markets – and hence the partial decommodification of labor, land and money – is manifest in the expansion of a social-market economy, a concept I elaborate in the following chapter.

But the goal of the Left is not only decommodification but also to enlarge the sphere of democratic decision making. The challenge is to reduce the scope of both technocratic planning and market forces. Strategic economic considerations, such as whether to promote one sector of manufacturing (perhaps automobiles) while allowing others to decline, or to realign investment priorities as between agriculture and industry, should be subject to the democratic process, not left either to the technocrats or to blind market forces. Much scope for creative thinking remains even if the Left accepts markets and limited property rights.

The culture of possessive individualism

Markets may be essential in modern economies, but even a Polanyian "society with markets" may inculcate values and attitudes at odds with the Left's mission. Markets, though usually understood merely as economic institutions, also mold cultural norms, forging a market mentality. Will greed and selfishness sabotage the Left?

Possessive individualism, which initially held sway in Europe and North America, has now spread worldwide. It is fostered by capitalist relations, but it also, in turn, reinforces capitalism. Possessive individualism is the culture that associates well-being with a "personal quest to acquire, to consume, to indulge, and to shed whatever constraints might interfere with these endeavours" (Bacevich 2008: 16; see also Cunningham 2005: 132–3). It is the internalized notion that a person's self-worth is measured by his/her privately held assets, and that there is never "enough." The market mentality reaches its fullest expression when individuals see themselves as commodities, things to be burnished so as to raise their market value and thus their self-esteem. This instrumental, individualistic rationality may not be the "natural" orientation of human beings, but living in a market society may erode the bonds of community and social obligation to the point that it appears to be so. This culture, in breeding indifference to the interests of others, is inimical to the solidarity that the Left seeks to foster.

A detailed study (Boo 2012) of the poor in Annawadi, a Mumbai slum, graphically illustrates how the undermining of reciprocal obligations can turn the poor against each other. Mumbai's poor today are apparently even more desolate than in-migrants in earlier decades when the solidarities of kin and village remained strong. According to the author, the struggle to get ahead and ward off a predatory, corrupt state fuels a competitive ethic in which poor individuals become indifferent to the suffering of their neighbors. Life among the poor resembles a war of all against all, where the material success of one is gained at the expense of others. The disabled, the ill, those with bad luck just disappear. Those who get one leg up on the ladder of success are not inclined to assist those left behind. And the well-off withdraw into their insulated sphere, into gated communities if affordable, with reliance on private security, private schools and private medicine. Meanwhile, party politics, rather than address the entrenched problems, retreats into make-believe. The fantasy of personal wealth and consumption, in the midst of mass poverty, undermines cooperation and empathy.

This portrait, though vivid, underplays the many instances of collective action on the part of the urban poor. Slum-dwellers' groups, housing rights movements, sex workers' unions, and small vendors' associations are active in Mumbai (Sengupta 2012). Nonetheless, a cultural shift may well be taking place as the sphere of social responsibility shrinks.

While Annawadi may be an extreme case, the vast literature on social change suggests many similar cases of atomization exist together with others in which a more solidaristic ethos survives. A massive World Bank study (Narayan 2000) of the "voices of the poor" worldwide concludes that "the disintegration of social order is compounded by the fact that for many the old coping mechanisms based on traditional networks are fast disappearing. The poor speak of a loss of community, which was once a partial substitute for the lack of assistance from distant state regimes the poor felt powerless to change." Among the Ladakhi of the Kashmiri Himalayas, a thirteen-year study (Norberg-Hodge 2009) finds that the rapid and belated penetration of this remote region by Indian administration and market relations led to the unraveling of close-knit communities and the rise of individualism. "The fabric of local interdependence is disintegrating, and so too are traditional levels of tolerance and cooperation" (Norberg-Hodge 2009: 123). A comparative study of Africa (Hyden 2006: 151–2) notes that reciprocity at the level of the extended family is in decline. Evidence of social breakdown abounds in the cities and increasingly in the countryside too.[19] Other research suggests a more variegated picture. MacLean (2010), in an incisive study of four Akan villages (two in Ghana and two in Côte d'Ivoire) finds that the informal bonds of reciprocity have loosened in all the villages, but the nature of the remaining ties depends on divergent colonial experiences. In-depth analysis of a series of villages in Senegal and Burkina Faso (Bernard et al. 2008) discovers a remarkable survival of solidarity. A variety of voluntary associations exist to promote the common interests of villagers, including the poorest. Clearly, the degree of individualism, though generally on the increase, varies markedly, even from one village to the next.

The sway of possessive individualism is also revealed through surveys of consumption trends. Personal indebtedness in Latin America – Brazil and Chile for instance – has mounted rapidly since 2000, driven by competition among banks to press their credit cards on consumers. Credit-fueled consumer spending supported rapid economic growth, but also led to high levels of indebtedness by 2010 (70 percent debt-to-income level in Chile, for example). Consumption has also surged in China and India as incomes of the middle classes rise. The Economist Intelligence Unit applauds the trend toward more "viable consumers" during the next two decades. China's government presses for growth above all, living as it does with the fear that a decline in the country's high growth rate will destabilize the political system. India's affluent class, the Unit reports (with apparent approval), has "shrugged off" any "traditional qualms about displays of wealth" (Economist Intelligence Unit 2011). When traditionally tight-knit communities bound by social obligations turn to an ethic of self-gratification, the world is changing.

What are the implications of this change for the Left? Some may argue that the possessive-individualist ethic has become so deeply ingrained that it will require a totalitarian government and "re-education centers" to eradicate. However, this option runs counter to the democratic stance of the new Left. In fact, the loosening of traditional solidarity offers an opportunity to progressive movements. With the atrophy of the social obligations that provided people with an informal safety net, insecurity and vulnerability grow. Progressive movements aiming for universal social protections, accessible and high-quality public services and other assistance can gain popular support by offsetting the vagaries of market forces. This program may have appeal even to the emergent middle class. In effect, the Left offers a modern, institutionalized system of social insurance to replace the desiccated traditional system of reciprocity. Perhaps a "fearless society" can counteract the influence of possessive individualism by demonstrating the benefits of mutuality (Cunningham 2005: 132–3).

Conclusion

To achieve its goals, the Left in the Global South must cope with more exigent social, political and cultural conditions than European socialists earlier encountered. Opportunity structures vary considerably from country to country and time to time, however. Shifting global power structures foster a greater or lesser leeway for national decision-making and heterodox models. And national opportunity structures vary widely, within regions and across regions. Within these parameters, leftist politics, if effective, exploits hidden possibilities for progress.

Yet the left wing of the possible is, in most liberal-democratic cases, moderate social democracy. This outcome is readily explicable in terms of the difficulties involved in forging a coherent, well-organized and programmatic party, shaping a synergistic relationship with social movements, overcoming structural constraints, and surviving within a hostile global order. Only in a few countries, where opportunity structures are more open, do governments gain the policy leeway to pursue a sustained radical path.

The following two chapters assess the nature, challenges and circumstances of the strategies of the Left, beginning with moderate social democracy.

NOTES

1. For an overview, consult Munck (2013); concerning Latin America, see Silva (2012: 9–10).
2. Salvation in both cases involves personal conversion and piety, not collective political action to build a just world.
3. On the Latin American situation, see Silva (2012: 12).
4. This conceptualization, which avoids determinism, is close to the position recommended by Fernando Cardoso and Enzo Faletto in their classic study *Dependency and Development in Latin America* (1979: xvi): "We conceive the relationship between external and internal forces as forming a complex whole whose structural links are not based on mere external forms of exploitation and coercion, but are rooted in coincidences of interests between local dominant classes and international ones, and, on the other side, are challenged by local dominated groups and classes."
5. Many scholars, including some in the mainstream of economics, have contended that the existing pattern of globalization works against the interests of the poor in the Global South, and needs major reform. See, for example, Stiglitz (2002) and Evans (2009).
6. For the case of the North American Free Trade Agreement, see Swenarchuk and Sinclair (2014).
7. For a concise overview of the various theories, refer to Kettel and Sutton (2013).
8. The following analysis draws on Gallagher and Robinson (1953) and Prasch (2005).
9. A policy that continued under President Barack Obama. In 2010, the US deployed Special Operations forces in 75 countries, up from 60 in early 2009 (DeYoung and Jaffe 2010).
10. India lagged far behind China as an economic partner to African governments until the late 2000s. India–Africa trade rose from just $3 billion in 2000 to $46 billion in 2010. By that time, China's trade with Africa reached $110 billion (York 2011).
11. Baran (1957: 9). For the same conclusion, see Harrington (1972: 288–95).
12. Consider the case of Brazil. Fourteen families own 90 percent of the country's communications media. The *Globo* group alone owned 61.5 percent of the TV stations and 41 percent of newspaper circulation in 2006. In 2010, President Lula da Silva drafted a media bill to establish basic ground rules for the media. A storm of criticism mounted by the media led to the shelving of the bill in 2011 (Lambert 2013a: 14–15).
13. For a concise review of this debate, refer to Bieling (2007).
14. An impressive defense is provided by Hahnel (2005), especially chaps. 7–9. See also Devine (1992).
15. Although the satisfactions of cooperation with others in a joint exploration and the joy of discovery are also important motivations, as I contend in Chapter 2.
16. For a graphic illustration of how the commercialization of fisheries in southern India created new opportunities for women, lower castes and youth, see Sundar (2012: especially chap. 1). See also Muller (2006: 12).

17. For a comprehensive discussion of the merits and problems of market socialism, refer to Wright (1996), especially the chapter by Roemer. See also Miller (1989).

18. "[T]he end of market society means in no way the absence of markets. These continue ... to ensure the freedom of the consumer, to indicate the shifting of demand, to influence producers' incomes, and to serve as an instrument of accountancy, while ceasing altogether to be an organ of economic self-regulation" (Polanyi 2001 [1944]: 260).

19. For case studies of the decline of solidarity in Africa, see Schaffer (1998: 70–4), Sseguya, Mazur and Masinde (2009) and Van Binsberger (2001).

5   Pitfalls and promise of the moderate Left

Although analysts in the Global South as well as the North have long accepted "the Left" and "socialism" as denoting political tendencies in their regions, "social democracy," another European-derived term, is more controversial. The first two terms have passed into common usage globally, but the last term has not – as yet. Some social scientists deny the validity of extrapolating this concept beyond its Western bailiwick. They claim that the context of social democracy in Europe, especially the existence of a large and well-organized working class and corporatist arrangements, does not obtain in the developing world, and that the term should therefore be avoided (e.g. Levitsky and Roberts 2011: 23–4). To the contrary, I contend that social democracy represents a political tendency within capitalism globally. This chapter focuses on the pitfalls and promise of moderate social democracy in the Global South.

The pitfalls arise, I contend, from a leftist government's response to what I identify in Chapter 1 as an intrinsic conflict within capitalism between the liberal movement and the societal counter-movement. I argued earlier that this conflict is more in the nature of an inherent, persistent tension than an irreconcilable contradiction. In essence, the clash is between the logic of disembedding the economy (giving priority to commodification, liberalization and efficiency), on the one hand, and, on the other, the counter-logic of re-embedding markets (protecting society and nature by decommodifying labor, land and money and promoting redistribution and reciprocity). This conflict can intensify into a deadlock, leading to economic crisis and eventually a political crisis, as in Germany in the 1920s and early 1930s. Alternatively, a refurbished modus vivendi may arise – championed by a well-functioning democratic system, as in the case of President Roosevelt's government and its New Deal, or an enlightened dictatorship, as in the East Asian developmental states. A modus vivendi can flourish for a considerable time: the Keynesian era of state-directed capitalism, for example, lasted throughout the golden age of capitalism from the late 1940s until the early or mid 1970s, before running into trouble. In the Global South, this era encompassed state-directed import-substitution industrialization as well as socialist experiments, some more genuine than others. However, *any modus vivendi is only provisional,* because inevitable shifts in economic performance, technology, class power and ideology, and global power dynamics will spur either the movement or the counter-movement to demand a fundamental realignment of priorities.

Leftist parties and their supporting social movements initially form part of the counter-movement, but as they move closer to the levers of power they become enmeshed in the underlying dialectics. The leftist forces face a strategic choice fraught with dangers: to forge within capitalism a new modus vivendi more favorable to their constituencies or to attempt to abolish the dialectic by transcending capitalism. The factors that shape the choice of strategy are diverse and embedded in the history of the countries concerned; they cannot neatly be summed up in a formula relying on a small set of independent variables. In general terms, we can say that a country's global and national opportunity structure (as clarified in the previous chapter) constrains the range of choices that a left-of-center party can realistically pursue. However, the party's leadership may misconstrue the opportunity structure, which often leads to disaster. Alternatively, an exceptionally well-organized, ideologically cohesive and well-led party may find hidden possibilities for change that sometimes emerge from a long period of strife. Dominant policy paradigms, which change from time to time (see Chapter 2), also shape the decisions of the Left. When a progressive party assumes power, it may find itself subjected to consistent advice from governmental technocrats and advisors from the international financial institutions, In the event of a crisis, such as a major balance-of-payments deficit, high unemployment or a depreciating currency, this advice may be seen as pointing out the only prudent path. Moreover, a moderate path may promote new classes, which then gain an interest in its perpetuation. If close ties link the emergent elite to the political elite, a new governing coalition may underpin the new modus vivendi between the movement and the counter-movement. The comparison below of the South African and Brazilian paths since the 1990s illustrates the complex factors shaping the Left's strategic decisions.

Whatever path is chosen, it is fraught with complex tensions and unintended consequences. Unsatisfactory outcomes, from the viewpoint of the counter-movement, are manifest in several tendencies: the decay of social democracy into macroeconomic populism, or the slide from socialist or social-democratic intentions to an implicit embrace of social liberalism, or the decline of socialist transformation into bureaucratic collectivism. This chapter focuses on the first two pitfalls; the next chapter considers the bureaucratic-collectivist tendency.

Certain social-democratic administrations, however, succeed in managing the inherent tensions. I explore what constitutes success in these cases, both by surveying actual cases and by constructing an abstract model of redistribution with growth. Although the social democratization of capitalism involves false starts and messy and unheroic compromises, its justification lies in the absence of any superior and practicable alternative.

The challenge of the moderate social democrats is to advance equal freedom, involving redistribution, decommodification and inclusive democracy, without undermining the productivity of capitalism. On the one hand, the Left, to retain its popular support, must extend and deepen the rights of political and social citizenship in accordance with its ideological commitments. On the other hand, it must attend to the efficiency/ accumulation imperative because the party's continued success depends upon robust economic growth and the ensuing jobs and revenues. Yet growth, according to neoliberal doctrine and the corporate elite, depends on creating an orderly market system. A robust market order involves respect for private property, enforceable contracts, deregulated markets for labor and money, adequate economic infrastructure, tax incentives, and conservative monetary and fiscal policies. It is clearly a difficult feat to reconcile the movement and the counter-movement in the circumstances of the Global South.

These dual imperatives, of course, are not wholly contradictory. Developmental states, such as formerly in Japan, Taiwan and South Korea, managed to achieve rapid industrial growth with policies that also maintained distributional equity. Public investment in "human capital" (education and health care) not only fosters equality but also raises productivity. Redistributing concentrated land holdings from a landed oligarchy to formerly landless or near-landless peasants usually increases agricultural output while enhancing equity. Higher wages for workers can promote both equity and accumulation because they spend a higher proportion of their incomes than the rich. Investors then have an incentive to expand production oriented to the local market – though export-oriented firms producing primary commodities and labor-intensive goods demand low wages to maximize their competitiveness. Finally, egalitarian social policies build social harmony; the resulting governmental legitimacy and peaceful industrial relations, in principle, encourage further investment and growth. But, despite the theoretical compatibility of the dual imperatives, it is politically challenging to reconcile them, especially in highly unequal societies oriented to export markets.

The first pitfall emerges when leftist governments champion the counter-movement in a populist challenge to the economically powerful, flouting the conditions for capital accumulation within a global market system. This is largely a twentieth-century pitfall; most instances occurred in the state-dominant era of import-substitution industrialization and state socialism. Before 1980, both mainstream development thinking and socialist theory accorded an important role to the state in modernizing the economy and building a more just society. Closely fought elections, where democracy survived, prodded leftist parties to escalate their promises and material enticements to attract support. If the new administration then yielded to the populist temptation – inflammatory rhetoric combined with redistributive programs, expansionary economic policies, and increases in minimum wages while controlling prices – disaster was the likely outcome. The unpredictable environment and threat to profits undermined "business confidence," triggering capital flight and capital strikes. The consequent inflation, balance-of-payments deficits, growing unemployment and falling state revenues precipitated a downward spiral and eventual economic breakdown. A political crisis often accompanied the economic crisis. At the worst, "macroeconomic populism" (Dornbusch and Edwards 1990) perversely victimized the very people that the policies were designed to help.

My contention is not that the Left should always avoid radical redistributive programs because they invariably provoke an accumulation crisis. One can argue that stimulating economic growth through expanding local demand for necessities is a theoretically sound economic policy. But the harsh reality is that developing countries that are heavily dependent on foreign markets, foreign investment and foreign credit can rarely succeed in such a provocative action. Such governments miscalculate their global opportunity structure or proceed regardless of the obvious constraints. To ignore the disruptive power of local and transnational capital in such circumstances is to court disaster.

Alternatively, leftist leaders in power, intimidated, rightly or wrongly, by the structural power of capital or enticed by the opportunities for personal and group enrichment, may cater to the liberal movement's efficiency/ accumulation imperative at the expense of equity and redistribution. This is largely a twenty-first-century pitfall: purportedly leftist governments, driven to reassure the local business class, foreign investors, financial markets and the IMF, implicitly move to a centrist position – social liberalism or the Third Way. The Left effectively makes peace with neoliberalism (however it portrays its ideological commitments), adopting palliative measures that do not challenge inequalities in life chances. Politically, of course, a leftist administration may find itself so constrained that adhering to the Post-Washington Consensus is its only realistic option. Yet the party's rank and file and supporters, inspired by a vision of a just society, react antagonistically to its leaders' pragmatic accommodation of the "enemy," its placating of clientelistic and corrupt coalitional partners, or its enriching of narrow elites. Disenchantment may not surface during boom times, when prosperity trickles down; however, hard economic times may precipitate a crisis as supporters defect.

The problem in this case is not that the social-democratic party/coalition seeks a class compromise – this is inevitable – but that it settles for too little in the bargain. The government may implicitly assent to oligopoly, financialization and even rent-seeking behavior, despite the fact that these tendencies are both economically and socially suboptimal. To be on the Left surely means (ironically) that the government uses the state, at a minimum, to discipline the business class so as to realize the theoretical advantages of markets.

Has the moderate Left found a way to balance the movement and the counter-movement, avoiding both old-style populist and Third Way snares? Steering clear of both provocation and intimidation requires a delicate touch and considerable good fortune. I contend below that we can discern the outlines of such a balance in certain contemporary cases. Political ingenuity has allowed some social-democratic regimes to live with neoliberalism, without being destroyed or swallowed by it.

Before discussing these tensions in concrete cases, I pause to consider what distinguishes moderate social democrats from the social liberals with whom they are often confused.

What is moderate social democracy?

Many leftist parties in the Global South, the majority of them in Latin America, not only identify themselves as social democratic (and belong to the Socialist International), but also have pursued what appear to be social-democratic strategies.

These strategies manifest the following traits. They install a particular *regime* in a capitalist society: one that comprises a widely supported set of norms, procedural rules and organizational arrangements designed to deepen democratic control of the state and to employ this state to regulate markets and otherwise intervene to enhance social equality, institute universal social protection and (partially) decommodify labor. A *social-market economy*, sometimes referred to as a social or solidarity economy or social capitalism, thus expands as the pre-existing liberal-market economy shrinks. In principle, the invisible hand of social norms shapes markets, via the state, to serve the common good. Furthermore, moderate social-democratic regimes rest on an implicit or explicit social or *class compromise*, sometimes minimal, which may be periodically renegotiated.[1] As new challenges arise, the compromise will need to be renegotiated to accommodate new policy directions or organizational arrangements. Finally, social-democratic parties depend for their success on building *trans-class electoral coalitions*. Similarities in political vision, policy packages and trans-class orientation suggest certain parties in the Global South belong in the same category as the longer-established social-democratic parties of Europe.

However, the social context does differ, as I discussed in the previous chapter. Today's European social democracies rest on a higher level of capitalist development, much higher revenues per capita, a longer experience of democracy, and substantially lower poverty and inequality than putative social democracies in Latin America and elsewhere. In the Global South, where poverty and inequality are severe, low public revenues are a major constraint on building effective states and mounting universal social programs. In addition, many or most of the poor are found outside the ranks of organized labor in the burgeoning informal sector; this bifurcated labor market complicates the task of extending social rights to all citizens.[2] Moreover, ethnic, religious or regional divisions are often deep-seated in the Global South, confounding the task of mustering class solidarity behind a leftist project. Fragmented class structures in the Global South, together with the common simultaneity (rather than the sequencing) of industrialization, democratization and demands for social rights, mean that cross-class compromises will be particularly complex and fragile. And the global opportunity structure is unpropitious, though less so than in the days of a unipolar world. However, the European parallels to the Global South are stronger if one considers the challenges facing social democrats in Europe in the early decades of the twentieth century, when their movements struggled to establish themselves in rapidly industrializing societies (Lindbeck 2002). Both sets of parties have striven to reconcile capitalist growth and macroeconomic stability with social rights, a deepening of democracy, and the alleviation of human deprivation in onerous circumstances.

The counterpart of a social-democratic regime is the expansion of a social-market economy. The government faces simultaneous pressures from the liberal movement to disembed the economy, thus fortifying the liberal-market system, and from the societal counter-movement to re-embed it, thus extending the realm of decommodification. The provisional balance it attains depends on such factors as the terms of the national economy's incorporation into the global market system and the governing party/coalition's ideology, unity and strength. Decommodification of labor, land and money is, in any event, only partial. People continue to engage in calculating, economizing behavior. Most household consumption still involves the purchase of commodities. People must still compete for jobs or support themselves through small businesses or self-employment. What develops is not so much a variety of capitalism – too static a concept – as a dynamic hybrid economy, with a sphere governed by market exchange coexisting with spheres regulated by the Polanyian principles of reciprocity and redistribution.[3]

Polanyi's main inclination, to reiterate an earlier discussion, was to hold that only democratic socialism could avert the dangers of unleashed market forces. But sometimes he accepted a more nuanced position, claiming that what he opposed was market society rather than a society with markets. This latter formulation, which I elaborate later, acknowledges the possibility that the social-democratization of capitalism might serve to protect society and nature without undermining accumulation.

The subjection of markets to social norms – that is, the expansion of the social-market sphere – can occur through the independent actions of civil society. The "fair trade" movement is a case in point. Purchasers of various agricultural products use norms of fairness to govern the prices they pay to producers (usually in developing countries). Or, in marketplaces catering to clan-based, ethnic, religious or ideological communities, norms of honesty, fair treatment and respect constrain transactions. Consumer cooperatives of various sorts also immerse their transactions in non-commercial norms stemming from community bonds. And producer cooperatives have long been seen as a way of mitigating or eliminating the subordination and exploitation of workers through cooperative decision making, including the allocation of tasks and benefits. (Of course, if producer cooperatives have to compete with capitalist firms, they will have to mimic the latter's focus on profitability.) Diverse activities in civil society thus fall within the ambit of the social-market economy.

Social-democratic governments also extend the social economy by implementing modern forms of non-market relations in the form of institutionalized reciprocity and redistribution. For Polanyi, *reciprocity* and *redistribution* are ways of satisfying material needs that, unlike market exchange, are submerged in social relations and thus regulated by social obligations.

Reciprocity derives from the social obligations stemming from community solidarity. Since anthropologists studying small-scale societies have most often used this concept, a misconception arose identifying reciprocity with such traditional practices as gift-giving in small-scale societies. Reciprocity is characteristic of small peasant communities. And the rise of market society does undermine these traditional practices. Nevertheless, Polanyi does not espouse an evolutionary approach, in which different principles of integration appear in successive stages. Reciprocity does not necessarily involve gift-giving, nor does it necessarily entail face-to-face relationships

(Servet 2007: 261–3). The community involved might be a village, a clan or a religious group, but it might also be a set of friends, a voluntary association or even a national citizenry. Mutuality is the core principle: one is obliged to assist others in the community in their times of need, without any expectation of receiving an equivalent return from the recipients at a later point (Schaniel and Neale 2000). However, should a donor later suffer a calamity, (s)he can expect to receive assistance from others in the community who can affcord to provide it. Reciprocity is thus a system of mutual assistance; it is underpinned by the social standing accorded those who fulfill their social obligations.

In the case of contemporary social democracy, we can speak of *institutionalized reciprocity*. National populations, in effect, agree that citizens facing catastrophic situations – such as ill health or disability, an impoverished old age, childhood poverty, or prolonged unemployment – will receive state assistance without the need to repay their financial debt. Institutionalized reciprocity socializes certain risks via social protection schemes.

Redistribution, which assumes the existence of a state and centralized power, denotes a system in which resources (goods, natural resources and/or money) flow to a central node, and are then redistributed by the authorities in accordance with "custom, edict or ad hoc central decision" (Polanyi 1977: xxxiv). Polanyi adds that the "collecting" of goods is only notional: what is crucial is that the central authorities have the power to allocate certain resources. The rules governing the flow of resources are well understood within society, nowadays formalized in constitutions and welfare legislation. Although historically redistribution is often associated with empires and kingdoms, we should not equate this principle of integration with autocracy and oligarchy. Redistribution may also operate in societies governed through democratic procedures. The social-democratic state engages in extensive redistribution in the form of progressive-tax-financed cash transfers, high-quality and accessible public educational and health facilities, public housing schemes and even land transfers from the wealthy to the poor via state programs. Markets persist, and calculating, economizing behavior continues in certain spheres of material needs production and distribution. However, regulations, statutes and transfers embodying norms of equal opportunity, solidarity, healthfulness and (perhaps) ecological sustainability partially re-embed economy in society.[4] State-owned banks, utility companies and energy corporations also moderate the play of market forces.

Social-democratization thus leads to a hybrid economy in which the three principles of rational behavior – reciprocity, redistribution and market exchange – coexist. With the rise of capitalism, market exchange predominated. Motives of personal gain and fear of hunger guided economic activity in a world in which labor and land, in addition to capital, consumer goods and services, were available to the highest bidder. People assumed a market mentality of possessive individualism. But the damage incurred by such a system led people to push back. The result, in the case of the social-democratization of capitalism, was some degree of decommodification of labor in particular and a redistribution of power and resources. Clearly, this arrangement cannot develop without a mobilized civil society and a deeply democratic system. A watchful and organized civil society is crucial in "norm maintenance," in pushing the social-democratic party/coalition to maintain or extend reciprocity and redistribution. It is the ensemble of regulation, institutionalized reciprocity and redistribution, in addition to the independent activities of civil society, which decommodifies labor, and sometimes land, education and health services as well.

To add further complexity, moderate social democracy (the right wing of the Left) is often conflated with social liberalism or the Third Way (the left wing of the Right) (see Chapter 1). Social democrats and social liberals appear similar insofar as both work within familiar liberal-democratic institutions and political freedoms. They both respect property rights, though social democrats are more likely to engage in land redistribution, nationalization (with compensation) and the direction of market forces. Today, they both self-defensively adopt fiscal discipline, a monetary policy to keep inflation under control, freer trade, and openness to (selective) foreign investment. But, as ideal types, one also finds significant differences.

Three features in particular distinguish social democrats from social liberals.[5] First, social democrats talk about forging a new social contract featuring an acceptance and expansion of social rights. The aim is universal and comprehensive social protection and accessible and good-quality public services. Social liberals are wary of social rights, preferring to talk about social needs and how they may be reconciled with the imperatives of economic growth. The focus is on targeted social programs. Second, social democrats promote a vision of a more egalitarian society, whereas social liberals feel more comfortable embracing poverty reduction than social equality. Insofar as the latter do address inequity, they do not generally embrace the means adequate for realizing this goal in highly stratified societies. Although the poor certainly deserve a better life, vast inequality is immensely burdensome too. Inequality is positively correlated with persistent poverty, poor health and morbidity, criminality and violence, illiteracy, diluted or quasi-democracy and ecological degradation, as discussed in Chapter 3. Declines in inequality can reduce poverty more quickly because the same rate of economic growth directs more income to the poor when income inequality is falling. Yet attacking inequality is more controversial than reducing poverty as the former, unlike the latter, focuses on conflictual relations among classes. Finally, rhetorically and to some extent in practice, the social democrats are committed to expanding democratic participation beyond the civil rights and periodic, free and fair elections championed by the social liberals.

Equal freedom, I have suggested, is an inherently radical idea. It aims to redistribute freedom to the dispossessed, the marginalized and the vulnerable, to those who currently lack capabilities, opportunities, assets and, in most cases, power. When interests conflict, rights are usually seized, not benignly granted. Disadvantaged groups and classes generally have their claims recognized when well-organized political movements challenge the existing dispensation. Yet social liberals, adhering to the Post-Washington Consensus, contend that equalizing opportunities can be achieved through the mundane means of neoliberal capitalism – a liberal-market economy, good governance (liberal democracy, the rule of law, and a Weberian-type bureaucracy), targeted safety nets and openness to global markets. They typically focus on individual action and market dynamics. But inequality and poverty are primarily the outcome of power disparities and cultural norms.[6] Dominant groups institutionalize their control; this power disparity allows the latter to horde opportunities and to transmit them intergenerationally. This process unjustly restricts the life chances of those outside the governing alliance.

The implication is clear. Building and sustaining equal freedom entails what social democracy (even its moderate version) offers – the primacy of politics, collective action and the progressive subordination of the economy to democratic control, rather than market primacy in the allocation of rewards and individual action. It requires universalistic and inclusive approaches to social provision, not targeted safety nets together with privatized social security and private educational and health schemes for the well-off. Although it is sometimes difficult to distinguish between moderate social-democratic and social-liberal regimes, in principle the distinction is basic.

I turn now to the pitfalls of the moderate Left, before considering recent successes in expanding social economies.

The populist temptation

In the difficult economic times of the 1970s and 1980s, several moderate, ostensibly leftist governments yielded to the populist temptation. In the context of hard-fought electoral contests, leftist leaders resorted to redistributive, populist appeals that alienated investors and foreign governments. They engaged in fiery denunciations of the national economic elite and their foreign allies and advocated popular expansionary and redistributive measures. Such a strategy often miscalculated the global opportunity structure. Volatile world prices for commodity exports and the inordinate power of foreign investors, bankers, the international financial institutions and an obsessively anti-Communist superpower worked against the politicians. Political as well as economic breakdown was the common outcome.

Rudiger Dornbusch and Sebastian Edwards (1990) capture the economic side of the old-style populist pitfall in their analysis of "macroeconomic populism." It involves the following measures:

- expansionary fiscal and monetary policies designed to stimulate domestic demand, which create major budget deficits;
- increases in real wages together with price and foreign-exchange controls, designed to redistribute income while holding inflation in check;
- an unwillingness to devalue the currency when inflationary pressures arise, owing to the concern that devaluation would erode the living standards of supporters.

Dornbusch and Edwards also identify four phases of populist policy. The initial phase manifests success: output, real wages and employment grow while inflation remains low. But other phases rapidly follow, featuring high rates of inflation and unsustainable budget and balance-of-payments deficits. Phase 4 witnesses the collapse of the populist government – often displaced by a coup or political violence – and a return to macroeconomic orthodoxy amidst deeper poverty than at the outset. (Although Dornbusch and Edwards refer only to Latin America, macroeconomic populism actually occurs more widely.)

Venezuela in the 1980s is one instance. This country has a long history of social-democratic ventures. Acción Democrática (AD), the party that emerged in 1941 from the movement that had opposed the Goméz dictatorship, adopted a social-democratic agenda. Its first electoral success in 1945 inaugurated a brief period of radical reform, interrupted by a coup in 1948. The 1958 pact that reintroduced electoral democracy reflected a consensus that the country's oil revenues should be used to fuel both industrial growth and a welfare state (Gómez Calcaño 1993: 189–90). Oil revenues, especially during the boom in the 1970s, allowed Venezuelan governments, whether social-democratic or Christian Socialist, to reconcile redistribution with accumulation. Governments protected and subsidized inefficient import-substitution industries, spawning powerful, interlinked oligopolies, and channeled resources to a burgeoning welfare state and expanding public sector.

Owing to the collapse in oil prices in the early 1980s, the AD government that returned to power in 1984 struggled to fulfill its campaign promises to reignite economic growth and accelerate social development. Expansionary policies combined with subsidies and controls on prices, interest rates and foreign exchange rates led to massive budget and balance-of-payments deficits. Economic problems were compounded by rampant corruption and clientelism, which spread mismanagement throughout the civil service and state-owned enterprises (Gómez Calcaño 1993: 196). The final act in widely discrediting both AD and the conventional party system featured the AD leader Carlos Andrés Pérez, who won the presidency in 1988 on a populist platform. His desperate attempt to implement an orthodox austerity program, abandoning his election platform, touched off several days of heavy rioting and looting in Caracas and elsewhere. This debacle, together with continuing economic crisis, corruption and machine politics, led to two abortive coups in 1992 and the eventual rise to power of Hugo Chávez (Ellner 2003: 10–11).

Interestingly, Chávez himself contrived another period of macroeconomic populism in Venezuela beginning in 2002 (Rodriquez 2008). Expansionary fiscal and monetary policy vastly inflated spending and liquidity, outstripping even the rapid growth of oil revenues. An overvalued currency led to a massive increase of imports. The government attempted to control the resulting inflation by means of price and exchange controls, though not very successfully. Already severe fiscal and balance-of-payments deficits, high inflation and a decline in real wages worsened during the world recession (and decline of oil prices) in 2009–10. Though losing electoral strength, Chávez managed to ride out this economic crisis through further economic controls, blaming his enemies and tightening restraints on freedom of expression and the opposition. The recovery of oil prices in 2010 helped his regime recover. The populist temptation did not end with the old regime.

Nor is the populist temptation restricted to Latin America. Sri Lanka (Ceylon during the colonial era) is a case in point. From the 1930s, a vibrant civil society and a leftist political movement pressured Britain to accept elections based on universal adult suffrage and institute progressive labor and social legislation (Lakshman 1997: 3–4). Independence was won in 1948. Thereafter, the reformist Sri Lankan Freedom Party (SLFP), under pressure from its more radical coalition partners and its union allies, extended the welfare state and undertook land reform, heavy state regulation, protectionist measures and widespread nationalizations. Electoral competition drove even the center-Right United National Party (UNP) to accept the statist, quasi-social-democratic framework when it held power. But the Left degenerated into populist posturing and clientelistic practices in the late 1960s as the economy stagnated. Growing unemployment, a balance-of-payments crisis and a shortage of consumer goods delivered a victory to the UNP in 1977 with its new platform of economic liberalization.

Extensive neoliberal reforms, beginning the following year, soon frustrated the high expectations of the large cohort of educated youth by reducing their access to welfare-state benefits and job opportunities. When economic reforms accentuated regional inequalities and when the government also instituted pro-Sinhalese cultural policies, Tamil separatists succeeded in framing the relative deprivation in ethnic terms with the Sinhalese majority as the enemy. Hence, a bloody civil war (1983–2009) had its roots partly in the failure of the leftist experiment and the neoliberal reforms that followed (Abeyratne 2004).

Jamaica provides another illustration of the populist pitfall: the dangers of a rhetorical focus on redistribution and rejection of capitalism in a highly dependent, small economy. Michael Manley's People's National Party (PNP) government in Jamaica between 1972 and 1980 provides a cautionary tale. Swayed by the then-influential radical dependency theory and the sense of Third World grievance underpinning the demand for a New International Economic Order (Keith and Keith 1992: 9), Manley revived the PNP's democratic socialist tradition in 1974. In practice, the PNP, like the rival Jamaica Labour Party (JLP), was a populist party that relied heavily on patronage; it had won the 1972 election with a vague, non-committal platform ("better must come") that played on widespread discontent with the governing JLP. Yet Manley's rhetoric in 1974–6 embraced democratic socialism, denounced imperialism, supported Castro's Cuba and demanded a more just international economic order. His actual policies, however, were less radical than his rhetoric. They amounted to a moderate social-democratic agenda for its time: an expansionary fiscal policy, more extensive regulation of private firms, and more scope for state-owned enterprises, higher taxes for the rich, and an export levy on bauxite to support more generous subsidies and social services for the poor (see Stone 1989). Manley provoked the ire of the local business community, transnational corporations and the US government, with devastating consequences.

Jamaica's opportunity structure made the PNP government highly vulnerable to the hostility of its opponents (Stephens and Stephens 1983). It had a small economy heavily dependent on US tourists, imports, foreign investment, and the export of mainly one commodity (bauxite/alumina) to only two importers: the United States and the European Union. Its balance of class forces did not favor social democracy or socialism. The working class was both small and divided in allegiance between the PNP and the JLP. Foreign capital was powerful, based on the major export industries. Land ownership was highly concentrated. Furthermore, the PNP had largely operated as a political machine. Manley thus could not rely on a unified socialist party with a coherent ideology and a programmatic appeal. Moreover the state bureaucracy lacked managerial capacity; patronage appointments had sapped its competence, and state agencies were fragmented and uncoordinated. Opponents were in a powerful position.

Consequently, Jamaica quickly spiralled into an economic crisis (Ambersley 1981: 81). The country's share of the world market for bauxite fell from 27 percent in 1970 to 17 percent in 1975, as the transnational corporations responded to the bauxite levy by shifting production elsewhere. Capital flight and curtailed foreign investment reduced the foreign capital inflow from just under 10 percent of GDP in 1973 to just under 1 percent in 1976. The US government cut off its foreign aid to Jamaica in 1975, while its Import-Export Bank reduced the country's credit ranking to the lowest category. The tourist trade dwindled. Some local businesses closed. The result, by 1976, was an economic crisis, manifest in a 16 percent decline in GNP (between 1974 and 1980), high inflation, an unemployment rate of 31 percent, an increase of 47 percent in the foreign debt, and shortages of consumer goods (Ambersley 1981: 83).

Jamaica had little option but to approach the IMF for a loan. The 1977 IMF agreement rescinded many of the social-democratic reforms and imposed a harsh economic stabilization program. Although the Manley government withdrew from this agreement in 1979 to revive its fortunes with a renewed radicalism, the JLP won the 1980 election by portraying the PNP as a dangerous, communist-inspired movement. The ensuing neoliberal adjustment program gained US support, but failed to reignite prosperity.

Today, as the doctrinal pendulum is swinging back to accept a rejuvenated role for the state in capitalist development, these vignettes remind us of the dangers posed by populism. It is not that radical rhetoric, state controls, tax reform, and redistribution of services, assets and income are unwarranted in many countries. But without a cohesive, ideologically united and programmatic party and/or a favorable opportunity structure, flouting the efficiency/accumulation imperative of liberal-market economies can prove disastrous. Perversely, it is precisely those who the Left sought to help who pay the highest economic price: in high unemployment, rampant inflation, and falling real incomes, shortages of consumer necessities and growing criminality. Yet this danger can be avoided.

The resurgent Left of the past decade or two has largely steered clear of macroeconomic populism. Another pitfall loomed, however, as the Left adapted to global neoliberalism and, in particular, embraced the efficiency/accumulation imperative of liberal-market economies.

Power relations and the pull of social liberalism

Most leftist governments since 1990 have selectively adopted neoliberal policies or accepted most of the pre-existing market reforms. In some cases, these governments have accommodated neoliberalism to the point of instituting social liberalism or the Third Way, a centrist position. They have gravitated toward this approach for various reasons: to avoid an investors' panic and the antagonism of the US government and the IMF, to respond to the advice of economic advisors and technocrats who contend that neoliberalism is the only game in town, to cater to the material interests of their middle- and even working-class support base, and to emulate the post-1978 Chinese model of "socialism with Chinese characteristics" – in other words, increasingly market-friendly, accelerated growth. Examples of social liberalism include Costa Rica since the 1990s, Uruguay between the end of military rule in 1985 and the election of the Frente Amplio in 2004, Chile during the two Christian Democratic administrations of the Concertación in the 1990s, Brazil during the presidency of Fernando Henrique Cardoso (1995–2002) and Lula da Silva's first presidential term (2003–6), and South Africa since the end of apartheid in 1994. Yet a programmatic party's dilution of its egalitarian vision undermines the élan of its grassroots militants.

When vast inequities persist as the "leftist" leadership pragmatically accedes to social liberalism, disenchantment of cadres and supporters commonly follows. The party's rank and file chafe at capitulation to the IMF or corporate power and the party's harboring of opportunists in the government, party or allied parties. Sustained economic growth may hold this disenchantment in check because people have reason to hope for a more prosperous future. But hard economic times starkly reveal the divisions between the elite, the middle class and the poor, leading often to infighting within the leftist party/coalition and a drop in its electoral support. A right-wing party or coalition may then win an election, further entrenching the inegalitarian order and market primacy.

To illustrate the pressures playing on progressive parties that adopt the Third Way, I refer to two important cases – Brazil and South Africa. In both countries, purportedly socialist parties won electoral power but then adopted a social-liberal agenda. They followed a similar accommodative approach between 1994 and 2005. After 2006, their paths diverged. South Africa continued in the Third Way mold and, in the period after 1993, achieved only a marginal decrease in poverty while income inequality grew. In contrast, Brazil made a transition to moderate social democracy after 2005 and significantly reduced both poverty and inequality (Barrientos et al. 2013). Why this recent divergence?

Comparison of the experience of Brazil and South Africa is fruitful because of their many similarities, despite this divergence. Both countries are upper middle-income developing countries with similar per capita incomes and similar economic growth rates (1994–2011). They both exhibit extreme inequality and extensive poverty in racially stratified societies.[7] Both countries are a dominant presence within their respective regions. Latin America's largest country both in territory – 42 percent of the total landmass – and in population (more than 190 million), Brazil is not only the region's largest economy but also the sixth-largest in the world. Similarly, South Africa has a relatively large population (50.5 million people) and is (or was until recently) sub-Saharan Africa's largest economy. Like Brazil, the country is both well-endowed with natural resources and economically diversified, with relatively well-developed financial, legal and manufacturing sectors in addition to mining. Both countries undertook economic reform in the same year – 1994.

Their political and economic circumstances have significantly differed, however, constituting one important reason for the divergence. In South Africa, unlike in Brazil, the left-of-center party that won electoral power and implemented a social-liberal agenda was primarily committed to national liberation. Although many activists in the African National Congress (ANC) and its allied organizations have held, and still hold, firm socialist and social-democratic commitments, what united the party in the years of struggle was opposition to the injustice and oppression of apartheid. With that battle won and in the absence of any significant electoral opposition since 1994, ANC elites have had latitude to enrich themselves and cater to the vested interests of the party's best-organized and relatively privileged supporters to whom they are intimately linked. In contrast, the administration that moved toward moderate social democracy in Brazil – the Workers' Party (PT) – originated as a socialist party. And, unlike the ANC, it has faced continuous electoral challenges, including from parties to its left. This pressure, when combined with the commodity boom beginning in 2004 and the reduction of unemployment, gave the PT administration the leeway to move closer to its ideological origins. South Africa, in contrast, experienced capital-intensive growth with unemployment hovering above 20 percent. Alienating employers might have made a bad situation worse. These differences account in part for the policy divergence.

South Africa

Few would have predicted in the 1980s that the revolutionary ANC would (a) soon attain power via elections, and (b) adopt neoliberal economic policies. The party, formed in 1912, was banned by the apartheid government in 1960, which arrested its leaders a year later. Long years of guerrilla struggle and underground activities followed. The Freedom Charter of 1955 articulated the fundamental principles of the anti-apartheid forces led by the ANC. The Freedom Charter demanded equal rights for all South Africans and envisaged a quasi-socialist future. "The mineral wealth beneath the soils," it stated, "the banks and monopoly industry shall be transferred to the ownership of the people as a whole; all other industries and trade shall be controlled to assist the well-being of the people." The ANC later affirmed its affinity with socialism in policy statements and in the Tripartite Alliance with the South African Communist Party (SACP) and the Congress of South African Trade Unions (COSATU). Senior Communist Party and COSATU leaders have filled ministerial posts. Communists, socialists and trade unionists form the left wing of the ANC. Yet, as it negotiated its way to governmental power after 1990, the ANC leadership shifted to accept neoliberal orthodoxy combined with racial affirmative action, black economic empowerment, augmented social spending, targeted safety nets and liberal-democratic institutions – social liberalism in essence.

This shift was evident in the Reconstruction and Development Programme, a White Paper issued in November 1994 by the Government of National Unity (GNU) headed by Nelson Mandela. Construed as a policy framework, it emanated from intensive consultations with many groups, including the ANC's allies, COSATU and SACP. It wrestled with the question of how the new government could best address the major problems of poverty, high unemployment (then 30 percent), inequity in the delivery of social services, and a large public debt. The White Paper's first draft had a firmly social-democratic thrust, but each successive draft further diluted this stance (Taylor and Williams 2000: 31). The published version opted for a "unified programme" in which economic growth and poverty alleviation would be mutually supportive goals. The measures to boost the economy fitted with neoliberal orthodoxy. The White Paper did not call for nationalization of assets, but rather for privatization and fiscal discipline. To augment social services, it envisioned higher tax revenues financing a major infrastructural program to enhance the delivery to all the people of water, electricity, telecommunications, transport, health services, and education and training. In addition, further "democratisation" would be needed to empower the marginalized black population and overcome "minority control and privilege." The White Paper was vague enough to (barely) mollify COSATU and SACP without alienating the National Party (apartheid's architect), which held cabinet seats along with the ANC and others within the GNU (until 1997).

The ANC-dominated GNU's adoption of the "Growth, Employment and Redistribution Programme: A Macroeconomic Strategy" (GEAR) in June 1996 confirmed a centrist position. GEAR was a fairly orthodox structural adjustment strategy that stressed deficit reduction, tight monetary policy, deregulation, privatization and trade liberalization. The aim was to increase economic growth to 4.2 percent per annum. Redistribution was to be a by-product of economic growth, not a separate goal. In its acceptance of the Washington Consensus and its limited attention to redressing major racial inequalities, it represented a departure from earlier ANC thinking. By 1996–7, the ANC government, like the Cardoso government in Brazil, had adopted a developing-country version of the fashionable Third Way (De Beus and Koelble 2001). The neoliberals had won the policy debate.

Why did this ideological shift occur? Some ANC leaders did not regard themselves as committed socialists or social democrats but were drawn to the ANC mainly as a liberation movement. Liberation of the black majority could be interpreted in ways that were congruent with neoliberalism (for example, the Black Economic Empowerment program). Whether Nelson Mandela initially intended, after a peaceful transition to majority rule had been completed, to drop his conciliatory approach in favor of radical egalitarian measures is not known. What is clear is that global neoliberalism and the resistance of the local capitalist class exerted considerable influence on the ANC leadership. The influence of global capitalism stemmed not so much from coercive measures such as conditionality on IMF loans, as indirectly through "policy dialogue."[8] Mandela's government arrived in power without a detailed progressive program or a strong economics unit within the ANC. It immediately found itself in dialogue with technocrats – from local think-tanks, the civil service and the international financial institutions – who did have a coherent program and who confidently believed that neoliberalism was the only game in town (Hanson and Hentz 1999; Peet 2002). The contemporaneous collapse of state socialism in the Soviet Union and elsewhere lent credence to this message. The well-organized South African business class also lobbied for privatization and deregulation. Finally, South Africa's economy was vulnerable; it had a volatile exchange rate following the removal of exchange controls in 1994, a moderately high debt burden (mostly left by the preceding apartheid government), high unemployment, and minimal new investment. It was plausible that a leftward move would lead to disaster.

These were the circumstances that shaped the debate over the ANC's economic policy. Activists in the ANC, COSATU and SACP advocated widespread nationalizations and a regulated economy in the early years of negotiations and joint power sharing. But Nelson Mandela quelled dissent by firmly supporting privatization and fiscal austerity in 1994–6, backed by key ministers such as finance minister Trevor Manuel (Taylor and Williams 2000). When the rand plummeted in February 1996, losing 25 percent of its value in six months, the economic debate was over. COSATU, which had continued to attack the neoliberal thrust of the ANC, muted its criticism in the face of the crisis. Mandela was under pressure to restore investors' confidence, and he did so by affirming orthodox economic policies. Social liberalism was the outcome.

When the ANC's new populist leader Jacob Zuma assumed the South African presidency in 2009, there was the possibility of a change in direction. But the New Growth Path, adopted by the government in 2010 as a framework for economic policy, though proclaiming a welcome set of social and economic objectives, did not break with neoliberal orthodoxy. It did not, as economist Ben Fine (2012) observes in a commentary, tackle "financialization" and illegal capital flight – a major constraint on economic growth – or propose any fundamental change to the "mineral–energy complex" that dominates the economy, or acknowledge the power of a privileged black elite that blocks fundamental change.

Power relations are critical in understanding the ANC's social-liberal orientation. The Third Way has offered the ANC, which has had no credible challenger on the Left (or the Right), a viable formula for governance and the economic advancement of political insiders. Neoliberal economic policies uneasily align the government with big and medium business, both domestic and foreign (and mainly white), whose continued investments might be expected to spur growth. The party can cater to its well-organized and relatively privileged constituencies and still win elections, helped by its nationalist aura, the progressive patina stemming from its Tripartite Alliance, its populist appeals, and its well-publicized expansion of basic services in favor of the poor. The Communist Party acted in the 1990s as a strong critic of the ANC government's neoliberal policies. It is still rhetorically committed to socialism. In practice, however, the SACP has been increasingly incorporated into government and parliament at the national, provincial and local levels. Its secretary-generals, for instance have been appointed cabinet ministers and thus share responsibility for the ANC's economic policies.

COSATU and its affiliates have also largely become a conservative force, though certain union leaders retain a strong and vocal support for socialism. During the era of ANC rule, unemployment has remained exceedingly high (20–25 percent) and casual employment has grown. COSATU has increasingly become a federation of unions catering to white-collar employees, skilled and semi-skilled workers and those in full-time employment

(Gentle 2013). Unionized employees form a "semi-privileged" group in South Africa (Seekings 2013); few union members fall into the poorest half of the population. Among workers, it is mainly the unorganized farm workers, domestic employees and, above all, the many unemployed and casually employed people who are "poor." Teachers, who numbered about 350,000 in the early 2000s, are a particularly well-organized and politically powerful force. The vastly increased public funding of education under the ANC has benefited teachers in the form of higher salaries. Other unionized white-collar and manual workers have gained from a Labour Relations Act that protects their jobs. In addition, critics complain both of a "bureaucratized" union leadership that bypasses democratic procedures, and of the disillusionment of rank-and-file members with union officials who seem preoccupied with careerism and self-advancement (Beresford 2012; Meintjies 2013). Shop stewards are often full-time officials with good benefits. Top officials in COSATU and its affiliated unions have joined the ranks of the wealthy by moving into the private sector. These criticisms apply to the National Union of Mineworkers (NUM), one of COSATU's largest and most influential affiliates (Beresford 2012: 575, 584).

Yet, it must be added, COSATU has championed such pro-poor policies as extensions of the welfare state, and a Basic Income Grant, despite the relative well-being of its members. This pro-poor stance not only fits with COSATU's ideological tradition, but also indirectly assists union members who are obliged to financially support poor relatives and who are eager to legitimize their relatively secure position (Seekings 2004: 303). Nevertheless, as the established unions have become more distant from the concerns of the poor and near-poor, splits within unions have given rise to new, more militant, voices on behalf of ordinary workers and the poor.

Finally, social liberalism caters to the ambitions of a growing black upper- and middle-class constituency of professionals, managers, skilled technicians, and business people, who have moved into positions of power and relative affluence.[9] Many of the wealthiest black South Africans are present or former leaders of the ANC or COSATU. Black Economic Empowerment and affirmative action in the civil service have coincided with the drop in *interracial* inequality even as overall inequality, already very high under apartheid, has grown further (Duclos and Verdier-Chouchane 2011: 142).[10] The state has used its leverage with big business to expand the inclusion of black economic and political elites through lucrative jobs, contracts and share holdings (Seekings 2013).

Yet, in the 2009 elections, the ANC retained significant support in the bottom half of the population that has not prospered since the end of apartheid.[11] Rural workers have gained little, while the share of national income received by the vast pool of unskilled urban migrants and the urban poor has actually fallen (Duclos and Verdier-Chouchane 2011: 141). Lackluster growth in the first post-apartheid decade (1994–2003) did not improve poverty statistics, though generally higher growth in 2003–8 has helped.[12] The absence of a credible pro-poor or leftist alternative to the ANC, together with the party's status as the liberation movement, continued to win the party votes. So does its populist and xenophobic rhetoric, with some leaders blaming high unemployment and crime on foreign Africans and portraying the class division as pitting poor blacks against rich whites.

Where the poor and near-poor have benefited is in the delivery of social assistance and service provision. Although ANC governments have neither reduced the abysmal unemployment rate nor lowered overall income and wealth inequalities, they have driven down the poverty rate and delivered services. Social spending on the poorest 40 percent of households rose by about 50 percent between 1993 and 1997 alone, especially in the fields of public education and health services (Seekings and Nattrass 2002: 8). Respectable economic growth in 2003–8 augmented tax revenues, which allowed the government to increase social spending and mitigate poverty. Health spending, for example, became considerably more pro-poor in the post-apartheid era. Not only has a rising proportion of expenditures on health been allocated to public clinics, but also an increasing share of public health facilities have been built in poor areas (Burger et al. 2012). In addition, the educational system has been expanded to make public education accessible to the children of the poor. Two and a half million people have also benefited from social housing. And millions of people, for the first time, have access to electricity and running water (Polgreen 2012: 5). However, reforms to improve the *quality* of public services, especially education and health, have floundered owing to opposition from powerful public-sector unions (Seekings 2013).

Indeed, the educational system contributes significantly to the intergenerational transmission of inequality, despite attempted reforms. During the apartheid era, the educational system was racially stratified with schools for the black population providing an inferior education. The government has redirected educational funding to the benefit of schools in poor areas and to the benefit of poor parents who are exempt from certain direct educational expenses. However, the majority of black South Africans who attend schools in the townships and the rural areas still receive an inferior education. As a World Bank study (2005b: 4) concludes, "there is every indication that basic education in South Africa remains one of the most inefficient and ineffective in Africa, despite the disproportionate per capita amounts spent on South African pupils." Many unqualified teachers were hired in the last years of apartheid and the first years of independence, and it has been difficult to monitor, retrain or replace them owing to their powerful teachers' union. Also, children in higher-income areas attend either private schools or public schools which supplement government grants with significant tuition and other fees. Educational resources need to be redistributed, and yet it is difficult to achieve this goal.

Finally, it should be noted that South Africa devotes a higher share of GDP to social assistance – about 3 percent – than most other governments in the Global South (Seekings 2008). In 2010, more than 14 million people (28 percent of the population) received cash transfers, which together accounted for 10 percent of government expenditure (van der Westhuizen 2013: 87). Most important are the Old Age Grant and the Child Support Grant because they are relatively generous and tend to be shared within the household. Although the children, the elderly and the disabled are well provided for, able-bodied men and women between the ages of 16 and 60 have no safety nets – and many of them are unemployed. A universal Basic Income Grant, debated since the early 2000s, has not been embraced by the ANC. In short, the ANC's record of social equity appears somewhat more favorable when public services and cash transfers are included in the assessment. But the high unemployment, the lack of a comprehensive welfare state, and the poor quality of public services create widespread dissatisfaction.

By 2012, the ANC was clearly paying a high price for failing to do more to translate its egalitarian ethos into practice. Beginning in August, a spreading wave of wildcat strikes by gold, platinum and iron ore miners revealed a deep vein of anger and disillusionment with the governing party and COSATU and its affiliated unions. A pivotal event was the police killing of 34 miners during a protest action at Lonmin's Marikana mine. An economy already in poor shape in consequence of the crisis in Europe, its largest trading partner, suffered further decline and rising unemployment as a result of a crippled mining industry. Public anger stemmed not just from the persistent high inequality, unemployment and violent crime, but also from the perception that their leaders were enriching themselves at the public's expense (Polgreen 2012: 5). The ANC's support of black businesses under its empowerment schemes has blurred the line between legal promotion and illegal cronyism (Hyslop 2005: 786). Families of top leaders have done extremely well. President Jacob Zuma's nephew, for instance, was a director of 26 companies in 2012 (including mining companies). President Zuma himself engaged in questionable dealings. Although he already had three residences in 2012, he required $27 million from public funds to upgrade his extravagant compound in his home village. Cyril Ramaphosa, the former head of the powerful COSATU-affiliated NUM, had become a wealthy businessman with assets valued at $275 million (York 2012: F7). Indeed, many miners had come to regard the NUM and COSATU as cronies of the ANC, which is why they refused to accept guidance from either in their dispute with employers, turning instead to a breakaway union. Finally, accusations of outright corruption tarnished the ANC's image.

The danger for the ANC is deinstitutionalization as its élan and unity erode. Until recent years, the party, with a long and storied history, has been well institutionalized. The decades of guerrilla warfare bred an "ethos of organizational loyalty" (Hyslop 2005: 783). This united front continued even while Mandela made unpopular concessions to the white minority after 1990, though grassroots activists in the ANC, SACP and COSATU objected to the change of direction (Webster and Adler 1999: 367). The ANC has largely maintained its organizational integrity at the national level. Two changes of leadership (in 1999 and 2007) were made according to the rules, though acrimony attended Zuma's ouster of Thabo Mbeki in 2007. At the provincial level, however, the party operates as a patronage machine, and the provincial administrations are "extensively afflicted by corruption" (as they were in the apartheid era) (Hyslop 2005: 786). Indeed, the accusations of corruption and self-seeking at all levels are undermining the party's and the Triple Alliance's moral authority.[13] Finally, the level of disorder and violence is growing, with a rising incidence of riots, protests and political assassinations (Cessou 2013: 10–11). There is a danger that social liberalism may be succeeded, not by social democracy or socialism, but by populism, clientelism and semi-authoritarianism.

Brazil

In Brazil both President Fernando Henrique Cardoso (1995–2002) and President Luiz Inácio (Lula) de Silva during his first term (2003–6) followed social-liberal policies despite their professed leftist positions (Farias 2003; Tavolaro and Tavolaro 2007: 31–5; Barros Silva, de Souza Braga and Costa 2010; Morais and Saad-Filho 2011: 32–4). They both combined macroeconomic orthodoxy with largely targeted social assistance and some extension in the accessibility and quality of essential services, especially health care and education. They both worked through liberal-democratic institutions, forging limited participatory mechanisms. Constraints stemming from global neoliberalism, together with an unpropitious domestic opportunity structure featuring a powerful business class, a clientelistic political tradition and the coalitional basis of government, militated against a more redistributive approach. High and sustained capitalist growth from 2004 kept distributional issues largely at bay. Given Brazil's circumstances, social liberalism was actually an accomplishment.

Although Cardoso's intention was to implement a moderate social-democratic agenda (or "globalized social democracy" [Cardoso 2009]), the constraints facing his administrations pushed him in the direction of the then influential Third Way. His "National Project" essentially committed him to accept the imperatives of global capitalism. But, within these limits, he sought a more responsive and democratic state together with a progressive social policy, including accessible health and educational facilities, guaranteed social benefits in an enhanced welfare state, and redistributive tax and land reforms (Cammack 1997: 236; Cardoso 2009). Cardoso realized that, to carry through his social program while promoting investment and growth, he needed to reform Brazil's archaic political system (Smith and Messari 1998). Pervasive clientelism, populist appeals and a fragmented state apparatus had long obstructed any meaningful change. In the end, however, politics as usual and its privileged beneficiaries prevailed, sabotaging much of Cardoso's program. To buttress his chances of winning a second term, he temporized, believing it preferable to play the clientelistic game and accommodate the elites than confront them (Cammack 1997; Smith and Messari 1998). But things did not work out as planned. An aspiring social-democratic president implemented a thoroughgoing neoliberal reform program, including privatization, while achieving some modest social reforms.

Cardoso's goal was to pursue a "made in Brazil" approach to neoliberal globalization, one that did not surrender to orthodoxy (Cunningham 1999). Brazil would need to attract foreign investment and build its competitiveness in export markets in an open market economy. That would require an anti-inflationary monetary policy and fiscal conservatism, in addition to opening the Brazilian economy to global market forces. But the state would not simply accept the discipline of the market; it would intervene to overcome market deficiencies. The state would not own productive assets (hence, the privatizations), but would act as market regulator and facilitator of new economic activities and new export markets. Brazil in 1998, however, was sideswiped by the East Asian financial collapse. Capital flight and major devaluation of the *real* in January 1999 drove Brazil to seek an IMF loan, undercutting the made-in-Brazil rhetoric. The economic downturn, which persisted until 2003, restricted what Cardoso could achieve in social policy.

Cardoso's record in government is thus controversial. He succeeded in slaying hyperinflation and carrying through market-oriented economic reforms. But many of his social reforms languished. He achieved success in expanding access to educational and health programs. He initiated a cash transfer scheme to benefit poor families (Bolsa Escola), the predecessor of Bolsa Família. However, his tax reform legislation and social security law were heavily diluted before approval by Congress. Low economic growth, high unemployment and a growing public debt characterized the period 1999–2003. Cardoso's own priority of opening Brazil to global market forces severely restricted his leeway in social reform, for fear that any "radical" measure would deter investment or precipitate capital flight. In addition, Cardoso lacked the political base for a social-democratic government (Cammack 1997: 241). His Social Democratic Party (PSDB), founded only in 1988, held a small minority of legislative seats. Cardoso not only had to employ traditional clientelistic methods to expand his popular support, but also had to negotiate with his coalition partners – four right-wing and centrist parties – to achieve his legislative agenda. Making progress in such circumstances was difficult.

Contrary to earlier expectations, continuity with Cardoso's Third Way approach characterized President Lula da Silva's first term. "Leftism without a leftist Project" is one colorful characterization of this period (Tavolaro and Tavolaro 2007). The continuity is remarkable insofar as Lula da Silva, in contrast to Cardoso, headed a well-organized, programmatic party with socialist sympathies and considerable grassroots activism. The Workers Party (PT) originated as a social-movement party. Taking advantage of Brazil's political liberalization in 1979, a coalition of left-of-center intellectuals, Catholic radicals, trade unionists and social-movement leaders founded the PT. It was to be a grassroots-oriented party, not just another vehicle for ambitious middle-class politicians, and its appeal would derive from ideology and policy, not patronage. The PT strongly opposed neoliberalism and stood for democratic socialism in its early years. A resolution of its national conference in 1993 contended that "capitalism and private property cannot provide a future for humanity" (Samuels 2004: 1,003). The party espoused several radical positions in the 1980s and 1990s: a repudiation of Brazil's external debt, the nationalization of the country's banks and mineral wealth, and radical land reform. The party, led by the former trade unionist Lula da Silva, became an increasingly powerful force in Brazilian politics. But the leader's defeat in the three presidential elections preceding his successful campaign in 2002 led him to progressively moderate his positions. In the 2002 campaign, the party dropped all references to socialism and adopted moderate social-democratic policies – but still located itself to the left of Cardoso's PSDB.

Yet the new president faced many of the same constraints as his predecessor when he assumed power in early 2003. He inherited a difficult economic situation, including economic stagnation, a heavy public debt, a major current account deficit and high interest rates to stem inflation. He had to reassure investors in order to forestall a disastrous capital flight, which might have been precipitated by Brazil's tenuous economic position and the accession of a "socialist" president. Lula da Silva had published a "Letter to the Brazilian People" during the 2002 election campaign, in which he undertook that a PT administration would honor its obligations to repay IMF loans and would continue Cardoso's conservative macroeconomic policies. The reassurance seemed to work, for Lula da Silva won the election handily. To the consternation of many Brazilian and foreign leftists, the president then appointed neoliberals to the central bank and finance ministry, pushed interest rates even higher to curb inflation, cut public expenditure to achieve a budget surplus, and refrained from reversing any privatizations. Even after the resumption of economic growth in 2004, the president persisted with cautious economic policies designed to keep inflation at bay. The middle class, top professionals, the financial sector and business people prospered. As the Brazilian stock markets soared, so did Lula da Silva's stock with these powerful groups (Anderson 2011: 9).

To keep faith with the masses who had voted for change, Lula da Silva had to reconcile neoliberal economic orthodoxy (focused on accumulation/efficiency) with social justice (an agenda of equity/redistribution) in a highly stratified capitalist society. Economic orthodoxy – with its priority to fighting inflation and balancing budgets – inhibits social policy initiatives. Economic caution to reassure the rich does not mix well with bold redistributive measures, such as land redistribution, universal social protection, and tax reform. Reinforcing caution were several moderating political factors (see Hunter 2010). Among the PT's cadres were those who had held office in the 1990s as mayors, state governors and assemblymen. They injected a pragmatic note into party debates because they were aware of the policy compromises required to hold power. Furthermore, Lula's administration needed to attract the support of other parties, owing to its minority status in Congress, to advance its legislative agenda. The necessary compromises and shady deals alienated the PT's more progressive cadres, whose resignations further fortified the party's moderate tendency.[14] Finally, the appointment of leaders of the PT's supportive social movements to political office moderated the militancy of those movements as well (Morais and Saad-Filho 2011: 32). Similar mechanisms had pushed Cardoso's PSDB in a moderate direction, especially the need to win support in the legislature.

Hence the first Lula da Silva administration achieved only modest social gains (see Kingstone and Ponce 2010: 112–15). The regressive public-sector pensions, which accounted for about half of social spending, were only minimally adjusted in 2003. The fiscal burden continued, to the detriment of other social programs. The public expenditure in health and education increased only minimally from that under Cardoso. Land redistribution was modest compared to Cardoso's record (Hunter 2010: 113–14). Bolsa Família, considered to be Lula da Silva's most popular program, really only amalgamated several pre-existing welfare transfers to poor families, though it became more generous and more widely distributed over time. Continuity with Cardoso's approach was foremost.

Rapid and sustained economic growth offered the easiest escape from the acute tension between the liberal movement and the counter-movement of societal protection. Unemployment remained high in da Silva's first two years, but then fell as growth accelerated. By the time of the 2006 election, the well-being of the majority of Brazilians, including the poor, had improved, partly as a result of the trickle-down effect (see Amann and Baer 2006). In his second term (2007–10), a more secure president at the head of an emerging economic power assumed a more proactive, social-democratic agenda and a more assertive foreign policy.

The paths of Brazil and South Africa diverged in the 2000s. The average rate of growth of GDP in both countries between 2004 and the world recession in 2009 was nearly identical, according to the World Bank's Databank: 4.8 percent in Brazil and 4.9 percent in South Africa. Both economies suffered negative growth in 2009 and modest growth in 2010–12 (an average of 2.9 percent in South Africa and 3.8 percent in Brazil). The two countries diverged markedly, however, on three key indicators: unemployment, inequality and poverty. Massive unemployment continued to plague South Africa (22.9 percent just before the world recession), whereas Brazil created many new jobs, moving from 9.7 percent unemployment in 2003 to 7.1 percent in 2008 and 6.2 percent in 2011. Also, overall inequality grew in South Africa (from a Gini of 57.8 in 2000 to 63.1 in 2009),[15] while it fell significantly in Brazil (from a Gini of 60.1 in 2001 to 54.7 in 2009). Finally, Brazil has recently experienced a dramatic reduction of poverty whereas, in South Africa, poverty reduction has been marginal (Barrientos et al. 2013 provide the data). This divergence cannot simply be attributed to varying growth rates; the shift to social-democratic policies in Brazil was an important factor.

Lula da Silva's second term ushered in a more proactive state developmentalism (see Morais and Saad-Filho 2011; 33–5; Muir 2011: 58). The government took credit for expanding the number of good (productive, remunerative) jobs and redistributed the augmented revenues from growth in the form of cash transfers to the poor, progressive raising of the minimum wage, new infrastructure, and augmented public services and social protection. It halted further privatizations. In 2007, it launched a "Growth Acceleration Program" to bolster public and private investment in infrastructure and reduce disparities between the country's north and south. Roads, railways and hydroelectric facilities were constructed. In pursuance of an industrial plan, the government subsidized loans to strategic firms through a state-owned development bank – Banco Nacional de Desenvolvimento Econônomico e Social (BNDES). The BNDES became the largest development bank in the world, with more than $US100 billion in loans in 2010 (whereas the Interamerican Development Bank lent only $US15 billion) (Lambert 2013b: 12–13). Strategic enterprises also benefited from preferential state contracts and share purchases by public pension funds and state-owned banks, especially BNDES. The government increased the public stake in previously privatized utilities. It established a sovereign fund to make further purchases. It created a new state-owned oil company in 2008 to participate in exploiting newly discovered oil deposits. It also augmented consumer demand for Brazilian goods and services by putting more money in the hands of the poor, workers and the middle class. The mechanisms included cash transfers to a growing number of poor households, significant increases in the minimum wage, and the expansion of consumer credit (especially *crédito consignado* for those lacking bank accounts). Brazil's investment rate thus grew from 16 percent of GDP in 2005 to 19 percent in 2008.

Tax revenues also expanded. In the 1990s, South Africa had a more efficient and more progressive tax system than Brazil (Lieberman 2003: 2). Tax evasion was a major problem in Brazil, but not in South Africa. Tax reform, carried out mainly under President Cardoso, wrought a significant change. Although the tax system continued to depend heavily on consumption taxes instead of a progressive income tax, tax revenues surged from 25 percent of GDP in 1993 to 37 percent in 2005 and stayed at about that level (Pereira and Melo 2010). By the late 2000s, Brazil's revenues as a share of GDP were twice the average in Latin America and higher than such industrialized countries as Japan, the United States and Canada. Tax increases together with healthy economic growth between 2004 and 2010 have thus generated a bonanza that the government has deployed to pay down its heavy debt, advance its industrial policy, and support more equitable and generous social assistance, universal categorical benefits and services.

Brazilians thus reaped benefits from the strategy of redistribution with growth under Lula da Silva (Morais and Saad-Filho 2011: 35–8; Anderson 2011: 3–5). Employment growth expanded from 156,000 jobs per year during Cardoso's years to 499,000 per year in the mid

2000s. Minimum wages cumulatively rose by 67 percent in real terms between 2003 and 2010 (even while employment grew) (van der Westhuizen 2013: 87). These increases directly benefit the worst-off workers in the formal sector. They also have a positive impact in the informal sector where employees use the minimum wage as a benchmark for their own wage demands, and in triggering linked raises in publicly provided pensions, unemployment insurance and disability insurance. Between 2004 and 2010, those below the poverty line fell from 50 million to 30 million while the number suffering extreme poverty was cut in half (Anderson 2011: 5). Social security coverage expanded from 45 percent of the population when Lula da Silva assumed office to 51 percent in 2010. In addition, the public investments in infrastructure spawned further growth in employment. Government expenditure on education surged between 2005 and 2011. The number of university students doubled (with many more bursaries and scholarships available to applicants from poor households). Some 32 million Brazilians entered the middle class, defined in income terms. And income inequality gradually declined.

Lula da Silva's protégée Dilma Rousseff, who assumed the presidency in 2011, continued in the same vein, delivering a more comprehensive approach to abolishing poverty. Bolsa Familia, the conditional grant offered to poor households with children since 2003, expanded rapidly, with more than 12 million households receiving between US$23 and US$178 each month in 2011 (Barrientos et al. 2013: 59). It has become a minimum income guarantee as well as a targeted child allowance. All families living in extreme poverty, regardless of whether they contain children, receive a basic grant. In addition, a child allowance is paid to poor and extremely poor families for each child less than 18 years of age. To be eligible, the children must attend school and report for periodic health check-ups. President Rousseff launched an integrated anti-poverty program entitled Plano Brasil Sem Miséria in 2012. It involves an enhanced payment to households in extreme poverty with young children through the Bolsa Família, together with improved access to pre-school care and health facilities. About 2.5 million families are expected to benefit from this program (Guerreiro Osório and Ferreiro de Souza 2013). Rousseff's Plan also includes improvements in access to, and the quality of, educational and health services and social protection schemes, together with programs to raise the productivity of poor farmers and the poor in the urban areas and expand productive jobs (Paes-Sousa 2013). The Bolsa Família program has not only succeeded in breaking with traditional patterns of clientelistic distribution, but also has reduced inequality modestly and extreme poverty considerably.[16]

Comparison

Whereas South Africa continues in the Third Way mold, though with increasing disorder, Brazil has made policy changes in the direction of moderate social democracy. A full explanation of this divergence would require more space than I can afford. But several broad points bear mention. The global and national opportunity structures confronting both "progressive" governments after 1994 were equally challenging, but they became less so for Brazil over time owing partly to design and partly to good fortune. And the progressive governments in Brazil, in contrast to South Africa, had strong incentives to remain attuned to their long-term egalitarian goals.

The governments of both countries faced a daunting challenge after 1994. Powerful business and middle-class interests and international financial institutions demanded commitment to neoliberal orthodoxy to spur accumulation, whereas the progressive parties' restive and underprivileged electoral bases, including the organized working class, demanded attention to redistribution and decommodification. It is not surprising that, in both cases, a cautious, social-liberal program characterized the early years. Governments in both countries in the 1990s and early 2000s stressed the concerns of the liberal movement: fiscal discipline, an anti-inflationary monetary policy, a positive balance of payments, trade liberalization, and avoidance of nationalizations. However, since 2006, development trajectories have diverged.

Economic structure partially explains the divergent trajectories. Economic policy in South Africa has supported capital-intensive growth that raises labor productivity but also enables lay-offs. Rigidities in the labor market have encouraged the substitution of capital for labor (Barrientos et al. 2013: 63). The result, when combined with the secular decline of the all-important mining industry, has been a very high level of unemployment.[17] The persistence of the apartheid-era practice of suppressing the unregulated informal sector, thus minimizing the opportunities for earning a modicum of income, has exacerbated this problem.[18] Brazil, in contrast, has exhibited a more inclusive pattern of growth that has generated many jobs, as indicated earlier. Both favorable economic conditions – a commodity boom that raised demand for Brazil's many agricultural and mineral exports – and an effective state developmentalism, as discussed earlier, account for the successful redistribution with growth approach. Agribusiness, in particular, grew exponentially, with Brazil becoming the third-largest agricultural exporter after the US and the EU.

Furthermore, with declining unemployment, Brazil's successive increases in the minimum wage had a major impact on the earnings of the poor. The increases affected not only workers in the formal economy, but also those receiving incomes pegged to the minimum wage – especially people depending on non-contributory pensions or contributory pensions with minimum guarantees and bargaining for wages in the informal sector (Barrientos et al. 2013: 63–4). Finally, both countries have expanded social assistance, but the combination of this expansion with job creation and major hikes in the minimum wage in Brazil has led to strong growth in the incomes of the bottom 40 percent of the population, significantly reducing both poverty and inequality.

Political factors play an important part in explaining why the PT, unlike the ANC, pursued inclusive growth via state developmentalism. Whereas stiff competition in electoral contests at the federal, state and municipal levels induced the PT to remain attuned to its largely poor political base,[19] the ANC and its Tripartite Alliance, with broad appeal stemming from the struggle for national liberation, lacked the same urgency. The ANC came to power with overwhelming popular support as a triumphant national liberation movement. It promised "a better life for all" rather than a specific program for socialist/social-democratic transition. Black economic empowerment, affirmative action and political cronyism soon built prosperous and politically influential black middle and upper classes that have fared well under social liberalism. Even much of the organized working class did well; wage increases in the formal sector have outstripped productivity gains, impeding job creation (Selassie 2011). The PT, in contrast, originated as a socialist party, forged by an alliance of leftist intellectuals, trade unionists and social movements. Although the party moderated its ideological position to attract broader electoral support, it remained a well-organized party of the Left – in fact, Brazil's first modern political party.[20] After winning the presidency in 2002, the PT had to struggle to maintain its popular support against opponents on its left as well as its right. In contrast, the ANC has not yet faced a credible opponent. The PT was thus under more intense political pressure to turn left than the ANC.

Do the mass protests that swept Brazil in June and July 2013 not contradict this positive assessment of the Brazilian experience with social democracy?[21] They began with a small protest in São Paulo in early June, sparked by a modest hike in urban transit fares. The repressive response by the military police incensed Brazilians, some of whom remembered the role played by this force in support of the junta that ruled from 1964 to 1985. The protests subsequently spread to all of Brazil's major cities, drew in protesters from the *favelas* as well as large numbers of young people, and became increasingly diffuse in focus. At the peak, an estimated million Brazilians participated in the actions. As the protests spread, the demands proliferated; no central leadership existed to develop a coherent set of grievances. In this respect, the protests resembled the mass demonstrations in Chile in 2010 and the Occupy movement in North America. Some protested violent police repression. Others expressed their frustration with the exorbitant public funds lavished on building facilities for the forthcoming soccer World Cup and Olympics while public services and infrastructure remained inadequate. Yet others, especially young people, objected to what they regarded as their bleak prospects, despite the enormous gains Brazilians had recently made. Poverty had declined, average real wages had risen and many jobs had been created. In fact, Brazil achieved the world's fastest rate of reduction in unemployment between 2008 and 2012, together with an increase in average real wages of 3.2 percent in the latter year (IMF 2013). The country had experienced, in the words of the IMF, "a remarkable social transformation" (IMF 2012: 4). The protests apparently took President Rousseff completely by surprise. So what was the problem?

The protests were not directed specifically at the federal government, the PT or Rousseff personally – her approval ratings remained high[22] – but registered a general frustration with traditional politics in Brazil, the persistence of high inequality, and expectations that had outrun the means to satisfy them (Baiocchi and Teixeira 2013; Saad-Filho 2013; Zibechi 2013). Brazil had experienced two years of lagging growth while the vast expenditures on World Cup and Olympics facilities had spurred inflation. Moreover, the decline in income inequality had only just begun the task of creating a fairer society. Many Brazilians were disappointed that, despite free electoral democracy and an incumbent socialist party, not enough had changed. Finally, the private media empires used the protests to bludgeon the PT administration with charges of incompetence and corruption. The protests signaled anger, demands for better services, cleaner politics and improved opportunities, but no coherent idea of how to change the situation.

The Brazilian protests, together with the earlier ones in Chile, illustrate the limitations of moderate social democracy. Its plight is similar to that of Sisyphus, who is condemned by the gods to push a boulder up a hill for eternity, only to see it roll back each time it approaches the summit. Despite its achievements, the party must deal with constituencies that expect more. Yet the progressive government is highly constrained. Private media empires dwell on every supposed deficiency of the Left to stir up popular opposition. The Left, broadly defined, usually holds a minority of legislative seats, requiring the government to make dubious concessions to opportunistic parties to fulfill its legislative agenda. All parties need campaign funds to fight elections, but that usually means cultivating private firms and

wealthy individuals. It is challenging, to say the least, to make the rapid progress toward equal freedom that the people expect.

Hence, many promising progressive experiments in the Global South have foundered. Some regimes have succumbed to old-style populism, misjudging their global and national opportunity structures by focusing on redistribution at the expense of accumulation. Others, for a variety of political and economic reasons, have opted to accommodate neoliberalism in the form of the Third Way. Balancing the conflicting demands of the liberal movement and the societal counter-movement demands a deft touch. Democratic regimes that make a determined and effective attack on inequality, insecurity and commodification are scarce, but they do exist.

Moderate social democracy: cases

Latin America has been the main site of the Left's recent revival. Several reasons account for this region's prominence: more favorable structural conditions, the depth and severity of the neoliberal impact since the 1980s, and the continent's lengthy history of resistance to imperialism and capitalism. Latin America's tradition of resistance includes revolutions, as in Mexico in 1910 (a peasant-based revolution with diverse causes), Cuba in 1959 and Nicaragua in 1979. It also has involved leftist insurrections (in most Latin American countries in the 1970s, directed at overthrowing brutal, pro-capitalist regimes), uprisings against neoliberalism (such as the *caracazo* in Caracas in 1989 and the Zapatistas' rebellion in Mexico in 1994) and historic electoral victories (notability the election in Chile of Socialist Salvador Allende's Popular Unity [UP] administration in 1970). These events are the historical context for today's politics.

Although Latin American countries share this common background, their political trajectories also depend upon historical experiences peculiar to each country. Where neoliberal reforms proved disastrous, where the traditional party system fell into disrepute, and where social protest was widespread, the radical Left has seized electoral power (as in Venezuela, Bolivia, Ecuador and Argentina). But where market reforms ultimately achieved economic growth and where an institutionalized party system channeled social demands, social liberalism or moderate social democracy has prevailed (as in Chile, Uruguay and perhaps Brazil). Social upheaval and widespread disaffection have provided impetus to radical-leftist leaders, in Latin America as elsewhere (Weyland 2010: 19–21; Levitsky and Roberts 2011: 16–18). Beyond these broad patterns, other specific events have proven influential. I indicate some of these specificities in the following sketches of leading examples of the moderate Left today, including those outside Latin America.

West Bengal and Kerala, states in India governed for many years by coalitions headed by the Communist Party of India (Marxist) (CPM), are prominent Asian cases of the social-democratic Left in power. Kerala, originally a radical social democracy, moderated its approach in the 1990s (a case I explore in Chapter 6). West Bengal followed a similar trajectory. Beginning in 1942, the Communist Party of India and later its CPM offshoot operated first as a revolutionary movement in West Bengal and later (implicitly) as a radical social-democratic party. The CPM governed in two brief and tumultuous United Front coalitions in the 1960s and then from 1977 until its electoral defeat in 2011. It engineered radical land redistribution, the abolition of tenancy, and labor market reforms in the late 1970s and early 1980s. It then shifted from a radical strategy of mobilizing sharecroppers, agricultural workers and near-landless peasants to a moderate strategy of class conciliation under the slogan of "peasant unity" (Varughese 2012: 118–26). This shift reflected the growing power of the middle and rich peasants, on whose leadership the party depended in the rural areas. Radical land reform had eliminated the landlord class, while the Green Revolution increased the prosperity of medium and rich peasants. "Peasant unity" thus came to mean that the interests of the latter took precedence over those of agricultural workers and poor peasants.

In the 2000s, West Bengal's CPM emulated the Chinese Communist Party in its promotion of industrial development. This policy brought the government into conflict with peasants, especially in its acquisition of land for private ventures. Depending ever more heavily on a clientelist mode of politics, the party went down to defeat in 2011 (Varughese 2012: 133). West Bengal's CPM was not as successful as Kerala's in improving social indicators or progressing on gender equality (Kohli 2012: 205–7; West Bengal, Government of 2004). Historical differences and strategic choices account for the different approaches, as the Kerala case study in Chapter 6 indicates.

Mauritius, an island in the Indian Ocean usually considered part of sub-Saharan Africa, has followed a moderate social-democratic approach since soon after independence in 1968. The three major parties all subscribe to this political stance. A developmentally oriented state has shaped market forces insofar as it identifies lucrative niches in the global economy and coordinates public and private investment to fulfill its industrial plan. The country, thanks to a proactive state and strong institutions, has undergone a dramatic transformation from a typical racially stratified sugar colony at independence to a diversified, middle-income and relatively egalitarian country today (Sandbrook et al. 2007: chap. 5;

Duclos and Verdier-Chouchane 2011). The economy is now based on tourism, financial services (declining), clothing and textile exports, a deep-water port facility, and a fledgling information technology sector, in addition to sugar exports. Though the Mauritian economy in the 1970s was highly regulated, it had by 2009 become one of only two African economies judged to be "mostly free" (Ulriksen 2011: 200). Yet trade liberalization has been a wrenching experience. The phasing out of preferential rates by the European Union for a set quota of Mauritian sugar led to the loss of more than one-third of the country's sugar revenues by 2010 (Mauritius, Republic of 2010). And the ending of preferences for clothing exports has exposed Mauritius to intense competition from cheaper producers, such as China and Madagascar. Consequently, unemployment has remained high at about 8 percent in recent years.

Mauritius balances its open economy with a relatively generous universal welfare state. A democratic developmental state, responsive to a well-organized civil society, tries to build opportunity by honing the capabilities of citizens through free public education, training and health services and through generating well-remunerated new jobs.[23] In addition to universal social protection schemes, the government targets the marginalized stratum of the population with augmented safety nets and scholarship assistance. Trade liberalization did thus not lead to higher inequality, as it has elsewhere (Duclos and Verdier-Chouchane 2011: 142). Nonetheless, this small island economy is highly vulnerable to the vicissitudes of global market forces.

Latin America has witnessed the largest expansion of the moderate Left since 2000. Costa Rica is a trail-blazer; it embarked on a social-democratic trajectory in the late 1940s following a brief civil war. Chile, Uruguay and Brazil are exemplars of the moderate Left in recent years. Argentina under the Peronist presidencies of Néstor Kirchner (2003–7) and Cristina Fernández de Kirchner (2007–15) falls between the moderate and radical Left. I do not explore this anomalous case. Nor do I consider the case of Nicaragua, in which Sandinista leader Daniel Ortega was elected president at the head of disparate coalitions in 2006 and 2011. It is still difficult to pin down his government's political orientation.[24]

Costa Rica, a highly regulated social democracy from the 1950s to the early 1980s, depended mainly on volatile primary exports until the mid 1980s. Like Mauritius, Costa Rica has had a democratic developmental state that has taken advantage of its healthy and well-educated population and political stability to diversify the economy toward higher-value-added exports and high-end tourism (Sánchez-Ancochea 2009). By 2005, primary exports accounted for only 23 percent of total exports.

Nevertheless, since an economic crisis in the early 1980s, the government has been under relentless pressure to liberalize from the international financial institutions and the US government. Its acceptance of a neoliberal agenda has remained half-hearted, however. This hesitant reform reflected "an ongoing political impasse between elites who favor neoliberal reforms and citizens who, to varying degrees, recognize and remain attached to benefits derived from welfare-state institutions" (Sandbrook et al. 2007: 95). As the traditionally social-democratic Partido Liberación Nacional (PLN) pragmatically diluted its ideological position, political disenchantment grew and the two-party system broke down. The referendum campaign concerning the country's adhesion to the Central American Free Trade Agreement in 2007 became a national debate as to what path Costa Rica should follow. The victory, albeit narrow, of the "Yes" side confirmed the social-liberal approach. Yet the PLN, which had supported the "Yes" side, lost significant support as a new progressive party – Partido Acción Ciudadana – rose in popular esteem (Cupples and Larios 2010).

Chile, which emerged in 1990 from the dictatorship of General Augusto Pinochet under a center-Left coalition – Concertación – adopted an incremental, moderate approach. During Salvador Allende's Popular Unity administration (1970–3), the pursuit of a democratic route to socialism polarized society into warring factions, undermined the economy, and precipitated a US-backed coup in September 1973 (Harmer 2011). Then followed sixteen years in which Pinochet's military government brutally suppressed the Left and trade unions and implemented a neoliberal counter-revolution of massive proportions. Following an economic collapse in 1982, a less doctrinaire neoliberal strategy brought sustained economic growth. Thus, the desire of Chileans to avoid a repetition of the polarization, chaos and repression of the 1970s and 1980s, together with the limitations imposed by Pinochet's 1980 constitution, dictated a moderate stance.

When Concertación assumed power in 1990 following an election, it faced immense challenges. Society was deeply divided, with nearly half the population favorably inclined toward Pinochet. Pinochet's constitution not only systematically fortified the political Right, but also could not be amended without the cooperation of conservative parties and senators. Inequality was extremely high (the income Gini coefficient was 56). Poverty was widespread (40 percent of the population). A free-market economy prevailed. No social rights were legally recognized. Privatization of social services such as health and education had created two-tier systems with the public systems woefully inferior. Finally, Chile's business elite was organized into powerful associations with close links to right-wing parties. The trade union movement, in contrast, had been legally hobbled by Pinochet and its leadership had been decimated. Given these constraints, a gradualist approach was realistic.

The decade of centrist Christian Democratic presidents (1990–9) was a social-liberal era. Concertación was and remains a coalition of several parties; the main partners are the centrist Christian Democratic Party (PDC) and the moderately leftist Socialists (PS). The PS, the party of Allende, originally located itself to the left of Chile's Communist Party. But it moved toward the center during the Pinochet years, in recognition of the need to avoid the errors of state socialism, to appeal to the Chilean middle class, and to forestall provoking the military (Muir 2011: 59–60, 63). Hence the PS broke with its socialist traditions to support "growth with equity" in the 1990s. Orthodox monetary and fiscal policies, liberalized markets, and free trade continued; indeed, the government negotiated new free-trade deals and further lowered tariffs. Pinochet's liberal-democratic constitution limited the scope of reform by buttressing the Right, but growing revenues and a limited tax reform financed enhanced social programs.

The period 2000–10, when two Socialist presidents held office, nudged policy to the left. In light of the continuing high inequality and the limited successes in achieving social rights, Chile during this decade stood on the boundary between social liberalism and social democracy. Although the center-Right that acceded to power in 2010 retained most pre-existing social programs, Chile under the Sebastián Piñera administration approximated the social-liberal model. In 2014, Socialist president Michelle Bachelet returned to office.

Consider the scope of reform under the Socialist presidents. Constitutional change finally neutralized many of the institutional constraints on majority rule. Many former military officers were punished for human rights abuses during the Pinochet dictatorship. The state played an increasing role in orchestrating investment in new industries. "Growth with equity" evolved into efforts to assert social citizenship in this highly unequal society. The government persevered in pressing the principle of universal coverage in health care (meeting with some success in 2004 and extending coverage to cover many serious conditions thereafter), unemployment insurance (in 2002, though restricted to formal-sector employees), paid maternity leave (2009), day care and pre-school nurseries (2009), and pensions (a basic universal pension in 2009, described as the "most important achievement of President Michelle Bachelet").[25] The government also promoted Chile Solidario, a conditional cash transfer scheme targeted to the poorest households that lifted many families out of extreme poverty. It expanded the public housing program, though the latter remained a targeted program governed by complex rules. Finally, President Ricardo Lagos's efforts to reform the restrictive labor code in 2001 met with limited success, thwarted by intransigent employers' associations and right-wing parties. In sum, the Left incrementally resuscitated "the bonds of solidarity" under very difficult conditions until its defeat in 2010 (Weyland 2011: 89), but inequality remained very high.

Public dissatisfaction with the scope of the reforms precipitated a series of political protests, beginning in 2006 and continuing with greater intensity following the election of President Piñera. The election of President Bachelet in 2006 raised expectations. Both Bachelet's campaign rhetoric and her personal history as a member of a family persecuted and destroyed by the Pinochet regime suggested a radical attack on injustice. But she was unable to deliver on many of her promises. Bachelet, even more than Lula da Silva and Rousseff in Brazil, was trapped by the system (Fernandez and Vera 2012). Moreover, with the Socialist Party's technocratic approach and lack of participatory mechanisms (the better to ward off populist pressures), the system offered no institutional outlet for grievances other than voting. The protests (discussed earlier) concerned the lack of equal opportunity and the commodification of public goods, especially education. Protesters demanded greater financial support for public education at the secondary and post-secondary levels, the halting of environmentally destructive mega-dams, aboriginal rights, and lower gas prices. The rejuvenation of social movements and engagement on the part of civil society augur well for a stronger social-democratic impetus in the future. It is significant that Bachelet won a second term in 2013 with two promises that reflected the demands of the protesters: free higher education and higher taxes on corporations.

Uruguay has followed a more "radical" moderate approach than the cases just sketched. Since the 2004 victory of the Frente Amplio (FA), Uruguay has forged the most progressive social-democratic regime in Latin America (see Lanzaro 2011; Muir 2011). Tax reforms reduced the sales tax while making income taxes more progressive. Public investment in educa-tion, infrastructure and strategic industries expanded markedly. Labor market changes included dramatic increases in the minimum wage, the reinstating of corporatist wage councils and compulsory collective bargain-ing (leading to major wage increases), and the legal enshrinement of union rights. Various universal, non-contributory transfer programs, including a new family allowance, were instituted (for the details, see Cruces and Bérgola 2013). Democratic reforms included the prosecution of former military officers for human rights violations during the time of the junta, the forging of participatory institutions at the local level, and the establishment of corporatist institutions for making economic policy. Finally, FA rejected a bilateral trade agreement with the United States in favor of joining the regional trade bloc Mercosur. The overall effect was significantly to reduce poverty and improve income distribution (see Amarante, Colafranceschi and Vigorito 2011).

Uruguay's progressiveness flows from two sources. First, the country's long tradition of social democracy, a trajectory introduced by a civil war that ended in 1904, is highly influential (Weinstein 1975). By the 1950s, Uruguay is reputed to have had one of the most comprehensive welfare states in the world. But economic problems in the 1960s precipitated by a highly protectionist state and incompetent and corrupt politicians led to polarization (including the emergence of the Tupamaros revolutionaries). A military dictatorship in 1973–84 sought to suppress the fledgling Frente Amplio (FA) and the Tupamaros, but did not undertake an ideological transformation (as Pinochet did in Chile). Redemocratization in 1984 returned the traditional parties to power; they instituted a social-liberal program through phased liberalization, privatization and retrenchment of the welfare state (Kaztman, Filgueira and Furtado 2000: 83, 93). In the 1990s, the FA abandoned its Marxist-Leninist position and portrayed itself as the defender of the original social-democratic tradition ("Batllismo"). Its electoral victory in 2004 ushered in a major shift to the Left.

The second reason for Uruguay's decisive progressiveness is political. The Frente Amplio encompasses all the elements of the Uruguayan Left, commands a slim majority in the legislature, and operates within an institutionalized party system (Luna 2007). This institutionalization and the clear ideological differentiation of parties foster a programmatic rather than populist and clientelist appeal. The result has been one of the most left-leaning social-democratic governments in Latin America (Lanzaro 2011: 360).

In sum, progressive administrations in Brazil and elsewhere have demonstrated the strengths as well as the weaknesses of the moderate Left. In highly unequal societies with powerful business classes and globally integrated economies, social-democratic governments have still been able to augment the well-being of the poor, the vulnerable and the middle class, though not to the extent these constituencies desired. Healthy rates of economic growth since 2003 have certainly helped in achieving this result, but they are not the whole story. A close examination of the social-democratic experience reveals the outlines of an astute model.

Moderate social democracy: a model

Social-democratic regimes have attempted to reconcile accumulation with equity in an open global economy by combining orthodox macro-economic policies with state developmentalism and social citizenship.

They have also promised to reinvigorate democratic participation, both as an end in itself and as a means of buttressing the state's focus on poverty and inequality But leftist parties have been wary of fulfilling this promise. Concerned to allay populist pressures that might undercut delicate class compromises and pragmatic politics, the regimes have opted only to expand public consultations and restrict participatory decision making to the local level. This finely balanced hybrid strategy may, however, work only in prosperous times. Prolonged stagnation is likely to throw inherited inequalities into stark relief, potentially pitting redistribution against capital accumulation in the guise of Left populism, radical social democracy or leftist insurgency.

Macroeconomic orthodoxy

To reassure domestic and foreign businesses, the IMF and bond-holders, and to ward off financial crises, the moderate Left accedes (paradoxically) to certain neoliberal economic policies. Their governments respect existing property rights and the rule of law; any nationalizations (which are rare) proceed only with full compensation. Selective trade liberalization and a welcoming environment for direct foreign investment complement this pro-business strategy. Finally, strict monetary and fiscal policies keep inflation under control and debt manageable. To safeguard macroeconomic balances, left-of-center governments buttress foreign-exchange reserves, keep interest rates relatively high, avoid expansionary fiscal policies and (since the 2008 global financial crisis) often employ capital controls to regulate the volatility of capital flows.[26] Such policies are designed to attract investment and, by reducing macroeconomic vulnerability, to keep the IMF at bay.

However, these policies exact a cost: they restrict the redistributive thrust of governments. High interest rates discourage investment and consumption that, in producing more sluggish growth than a less austere monetary approach, leads to higher unemployment and lower wages. Mild inflation can be beneficial from a redistributive viewpoint. Inflation of less than 15 percent per annum does not adversely affect growth, whereas it can spread prosperity more widely than adherence to a low-inflation target (Stiglitz 1998). Budgetary and current account deficits are not necessarily a bad idea – provided that the extra resources fund public investments that raise productivity. Also, these governments need higher and more progressive taxes not only to fund enhanced social programs, but also to pay down the public debt. Yet progressive income taxes face stiff resistance and effective tax evasion strategies from the wealthy, who usually can count on the private media to support their cause. Finally, trade agreements often introduce restrictive intellectual property rights and investor rights regimes. Yet the need to reassure investors and attain economic growth in a neoliberal world order argue in favor of orthodoxy.

State developmentalism

State developmentalism, though less obvious than the market-friendly policies, is the side of economic policy that reflects the primacy of politics. During the heyday of import-substitution industrialization from the 1950s to the 1970s, states played a proactive role in the Global South. The Washington Consensus brought a halt to directive states outside East Asia. But industrial policy experienced a renaissance in the 2000s, spurred by disillusionment with the efficacy of neoliberal policies in the 1990s and admiration for the achievements of the developmental states of East Asia. Social-democratic forms of state developmentalism aim to promote economic growth – in particular, inclusive growth that generates many productive jobs through diversification and moving to higher-value-added products. If this strategy succeeds, as in Brazil in the 2000s, major increases in the minimum wage will then mitigate both poverty and inequality.

State developmentalism lies between free-market orthodoxy, where the ideal is the self-regulating market, and the developmental state, where the state governs the market even to the extent of picking and promoting "winners." The developmental state, as exemplified by Taiwan and South Korea between the mid 1960s and early 1990s, requires stringent conditions: political and bureaucratic elites with a developmental mission; an efficient, coherent and skilled bureaucratic apparatus; a robust tax base to support a strong state; and a balance between the bureaucracy's autonomy and its embeddedness in society that imparts coherence and effectiveness to the state's industrial plan (Evans 1995). Few countries in the Global South and Latin America in particular exhibit all these conditions. Commonly, states lack bureaucratic effectiveness, or the degree of autonomy needed to succeed at this strategy, or a strong tax base (owing to widespread tax evasion) (see Chapter 4). Furthermore, the Left clearly requires a *democratic* developmental state, not an authoritarian and repressive developmental state on the South Korean pattern. A democratic developmental state introduces another level of complexity to an already ambitious agenda (see Sandbrook 2005).

But progressive governments can succeed without this rare species. "Good-enough" states can play a developmental role. They can promote policies to create productive and well-remunerated jobs, democratize the market, and expand the welfare state. If social-democratic governments cannot "lead" the market, they can at least "nudge" it to conform to their inclusionary socioeconomic agenda.[27] Nudging rarely involves "picking winners;" it does include creating incentives for existing enterprises to enter foreign markets or for foreign firms to switch to domestic suppliers of intermediate goods. It involves more in the way of enhancing global competitiveness than retreating to protectionism. We thus find state developmentalism, though rarely a democratic developmental state.

State developmentalism takes advantage of the beneficial legacies of social democracy – advanced human capital, good social and physical infrastructure, legitimate and relatively effective government – to find lucrative niches for local producers in the global economy. The social development associated with such regimes provides advantages to firms engaged in the more sophisticated, higher-technology products and services. Such firms pursue not just the lowest wages, lowest taxes and most lax environmental standards, but also the potential profits to be derived from high labor productivity. A well-educated workforce means a large pool of potential employees with the literacy and analytical skills to innovate and master complex production processes. Superior health indicators are also pertinent, not only for narrowly instrumental reasons – reduced absenteeism and the enhanced ability of employees to learn and concentrate on complicated or repetitive tasks – but also for their positive impact on social stability. Health care, along with social protection against such risks as disability, old age, and unemployment, mitigate income inequalities and fortify the social cohesion and generalized trust that facilitate high productivity (Garrett 2003).

In addition, state developmentalism fosters further competitive advantages for local firms and new investors through supply-side measures, (Sandbrook et al. 2007, chap. 8; Kurtz and Brooks 2008: 238–41; UNRISD 2010: 310). A proactive state can channel cheap credit to firms that accord with the state's industrial policy, often from state-owned banks. I mentioned above the important role played by the development bank in Brazil – the BNDES. It provided 2,115 loans between 2002 and 2011. Although the BNDES continued to direct large loans to some of Brazil's largest firms, it also directed smaller loans to support innovation and global linkages in a range of firms in all sectors of the economy (Hochstetler and Montero 2013). The state can also furnish subsidies to compliant firms in the form of tax concessions or low rates for electricity or other services. It can provide information on export market opportunities and insure corporations against the risks of entering foreign markets. It can supply appropriate job training programs. Although the tax holidays and other incentives associated with export-processing zones are well known, public investments in physical infrastructure have received less attention. Yet the construction of appropriately situated roads, railways, airports and sea-ports, and the provision of reliable electricity, water, telephone and internet communications, sometimes at artificially low rates, constitute major lures for investors. The intrinsic comparative advantages of moderate social democracies, in combination with astute developmentalist policies, can prove attractive to high-value-added firms.

Moderate social-democratic regimes have thus learned to live with neo-liberal globalization. State developmentalism is not a new development approach; it is an updated strategy to grapple with the challenges and opportunities of global markets. Under pressure to prove their pro-business credentials, these regimes have not engaged in much outright redistribution of assets. But they have indirectly improved income distribution and reduced poverty by generating good jobs, regularly raising minimum wages above the rate of inflation, and raising tax revenues to finance (among other things) higher social expenditures.[28] Creating industrial employment, moreover, is not only redistributive but also expands the potential political base of the Left.

Social citizenship

Social-democratic regimes, besides promoting growth, employment crea-tion and innovation, introduce measures to provide basic income security, engineer universal access to affordable basic services and extend labor-market guarantees. These measures expand the social-market economy by subjecting certain markets, especially those for labor, education, health services and basic housing, to solidarity-oriented norms and regulations. Social democrats, in pursuing redistribution and decommodification, are more likely than social liberals to talk of social *rights* rather than social *needs*.[29] Social rights assume the universal access of citizens, though limited resources generally permit only a phased movement toward universalism (Yashar 2011: 190). Social citizenship, in the sense of universal political and social rights, advances the goal of equal freedom by reducing poverty and the fear of impoverishment, building the capabilities of citizens, incor-porating the socially excluded in a decent, respectful life, mitigating inequality and erecting a political process to guard against domination.

Of course, redistributive social spending depends not only on who receives the benefit, but also who pays for it. Ideally, tax reform would include a reduction in regressive sales taxes, with more of the tax burden shifting to progressive income taxes. But this ideal is elusive. The wealthy often pay low income taxes or evade taxes, as in much of Latin America and Africa. In Uruguay, tax reform is quite successful, but in other moderate leftist countries, less so.

Social protection is a vague concept. Analysts do not agree on the range of programs, and different programs exhibit different degrees of redistribution. Usually, social protection assists citizens who become unemployed, suffer debilitating illness or disability, are born into a destitute family, endure social exclusion due to caste, ethnicity or religious status, or are unable to work owing to old age. Social insurance schemes, based on contributions from the employer and employee, are the least redistributive in that they exclude the large portion of the labor force employed in the informal sector. Latin American and African countries were notorious for regressive schemes in which employees in the large public sector received pensions and health care paid from government revenues dependent on sales taxes. Equity in the social democracies demanded movement toward social assistance and "universal categorical benefits" (Piachaud 2013: 34).

Social assistance programs are more redistributive than social insurance; they are paid out of general revenues and target the poor, the extremely poor or the socially excluded. President Rousseff of Brazil, as earlier mentioned, undertook in 2012 to eliminate extreme poverty through a variety of measures included in her Brasil Sem Miséria program, especially increasingly inclusive income supplements. Mauritius has a large fund dedicated to the uplift of the poorest citizens, including educational grants and post-secondary bursaries. Public housing programs are also common. Social assistance for the disabled and unemployed is still rare. Universal categorical benefits, redistributive if supported by progressive income taxes, include basic income grants paid to all citizens or grants to those who fall within a certain category, such as the elderly and children. In principle, though not yet in practice, basic income grants replace non-contributory social assistance – avoiding the costs and stigma of means testing (UNRISD 2010: 140). Public old-age pensions, however, are becoming common. And child allowances have grown in popularity. Some conditional cash transfer programs (as in Brazil) progressively broaden eligibility for receiving cash transfers, so that eventually they may become basic income grants. Even modest cash transfers to the elderly or children may reduce poverty and inequality, because the households receiving these grants may be worse off than the general population. Measures channeling money to mothers tend also to empower women within the household.[30] All these measures may, as well, foster economic growth, by augmenting demand for basic goods.

Providing universal access to high-quality public services is another basic redistributive mechanism. Social democratization, in principle, transforms education and health care from commodities into universally available public goods. A high priority is to extend high-quality schooling and health clinics to the informal urban settlements and the countryside, where the poor mainly live. However, two- or sometimes three-tier service provision usually persists, with the well-off having access to higher-quality publicly supported facilities or private provision (as in Kerala, Brazil and Chile). Insofar as educational systems transmit privilege across generations, this inequality flouts the ideal of equal freedom. Sanitation, clean water, adequate housing, and subsidized public transport and electricity are also extended as social rights in some cases. Leftist regimes generally resist advice from outside agencies to privatize health provision or water supply or raise user fees for essential services.

Universal social programs advance social goals, but they are also critical in building solidarity across classes (UNRISD 2010: 136–7). They appeal to everyone with insecure livelihoods and hitherto minimal safety nets – including the lower strata of the amorphous middle class. Many middle-class employees and small-time entrepreneurs experience livelihood insecurity, fear urban criminality, and see their children subjected to inferior public educational and health institutions. Social-democratic parties have thus been able to construct cross-class coalitions in which the middle class has been a substantial element (Deacon and Cohen 2011: 233–42).[31]

But can developing countries afford universal programs? Contrary to conventional wisdom, studies undertaken by the International Labour Organization, UNICEF, the World Health Organization, the Economic Commission for Latin America and the Caribbean, and the United Nations Research Institute for Social Development attest to the affordability of basic programs.[32] Basic social protection (targeted social assistance plus a basic old-age pension and child benefits) costs only 1–2 percent of gross domestic product in developing countries (ILO 2011: xxvii). Other affordable benefits include free school lunches, free basic health care, and subsidized transport (UNRISD 2010: 180). Foreign aid donors often help in meeting the costs.

Universal programs are more affordable if they are phased in. Even phased universalism promotes solidarity as well as equal freedom. Equity requires that these programs cover the neediest groups first; they may later extend their coverage progressively to higher-income groups. "Universalism in phases" was Costa Rica's path (Franzoni and Sánchez-Ancochea 2013: chap. 3). The building blocks of universal social policies were health and pensions. In 1941, a government under a progressive leader (President Calderón) implemented a modest social insurance scheme without provoking much opposition from employers. The scheme required employees and employers to contribute to a fund providing health benefits for employees, while the government drew on general tax revenues to cover the lower income groups. Governments gradually expanded the programs to encompass progressively higher income groups. This gradualism, which slowly increased the financial burden on employers, did not provoke strong resistance (Franzoni and Sánchez-Ancochea 2013: chap 3). Consequently, by 1960 Costa Rica had outperformed the other Central American countries in health and living standards whereas, in the 1930s, the country had relatively poorer conditions. Comparatively low national incomes do not rule out phased universalism; to achieve universal programs in highly unequal societies, however, is still a daunting political task.

A final form of social protection is labor-market intervention. Moderate social democrats all aim to extend trade union and workers' rights, especially rights to organize, bargain collectively and enjoy employment guarantees (so that lay-offs follow procedures and generate compensation). Uruguay has achieved major success in these regards, whereas Chile has achieved little in the face of strong and united business associations. The moderate leftist regimes also raise minimum wages, which indirectly influences wage levels in the large informal sector as well. They enforce minimum standards of employment, especially workplace safety rules. These interventions, when combined with retraining opportunities for the unemployed, social protection schemes, and universal access to essential services, partially decommodify (formal-sector) labor. They shrink the scope of employers' unilateral control of labor.

Social democratization is unavoidably fraught with tensions as decommodification and redistribution proceed (Standing 2007: 69–71; Esping-Anderson 1990: 23). Decommodification incrementally decouples the life chances of individuals from their market position and – when extended to land and money markets – restricts private-property rights in land and financial assets too. At some point, decommodification in combination with redistribution obstructs accumulation within a capitalist economy. But the clash between the logics of profitability and decommodification, the movement and the counter-movement, is rarely terminal as Polanyi supposed. The relative influence of the movement and the counter-movement will wax and wane as economic fortunes change, but without necessarily precipitating a breakdown of the capitalist system.

Democratic deepening

Finally, social democrats everywhere have keenly advocated extending democracy. They generally understand democratization of state and society as not only an end in itself – a way of exercising freedom – but also an important means of shaping a more egalitarian society. Much research confirms the potency of robust democratic institutions. For example, a recent empirical study of Latin American countries reached the unsurprising conclusion that the more robust the democracy, the more egalitarian the outcomes (Porzecanski 2005). Yet moderate social democrats have generally balked at extending participatory mechanisms beyond the local level, either within the party or the state.

Why this reluctance? The most likely explanation is the leaders' concern that a more participatory democracy may unleash "unreasonable" populist demands. Governing in the neoliberal era presents major challenges to the moderate Left. Typically, its leaders seek to retain the confidence of financial markets and foreign and local business through a "responsible" approach to monetary and fiscal policy and private property. In addition, the harsh realities of legislative power often dictate that progressive parties forge coalitions involving centrist and center-Right junior partners. The latter demand a quid pro quo for their loyalty, in the form of policy or personal accommodations. Electoral success, furthermore, may require leaders to engage in (normatively decried) clientelism, in addition to a programmatic appeal, to win votes in an electorate accustomed to such practices. But these pragmatic accommodations do not sit well with party activists and allied social movements. Consequently, needing to make pragmatic compromises, professional politicians do not want to be encumbered by (what they construe as) naïve grassroots demands for rectitude and fiery rhetoric. Also, the uncontrolled mobilization of popular forces into politics might introduce chaos. Populism, the leaders fear, might sabotage all their patient preparations for social advancement.

Hence, left-of-center parties in power usually expand participatory mechanisms at the local level, but rarely transfer them to higher levels (Goldfrank 2011: 161–6). Brazil is a partial exception in that the constitution mandates policy councils at the local, state and national levels. Lula da Silva expanded the number of national forums in which the government consulted civil society, and endorsed certain of their policy recommendations. In the main, however, the PT at the center has governed in the conventional manner, though with less corruption and clientelism (Muir 2011: 59). Even at the local level, the degree of public involvement in policy making varies widely. The Communist Party of India (Marxist) in Kerala, the Workers Party in Brazil and the Broad Front in Uruguay have all undertaken experiments in democratic decentralization. In contrast, Chile's Socialist Party has resisted building participatory structures within the party or the political process. Its ties to social movements, including labor, have been weak. The hypermobilization that characterized the Socialist Allende era (1970–3), and the repression that followed, have made the party's leadership resistant to popular pressures (Roberts 2011: 335).

In Kerala, the situation was very different. In the 1990s, as the radical thrust of the CPM waned following three decades of (successful) struggle, younger party members persuaded the party to rekindle popular enthusiasm. The centralized CPM in 1996 broke with its top-down approach to construct radical, participatory decentralization in the form of the People's Campaign for Decentralized Planning (see Isaac and Franke 2002). The local *panchayats* in villages and towns receive 35–40 percent of the state's development planning budget to fund the public goods identified as the highest priorities through participatory planning exercises. This scheme has mobilized an average of 1.7 million of Kerala's 30 million people in biannual People's Assemblies at the village and city ward level to set priorities for local infrastructural and service development. These assemblies are preceded by comprehensive assessments of their localities' natural resources, with a view to their conservation and optimal use. Projects prepared by elected officials with the assistance of experts are then sent to a District Planning Committee for evaluation and acceptance. Implementation is then carried out by local authorities.

The People's Campaign is generally regarded, by the World Bank among others, as a successful experiment in democratic decentralization (Sandbrook et al. 2007: 88–90). It emerged as Kerala's CPM came to terms with liberalization in India and the growth of the middle class in Kerala.

Brazil's Workers Party, formed in 1979, originally committed itself to a deep democratization of state, society and economy. Participatory budgeting was initially conceived as a radically participatory program, a "counter-hegemonic strategy to overcome capitalism" (Novy and Leubolt 2005: 2,026). In 1988, when the PT won both the mayor's office in Porto Alegre and control of the state government of Rio Grande do Sul, the stage was set to introduce participatory budgeting at the municipal level. Porto Alegre was an ideal testing ground, for the city of 1.3 million people was not only relatively wealthy and well-educated, but also had a strong democratic tradition and a history of leftist movements. The municipal government could also count on the support of the PT-controlled state government. Between 1989 and 2004, when the PT lost control of Porto Alegre, participatory budgeting operated in a manner that drew praise at home and abroad as well as emulation in dozens of cities in Brazil and worldwide. (The model was endorsed by the World Bank.) Participatory budgeting succeeded in transforming clientelistic politics into an accountable, participatory and deliberative budgetary process in Porto Alegre and elsewhere in Brazil (see Baiocchi 2005). However, as the PT moved from a strategy of class struggle to overthrow capitalism to a strategy of class compromise within capitalism, the party did not (as it initially intended) make a sustained effort to replicate participatory government at higher levels. Moreover, participatory budgeting at the local level did not challenge the status quo.

The achievements of participatory budgeting were nevertheless considerable (Baiocchi 2005; Novy and Leubolt 2005: 2,028–31). In Porto Alegre, a progressive tax reform augmented municipal revenues, and the municipal government redirected expenditures to poorer neighborhoods. The poor benefited in the form of water connections, more schools, and improved roads and sanitation. Participatory budgeting curbed clientelism and corruption at the municipal level. Excluded groups, especially women, blacks and the poor, participated in negotiating an infrastructural budget each year. The system thus acted as a school of democracy, mixing direct democracy with representative democracy, and provided important local services in poor neighborhoods. But it could not address the structural basis of poverty, inequality and unemployment, which was rooted in the broader political economy of Brazil. Furthermore, participatory budgeting was vulnerable to changing political fortune at the city and state levels. After a right-wing party won control of Porto Alegre's government in 2004, participatory budgeting was progressively marginalized.

In Uruguay, the FA in opposition developed mechanisms for involving its rank and file in policy formulation and coordinating action between the party and civil-society organizations, especially its trade union allies. It also transformed governance in Montevideo when it won control in the late 1990s. Until then, the capital city was run in a top-down, bureaucratic manner by politicians who typically engaged in clientelism. Through "participatory decentralization" the party sought to forge bottom-up institutions that would obviate corruption and clientelism and redirect resources to the poor neighborhoods. Major success was achieved in certain districts of the city (Canel 2010). Since 2004, however, the FA has not developed participatory institutions at the center other than the (traditional) tripartite salary councils, the appointed National Economic Council to advise on social and economic policy, and occasional "national dialogues" to discuss specific sectoral reforms. In addition, the party's rank and file are consulted on policy through regular public deliberations and standing committees. In comparison to Chile, which has had much weaker channels for participation or consultation,[33] the Uruguayan approach is bold (see Pribble and Huber 2011: 130–1).

Although the degree of participation and consultation varies from case to case, the moderate Left in power acts cautiously. It makes social progress, but slowly, well aware of the forces arrayed against it. This caution, evidenced in pragmatic accommodations and the sidelining of militants, leads to dissent among the party's rank and file and disillusionment among the Left's constituencies. The regular opinion surveys undertaken by *Latinobarometro* show declining popular approval of democracy in Chile, Brazil and Costa Rica while they were governed by the moderate Left (Weyland 2010: 15). Reconciling the imperatives of accumulation with redistribution demands a deft touch, but alienating activists exacts a cost.

Conclusion

Karl Polanyi feared that deviations from an unfettered market model would, by impairing the price mechanism and undermining business confidence, precipitate economic and, subsequently, political crisis (Polanyi 2001 [1944]: 3–4; Dale 2010a: 62–3). In light of the many instances of disastrous macroeconomic populism in the developing world, this anxiety is not misplaced. But it is exaggerated: economic (and political) crisis is not the invariable outcome of deviations from market purity. A democratically controlled state can actually play a contradictory dual role: support an institutional and policy framework for efficient markets (accumulation), while protecting society and nature from the market's corrosive effects (equity). Moderate social democracies, I contend, achieve this feat by shaping class compromises that combine neoliberal policies with proactive state developmentalism, a commitment to universalism in social protection programs and pro-poor policies, and democratic decentralization. This compromise may persist without severe crisis for one or more decades, though periodic economic downturns are inevitable under capitalism. But any modus vivendi between the movement and the counter-movement is only provisional.

False starts on the Left in the shape of macroeconomic populism or social liberalism occur for several reasons. It is the task of the progressive party or coalition either to manage the tensions between the movement and the counter-movement or seek to abolish the tensions by transforming capitalism. What path the party chooses, and whether it succeeds, depends above all on the prevailing global and national opportunity structure and the party system in a particular country. The prevailing development policy paradigm, articulated by local bureaucrats and interest groups and foreign technocrats, will also shape what is seen as possible. Dependency thinking in the 1970s and early 1980s, influential in Latin America and the Caribbean, led in one direction, neoliberalism later on in quite another. However, leaders may miscalculate the opportunity structure, especially the structural power of domestic and foreign capital, or they may misjudge the ideological coherence, cohesive leadership and organizational prowess of their leftist party or movement. They may thus precipitate macroeconomic populism or settle for the Third Way, though other leftist options may have been possible.

Redistribution with growth, the essence of the moderate social-democratic approach, is a gradualist program. Far from repudiating capitalism, it involves deliberate state action to foster the deeper and more efficacious integration of national firms into the global market economy. The rich typically continue to do well, in accordance with an implicit class compromise. What the strategy achieves, if it works, is the following:

- the expansion of higher-productivity, better-paid jobs;
- the deployment of rising tax revenues to alleviate misery, hone the capabilities of poorer citizens, and enhance economic security;
- the extension of the social-market economy with the partial decommodification of labor (and perhaps land and money as well), the promotion of cooperative forms of production, and measures to augment access to credit on the part of micro-enterprises;
- democratic decentralization.

Moderate social democracy thus offers to its political base material improvements and new opportunities, social order, civil and political liberties, and movement toward universal social protections – but limited empowerment beyond the local level.

Is this program enough? Under the moderate Left, a small class still controls the means of production. The intergenerational transfer of privilege is only gradually restricted; access to elite schools, money and social contacts continues to provide the children of the rich with vastly superior life chances to those of the general population. The corporate elite exercises disproportionate political influence owing to the power of money and concentrated control of the mass media. Inequality thus persists (though it declines), despite the commitment to equal freedom. What is needed is a redistribution of wealth, educational resources and political power, in addition to income. But to attack the inherited inequalities in such a fundamental manner introduces a tumultuous and conflictual process with unpredictable consequences. It is little wonder, then, that democratic leftist parties usually settle for class compromise over class conflict.

Moderate social democracy, however, may prevail only so long as economic growth continues. The economic boom since 2003 has served the Left well (though in Chile the center-Left went down to defeat following an economic downturn in 2009). When growth ceases, the leadership loses its ability to promote both accumulation and redistribution. The moderate Left's choices then are to champion the accumulation imperative, probably sacrificing further social gains, or to embrace redistribution with the social dislocation, conflict and uncertainty that will ensue.

Despite the uncertainties, some progressive governments do unleash class struggle to redistribute wealth and power, in addition to income. The path of the radical Left usually entails confrontations with both national and global power structures. I turn now to these cases.

NOTES

1. A classic statement on social-democratic class compromises in the Western context is Przeworski (1985: 136–7). Leftist parties accept the institution of private property (providing fair compensation for any nationalization of private firms or lands) and the obligation to discipline followers who fail to respect the limits of reform within capitalism. The economic elite thereby gain social and political peace, enhanced human capital, and potentially harmonious industrial relations. In exchange, capital and its allies accept a regulatory state, the exemption of certain spheres that are essential to equal rights from the play of market forces (especially health care, education and social protection), the partial decommodification of labor to ensure that a person's life chances are not wholly determined by market position, and the allocation of a portion of profits to finance universal social entitlements.
2. Nevertheless, references by Marx and his followers to an "industrial reserve army of labor," a "lumpenproletariat," a "sub-proletariat" and the "laboring poor" suggest that something akin to what we now term an informal sector also existed in Europe in the early stages of capitalist development.
3. In this exposition, I draw in the next few paragraphs on the following sources: Polanyi (1957); Polanyi (1977), especially the editor's Introduction; Stanfield (1986); and Schaniel and Neale (2000).
4. In practice, it is difficult to distinguish between reciprocity and redistribution in the case of the modern centralized state.
5. This section is a brief summary of the discussion in Chapter 1. The distinction is developed below in the cases of South Africa and Brazil.
6. For a concise and recent statement of this viewpoint, see Carroll (2011). For an illustration of how power structures at the local level distort even "participatory development" projects aiming to alleviate poverty, see Mosse (2005).
7. In 2011, the gross national income per capita, expressed in purchasing power parity (current international dollars), of South Africa was $10,790 and of Brazil $11,500 (World Bank, Databank, data.worldbank.org/indicators/). Both countries rank among the countries with the highest inequality in the world, though Brazil, unlike South Africa, has experienced a decline in income inequality (as measured by the Gini coefficient) since the early 2000s.
8. The government negotiated an IMF loan in 1993 for $750 million, conditional on tight monetary policy and a commitment to low inflation.
9. The South African economist Solomon Terreblanche estimates that ANC politics have forged a black elite of 2 million and a black middle class of 6 million (Cessou 2013).

10. Poverty increasingly became an urban phenomenon as people moved to the towns and cities in search of a better life since 1994. In the period 1995–2005, the Gini coefficient for the urban areas moved from 55 to 65, indicating a major increase in inequality.
11. The ANC won 66 percent of the popular vote in this election.
12. World Bank data indicate that 31 percent of the population fell below the poverty line in 1995, rising to 38 percent in 2000. By 2006, 23 percent of the population lived in poverty. (World Bank, Databank at data.worldbank.org/indicators/)
13. The rise in corruption is widely acknowledged, even by some insiders. For instance, COSATU's Secretary-General Zwelinzima Vavi recently criticized the ANC's "corruption, mediocrity and bad policies," claiming that ANC stands for "Absolutely No Consequences" for corrupt and arbitrary actions (Cessou 2013: 11).
14. The darkest moment occurred in 2005, when it was revealed that staff in the president's office had been buying the votes of about thirty deputies with monthly payouts. However, the top officials engaged in this exercise were held to account in court.
15. However, interracial inequality fell.
16. The Bolsa Família has not been diverted into patronage distributed by the PT, according to investigative studies. With 14 million beneficiaries, the cases of fraud number in the "hundreds or at most thousands" (Soares 2012: 17; Fried 2012). For the impact on inequality and extreme poverty, see Soares (2012: 29).
17. Mining contributed 21 percent of GDP in 1970 but only 6 percent in 2012. Gold production in 2012 was barely one-fifth of its peak level in the early 1970s. The mining sector has shed about 900,000 jobs since the early 1990s (*Globe and Mail*, March 12, 2013, B1).
18. Personal communication, Professor Nicoli Nattrass, University of Cape Town, July 24, 2013.
19. An opinion poll a week before the 2006 election in Brazil found that Lula da Silva drew most of his support from the poorer sections of the population, especially from those earning less than twice the minimum wage and those living in the poorer north of the country (Tavolaro and Tavolaro 2007: 437).
20. The PT's major scandals have involved payments to secure the votes of minority parties, not self-enrichment.
21. This analysis draws principally on Baiocchi and Teixeira (2013); Rohter (2013); Saad-Filho (2013); and Zibechi (2013).
22. A poll conducted by one of Brazil's largest newspapers in August 2012 found that Rousseff's government was assessed as "excellent" or "good" by 62 percent of those surveyed (MercoPress, August 16, 2012).
23. However, this strategy has not helped the unskilled and less educated segment of the population, which for historical reasons comprises mainly the Afro-Creoles.
24. As one close observer remarked in 2012: "Nicaraguan politics are not clear-cut, and the traditional left–right divide is complicated by rivalries between former allies" (Lemoine 2012: 10).
25. For the details of all these programs, refer to Huber, Pribble and Stephens (2010).
26. However, Chile phased out its capital controls in the early 2000s.

27. For the distinction between leading and nudging the market, see Wade (2010).
28. For a detailed case study of Brazil, see Kroger (2012).
29. In Chile, this is less true than in the other cases, especially for rural labor.
30. Although conditional cash transfers have beneficial effects, they do not address the underlying structural causes of poverty, not even in the comparatively radical case of contemporary Uruguay. See Sandberg (2012).
31. I am not suggesting that these voting blocs are permanent. Center-Right candidates who promise to retain many of the social-democratic protections while giving more scope to markets and fighting crime may defeat social-democratic opponents, as in Chile in 2010.
32. For summaries of the first four sets of studies, see ILO (2011). For the final study, see UNRISD (2010: 153).
33. In Chile, the Concertación governments (1990–2010) acquiesced to the 1980 constitution with its over-representation of the Right, and thus accepted that it would need to bargain with the Right in the Senate to pass its legislation. This decision, in tandem with its acceptance of macroeconomic orthodoxy and free trade, meant that the center-Left would resist opening up the political system to potentially disruptive participation (Ruiz 2012: 72–3).

6   The radical Left: moving beyond the socialist impasse

Twentieth-century socialism stands as a cautionary tale of the pitfalls into which socialist movements can fall. In the Global South, the wave of socialist regimes of the 1960s and 1970s soon subsided. Many of them descended into civil war or chaos in the 1980s and 1990s. With rare exceptions, socialist experiments devolved into an authoritarian and statist route that subordinated society and economy to centralized edicts. This degenerative form of socialism has aptly been termed bureaucratic collectivism.

From today's perspective, this outcome is not surprising. Socialism, we realize, involves an inherently complex and conflictual reorganization of economy and society. This transformative approach might be expected to work best in countries with well-developed class identities, traditions of autonomous political and social organization on a non-parochial basis, a civic culture, an economy productive enough to lift the population out of poverty, and a state with high administrative and fiscal capacity. Yet, as sketched in Chapter 4, most countries in the Global South, especially those with low-income or "fragile" states, lack all or some of these characteristics.

Nevertheless, an early strand of socialist thinking, which traces its origins to the utopian socialists of the early nineteenth century, held that even economically backward societies could achieve socialism. The Narodniks of Russia in the late nineteenth century were an exemplar of this view. These leftist intellectuals believed that largely agrarian Russia could skip the capitalist stage and directly enter socialism. In effect, the country could move from "primitive communism" to modern socialism, if the peasantry could be aroused to overthrow the tsarist order. The village commune was seen as the embryo of the new society. Local peasant solidarity and the communal land tenure system would be extended to the society as a whole to form a collective system of production and exchange. The Socialist Revolutionary Party represented this viewpoint at the time of the Russian Revolution, but the Bolsheviks swept it away.

A similar view animated some socialist parties in the newly independent former colonies in the 1960s and 1970s, especially in Africa. African socialists claimed that they would extend the solidarity norms characterizing social relations at the level of the extended family, village or clan to encompass the nation as a whole. Underdeveloped countries could thereby bypass the individualism and exploitation of capitalism by making a direct transition to socialism. Tanzania under Julius Nyerere had the best conditions for realizing this vision, I argue below, but the experiment dismally failed. Although the strategy envisioned peasants voluntarily joining together in villages and adopting cooperative forms of production, in reality *ujamaa* socialism became top-down, authoritarian and coercive. Understanding this failure illuminates the challenges of attaining socialism in poor counties.

With the collapse of the Soviet Union and other Communist and socialist experiments in the late 1980s, and with the implicit conversion of the Chinese Communist Party to the task of building state capitalism, socialism went into eclipse in the 1990s. Socialism seemed to have reached an impasse: efforts of socialists to transcend capitalism actually brought about authoritarianism and the rule of a new class, thus contradicting socialism's emancipatory principles. Is there a way out of this impasse?

Hugo Chávez and his followers in Venezuela and acolytes elsewhere have proclaimed their intention to find a way. In 2005, Chávez proclaimed his commitment to "twenty-first-century socialism." Newly elected presidents in Bolivia and Ecuador soon followed suit. Chávez and the others have asserted their resolve to avoid the previous century's top-down, authoritarian form of socialism by building on a democratic foundation. The three leaders have adopted an experimental approach, changing policy direction from time to time and harboring dissenting voices within the governing party. They have succeeded in improving the lives of the indigenous peoples, the poor and elements of the middle class. They have so far avoided bureaucratic collectivism, but have acceded to a new form of populism: Left populism. Particularly in the cases of Venezuela and Ecuador, Left populism has involved a top-down and sporadically heavy-handed approach as well as vulnerability to political crisis when the original leader departs. Twenty-first-century socialism, though not without achievements, is not yet a robust model of socialist transition.

Insofar as means and ends are closely entwined, can socialism be achieved democratically? More specifically, is it possible for socialists to work within liberal-democratic institutions while challenging their limits through popular mobilization, attacks on inherited privilege and property relations, and extending participatory decision-making? The means–ends dilemma is particularly acute in countries in which the commitment to liberal democracy on the part of both entrenched elites and the radical Left is tenuous and conditional.

I suggest that, if there is to be a democratic socialism, it will probably be achieved through the strategy of what is most aptly characterized as radical social democracy. This conclusion flows from both historical experience and the logic of an attempt to achieve socialism democratically. According to this model, a socialist party/coalition mobilizes a cross-class (and, in many cases, cross-communal) constituency to take control of government through free and fair elections. The government then institutes a process of domesticating capitalism, expanding the scope of collective decision-making and cooperative production, and introducing opportunities for citizens to enhance their capabilities. In time (according to the logic of this model), these incremental changes shape subaltern classes with the abilities, sense of efficacy and solidarity to assume a self-determining role in political and economic life. Social-movement activism, based on autonomous, encompassing movements of the subordinate classes and other groups, is key to sustaining a democratic transition. A synergy between civil society and political society, especially the leftist party/coalition, blocks the oligarchical tendency inherent in a party-led revolutionary struggle. Socialism, in this view, is thus more in the way of an open-ended, long-term process than a fixed destination. It is a process of building solidarity, citizens' capabilities and participatory structures while fostering equality, social protection and economic development. In principle, the social-market economy expands and, at some point, becomes a socialist-market economy.

I employ the case of Kerala, India, to illustrate the process and its inherent problems. I am fully aware of this case's peculiarities and the shortcomings of its socialist process. Yet Kerala's history illuminates the trajectory of radical social democracy better than any other case. Indeed, it is a "pure" case owing precisely to its peculiarities. Kerala was buffered from imperialism, global capitalism and violent or undemocratic politics by its status as a state within a federation led, for many years, by a Congress Party rhetorically committed to socialism. Of course, this provincial status also meant that the ultimate goal of socialism was unattainable in Kerala; violent class struggle or unconstitutional seizures of property would have led (in fact, did lead) to the imposition of central rule by New Delhi. The radical path ultimately gave way to moderate social democracy – for reasons, I suggest below, that are of broader significance.

The radical social-democratic strategy is unlikely to succeed in the contemporary world. Today, even more than in the past, socialism is unlikely to survive in a single country. A socialist government would be called upon to prevent a meltdown of the economy, while fending off the hostility of the hitherto dominant classes, the US government and governance institutions of the neoliberal global order. Realistically, the radical social-democratic model could only survive in the context of a regionally based counter-hegemonic alliance. If there is an escape from the socialist impasse, it lies in this direction.

The dead end of state socialism

The statist approach to socialism, we now know, leads to a dead end. A state-socialist tendency is particularly strong in socialist regimes attaining power through revolutionary violence. This pattern typically involves a monopolistic and centralized vanguard party. The party, comprising those who have a more highly developed consciousness, forge unity to defeat enemies and guide the people toward a collectivist mentality and cooperative institutional arrangements. Though an effective instrument in overthrowing tyranny or oppressive colonial rule, this sort of party was ill suited to fostering democracy. The vanguard party, after seizing power, commonly imposed an authoritarian revolution from above. Various circumstances combined in the twentieth century to shape this outcome: the leadership's alleged superior grasp of historical laws, the party's need to close ranks against external and internal enemies, the absence of autonomously organized social movements to check oligarchy, and the inevitable decline of revolutionary fervor among cadres faced with the temptations of office. In time, the self-interest of the dominant bureaucrats of party and state trumped the solidarity and equality norms to which, rhetorically, they were dedicated. The result of adopting the top-down strategy was not socialism, but an oppressive bureaucratic collectivism.

Bureaucratic collectivism involves the merging of political society with the state apparatus, forming a party-state. This party-state eliminates (or severely reduces) the autonomy of civil society and the sway of private property, subjecting the economy to centralized control. Unconstrained by the market or civil and political society, the monopolistic party becomes tyrannical, concentrating power and privilege in a narrow coterie. At the extreme, this control entails a central plan and a command economy. However, centralized, top-down planning fails in the context of complex economies and increasingly venal bureaucrats. Eventual economic devastation as well as political tyranny is associated with this model.

Michael Harrington, who thoroughly explored this syndrome, does not conclude that the bureaucratic-collectivist outcome is inevitable (Harrington 1972). However, to avoid it, socialist *ends* of enhanced equal freedom demand adherence to democratic *means* – advice that poses a major strategic challenge for parties pursuing socialism in societies dominated by repressive regimes and/or entrenched possessive individualism.

Significantly, the violent revolutions in the 1960s and 1970s that defined themselves as socialist primarily mobilized the masses to oust a detested tyrant or colonial master, rather than to introduce socialism (see Colburn and Rahmato 1992: 161–2). In Cuba (1956–9), Nicaragua (1972–9) and Ethiopia (1974–8), the armed struggle was directed at defeating tyrants and crushing opponents. In Mozambique (1964–75), Angola (1961–75) and Guinea-Bissau (1963–75), the revolutionary movements mobilized people to oust the Portuguese colonial power. In Eritrea (1962–91), the fight was both to remove a tyrant in Addis Ababa and win independence from Ethiopia. Socialism was a subsidiary goal; the people sought liberation, but not necessarily state ownership of the means of production. A strong class base committed to the subsequent socialist revolution was thus lacking.

Peasants, forming the largest social class in most of these cases, were generally not favorably disposed to collective agriculture. They clung to a desire to work their own land.[1] The pattern was different in Cuba, where a large rural and urban proletariat provided the basis for a more far-reaching socialization of the economy. In Ethiopia (Clapham 1988) and Mozambique (Howe and Ottaway 1987), the peasants initially enjoyed considerable autonomy and democratic participation; however, this permissive era soon ended, replaced by a top-down approach. The governments instituted socialist policies without much consultation and preparation. When peasants resisted collective forms of agriculture, the party-state responded with force rather than persuasion.[2] Civil wars, in which peasants fought on both sides, broke out in Mozambique, Angola, Ethiopia, Eritrea and Nicaragua, instigated or exacerbated by foreign interference. None of the socialist experiments, except that in Cuba,[3] has survived – though, it should be added, the displacement of "socialism" by neoliberalism has only rarely improved the lot of poor people.

A bureaucratic-collectivist tendency was also manifest in certain underdeveloped countries whose presidents, in the absence of violent revolutionary struggle, simply proclaimed their governments to be socialist. In some cases, these proclamations represented nothing more than ideological posturing on the part of military juntas or autocrats. Consider the cases of the "People's Republics" of Congo (Brazzaville) and Benin in the late 1960s and 1970s. Military officers in both countries discovered, shortly after leading coups d'état, that they were, after all, Marxist socialists. In both cases, a yawning chasm separated the Marxist rhetoric from the actual reality, a gap between a stridently vocal concern ... with ideological militancy, vigor, purity, and autocriticism ("Socialist rectitude") and a near-total failure of all leadership strata to direct or control socioeconomic development (in *any* manner, let alone along socialist lines) or to arrest corruption and mismanagement in their own ranks. Indeed, the immense gap between, on the one hand, ... ideologically derived policy-goals, incessantly hammered at with an insistence and ferocity reminiscent of the ideological clashes of early Stalinist Russia ..., and on the other, the pragmatism and continued dependency-relations with former colonial powers ... tempt the critical observer to discount African radical ideology as but "opium for the masses." (Decalo 1979: 231)

If Marxism was not "opium for the masses," it certainly served to mask the self-aggrandizement of the state-class.

Other cases, however, demonstrated a deeper attachment to socialism. In these cases, a tension arose between the professed *ideal* of people voluntarily choosing cooperation and collective production, and the *reality* that the political authorities, come what may, were firmly committed to a socialist path. Peasants, workers and the middle classes often resisted, however. Would the socialist elite respond by trying to win people over through persuasion, or would they contend that too much was at stake to permit the present generation, mired in a petty-bourgeois mentality, to block progress? The answer is clear. Arab socialism in Egypt, Baath socialism in Syria and Iraq, various African socialisms and Marxist socialisms all became, in time, a pretext for authoritarian rule by a new political class (see Kitching 1983).

One socialist experiment that attracted a great deal of foreign interest, as well as financial support, was engineered by Tanzania's first prime minster and president, Julius Nyerere. This experiment demonstrates that a single-party, top-down socialist initiative falters even under comparatively favorable conditions. Elsewhere, socialist experiences foundered owing to intense opposition from a powerful domestic business class, often in conjunction with an imperialist power, or the self-aggrandizing proclivities of the "socialist" elite, or intense ethnic rivalries that degenerated into civil war. But none of these contingencies applied to the Tanzanian case in the period from the Arusha Declaration in 1967 (which set the guidelines for socialist development) to 1985 (when Nyerere resigned from the presidency and the country abruptly changed course). If any country could leapfrog from peasant communities to socialism, it would be Tanzania in the 1960s and 1970s.

Ujamaa *socialism in Tanzania*

Although Tanzania was economically undeveloped, this lack of capitalist development paradoxically offered opportunities for socialism, as well as impediments. In 1967, Tanzania had a largely rural population of self-provisioning peasants, a minuscule industrial base, a reliance on several agricultural exports, a paucity of citizens with university-level education or with technical skills, and very low average incomes. All of these factors clearly impeded a skill-intensive, party-state-directed developmental socialism. However, Tanzania's lack of development also meant that the considerable equality and solidarity of the country's traditional acephalous communities remained largely intact among the widely scattered nine-tenths of the population who lived on the land. In addition, the domestic business class was far from an imposing opponent; it was small, mainly of Indian origin and not highly influential. Nyerere and his party (TANU/CCM)[4] sought to take advantage of these circumstances to bypass the capitalist phase by moving directly to an egalitarian socialist society – an idea that was taken seriously at the time not only by Tanzania's leaders but also by academics and NGO activists who succumbed to "Tanzaphilia."

Tanzanian socialism had other distinctive domestic advantages. Neither Nyerere nor his top lieutenants were self-seekers or prone to a cult of personality. Nyerere was widely respected in Tanzania and abroad for his humility, probity and dedication to his people's welfare.[5] His low-key, undogmatic approach to socialism made it difficult for anyone to pin an extremist label on him. In addition, Tanzania was not riven by ethnic rivalries. It was blessed with a multiplicity of small, mainly Bantu, ethnic groups, and with a lingua franca in the form of Kiswahili. No single group could thus aspire to dominate the country alone, or in combination with another. A potential Christian–Muslim split was pre-empted by an equitable distribution of leadership positions and public goods. National unity was, indeed, one of TANU/CCM's cherished achievements.

Finally, no capitalist power held a major economic or strategic interest in Tanzania that might motivate it to sabotage this non-Marxist socialist experiment. Following the Arusha Declaration, bilateral and multilateral aid dramatically *increased*. The World Bank allocated more loans to Tanzania than to any other African country in the 1970s (before the World Bank converted to neoliberalism), while bilateral donors, especially those from Scandinavia, became major supporters. Nyerere's rectitude, the leadership code that restricted the growth of a self-aggrandizing political class, and the emphasis on rural development reassured donors that aid money would be well spent (Clark 1978: 82). The rise of neoliberalism and the evident shortcomings of state socialism in the early 1980s bred a more hostile donor attitude, however.

A sketch of *ujamaa* socialism would include the following elements:
- "Modern African socialism can draw from its traditional heritage the recognition of 'society' as an extension of the basic family unit"

(Nyerere 1968: 12). Hence, to reiterate, socialist strategy aimed to pre-empt the class divisions, individualism and notions of private property associated with the rise of capitalism, and draw upon the egalitarianism, solidarity and mutuality that still obtained at the level of kinship groups in the rural areas. Community members did not generally "own" their land, but they maintained the right to use land for their sustenance. And everyone had an obligation to work to support the household. These values would continue to guide Tanzanian society (Nyerere 1968: 6–7).

- "One-party democracy," proclaimed in 1965, recognized the reality that the electorate voted overwhelmingly for TANU in national elections. Nyerere feared that a multiparty system would emerge that would divide the country into ethnic fragments and promote divisions as self-seekers advanced their own interests. Hence, only one political party would legally exist (TANU), but *intra*-party democracy would obtain with two or more candidates contesting most parliamentary seats. In practice, one-party democracy was not a mere sham: some incumbent MPs and several cabinet ministers lost their seats in parliamentary elections (Shivji 1991). However, centralized control of the legislature existed: a party committee vetted potential candidates, and the National Assembly simply ratified policies first adopted by party committees.

- The Arusha Declaration of 1967 spurred further public ownership of private firms along with closer state regulation. By 1973, the bulk of large and medium-sized firms in the formal sector had been national-ized, including banks, manufacturing firms, companies involved in the import and wholesale trade, and sisal plantations (Mwansasu and Pratt 1979: 11–12). However, the paucity of managerial expertise required that the factories operate as joint ventures with foreign capital or under management contracts. Thus, the relations of production in many firms remained much as before nationalization. Heavy state regulation included, most important, currency controls and a fixed exchange rate.

- A strict leadership code adopted in 1967 required that all full-time TANU/CCM officials, cabinet ministers and MPs, and top and middle-level civil servants should draw only one salary, not accept directorships in firms, and not own shares or houses for rent. This code successfully checked, at least in the early years, the common practice elsewhere of political insiders using their political influence for personal enrichment.

- *Ujamaa vijijini* was to govern rural development. The government would encourage peasants to regroup in villages rather than continue to live in dispersed households adjacent to the land they cultivated. Villagization would not only allow the government to provide basic services such as education, health care and clean water to the rural population, but also enhance the opportunity for villagers to develop communal rather than individual production. The early emphasis on peasants voluntarily choosing to form *ujamaa* villages and engage in communal agriculture was short-lived; in 1973, the government turned to heavy-handed coercive measures.

- Most important, the strategy from the mid 1960s was to use the state, and the party with which it was entwined, to move society toward a socialist future. The goal, established by the top leadership and especially Nyerere, was not open for discussion. The means of achieving socialism, however, might be debated, though within the confines of a single party with a limited tolerance for dissenting views and a largely powerless National Assembly. TANU/CCM was a mass rather than a vanguard party; any citizen could become a member as long as he/she accepted a broad statement of socialist principles. But the party was firmly under the control of its top leadership, many of whom were also government leaders. The press and all mass organizations – trade unions, women's groups, students and youth organizations, cooperative societies – were formally under the control of TANU/CCM. The party also tried to extend its sway down to the grassroots, in the form of ten-household cells.[6] And the security services were active: political commissars were placed in the armed forces, governmental critics were subject to surveillance and preventive detention, and constitutional protections of human rights did not exist until 1984 (Shivji 1991).

In sum, Nyerere's strategy was to consolidate and use state power to institute an egalitarian and cooperative society before capitalism eroded the equality and solidarity of traditional communities. Not surprisingly, in light of the vastness, poverty and administrative weaknesses of Tanzania, the experiment failed.

Tanzania suffered a severe economic crisis, beginning in the late 1970s, which nullified much of the social development achieved since independence in 1961. These social achievements, lest we forget, included universal primary education, an effective adult literacy campaign, vast expansion of primary health care, a major reduction of income differentials within the public sector, and the inculcation of a sense of nationhood. Nevertheless, from the late 1970s, Tanzania experienced chronic balance-of-payments deficits, budgetary shortfalls that curtailed development projects and infrastructural maintenance, a sharp decline in the quality of social services, and a precipitous drop in the real income of households (between 1970 and 1984) of about 50 percent overall and 65 percent for urban dwellers (Hyden and Karlstrom 1993: 1,399). Peasants could, and did, retreat into subsistence agriculture, but urban households, not having that option, bore the brunt of the collapse, having to find the money to purchase essential goods on the exorbitant black market.

A sympathetic observer illustrates the depth of Tanzania's collapse. Reginald Green noted in 1983 that "on the face of it nothing works and man is a plaything of forces beyond his or her leaders' control" and that the consequent despair, cynicism and incessant struggle for survival spawned "corruption, inefficiency and anomie" (Green 1983: 112. See also Hyden and Karlstrom 1993: 1,399). But did this economic disaster result from state socialism?

In large measure, yes. Certainly, Tanzania's economy suffered from exogenous shocks: two major price increases for its imported oil in the 1970s, a drought in the mid 1970s, and a costly war against the notorious Idi Amin regime in Uganda in the late 1970s. Still, the state-socialist strategy bears a major responsibility for the debacle. An increasingly sclerotic and highly centralized party-state pre-empted and undermined popular initiatives in a top-down effort to build socialism in the image promulgated by the party's leadership.

All sectors of the economy suffered from this bureaucratic-collectivist tendency. Because peasants were slow to realize the benefits of voluntarily resettling in villages and (eventually) engaging in communal production, the party-state undertook compulsory villagization in 1973. The passive resistance of peasants to a policy that threatened their way of life led to major food shortages in 1974–6 (exacerbated by a drought) – and that in a country that had hitherto been self-sufficient in food (Lofchie 1978; McHenry 1979; Briggs 1979). Also, state control of cooperatives catering to peasant needs, instituted in the late 1960s, undermined their former effectiveness. In manufacturing, parastatal enterprises not only failed to transform capitalist management practices (as was promised), but also abetted their disastrous inefficiency by inserting non-expert party officials into workplaces (Bienefeld 1977: 37–8; Clark 1978: 129; Samoff 1979: 39–40). State controls throughout the economy stifled both efficiency and the proclaimed commitment to participatory development.

Implications

Tanzania's experience suggests that a state-centric strategy of implementing socialism in a low-income country will fail – even if the leadership is relatively benign and the socialist party faces little domestic or external hostility. The monopolistic party not only lacks the managerial expertise and popular support to manage a complex economy and society, but also tends to become arrogant, corrupt and authoritarian. Avoiding this pitfall requires, at a minimum, that socialist movements be less paternalistic and coercive, and more receptive to autonomous social movements, political opposition, and small-scale, bottom-up, cooperative initiatives.

Nyerere's vision of Tanzania leaping from communal solidarity to socialism was romantic, but it did build on a certain sociological reality. *A deeper problem arises from the nature of solidarity in peasant societies.* Mutuality depends on face-to-face relationships at the level of the extended family, village or clan. Socialists wishing to scale up this intimate solidarity to the national population as a whole face a difficult, perhaps impossible, task.

An authoritarian tendency and economic shortcomings discredited socialism in the late twentieth century. Have more democratic and effective versions appeared in the twenty-first century?

Twenty-first-century socialism?

Venezuela's President Hugo Chávez, in declaring his commitment to "twenty-first-century socialism" in January 2005, emphasized that the new socialism would avoid the authoritarianism of old-style socialism. "We have to reinvent socialism," he declared. "It can't be the kind of socialism we saw in the Soviet Union." Instead, the new socialism would be democratic and based on local traditions rather than foreign models. Similarly, Evo Morales, after becoming president of Bolivia in January 2006, spoke of his commitment to "communitarian socialism" as a new form of socialism drawing on the traditional solidarity and communal orientation of the indigenous people (an orientation reminiscent of Nyerere's). A year later, the new president of Ecuador, Rafael Correa, claimed to be leading a "citizens' revolution." Neither these declarations nor the policies that followed provided a clear delineation of the new socialist strategy, though the leaders and their parties did reject capitalism and assert their intention to avoid the painful errors of earlier socialist experiments.

The search for an alternative path in all three countries emerged amidst economic and political turmoil. There was a popular yearning for change. Low economic growth, periodic economic crises, growing poverty, ineffectual and austere neoliberal recovery programs, political instability,[7] and massive inequality and corruption in the 1980s and 1990s discredited existing party systems and neoliberalism. The new leaders benefited from increased leverage within the global economy in the 2000s, stemming from their countries' exceptional hydrocarbon and mineral wealth in the context of a commodity boom and the rise of China and India as major trade and investment partners. More leeway in policy making permitted the three presidents to pursue radical solutions to their deep-seated problems – as long as commodity export prices remained high. But how do we characterize their approach?

The case of Venezuela

To simplify, I focus on Venezuela, a country of 29 million people with the longest-running record of radical change (since 1999). Even with a single-country focus, however, the analyst encounters ambiguity. Observers have variously characterized Chávez's regime (1999–2013) as populist, authoritarian socialist, and radical social-democratic. One source of ambiguity is the shifts in strategy over time. Studies of Venezuela under Chávez often refer to two or three phases: at least an initial phase (perhaps 1999–2004) of anti-neoliberal and nationalist policies, followed by a radical phase in which the goal is to transcend capitalism, not just neo-liberalism (e.g. Lebowitz 2007: 42–9; Ellner 2008: 111–19). A series of hostile actions marked the turning point: a US-supported coup attempt against Chávez in April 2002, followed by a general strike engineered by anti-Chávez unions and employers in the winter of 2002–3, and a recall referendum in 2004 organized by the opposition parties (which failed). In addition, contradictory policies and tendencies coexist in the same phase, reflecting both internal socialist divisions between hard-liners and soft-liners and Chávez's experimental style. Analysts, by highlighting certain tendencies, can thus find support for more than one interpretation. I consider each possibility in turn.

Some observers contend that the Chávez regime, beginning in 2005, moved toward a top-down and authoritarian socialist model, fueled by oil revenues (e.g. López Maya 2011: 236). How valid is this interpretation?

The "vanguardist" temptation surely exists in Venezuela, as a lengthy article by Marta Harnecker (2010) unintentionally reveals. Harnecker, a noted Chilean Marxist activist and theoretician, has lived in Venezuela and advised Chávez. In an article on twenty-first-century socialism, tellingly subtitled "Inventing to Avoid Mistakes," she acknowledges the well-known vanguardist shortcomings of twentieth-century socialism and observes that "the struggle for democracy cannot be separated from the struggle for socialism" (2010: 5). However, top-down control and the specter of false consciousness implicitly slip in near the lengthy article's end. She notes that contemporary socialism will work only "if we manage to impregnate present and future generations with a new humanistic and solidarity-infused ethics" (2010: 66). Although the long-term goal is self-government by the people, they will need an interim period of tutoring to develop a "culture" of participation. Building socialism, she observes, requires "a real cultural revolution ... and developing a revolutionary subject who is the bedrock of the whole process." The people must "undertake an apprenticeship in forms of self-government. These are not things that come spontaneously." Hence, a revolutionary party will need to devise an "educational strategy" so that people can learn how to assume their new responsibilities.

The problem is the old one: "we cannot build socialism without socialist men and women." Hence, those who have already transformed their consciousness should form the revolutionary party and use this instrument to prepare the people for their democratic role. People will be allowed to criticize their leaders, though "strong sanctions" will be applied to those "who make unfounded criticisms or denunciations" (Harnecker 2010: passim 66–77). This advice, if followed, would surely return socialism to the authoritarian mind-set that led to the earlier debacles.

Other Marxist analysts who have studied the Venezuelan experience have had equal difficulty in exorcising the vanguardist specter. Michael Lebowitz, in a book entitled *The Socialist Alternative* (2010), labors to shake the socialist transition free from the stigma of top-down control – to the point of devoting only three pages to the role of the socialist party. Despite this caution, the author refers to a vague "socialist mode of regulation" to develop a "new social rationality" of cooperation and solidarity (2010: 120). Lebowitz agrees with Che Guevara that "it is necessary, simultaneous with the new material foundations, to build a new man" (2010: 120). This acknowledgment leads to a guarded but nonetheless unmistakable embrace of vanguardism. He asserts (2010: 159), for instance, that "solutions relying upon individual rationality produce people who are fit to produce a society that is not socialist – and this is what a socialist mode of regulation must prevent." People will still be forced to be free.

Turning to the Venezuelan experience, we can glean some evidence supporting a bureaucratic-collectivist interpretation. Key elements include the following.

- *Extensive public ownership*: Aside from the renationalization of the state oil company (PDVSA) early on, the Chávez administration extended the public sector after 2007 to include other petroleum and mining assets, steelworks, cement, electricity generation, telecommunications, banking, food processing, sugar mills, refrigerated storage, coffee roasting, and a chain of supermarkets. In the 2012 election campaign, Chávez proposed extending the public sector to include commerce and transport as well by 2019 (Ellner 2012b: 4). However, extensive public ownership is not unique to socialism; in Latin America, it has been associated with populist regimes as well.

- *Promotion of worker-owned and managed cooperative enterprises*: Since 2005, the government has nurtured producer cooperatives through training programs, awarding them state contracts, preferential credit arrangements, and technical and administrative support. The ambitious goal is to promote egalitarian and solidaristic orientations not only in the workplace but also in the residential communities to which cooperative members belong. To foster this broader solidarity, Chávez attached "social clauses" to preferential credit agreements, requiring producer cooperatives to direct 10 percent of their revenues to funding high-priority projects in local communities (Piñeiro Harnecker 2009: 310). As many as sixty thousand cooperatives operated in 2007, though thousands more had collapsed.[8] Officially, 2.5 million Venezuelans (14 percent of the labor force) worked in cooperatives, producing 8 per cent of GDP by 2007.[9] The government has also experimented with co-management of state-owned firms.

- *A centralization of powers in the presidency at the expense of the legislature and checks and balances*: Bureaucratic collectivism, though not only bureaucratic collectivism, entails a centralization of power. In Venezuela, this process began with the new constitution approved by a referendum in 1999, continued with the National Assembly voting, three times, to empower the president to rule by decree for a set period, and was advanced by the successful 2009 constitutional amendment that, among other things, removed term limitations on the presidency and other elected officials. Also, judges are "routinely fired" for rulings contrary to the government's wishes (Toro 2012: A17). One judge, who outraged Chávez with a ruling favorable to a government critic, was arrested and sentenced to house arrest, an episode that Human Rights Watch claimed intimidated other Venezuelan judges (*Globe and Mail* [Toronto], September 22, 2012). However, in Latin America, centralization of power in the presidency, even including intimidation of the judiciary, has been a common trend regardless of regime type.
- *Restrictions on liberal-democratic institutions*: They include the weakening of institutional checks on power by appointing *chavistas* to non-partisan positions (such as the Supreme Court, the attorney general, the National Electoral Council, national comptroller); the erosion of freedom of expression to the point that, by 2007, the government controlled 85 percent of television stations, two national radio stations, a news agency, three thousand community radio stations, three print media companies and about a hundred internet portals (Corrales 2010: 34) – control that was extended in 2012 to incorporate the two further private TV channels sympathetic to the opposition; and governmental intimidation of state governors, mayors and local legislators elected from opposition parties in 2007 and later (Ellner 2010b: 79–80; Alvarado 2010: 1; López Maya 2011: 229–31; Johnson 2010). Nicolás

Maduro, Chávez's anointed successor, used this media apparatus to support his candidacy in the 2013 presidential election.

- *A blurring of the lines among state, government and party* has occurred. *Chavista* ministers and governors have filled the leadership positions in the Partido Socialista Unido de Venezuela (PSUV). Active-duty and retired military officers have been appointed and elected to governmental and state administrative offices.[10] Partisan civil servants have dominated certain governmental agencies, including those implementing social programs. However, these stratagems have also characterized populist regimes, such as that of Carlos Menem in Argentina.
- *The top-down establishment of various locally based participatory ventures since 2001:* These included 65,000 Bolivarian Circles in the early years, dozens of water councils, local planning councils, urban land committees, agricultural cooperatives, and community councils.

Yet, despite these trends, Venezuela under Chávez more closely resembles quasi-democratic state capitalism than a centralized and authoritarian bureaucratic collectivism (as in Cuba, for example). Organized opposition and political freedom, albeit attenuated, have survived. Parties continue to vie for power. The country has held a record number of elections since 1998: a recall referendum, two referendums on constitutional revisions, and party primaries, in addition to the regularly scheduled legislative and presidential votes and state and local elections. In the referendums, the government has adhered to constitutional rules even in those that sought, among other things, to augment presidential powers – in 1999, 2007 and 2009. Elections also are not rigged.[11] However, the fairness of election campaigns is questionable, especially in light of the publicly owned media's focus on Chávez and later Maduro, and the tight regulation of the remaining private media outlets. Yet the governmental side does not always do well. Chávez lost the first constitutional referendum in 2007; in the 2010 mid-term elections the PSUV coalition received only 48.2 percent of the popular vote; and in the 2012 presidential election, Chávez garnered only 54 percent of the popular vote. These poor showings are usually attributed to the country's dire economic problems, high and growing crime rate, and fear of Cuban-style socialism.

Opposition forces are far from blameless when it comes to democratic rules. The United States government has been overtly hostile, to the point of supporting an attempted coup in 2002, financially assisting opposition groups and augmenting its military presence close to Venezuelan territory. The domestic opposition has sometimes acted provocatively. Its leaders denied the legitimacy of the Chávez government during its first decade, resorting to extra-parliamentary actions (general strikes, support for a coup, and street demonstrations). A leader of a Venezuelan non-governmental organization nicely captures the ambiguity in describing his country as a "democracy with authoritarian traits" (Alvarado 2010).

Moreover, the PSUV is not a vanguard party, in the sense of an ideologically unified, disciplined and organizationally effective instrument for capturing power and ruling in a monopolistic manner to advance a socialist agenda. Mass organizations, such as the labor movement, are not arms of the ruling party. Instead, they have typically split into pro- and anti-*chavista* factions. Even Venezuela's Catholic Church has divided along these lines. Rather than Leninists, Chávez and most of his party supporters were engaged in a gradual, semi-democratic process to attain egalitarian, cooperative and nationalist goals. Radicals within the PSUV demand a frontal assault on the bourgeois state, but the mainly peaceful, electoral road prevailed (Ellner 2011: 445). This path is, however, sullied by corruption and opportunism. Although this is a common complaint throughout Latin America, it has particular significance in relation to a "socialist" transition.

As for Venezuela's economy, it remains a mixed economy with regulated markets. Nationalizations have been extensive, justified on the grounds that Venezuelans, not foreigners, should reap the profits. Chávez often emphasized that his government had no intention of interfering with small businesses. The President called for neither a centrally planned economy nor the elimination of private property; he sought, rather, a "strategic alliance" with private business (Ellner 2012a: 106). The government has, however, intervened heavily in the economy, using such tools as subsidies, price and wage controls, exchange controls and a government-managed exchange rate. Although the PSUV is publicly committed to fostering cooperation and solidarity norms via producer cooperatives and co-managed firms, this is a long-term goal in a state-dominated market economy.

If a bureaucratic-collectivist interpretation is unpersuasive, is the Bolivarian Revolution closer to a radical social-democratic experiment? Venezuela, after all, has a lengthy tradition of moderate social-democratic politics. Acción Democrática was the main social-democratic party after 1958, though it declined into corruption and populism in the economic upheavals of the 1980s and 1990s. That Chávez's main opponent in the presidential election campaign of October 2012, Henrique Capriles, positioned himself as a "progressive" candidate of the center-Left (citing Lula da Silva's government as his model), suggests the continuing attractiveness of this tradition.[12] One finds some evidence for an incipient radical social-democratic approach, but overall it is an unconvincing interpretation.

Chávez forged a cross-class coalition since the early 2000s, consistent with this approach but also characteristic of populism. The *chavistas* have not identified the proletariat as the main agent of social transformation. Indeed, Chávez had many conflicts with organized labor, which had benefited from the patronage of the two old parties in the 1980s and 1990s. The *chavistas*, like their counterparts in Bolivia and Ecuador, have instead pursued an inclusionary politics through a program of re-asserting national autonomy and redistributing benefits from the oligarchy and transnational corporations (especially oil revenues) to the broad public. Chávez certainly appealed to the urban and rural poor, indigenous people and Afro-Venezuelans for support. However, the middle class also responded to the nationalist and anti-oligarchical rhetoric, together with such policies as nationalizing utilities to reduce utility bills, extending public pensions and other forms of social protection, and expanding access to college education (Lupu 2010: 9, 26). A careful study of Chávez's first three successful presidential elections and a recall referendum indicates that, contrary to conventional wisdom, the socialists drew electoral support across class boundaries (Lupu 2010). Only in the 1998 election did the *chavistas* depend on disproportionate support from the poor for their victory. Thereafter, there was no clear class bias in voting patterns, except that the wealthiest Venezuelans were consistently more likely to vote for the opposition than for Chávez. Interestingly, in the 2006 national elections, the incumbent drew support disproportionately from the middle of the income distribution, *not* the poor (Lupu 2010: 23). Also, the poor were no more likely to vote in elections than eligible voters from the other income classes – a finding that runs counter to the popular view that the *chavistas* successfully mobilized the lower classes.

The presidential election of 2012, which Chávez narrowly won, and the even narrower victory of Nicolás Maduro in the April 2013 election are too recent for voting analyses to have appeared. It is likely, however, that rolling blackouts, high inflation and rampant crime alienated some of *chavismo*'s middle-class supporters. Overall, though, it is clear that the PSUV has depended for its success on a broad coalition of the poor, near-poor and middle class, with even some support among wealthy voters.[13]

Consistent also with radical social democracy is the *chavistas*' focus on advancing the capabilities and power of ordinary citizens. Only with self-development can citizens assume an active role in the governance of political and economic life. Beginning in 2003, Chávez channeled reve-nues gained from high oil prices into various "missions" (*misiones*) to augment the opportunity of poor and marginalized groups to attain liter-acy, education (including at post-secondary level), good health, adequate housing, and sufficient food, and in the case of *campesinos*, access to land

and agricultural training. Millions of people have benefited from these missions, the facilities for which are often located in the *barrios* (Ellner 2010b: 92). Social spending as a percentage of GDP almost doubled between 1998 and 2007.

Furthermore, the *chavistas* have opened up new arenas for participation on the part of formerly marginalized Venezuelans. Despite the defects of democracy noted earlier, Venezuela has held more elections and referendums since 1998 than ever before. More representatives are drawn from formerly under-represented racial groups. The 1999 constitution established new mechanisms for recalling elected representatives. Workers' cooperatives and co-management schemes have extended democracy, however tentatively and imperfectly, into the economic sphere.

In addition, Chávez introduced community councils (*consejos communales*) in 2006, which he identified as the basic cells of socialism. His idea was to decentralize power and financial resources directly to communities small enough (200–400 families) to practice participatory democracy (Gott 2008: 481). More than 35,000 such councils existed in 2008. Each community (in principle) diagnoses its own needs, whether a community center, road, sidewalks, family housing or a medical center, and applies for funding from central and municipal governments to implement the plan. Over $1 billion was reportedly allocated to the councils in 2006 alone. Although the councils were launched with high expectations, they often did not work as intended. Common complaints included the manipulation of community councils for clientelistic ends and misuse of government funds. Also, a constant struggle ensued between attempts to assert central control, on the one hand, and the assertion of autonomy from below, on the other (Ellner 2010a: 68; Goldfrank 2011: 178–82). Irrespective of these tensions, however, many poor Venezuelans still held a positive view of these councils (Levitsky and Roberts 2011: 420; Goldfrank 2011: 182).

Indeed, *Latinobarómetro*, which periodically samples Latin American opinion, has found a higher level of satisfaction among Venezuelans with their democracy than among the citizens of most other Latin American countries.[14] In light of the earlier discussion of the government's limited adherence to liberal-democratic principles, this finding is paradoxical.

The paradox dissolves, however, when one understands that ordinary Venezuelans, like many Latin Americans, conceive of democracy differently than Westerners. Liberal academics tend to equate democracy with *liberal* democracy. Democracy, from this viewpoint, is a set of procedures for fairly selecting political representatives at regular intervals and safeguarding the civil and political rights of citizens. But many Venezuelans mistrust liberal democracy and the traditional parties because they associate both with corruption, broken promises and growing inequality in the 1980s and 1990s (Motta 2011: 35–6). Instead, they tend to understand democracy as a type of society rather than as a way of selecting political leaders – a society characterized by inclusiveness, equality and opportunities for direct participation (Valencia Ramírez 2006: 178; de la Torre 2007: 384–5; Motta 2011: 42).[15] In this regard, Venezuelans are not unique. As one large-scale survey concludes, "what most distinguishes the Latin American version of democracy ... is its emphasis on social and economic equality and progress" (Camp 2009: 9). Indeed, the tendency of ordinary people to embrace popular or radical democracy extends beyond Latin America – to Africa, for instance.[16] Thus, Venezuelans, who feel today more included in political and economic life than formerly, respond positively to survey questions probing their judgment of their country's "democratic" system.

However, even if we give credence to this popular perspective on democracy, Venezuela has deviated from the radical social-democratic model in significant ways. For one thing, the PSUV is not a social-movement party. Not only did it develop as a top-down organization, but also the factionalization of social movements weakened the latter's ability to counter oligarchical tendencies in the PSUV. The labor movement, for example, is split along pro- and anti-Chávez lines, and even the pro-Chávez unions are factionalized. The community councils, though including many activists, are too small and decentralized to counter the top-down tendency. Furthermore, some of them have been infiltrated by criminal gangs, who use the councils for their own purposes (Burback, Fox and Fuentes 2013: 73).

Most important in disqualifying Venezuela as a radical social-democratic case are the absence of an institutionalized party system or an institutionalized socialist/social-democratic party. The opposition in 2012–13 was a loose coalition of ideologically diverse parties, united only by opposition to *chavismo*. The United Socialist Party of Venezuela (PSUV), dating only from 2007, is neither united nor much of a party: it is a loosely organized vehicle to advance the leader and his shifting doctrine (under both Chávez and Maduro). As I mentioned, the party is not institutionally separate from the government. Top state officials are also party leaders. The supposedly neutral attorney-general and Electoral Council are run by loyalists. Retired army officers play key roles in the administration and the party. There are no mechanisms to ensure internal party democracy. Most damaging is the emergence of a *boliburguesia* – a class composed of opportunists who have used their political influence to amass fortunes, all the while avowing their commitment to the revolution (Burback, Fox and Fuentes 2013: 71). There are many accusations of outright corruption at the top as well as lower levels of officialdom.[17] Chávez himself, in 2011, denounced the party for its corruption and "individualism," warning that a failure to clean house would lead to the dissolution of the PSUV (Burbach, Fox and Fuentes 2013: 75). But Chávez was part of the problem. By dominating the government, the party and the mass media, he identified the revolution with his person rather than with an institutional arrangement and a program.

Finally, in spite of educational programs to foster solidarity norms, Venezuelans of all classes have embraced a possessive-individualist mentality (as defined in Chapter 4) (Jiménez 2006). Venezuela has been a consumer-oriented yet class-divided society living off oil money for fifty years; the masses have now seized the opportunity to join in. This trend underlines another paradox: though Chávez was very popular, his followers expressed little interest in transforming capitalism in a socialist direction.[18] The radical social-democratic impulse thus remains weak.

If we reject the first two interpretations, are we left with the mainstream view that the *chavista* regime is just another instance of populism? Populism, as suggested in Chapter 1, is both a derogatory term used to denigrate opponents and a concept in scholarly discourse. For those seeking to dismiss *chavismo*, populism is a convenient label. It connotes a self-aggrandizing demagogue who manipulates the common people by denouncing the elite and foreign enemies. As a term in scholarly discourse, populism encompasses several dimensions: a form of governance marked by personalism – a link between the charismatic leader and his following unmediated by an institutionalized party; a rhetorical appeal to the *puebla* who are depicted as exploited and oppressed by a venal elite; a heavy reliance on dispensing patronage to popular constituencies; and ideological opaqueness and an ambivalent attitude toward democracy. One can certainly identify features of Venezuela under Chávez that support an old-style populist interpretation.[19]

Chávez was undoubtedly a personalistic leader who identified himself with the Bolivarian Revolution. He appeared to be a charismatic leader with a strong popular following. His fiery speeches condemned the country's wealthy oligarchy and its supposed patron, the United States, for oppressing and cheating the common people. Chávez never led a unified or institutionalized socialist party. Indeed, Chávez overshadowed the PSUV. His likeness appeared everywhere. Ministers came and went, but Chávez remained. His death in early 2013 threw his party into such disarray that his deputy promised to preserve Chávez's body for public viewing forever.

Furthermore, cronyism and clientelism have apparently played a major role in regime dynamics. Critics and ordinary people complained of an insider elite who corruptly accumulated wealth. Many voters also believed that the government favored Chávez supporters in the allocation of benefits via its various missions – for instance the mission that allocated public housing units (Weyland 2011: 76–7; Ellner 2012b: 4; Neuman 2012: 1). Also, those holding government jobs who signed the 2004 recall referendum were dismissed; government workers were expected to attend pro-Chávez election rallies; and the government boosted public spending in 2012 (election year) to expand social benefits and attract electoral support (Neuman 2012: 1). Nonetheless, simply to equate Chávez and twenty-first-century socialism with old-style populism is to underestimate the Bolivarian Revolution.

Chávez's electoral victory in 1998 was the culmination of a popular revolt against neoliberalism that opened with the *caracazo* in February 1989. This urban mass protest, suppressed by the army with hundreds of civilian casualties, arose from austerity measures imposed by a duplicitous government that had just won an election by *opposing* such measures. The uprising instigated two abortive coups in 1992, one led by Hugo Chávez. Chávez's electoral victory in 1998 reflected a popular demand for fundamental change.

Chavismo actually represents, not old-style populism, but a new type that is aptly described as *Left populism*. This populism differs from old-style populism in two ways, as noted in Chapter 1. First, it has shed the ideological opacity that characterized the earlier version; Left populism consistently and openly supports the positions of the radical Left. It does not seek to co-opt the Left but to buttress it. Second, it has dropped the original ambivalence, or even hostility, to democracy. Left populism does repudiate key features of liberal democracy (as well as neoliberalism), but it does so in the context of embracing an alternative conception of democracy – "radical" or "popular" democracy. Consider each feature in turn.

Left populism unambiguously endorses leftist positions – hostility to neoliberalism, capitalism and imperialism, the goal of socialism, and fundamental institutional change and redistribution. The institutional and redistributive changes wrought by the Bolivarian Revolution were deeper than one would associate with old-style populism. Consider a few examples (Ellner 2008: 132–3). Following the 2001 Land Law and especially with the rejection of private property as an absolute right in 2007, the government undertook major land reform involving the redistribution of 8 million acres, mainly uncultivated land. It has nationalized many large firms – and not just in the natural resource sector (the sector populists typically concentrate on). A government-controlled chain of subsidized grocery stores (MERCAL), serving 13 million people at its height, competed with private supermarkets. The government vastly augmented and redirected social spending and social programs toward the poor: oil revenues have enhanced the educational, health and nutritional status of the poor and near-poor. Millions of people have access to health care for the first time. Illiteracy has plummeted. A college education is more widely accessible. Four times as many people were eligible for pensions in 2012 than in 1998. Thousands of units of subsidized housing have become available since 2011. In addition, state loans and preferential contracts have promoted workers' cooperatives, while the land redistribution program, together with start-up capital for thousands of agricultural cooperatives, has benefited the rural poor. Consequently, Venezuela achieved the largest decline in income inequality in Latin America between 2003 and 2007, a decrease of 4.8 points in the Gini coefficient for household income (Cornia and Martorano 2009: 3). Over the decade 1998–2009, the country's wealthiest quintile saw its share of the country's wealth decline by 7.8 percent (Orhangazi 2011: Table 1). Poverty and extreme poverty have been significantly reduced, though the precise reduction is disputed. However, even the *Factbook* of the US Central Intelligence Agency acknowledges that Venezuela's poverty rate had been cut in half by 2011. In short, Chávez did not simply engage in empty rhetoric; his policies effectively challenged a highly inegalitarian status quo.[20]

Second, the populist Left rejects liberal democracy, but not democracy as such. Left populists repudiate liberal democracy because it excluded large segments of "the people" from both political power and a decent share of wealth, income and respect. Hence, Chávez (together with presidents Morales of Bolivia and Correa of Ecuador) emphasized egalitarian, redistributive measures and direct participatory democracy, as sketched earlier. The people also retain the opportunity to oust their leaders at regularly scheduled and freely conducted elections and through the medium of a recall referendum. Left populists are thus not inherently anti-democratic, if one accepts that liberal democracy is not the sole legitimate democratic system.

Nevertheless, Left populism does not offer a robust way to escape the socialist impasse. Twenty-first-century socialism, at its best, is an experimental and largely peaceful process of defying neoliberalism, rejecting oligarchy, empowering marginalized groups, and redistributing resources within a heavily regulated and hydrocarbon-dependent state capitalism. The dependence of the "Revolution" on a voting coalition that prominently includes the middle class places limits on a socialist push for a deeper and more comprehensive transformation – though such limits are not necessarily undesirable.[21] Even in its state-capitalist form, twenty-first-century socialism has led to economic turmoil in Venezuela, with high budget deficits, high inflation, scarcities of staple foods, a rampant black market and a continued dependence on volatile oil exports.[22] State controls and a large public sector have also created new channels for corruption and self-enrichment on the part of an insider elite.

Moreover, the personalism and loose organizational foundations of *chavismo* mean not only that it readily degenerates into messianic leadership,[23] but also that the departure of the paramount leader brings instability and threatens the survival of the leftist current. The death of Chávez in early 2013 threw the country and the governing party into turmoil. Maduro, who lacks Chávez's charisma, barely won the April 2013 presidential election, and even then in a campaign marked by a new level of incivility and an effort on his part to deify the deceased leader. In mid 2013, the PSUV still controlled the presidency, the National Assembly and 20 of the 23 state governorships. But observers speculated that only the threat posed by the strong, united opposition and the hostility of the US government held the disparate factions of the PSUV together (Wilpert 2013: 2). Maduro, unlike Chávez, does not command unquestioned loyalty. Whether the new president can maintain party unity in the longer term is doubtful, given the existence of powerful factions centered on ex-military leaders and Chávez family members.

Nevertheless, despite these weaknesses, if *moderate* social democracy falters or is co-opted by the economic elite in other countries, popular disillusionment may well find its outlet in Left populism.

Bolivia and Ecuador compared

The administrations of President Evo Morales in Bolivia (since January 2006) and President Rafael Correa in Ecuador (since January 2007) have also identified themselves with renewed socialism.[24] Both presidents have pursued strategies akin to Venezuela's. Like the Chávez phenomenon, both of these regimes grew out of economic and political turmoil. Morales and Correa, like Chávez, have capitalized upon widespread disillusionment with each country's conventional party system and neoliberal economic reforms to win elections. All three presidents engage in fiery anti-establishment and anti-imperialist rhetoric, though actual policy is less radical than the rhetoric. They all established, as their first priority, constituent assemblies to design a new constitution that not only centralized more powers in the executive, but also established new participatory and consultative mechanisms. However, Bolivia and Ecuador differ from Venezuela in the political salience of their indigenous communities. In both countries, Amerindians and mestizos (people of mixed Amerindian and white ancestry) comprise more than 80 percent of the population.

This ethnic profile has raised acute dilemmas in Bolivia and Ecuador that Venezuela (with only 1.5 percent of its population Amerindian) has largely escaped.

State-directed mixed economies prevail in the three cases in the context of heavy dependence on hydrocarbon and mineral exports.[25] Each regime has undertaken nationalizations and extensive regulation, though in Bolivia and Ecuador the extent of nationalization (mainly in the natural resource sector) has not matched that in Venezuela. Each administration has increased the government's share of revenues generated by hydrocarbons and captured windfall gains with the run-up in oil and gas prices in 2002–8. They have used these revenues to fund major expansions in social spending (suffering large deficits in 2009 as oil and gas prices fell). All three, with highly inegalitarian societies and substantial poverty (especially in Ecuador and Bolivia), have redistributed some land (the extent of redistribution, however, varies), extended social protection, improved services such as education, health care and public housing, raised minimum wages, and transferred cash to the most vulnerable (though the emphasis varies).[26] All three presidents have acted pragmatically on occasion. President Morales, for instance, has pragmatically responded to pressures from both Bolivian business organizations and anti-neoliberal social movements by joining both the regional free-trade associations (the Andean Community of Nations, Mercosur and UNASUR) and the more radical, solidarity-based ALBA (see below) (Mejido Costoya 2011).

In politics, each president has rallied coalitions including those social forces that historically lacked political voice. They have all continued to honor unimpeded national votes in periodic elections, though Morales has shown a stronger commitment to political and civil rights than Chávez and Correa. All three governments have subjected the mass media to regulation and/or state control. In each case, a charismatic leader with considerable powers has dominated the political system. But there are also significant differences.

Bolivia, in contrast to the Left populism of Venezuela and Ecuador, has developed a synergy between social movements and the socialist party within the framework of democratic contestation. In this respect, the arrangement resembles radical social democracy, at least in the early years (2006–10). Movimiento al Socialismo (MAS) originated as a movement-party in 1995, growing out of rural-based associations of indigenous people (Zuazo 2010). Evo Morales rose through the ranks of the *cocalero* movement, one of these allied rural associations, before he moved to politics, and eventually the leadership of MAS.[27] Coca cultivation is part of indigenous culture in a country where a majority of citizens are Amerindians. The coca union federation is a powerful body encompassing individual *sindicates* organized on a village or town basis. The *cocaleras*, headed by Evo Morales, formed an association in the 1980s to defend their livelihood as the US government pressed Bolivia to crack down on illegal planting of coca. Aymara and Quecha *campesinos*, mainly in the highlands, had already organized two separate peak organizations. The three associations combined to create MAS, which then added urban-based movements (two-thirds of the population dwells in towns and cities).

From 2000 onwards, MAS participated in a series of mass protests precipitated by neoliberal policies, especially privatizations. They included, famously, the "water war" in Cochabamba in 2000 and the "gas wars" of 2003 and 2005. MAS thus originated hand in hand with social-movement activism.

MAS quickly attained a relatively strong position in Bolivian politics. It won both the presidency and the assembly in the 2005 elections, and expanded its electoral support in 2009 to 64 percent, winning large majorities in the senate and the legislature (Zuazo 2010: 125). MAS built its support through its policy commitments, especially to respect and empower local communities, not just through the distribution of patronage (Yashar 2011: 190). The new constitution of 2009 not only recognized the autonomy of indigenous communities, but also formalized a consultative process whereby the relevant government ministry consults officially recognized movements on legislative initiatives (Zuazo 2010: 132–5). Morales sought to cast MAS as an independent political party, albeit one that remained responsive to strong and engaged social movements.

Yet Bolivia's experience of mass protests since 2010 illustrates the difficulty of combining social-movement activism with strong, developmental government in an extractive economy heavily dependent on the export of unprocessed natural resources (see Molero Simarro and Paz Antolín 2012). A conflict emerges between governmental undertakings to protect the rural lands, forests and way of life of indigenous peoples, on the one hand, and the need to extract revenues to support generous social programs in resource-dependent economies, on the other. Protests by coca farmers concerning threats to their livelihoods, by environmental activists and indigenous-rights activists opposing the building of polluting mines and roads through pristine rainforest, and by workers and the disabled demanding better welfare support, have rocked the government. MAS's indigenous supporters split over environmental issues in 2012, when one group of Amerindians opposing road building confronted a counter-demonstration in La Paz by other indigenous supporters of MAS. Social movements, well aware of the efficacy of popular protests, have turned this weapon against their erstwhile champion. Morales and MAS have remained attuned to popular demands; however, the need to find new sources of mineral rents and the divisions within the indigenous movement have presented acute dilemmas.

Ecuador and Venezuela are more distant from the radical social-democratic model than Bolivia. The parties created by Chávez (the MVR, in 1997, which merged with others in 2007 to form the PSUV) and Correa (Alianza PAIS, in 2005) are top-down, personal vehicles whose role is to fight elections. I have already discussed the situation in Venezuela in some detail. In Ecuador, President Correa has "regarded Ecuador's turbulent and intrusive civil society as an obstacle, not a building block, for his revolution. He took a dim view of all organized interests, regardless of class, identity, or ideological leaning" (Conaghan 2011: 274).

The president's top-down approach has alienated various organized interests, including major factions of indigenous communities. Relations between Correa's government and CONAIE (Confederation of Indigenous Nationalities of Ecuador) soon soured.[28] Indigenous people have engaged in a series of organized protests, stemming from the negative environmental and health impacts of current and proposed mining and oil projects in the Amazon supported by the central government. Since extractive industries account for over half of public revenues, Correa has not sided with the protesters.[29] He has continued to court foreign investment in the mining sector, including a Chinese oil company to drill for oil in Yasuni National Park. Political life is consequently tumultuous, though Correa won his third successive election in February 2013.

Given these internal divisions and conflicts, how have these regimes, especially the one in Venezuela, survived in the face of neoliberal globalization and US hostility?[30]

Dealing with neoliberal globalization

The commodity boom and the economic rise of China and India increased the three governments' leverage within the global market economy. Both trends reduced the leftist governments' dependence on Western trade, credit and investment. The hydrocarbon wealth of Venezuela, Bolivia and Ecuador has afforded the regimes greater policy autonomy than elsewhere, as well as the wherewithal to fund expensive social programs. That Venezuela was the fifth-largest oil exporter during an era of booming oil prices buttressed Chávez's ability to defy the United States and adopt a "socialist" agenda. By the same token, the drop in oil prices in 2009–10 led to major economic strains in Venezuela (which depended on oil exports for half of the government's revenue), and the retrenchment of some of its missions (Orhangazi 2011: 3; "Socialism on the Never-Never" 2009: 53). Bolivia and Ecuador have not enjoyed the same degree of leverage, though each has considerable reserves of hydrocarbons. Bolivia, as a recipient of substantial official development assistance, is more vulnerable than the others. Yet China's and India's willingness to assist and invest in resource-rich countries counterbalances US influence.

To buttress its autonomy from the United States and build a regional support base for an alternative to neoliberalism, Venezuela under Chávez promoted various regional organizations and foreign alliances. Chávez campaigned against the US-supported Free Trade Area of the Americas in the early 2000s, and in favor of the creation of alternative regional arrangements.

ALBA, the Bolivarian Alliance for the Americas, established in 2004, is one important instance (Riggirozzi 2012). Its current membership includes Cuba, Nicaragua, Bolivia, Ecuador, Dominica, Antigua and Saint Vincent, in addition to Venezuela. It forms a more radical grouping than UNASUR (the Union of South American Nations that integrates the Andean Community and Mercosur), formed in 2008 at the initiative of Brazil, to which Venezuela, Bolivia and Ecuador belong. Whereas UNASUR aims to develop a regional economic community on the model of the European Union, ALBA is broader in scope. It fosters mutual economic assistance, projects to advance social welfare in the poorer countries of Latin America and the Caribbean, and a barter system of trade. On the welfare side, it promotes literacy, health care, education, energy cooperation and a social emergency fund. Cuban medical specialists have served in Venezuela, Bolivia and elsewhere. Cuba offers medical scholarships to countries with limited medical facilities, such as Bolivia and the Dominican Republic. Governments undertaking literacy campaigns can draw on the experience and resources of member states. Venezuela has provided subsidized oil to countries experiencing economic difficulties. ALBA has also devised a new regional currency, the SUCRE, for settling commercial transactions between regional parties (though the currency has so far rarely been used). Its purpose is to replace the US dollar as a medium of exchange, thus reducing US influence over Latin American economies. In these ways, ALBA operates as a network of mutual assistance among supposedly Left-oriented governments.

BancoSur, a lending body that began operations in September 2009, is conceived as an alternative to IMF and World Bank lending in the Americas. The presidents of Venezuela and Argentina (Hugo Chávez and Néstor Kirchner) were the initial architects, joined later by Lula da

Silva of Brazil. Its members include Bolivia, Ecuador, Paraguay and Uruguay, in addition to the three founders. BancoSur specifically opposes the practice of the IMF and World Bank in linking emergency loans to the recipients' adoption of free-market reforms. Chávez has even advocated the withdrawal of Latin American countries from the IMF. With its head-quarters in Caracas, the regional bank is another institutional attempt to buffer Latin American governments from global neoliberalism.

Finally, Venezuela applied to join Mercosul/Mercosur (Southern Common Market) in 2006, attaining membership in 2012. Founded in 1991, the organization operates as a customs union. It, together with the Andean Community of Nations, is a component of a larger process of South American economic integration embodied in UNASUR.

Not only have Chávez and his allies tried to shield their alternative development strategies from neoliberal globalization through regional bodies, but Chávez also cultivated new alliances. On the premise that the enemy of my enemy is my friend, he cultivated warm relations with the Iranian and Syrian regimes and the more ideologically compatible Castro brothers in Cuba. All these initiatives suggest that radical leftist regimes are not necessarily passive victims of global neoliberalism. Under certain circumstances, national states can defy the dominant ideology in pursuing a progressive national agenda.

Yet this radical Left, with the possible exception of Bolivia's MAS, fits a Left-populist profile. Populism is vulnerable to both crisis and deteriora-tion into a messianic, anti-democratic regime. I suggested earlier that if a democratic transition to socialism is feasible, it will probably take a radical social-democratic route. It is now time to explore this proposition.

Radical social-democratic transition to socialism

In a radical social-democratic strategy, a cohesive and programmatic socialist party does not impose socialism from above, but rather works within a largely market economy and liberal-democratic institutions to challenge inherited privileges and power structures and deepen democ-racy. Civil and political liberties, competing political parties, autonomous social movements, and voluntary associations continue to function. As in Eduard Bernstein's (1961 [1909]) original notion of democratic revision-ism, the party builds a cross-class electoral coalition. It appeals to its constituencies on both the ethical grounds of social justice and the mate-rial grounds of class interest. Generally, the party's or coalition's agenda of redistribution includes the removal of discriminatory practices, the extension of social protections and high-quality public services to the poor, the democratization of markets, selective nationalizations, and land reform (where landholdings are concentrated). Democratic deepening involves the decentralization of powers and revenues, consultative or participatory mechanisms involving social movements, and producer and marketing cooperatives of workers and farmers. Radical social democracy is thus more a *process* – of building citizen capabilities, participatory structures, new economic opportunities, and decommodification in an expanding social-market economy – than a final *destination* ("socialism").

This strategy is unlikely to persist in the absence of certain (highly unusual) social and historical conditions. The socialist/social-democratic party, to be effective, must be cohesive, well-organized and programmatic in its appeal. It must operate within a class-divided society, even if communal identities also remain strong. Whereas moderate social democracy depends on a class compromise in which elements of the dominant business class participate, radical social democracy involves class struggle with a minimal or even nonexistent society-wide compromise. Accordingly, the party/coalition needs a strong, mainly non-communal, political base to persist under such conditions. Civil society must manifest a density, autonomy and purpose enabling its social movements to hold the social-democratic/socialist party true to its vision of attacking entrenched inequalities. Only this degree of mobilization can ensure that the party's commitment to equal freedom and democracy does not wane and a new privileged class of political insiders does not crystallize.

Also, the state must be both relatively effective and uncaptured by the dominant economic class, if the state is to implement complex and redistributive social and economic policies. The economy, though continuing to make extensive use of markets, must not be dominated by powerful oligopolies. A democratization of markets (via cheap credit, expert assistance and preferential treatment in state procurement) provides opportunities for small-scale and cooperative enterprises, while diffusing economic power. Socialism, under such circumstances, constitutes an open-ended process of popular empowerment.

Although these stringent conditions do not, *in toto*, obtain anywhere, a radical social-democratic approach has emerged in scattered cases. The social conditions in a few counties are more conducive to the class politics of the radical Left than in others (see Chapter 4). Organized industrial workers do not play as central a role in leftist politics today as they did in nineteenth- and twentieth-century Europe; instead, the class coalitions that emerge feature peasants, landless laborers, small and medium farmers, informal-sector workers and elements of the middle class, in addition to organized labor. Rapid urban growth means that the locus of politics has shifted, or is shifting, from peasants and rural protest to the burgeoning cities.[31] Vast inequalities, persistent poverty, corruption, and discrimination against indigenous peoples, castes and ethnic groups, feed a sense of popular grievance. In addition, the global opportunity structure varies from one country to another. Large industrial "emerging" economies and countries exporting valuable energy resources have more leverage within the global order than others. Global neoliberalism, as the previous section indicated, does not uniformly rule out radical experiments.

Consider the cases that might illuminate the dynamics and dilemmas of radical social democracy. Bolivia under Morales, as I proposed above, approximates this model, though it is too early to arrive at a firm judgment. The Sandinistas in Nicaragua, between the 1979 revolutionary seizure of power and their electoral defeat in 1990, also resembled radical social democrats. But the period is too brief and too muddled by the internal war against the US-supported Contras to draw conclusions.

The Popular Unity (Unidad Popular – UP) administration of President Salvador Allende in Chile (1970–3), which was terminated by a brutal military coup, is the most dramatic and famous exemplar. However, several factors argue against selecting this case (besides its brief duration). Allende, with just over 36 percent of the vote in 1970, never received a convincing popular mandate for revolutionary change. UP proved unable to control its supporters: peasants seized land, squatters established unauthorized settlements, workers occupied factories, and allies (especially the Revolutionary Left Movement – MIR) promoted illegal seizures of property. This chaotic mobilization of social forces into politics, combined with disastrous macroeconomic policies and a US embargo, polarized society and drove small business owners (famously including truckers) into the arms of the oligarchy. It is precisely the failure of UP to attract the support of the small proprietors that doomed the coalition to a minority status and laid the foundation for the eventual coup.

The unremitting efforts of the US government under President Richard Nixon to destabilize the Allende regime – by funding the opposition, sabotaging the economy and aiding the Chilean military – certainly made a bad situation worse (Harmer 2011). However, the problems were probably fundamental enough to unseat the regime irrespective of foreign influence. The UP administration, though bold, courageous and democratic, lacked the majority support, the discipline and the economic competence to carry off a non-violent, constitutional socialist transformation. All three potential cases – Allende's Chile, the Sandinistas' Nicaragua and Morales's Bolivia – thus demonstrate the dangers inherent in a radical social-democratic approach.

But they do not reveal its promise. Kerala provides a better illustrative case. Despite its peculiar status as a state within a federation, and despite the fact that Kerala's record is not stellar (inequality has grown substantially in recent years), this case nicely illustrates both the dynamics of radical social democracy and the paradox to which this strategy is prone. It is a case in which synergy long ago emerged between a cohesive socialist party and autonomous social movements. Kerala is a pioneer of radical social democracy in the Global South, guided initially by the Communist Party of India (CPI) until 1964 and then by its radical offshoot the Communist Party of India (Marxist) (CPM). The radical phase endured for more than three decades in part because Kerala was shielded from global capitalism and imperialist hostility and constrained to remain democratic by a federal state formally committed to democratic socialism (under Congress Party rule). We can gain insight into the nature, promise and challenges of the strategy by exploring this "pure" case in some detail.

The case of Kerala

Kerala's radical-democratic phase extended from the inaugural election of the newly amalgamated state of Kerala in 1957 until about 1990. But the story actually begins long before 1957. Radical socialists operated in (what became) Kerala within the Congress Socialist Party until 1939, when they split off to form the CPI. The CPI engaged in organizing peasants in Malabar (northern Kerala) and mobilizing them for protests (against landlords, upper-caste rule and eventually the British colonialists) from the early years, operating as an underground movement in the first two years of World War II. When Kerala gained statehood in 1956, the party decided to contest the elections and won the largest proportion of the popular vote. The radical social-democratic approach petered out in the late 1980s, when the dominant CPM moderated its ideological position to deal with economic strains and retain its middle-class support.

Kerala is atypical inasmuch as it is a state within a federation, rather than a separate country. This provincial status restricts the monetary, fiscal and regulatory powers that the Kerala government can employ in pursuing its goals. It also ensures that an outside arbiter (Delhi) will intervene, if necessary, to protect property rights and democracy. These limitations provide reassurance to capital in a state led by a communist party. Furthermore, Kerala's economy is also atypical in benefiting from a relatively high level of remittances from hundreds of thousands of its expatriate citizens, who are employed mainly in the Middle East.

Yet in other ways this state of 32 million people is typical of the Third World. It suffered widespread poverty in the 1950s and 1960s when its population was then mainly rural. Its economy depended heavily on a handful of agricultural exports in the 1970s (though of declining importance thereafter). Its population is highly heterogeneous – roughly three-fifths Hindu, one-fifth Muslim and one-fifth Christian, together with several castes and an indigenous population. Typical also was the elevated inequality of the state's population in the 1950s, the legacy of a rigid caste system, hierarchical rural relations, and the subordination of women. If Kerala's peculiarities prevent it from providing a model for socialist movements elsewhere, its experience nevertheless illustrates the state–society–economy relations underpinning radical social democracy, and the strains to which it is subject.

That Kerala followed a radical path can hardly be disputed. The CPI remained a militant, disruptive force after its coalition won the 1957 election. It inserted itself in conflicts between tenants and landlords, workers and their employers, and lower castes and upper castes. The CPI so successfully fused caste and class antagonisms that caste never became a separate basis for party formation in this state (in contrast to the situation in most Indian states). Kerala teetered on the brink of ungovernability, narrowly avoiding a slide into violence. The chaos led the central government to suspend the state government in 1959 and impose Presidential Rule (see Heller 2012). When returned to power in 1960, the CPI and then the CPM (from 1964) hewed to a parliamentary path. In 1969, its United Front government finally enacted, in the face of widespread protest, a comprehensive land reform bill. This legislation, true to the CPM's "land-to-the-tiller" promise, eliminated the landlord class, conferred ownership rights on tenants, undertook to redistribute land above the allowable maximum to the landless, and conferred ownership of their hut and accompanying garden to agricultural laborers (Varughese 2012: 214–19). Kerala, along with another CPM-governed state, West Bengal, achieved "the most radical land reform outside socialist countries" (Varughese 2012: 314).

Following this success, the CPM as leader of coalition governments turned its attention to workers' issues, especially wages and job security. The 1970s were years of labor protests, peaceful and violent, localized and statewide. The Kerala Agricultural Workers Act of 1974 was a landmark in standardizing working conditions, protecting jobs, and establishing wage determination machinery. Thereafter, CPM-dominated governments passed an array of laws institutionalizing a collective bargaining system and tripartite dispute settlement procedures, all overseen by industrial relations committees at the state, sector and local levels that gave labor an equal voice with employers (Varughese 2012: 225–8, 300–1). Vigilant trade unions and a proactive CPM ensured employers complied with labor legislation.

In addition, the CPM's Left Democratic Front (LDF) coalitions engineered a redistribution of public services (education, health care and housing) and social protection (especially pensions, which were extended even to those working in the informal sector). They backed the recognition of the rights of women,[32] lower castes and labor unions.[33] They expanded public ownership of firms, subsidized necessities for the poor, and provided free potable water to low-income neighborhoods. The CPM also radically decentralized power in 1996 to local democratic assemblies.

Closely fought state elections ensured that the CPM remained attuned to the interests of its constituencies. To win, the party crafted LDF coalitions that required accommodating the interests of various smaller parties, some communally based. The LDF thus constituted a trans-caste, trans-communal and trans-class coalition. The Congress Party forged its own powerful coalition, the United Democratic Front (UDF), and Kerala's electoral politics has featured an alternation in power of the LDF and UDF since 1982. The popularity of CPM programs has been such that the UDF rarely has done more than modify them when it formed the government. Though never acknowledged by the socialist CPM, it pursued a radical social-democratic strategy over several decades.

The Kerala case shows that a poor, agrarian and diverse society can deepen democracy, dramatically diminish poverty and significantly reduce social exclusion and inequality within three decades or so. Nevertheless, social conditions were far from ideal by 1990 – Kerala had comparatively high rates of suicide and violence against women,[34] its Dalits and indigenous people still felt aggrieved, corruption occasionally surfaced, remittances played an inordinate role in supporting families, and the state's economy stagnated from 1975 to 1985. Yet, despite these problems, Kerala's social and political record has won deserved praise.

Can we attribute the successes to a radical social-democratic strategy? It appears so. Until the late 1980s, the CPM regarded its long-term goal as the building of a socialist society, not simply the humanizing of capitalism. Its strategy involved an open-ended process of enhancing the capabilities of all citizens, promoting their access to assets (especially land), expanding their political and social rights, and forging participatory structures to progressively empower ordinary people. The goal, in essence, has been to create the conditions in which people share an equal opportunity to experience freedom, in the sense of the opportunity to pursue a meaningful and lengthy life. Underpinning this process is a synergy between *civil society* (social movements and civil associations) and a *political party/ coalition* that periodically controls the executive and legislative powers of the state. Another feature is a *mixed economy* in which markets still predominate, albeit restricted by a large parastatal sector and a social economy based on the partial decommodification of labor and land. Although the Communists set out to transform capitalism, they actually humanized capitalism in a rights-conscious, social-democratic welfare state.

Kerala has a vibrant civil society dense with voluntary associations. Autonomous organizations of subaltern groups, dedicated to redressing their grievances, emerged early in the constituent political units that amalgamated to form Kerala in 1956 (Sandbrook et al. 2007: 74–8). In the princely states of Travancore and Cochin in the south of what is now Kerala, caste movements mobilized in the late nineteenth century to seek advancement in a rigidly hierarchical caste system. As well, agricultural laborers (who were also from lower castes) organized to win better terms from (upper-caste and Christian) farmers. In Malabar, under direct British rule in the northern part of Kerala, parasitical landlordism was the main issue for the large segment of the population who earned their livelihoods as tenants. Hence, social movements in the late nineteenth and early twentieth century focused on agrarian issues, especially control of the land, in mobilizations against the landlords. Contingent factors also played a role in the forging of independent associations of subaltern groups. Royal leaders of Travancore/Cochin from the mid nineteenth century were of a progressive viewpoint, backing land reform, supporting lower-caste struggles to end caste domination, opening schools to children of all castes, and allowing Christian missionaries to open their own schools. Members of subaltern groups thus became literate and accustomed to organizational life from early on. Some of their movements, in both the north and the south, were later absorbed by, or joined with, trade unions as participants in further campaigns. Not surprisingly, then, the CPI developed as a social-movement party.

The CPI, as already mentioned, originally built its popular support by uniting an anti-colonial struggle with movements for caste uplift, land to the tiller, and the rights of workers. In Kerala, its leadership committed itself to a parliamentary route, calculating that, in multiparty contests, its organizational strength, ideological cohesion and mass base would allow it to triumph. A highly competitive political environment – in which the LDF and UDF alternate in power – has motivated the CPM to maintain contact with the grassroots and avoid venality and authoritarian vanguardism. As well, the Kerala public bureaucracy proved effective and autonomous enough to implement new programs. Hence, a synergistic relationship developed between an active and independent *civil society* and a movement *party* that pushed forward a radical agenda of change.

The final aspect of this radical social-democratic experience is a *mixed economy*. The CPI/CPM pragmatically accepted that markets must continue, but added that state regulation must keep the market in the role of servant rather than master. Kerala, along with most other states, developed an extensive array of parastatals during the era in India of heavy state controls, planning and protectionism. After the turn to liberalization by the national government in the 1980s and especially since 1991, this sector ran into trouble. In addition, legislation and regulation in Kerala partially decommodified labor and land. The social rights of citizenship mean that a person's life chances are not determined by his or her market position. The labor code regulates the circumstances in which employees can be laid off and many of the conditions of employment. Private ownership in land is hedged by environmental and other regulations. To a significant extent, Kerala had developed a social-market economy by the 1980s.

Yet there was a serious flaw in this strategy. It became clear with the onset of economic stagnation in Kerala in the early 1970s, a situation which persisted until 1985. Redistribution and policies to promote equity had brought results, but at the expense of capital accumulation. This, as acknowledged earlier, is the fundamental challenge facing the radical Left in general. The CPM could not bring about a socialist revolution (owing to Kerala's status as a state in a federation); yet its one-sided focus on redistribution in a capitalist economy was unsustainable.[35] The radical land reform law and labor militancy discouraged private investment and increased the unemployment and inflation rates. Hence, "class struggle" had led to a "crisis of accumulation" (Heller 1999), which in turn generated dissatisfaction with the CPM and its falling share of the popular vote. The question of what should be done divided the party into hard-line and moderate factions.[36]

In the 1980s, the moderate faction prevailed and the party's position gradually shifted from the earlier "class struggle" approach to "class compromise" (Heller 1999). What emerged was a *moderate* social-democratic model focusing on growth with equity – or, rather, maximizing growth while protecting social advances. Fostering investment and growth would yield more and better jobs and higher tax revenues. The latter would sustain widely accessible public services and universal social protections. Hence, militancy declined. The government, which participated with employers and labor in corporatist industrial relations institutions, used its influence to promote cooperation in raising productivity. It also offered tax incentives to encourage investment. It improved infrastructure. It paid attention to raising the productivity of small-scale producers. This change to a productivist strategy informed the LDF approach when it held power in 1996–2001 and 2006–11 (Varughese 2012: 237–45).

India's neoliberal turn, especially strong following the balance-of-payments crisis of 1991, imparted further impetus to moderation in Kerala's Left. Kerala had to cope with the consequences of a number of policy changes introduced by the central government (Sandbrook et al. 2007: 82–6; Tharamangalam 2010: 383–91):

- cutbacks in transfers from New Delhi and falling revenues, resulting in a dramatic decline in the quality of public education and health services and the expansion of private schools and private medical care to cater for the needs of the better-off;
- decrease and elimination of federal support for Kerala's many state-owned enterprises, leading to some privatization and the necessity for the state budget to fill the gap;
- reduction of federal subsidies to Kerala's successful food rationing system, requiring the state government to make up some of the shortfall so as to protect the nutritional status of the poor;
- the gradual decline of tariffs on imports has made Kerala vulnerable to market fluctuations since 80 percent of Kerala's agricultural crops are traded nationally and internationally; indeed, cheap imports have undercut smallholder production, especially in rubber production, with a resultant decline in state tax revenues;
- the decline of public investment in Kerala, much of which had formerly come from state-owned enterprises, forced the state government to attract private investment, a tough sell in light of the state's reputation for high minimum wages and militant trade unions;
- market liberalization has had significant cultural and political effects: the growth of a middle class, a marked increase in income inequality (though no rise in poverty), and the expansion of the culture of possessive individualism as the urban middle class embraced consumerism (Tharamangalam 2010: 391; Mannathukkaren 2010a: 159–60).

In sum, the CPM could only remain electorally competitive if it fostered *accumulation* within the context of India's capitalist economy

Kerala has undergone significant changes since the late 1980s. Its annual growth rate of gross state product reached 5.5 percent in the 1990s, and even higher in the 2000s. It has moved from a mainly agrarian economy to a service economy based on tourism, banking and finance, transport and communications. Only a quarter of the labor force now depends on agriculture. Yet demands for further liberalization persist.

Paradoxically, radical social democracy became a victim of its own success. Yes, the unavoidable entangling of Kerala in the global market economy, especially following 1991, and the quest to foster accumulation, pushed the state toward market-oriented measures. In addition, the collapse of the Soviet Union in 1989–91 and the neoliberalization of "Communist" China inclined the CPM's leadership toward the pragmatic, market-friendly approach of the Chinese. But the party's success in expanding Kerala's middle class through extensive land reform, labor-market interventions, universal education, and a generous welfare state was a decisive factor. It led to the "deradicalization and embourgeoisement" of part of the CPM's constituency (Mannathukkaren 2010a: 159). In Kerala as elsewhere in India, India's liberalization spread a culture of possessive individualism (Mannathukkaren 2010a: 159). As the state's enlarged urban middle class embraced the consumer society, the radical CPM shifted to a moderate agenda of promoting liberal-capital accumulation while mitigating the excesses of resurgent market society.

Hard-liner versus soft-liner divisions in Kerala's Left continued, however. In 1996, the CPM sought to respond to the challenges by adopting the People's Campaign for Decentralized Planning. This participatory program was designed to counter the malaise of militants and to reinvigorate the centrally controlled CPM. The People's Campaign radically decentralized power and resources to a system of local governance, which was empowered to build public facilities and services identified through a participatory decision-making system (see p. 180 for the details). A recent assessment of this experiment arrives at a generally positive view. Popular participation remained high more than a decade after the scheme's establishment. Moreover, the substantial funds transferred by the state government built much-needed infrastructure and eased the delivery of drinking water, sanitation and primary health services – all with a minimum of corruption (Mannathukkaren 2010b; Tharamangalam 2010: 391–2). However, this endeavor was perhaps the last innovative gasp of the radical-mobilizational model.

Indicative of the LDF's moderation was the coalition's acceptance, when it returned to power in 2006, of an agreement negotiated by the UDF government with the Asian Development Bank (ADB). The state was to receive a loan of more than $1 billion in exchange for implementing a number of neoliberal policy conditions (Raman 2009). The new government's position was that the state needed the loan to rebuild its fiscal balance and compensate for the lack of private investment. It further justified accepting the loan by renegotiating the more offensive conditions and undertook to mitigate hardships arising from the agreement. Although this position was realistic in light of the constraints, it confirmed that the CPM had implicitly conceded that its role was to mitigate the market's negative effects, not transform the system.

Does the Kerala case suggest the impracticability of a radical social-democratic route? On the one hand, this case illustrates that this route can succeed, for a lengthy period, even in a highly heterogeneous and initially hierarchical society with substantial poverty and dependence on agriculture.[37] On the other hand, an accumulation crisis is likely to result from the radical emphasis on eliminating historical inequities and promoting redistribution (a crisis that afflicts Left populism too). This crisis heightens pressures, including those from middle-class elements who benefited from earlier redistributive policies, to deradicalize the mobilizational model by assigning priority to the accumulation imperative. The middle class may switch its loyalty to the liberal movement, in Polanyian terms. The beneficiaries of radical social democracy find certain neoliberal policies attractive.

To follow a moderate path, even as a "tactical" maneuver, raises new problems for the Left. A major one is the rise of possessive individualism among not only the expanding middle class, but also small farmers and workers. This culture is inimical to the social solidarity and cooperative approach that the Left seeks to enhance. But what alternative to moderation does the party actually have? Kerala, as a state in a federation, does not have the option of deepening the revolution when the center is unsympathetic to this path. In sovereign countries, a radical social-democratic strategy could survive only in countries with significant leverage within the global economy, and then only if they are buffered from external pressures by regional associations of like-minded states.

But even if the radical impetus ultimately subsides into moderation, do we construe this outcome as a defeat? Probably not. Radical social democracy has transformed the lives of most of Kerala's (and West Bengal's) citizens in ways that marginalized groups elsewhere can only imagine.

Conclusion

Socialists today seek to avoid both the dead end of authoritarian and tutelary bureaucratic collectivism and the compromises with capitalist values and institutions that moderate social democracy entails. Proponents of twenty-first-century socialism have explicitly undertaken to blaze a democratic road. Yet a close examination of these Latin American cases reveals Left populism as the dominant approach. And this model offers an uncertain prospect. It has achieved some success in empowering formerly marginalized groups, redistributing income through social programs funded mainly by resource exports and redistributing assets, especially land and nationalized enterprises. For the most part, Venezuela, Bolivia and Ecuador have avoided the pitfall of bureaucratic collectivism.[38] But uncertainty arises because, where personalism and a weakly institutionalized party prevail, instability attends the demise of the supreme leader. Furthermore, popular democracy may have a dark side. Faced with a serious challenge, populists may react with repressive measures on the grounds that the regime's opponents are not part of the popular masses in whose name the leader speaks. Hence, Left populism does not constitute a reliable model for transcending the socialist impasse – though it is unlikely to be a short-lived phenomenon in regions with long histories of populist politics.

A more robust model for moving beyond the socialist impasse is offered by radical social democrats, though its success depends on a rare combination of circumstances and leadership. This strategy challenges, as does Left populism, the entrenched inequalities and power structures of capitalism. But in this case, a cohesive, organizationally strong and programmatic party/coalition is the major actor. It mobilizes, usually within liberal-democratic institutions, cross-class and cross-communal constituencies including the poor and near-poor as well as elements of the middle class. Social-movement activism is not co-opted by the socialist/social-democratic party, but continues to play a key role in representing interests and pressing the party to remain true to its goals. Significant redistribution flows from this political process, including redistribution of assets, universal social protections, and educational and health services and possibly the democratization of markets. I illustrated this model by reference to Kerala's experience. Although the CPM-based coalition achieved remarkable gains in this initially poor and heterogeneous society, it eventually moved to a moderate social-democratic approach. An accumulation crisis, economic liberalization in India, the consumer aspirations of Kerala's now-large middle class, and the positive example of business-friendly "Communist" China all pressed in this direction.

Will an eventual accommodation with capital always be the fate of radical social democracy? To the extent that the volatile middle class constitutes a significant segment of the Left's electoral coalition, this outcome is likely. It is, in any event, improbable that a state within a federation – or even a single sovereign country lacking extensive leverage within the global order – can proceed very far toward a socialist future. Socialism in one country remains an unlikely prospect in today's world. The probability of success will rise if a regional bloc of like-minded states buffers the radical experiment from the global neoliberal order, or if global neoliberalism is itself reformed in a facilitative direction (a possibility I discuss in Chapter 7). But even if the balance of class forces and economic crisis eventually shift a radical regime toward moderate social democracy, this shift does not negate most of the major social gains already achieved.

Many leftist intellectuals, however, are highly critical of "socialist" movements in the developing world that settle for the reform of capitalism rather than its transformation. Jeffery Webber, for instance, criticizes Evo Morales and MAS for not seizing the opportunity of moving Bolivia beyond capitalism, instead of merely "reconstituting neoliberalism"

(Webber 2011). Not only do such critiques fail to recognize the important social gains made by many leftist governments, but also they are unrealistic. How likely is it that small, resource-dependent and poor countries of the Global South can carry off – alone – a (vaguely identified) socialist transformation? The question answers itself: very unlikely. To understand why, one needs to look no further than the fate of the Sandinistas (Frente Sandinista de Liberación) under its leader Daniel Ortega. The revolutionary Sandinistas assumed power amidst great expectations in Nicaragua in 1979, and met electoral defeat amidst great turmoil in 1990.[39] External intervention, local class hostilities, and a fragile economic base usually condemn revolutionary movements, especially if democratic, to an early demise.

If bureaucratic collectivism is unacceptable and Left populism is uncertain, radical social-democratic development offers the best, albeit limited, hope of moving beyond the socialist impasse. It may be that radical social democracy, if it survives, tends to evolve into moderate social democracy. Analysts will disagree in their evaluation of this evolution – whether it is a betrayal or a recognition of hard realities. Radical and moderate social democracy may indeed alternate, reflecting changing priorities of accumulation (the liberal movement) and redistribution (the counter-movement) and shifting opportunity structures. But if democratic socialism has a future, it seems to lie in exploring this demanding possibility.

NOTES

1. For an extended discussion of the conservative mind-set of peasants, refer to Barrington Moore's classic study (1966: 495–506).
2. For example, a researcher, returning to two districts of rural Ethiopia in 1985 nine years after his initial study tour, found that the peasants' enthusiasm for socialism had waned: "Peasants today feel controlled from above, they complain they have no influence whatsoever over their own local affairs. They observe that their peasant associations are becoming increasingly a tool of the government ... Elections are in practice decided by the officials who select candidates who peasants have to endorse through their votes" (Pausewang 1988: 6).
3. Cuba has nevertheless experienced persistent problems of inefficiency and low productivity, especially in agriculture. Since 2008, President Raúl Castro has introduced a variety of liberalizing reforms in agriculture, though, as of early 2013, many controls and hindrances to the production and distribution of agricultural products remained.
4. TANU (the Tanganyika/Tanzania African National Union) became Chama Cha Mapinduzi (the Party of Revolution) in 1977 when TANU merged with Zanzibar's Afro-Shirazi Party.

5. The depth of Tanzanians' respect and affection for Nyerere was evident in the outpouring of grief by the hundreds of thousands who turned out to witness his casket following his death in 1999. For an appreciation of Nyerere's ethical commitments by someone who knew him well in the early years, see Pratt 2000.

6. As the important Mwongozo Declaration of 1971 noted, "the duty of a socialist party is to guide all activities of the masses."

7. Venezuela, in contrast to Bolivia and Ecuador, had a reputation as one of the most stable democracies in Latin America until the revolt in Caracas in 1989.

8. Statistics from Piñeiro Harnecker (2009, 310).

9. While some cooperatives work more or less as they were intended, others are inefficient, scams in which workers pocket start-up funds, and fronts for existing firms that take advantage of grants, tax exemptions and preferential treatment (Ellner 2010b: 67). Many cooperatives behave like capitalist firms, with little sense of solidarity with local communities (Piñeiro Harnecker 2009: 317–28).

10. In late 2012, 11 of 24 elected state governors were former military officers.

11. The esteemed Carter Center has judged that the casting and counting of ballots in elections over the years were conducted freely.

12. Caprilles received about 44 percent of the national vote, to Chávez's 54 percent.

13. A survey carried out in June 2006 by Venezuela Data Analysis Institute found that 12.8 percent of the "upper class" self-identified as pro-Chávez (*El Nacional* 2006). In May 2012, the same polling agency found that about one-third of "relatively privileged voters" intended to vote for Chávez (and 53 percent for Capriles) (Ellner 2012b: 5).

14. These periodic surveys of Latin American opinion are to be found at www.latinobarometro.org

15. Needless to say, this conception of democracy in the Western tradition goes back to Rousseau.

16. In Senegal, for instance, the Wolof term "democaraasi" connotes not only meaningful political participation but also equality (in style as well as outcomes), inclusiveness, mutuality and fairness in the distribution of resources (Schaffer 1998: 81).

17. Transparency International has ranked Venezuela as the world's tenth-most-corrupt country.

18. An AP-Ipsos poll in 2006 found that 84 per cent of Venezuelans reject the Cuban model, a similarly high proportion oppose expropriation of private property, and only 7 percent agreed with the notion that "being rich was a bad thing" (Jiménez 2006).

19. For a study contending that *chavismo* represents old-style populism, see Hawkins (2003).

20. For a contrary assessment, see Rodriquez (2008).

21. Periodically, Chávez proclaimed that he wanted to include the middle class and the private sector in his political project, which indicated a degree of ideological ambivalence. See, for example, BBC (2011).

22. In 2012, the inflation rate of 25 percent was among the world's highest, the fiscal deficit was massive at more than 16 percent of GDP, and the state-controlled oil industry experienced declining output (Naim 2013). The government devalued the currency by 32 percent in February 2013. Oil represents about 95 percent of exports.

23. Some observers argue that Left populism has a "dark side," inasmuch as messianism and a plebiscitary approach may decline into authoritarianism (March 2007: 73).

24. Argentina under the Kirchners lies between these cases and the moderate social democracies I discussed in Chapter 5. Argentina, since its collapse in 2001, has more radically rejected neoliberalism than Brazil, Chile or Uruguay; its economic strategy has been more heavily statist; and it has been more willing to confront powerful international organizations and domestic business interests than these three. The presidencies of the two Kirchners, though identified with the Peronist movement, have moved away from both old-style populism and the neoliberal populism of President Carlos Menem.

25. For details of the economic changes, see Molero Simarro and Paz Antolín (2012: 533–5); Conaghan (2011: 277–80); Cunha Filho and Santaella Gonçalves (2010).

26. For details of the redistributive programs, see Madrid (2011: 250–1); Urioste (2009: 113–14); Reygadas and Filgueira (2010: 184–7).

27. *Cocaleros* are coca leaf growers.

28. A quarter of Ecuador's population of 15 million is Amerindian.

29. Though, since 2010, he has encouraged foreign governments and charities to contribute to a trust fund managed by the government in exchange for Ecuador desisting from exploiting suspected oil reserves in sensitive ecological zones.

30. For the extent of US hostility to the Chávez regime, see Valencia Ramírez (2006: 175–6).

31. For an overview of grievances and protest in the urban areas, see Davis (2006), and for an intimate case study, Finn (2006).

32. Though, in the Indian context, Kerala women have unusually high levels of education and well-being, many problems remain. The Left in Kerala is often criticized for not doing enough to advance women's rights.

33. As Kerala's social achievements are widely known, I will not pause to itemize them. Refer to Tharamangalam (2010: 364–74), and Sandbrook et al. (2007: 68–70).

34. Paradoxically, women in Kerala have attained advanced social indicators, yet suffer from relatively high rates of suicide and wife abuse. These social ills usually indicate low female status. See Mitra and Singh (2007).

35. For a representative critique of the CPM's approach as too politicized, statist and oriented to redistribution, see Tharamangalam (1998).

36. For helping me sort out the competing claims of proponents of ultra-Marxist, moderate socialist and neoliberal interpretations, I thank Patrick Heller, Brown University, and Anil Varughese, Carleton University. Any remaining errors of interpretation are my responsibility.

37. A similar argument can be made in the case of West Bengal until its shift to moderation in the early 1980s.
38. Bolivia, to repeat, is least clearly in the Left-populist mold, manifesting elements of a radical social-democratic strategy.
39. Nevertheless, the FSLN survives as an ill-defined moderate social-democratic or Left-populist party, still under the leadership of Daniel Ortega. Ortega and the FSLN returned to power via elections in 2007.

7 Politics of the possible

History is an uncertain guide to the future. We may say that a strategy that succeeded under a certain set of conditions in the past will lead to similar outcomes in cases with similar conditions today. But, in reality, conditions are never fully the same and are constantly changing: global and national opportunity structures shift, dominant ideas concerning development and the economy rise and fall, technological innovation and political organization transform the balance of class forces, and well-organized progressive parties with far-sighted leadership emerge – or fail to emerge. Politics is the art of the possible, but it is never entirely clear in advance what constitutes the realm of the possible. Leadership and political vision are thus critical determinants of success.

Historical experience is more useful in offering warnings about what to avoid than "lessons" for successful action. The debacles of socialism and social democracy in the twentieth century suggest two warnings. First, to the extent possible, democratic means are required to reach democratic ends: means and ends cannot be separated.[1] This requirement undoubtedly places onerous restrictions on regimes attacking inherited privilege. Warding off hostile domestic elites and the external defenders of the existing economic order is a major challenge for democratic redistributive regimes. But there is little choice for movements truly struggling for equal freedom. Justifying extra-legal, authoritarian means on the grounds of self-defense is to start the slide to tyranny. Also, markets appear indispensable in modern economies. Central planning doesn't work, and participatory planning at the national level (though as yet untested) seems impractical. Markets, as I suggest in Chapter 4, not only adjust supply to demand and promote entrepreneurship, but also play a liberating as well as a destructive role in changing societies. Yet to accept markets does not entail embracing a self-regulating market *system*. Polanyi's distinction, discussed in earlier chapters, is apposite: we might oppose "market society," but welcome "a society with markets." The latter entails an economy in which the "fictitious commodities" of labor, land and money are decommodified by embedding markets for these factors of production in protective social norms and regulations. The Left in power, when it expands the sphere of the social-market or, potentially, the socialist-market economy, accords with this Polanyian principle.

If politics, as Max Weber famously observed, is "a strong and slow boring of hard boards," this analogy applies in full force to the politics of the democratic Left. Its politics of the possible operates at three interrelated levels. This book has focused on the national level, a choice I justify on the grounds that the national state is the broadest scale at which solidarity may readily be mobilized behind a redistributive program. Nonetheless, it would be a mistake to ignore the possibilities at the local and global levels. Small-scale experiments in equitable cooperation are significant, either as complements to national-level socialist/social-democratic strategies or as stand-alone initiatives. These experiments allow poor and vulnerable people to survive with dignity under harsh conditions, and/or they represent harbingers of a new, solidaristic society. The global level is also critical. Ultimately, regimes seeking to build social economies and egalitarian structures will need to pursue major reforms of the neoliberal global order to neutralize the still-pervasive constraints on leftist policies. At all three levels, leaders and movements must square their sense of what is just with their understanding of what is possible or, at least, can be made possible.

A discussion of the politics of the possible would be incomplete without broaching the most serious threat to the human prospect: climate change. Whether the Left in the Global South has anything special to bring to the mitigation of this challenge is a question rarely posed. A paradoxical judgment seems warranted: leftist movements in the Global South are pro-growth and pro-consumption, yet their critical stance vis-à-vis neo-liberalism and capitalism and their concentration on questions of distributional justice make them a potentially significant ally of the green movements.

The national level: adaptive versus disruptive strategies

Marta Harnecker's eulogy (2013) to Hugo Chávez neatly raises the issue of the appropriate response of the Left to neoliberal capitalism. Chávez, she asserts, saw "the art of politics" as "making the impossible possible, not by pure voluntarism, but by starting from the existing reality, seeking to create conditions for changing it, by building a correlation of forces favorable to change."[2] Others of the Left counsel making progress by coming to terms with existing realities, an idea vividly expressed by Michael Harrington in identifying his political stance as "the left-wing of the possible" (see Dorrien 2010). The first strategy is disruptive, mobilizing people behind a transformational program; the second is adaptive, working with existing forces and processes to bring about greater equality and deeper democracy. Each tendency has its own rationale and dangers.

The *disruptive/transformational strategy* is, from the viewpoint of the Left, the "first-best" solution, though in seeking to make "the impossible possible," its feasibility is highly questionable under current conditions. The disruptive strategy does not necessitate a revolutionary overthrow of the existing order (though this may occur). It does involve a democratic and evolutionary systemic transformation that will take years and probably decades (as in Kerala and, in a less satisfactory manner, Venezuela) to carry through.

Old-style insurrectionary Marxist-Leninist and Maoist movements remain active in parts of Asia (India, Nepal and Pakistan) and Latin America (notably in Colombia). Where corrupt dictatorships and powerful agrarian elites hold sway, revolutionary Leninism may offer the only real hope for the redress of social grievances. This book, however, has focused on the democratic Left, for the reasons indicated in chapters 1 and 4.

The ambitious aim of parties describing themselves as democratic socialist is to achieve a democratization of wealth as well as power, income and social protection, while avoiding top-down, great-leaps forward. Whereas the structural inequalities of class remain, though attenuated, under moderate social democracy, they are frontally challenged by democratic socialists (whether Left populist or radical social-democratic in character), as well as in violent revolutionary struggles. The rationale for this approach is straightforward. The concentrated economic power of the dominant transnational and national classes allows them to accumulate considerable political influence. The wealthy minority is thus able to offset the voices of the numerous poor, working-class and even middle-class voters and to influence policy to serve their own interests. Furthermore, they are usually able to pass on their privileged positions to their offspring, especially through access to private education and health care and through social contacts to secure superior business or employment opportunities. Class contention rather than compromise is therefore necessary to restrict this concentrated economic power and the mechanisms that facilitate the intergenerational transmission of privilege, such as elite private education.

One cannot (and should not) speak of a "one-size-fits-all" program of transformational change, though actual experience in scattered cases and debates on the Left suggest some key approaches. The scope and pace of reconstruction will depend on the level of public support and available resources. The goal is to avoid state socialism while augmenting the capabilities of ordinary citizens, deepening democracy, and democratizing the ownership of wealth.[3] Depending on the country and spread out over many years, "evolutionary reconstruction" (Alperovitz and Dubb 2013: 2) would include programs such as land redistribution, selective nationalizations of large firms benefiting from oligopolies or monopolies, the promotion of small businesses, legislation to break up media conglomerates, the expansion of the social-market or solidarity economy, and democratization, often through decentralization of decision-making powers to local and perhaps regional participatory institutions.

Extending the social-market economy, to be clear, involves expanding the sphere of production and distribution governed by the principles of reciprocity and redistribution, and placing limits on market exchange. The centerpiece of the social economy is a universalistic and comprehensive welfare state. Such a welfare state decommodifies, to a greater or lesser extent, labor, education and health services (at a minimum), as well as redistributes income and services and hones the capabilities of poor and socially excluded citizens through the provision of accessible, high-quality public education, health facilities and nutritional provision. Initiatives might also include (re)regulation of labor markets to permit generous minimum wages, the implementation of labor standards as established by conventions of the ILO, and perhaps co-determination at the enterprise level. Leftist governments can also embed markets in solidarity norms by democratizing the market: providing the poor in the rural areas and peri-urban slums with basic infrastructure (roads, transport, fresh water and electricity), making credit available to poor people, mounting literacy campaigns and cracking down on bribes for basic transactions (such as registering land). Other possibilities include promotion of worker-owned and -managed firms and agricultural and credit-union cooperatives, non-profit housing corporations and environmental codes that place restrictions on the rights of private land or resource ownership. Solidarity, mutuality and trust grow along with the institutions that presuppose these dispositions – or that, at least, is the expectation.

The deepening of democracy might focus first on enhancing popular participation in decision making at the local level, where the principle of subsidiarity would allocate specific decision-making power to the lowest feasible level. Participatory budgeting, as originally conceived by the Workers Party in Brazil (see below), or the People's Campaign for Decentralized Planning in Kerala (p. 80) might constitute models. Local assemblies would plan infrastructural investments or policy concerning city-wide or community-wide issues such as public transit or public health. Such assemblies might later be extended upwards, to the regional and national levels (as the PT in Brazil initially proposed). But this list is merely indicative of the scope of evolutionary change.

We should expect periodic shifts in policy, in response to both the changing priorities of accumulation and redistribution and the waxing and waning of avid new classes. The middle class, in particular, is a fickle ally of the Left, one which may prove unpredictable and even hostile as social transformation unfolds. It is probably true, as Michael Walzer concludes in his prospective analysis of socialism in the West, that "socialism-in-the-making . . . is the only socialism we will ever know" (2010: 43). These experiments will always introduce a tumultuous era of political conflict whose outcome is uncertain.

The radical social-democratic strategy is one of the two disruptive types explored in this volume. As an ideal type, it features a cohesive, organizationally strong and programmatic party/coalition that mobilizes, initially within liberal-democratic institutions, a cross-class and cross-communal alliance to challenge the entrenched inequalities and power structures of neoliberal capitalism. Social-movement activism, in this model, is not co-opted by the socialist/social-democratic party, but continues to play a key role in representing interests and pressing the party to remain true to its goals. Significant redistribution results from this political process, including redistribution of assets (especially land) as well as income, universal social protections and services, and the democratization of markets. The social-market expands at the expense of the liberal-market economy, thus producing in the early stages a hybrid economy in which the principles of market exchange, reciprocity and redistribution coexist. Because progressive parties and the processes they institute may always become corrupted, a synergy between the progressive party and government, on the one hand, and active and independent social movements, on the other, is essential.

Left populism is the other transformational tendency, exemplified by the Chávez regime in Venezuela (1999–2013) and the Correa government in Ecuador. This approach diverges from old-style populism in consistently championing a leftist agenda and hewing more closely to democratic norms. Left populist parties resemble radical social-democratic parties in several ways. They utilize socialist terminology, rhetorically champion the interests of the people vis-à-vis an exploitative oligarchy, condemn imperialism, embrace redistribution and an interventionist state, and claim democratic legitimacy. The populist conception of democracy essentially combines egalitarianism and inclusiveness with plebiscitary democracy. However, Left populism's reliance on a charismatic leader and clientelistic politics sets it apart from the programmatic appeal and institutionalized party of the radical social democrats. The messianic tendency inherent in the cult of the leader threatens to undercut the assertion of popular democracy. Also, the lack of institutionalization may precipitate the collapse of the socialist project when its charismatic leader dies. Contemporary Left populism is thus a less viable long-term alternative than radical social democracy.

If the strength of the disruptive approach is its challenge to the *structural* basis of inequality, poverty and commodification of fictitious commodities, its major downside is that the "impossible" often turns out to be truly impossible. The foremost challenge is to handle the inevitable tension between the liberal movement and the societal counter-movement during the extended period in which neoliberal logic continues to hold sway. Democratic socialism is not introduced overnight. Karl Polanyi, as discussed in Chapter 1, focuses above all on the social and ecological unsustainability of liberal-market systems. Sustainability requires the re-embedding of markets, especially those for the fictitious commodities, in non-market institutions that limit the scope of markets or replace market exchange with the principles of reciprocity and redistribution. While the party or coalition of the Left is in opposition, it acts as a key agent of the counter-movement. When it assumes office, however, it must either transcend the logic of a market system or attempt to mediate its persistent tension. Since social transformation is a drawn-out process, the government in the interim has no choice but to manage the tension. Radical activism within a largely capitalist economy will inevitably precipitate accumulation crises, with the likelihood of subsequent declines in political support for the democratic Left.

This dilemma poses knotty challenges to the Left. In Latin American countries, for example, the liberal movement usually seeks to commercialize land for the production of cash crops or the exploitation of natural resources, such as oil, gas, minerals, timber or water. But, as in Bolivia and Ecuador, many indigenous people and environmentalists combine to oppose this commercialization, in an effort to sustain collective rights to land and self-determination, as well as indigenous ways of life. Indigenous leaders reaffirm the traditional view that land is sacred. Leftist governments are thus caught between their need for revenues to finance the welfare state and the demands of a powerful Amerindian counter-movement that they oppose commodification (Roncallo 2013). There is no easy resolution of this basic conflict.

The power and tenacity of the neoliberal order make it difficult to overturn or transform. The Left populist route has so far survived only in countries with special leverage in the global economy deriving from ample hydrocarbon deposits (though this endowment poses its own dilemma). Radical social democracy persisted for several decades in Kerala, where it was shielded from antagonistic global forces. Nevertheless, conditions change, and what is impossible today may not be so tomorrow, especially if protective regional associations of like-minded states evolve. But, for now, the attempt to make the impossible possible (in Marta Harnecker's terms) often wreaks misery among the intended beneficiaries. One thinks of the suffering caused by the aftermath of macroeconomic populism or the repressive Pinochet dictatorship in Chile.

The *adaptive strategy*, in contrast, unheroically stakes its claim as the left wing of the possible. Moderate social democracy, to give the adaptive strategy a name, is found at one end of a continuum whose opposite end is occupied by radical social-democracy. The former's hallmark is an implicit or explicit class compromise, as opposed to the radical's class contention. The social-democratic party/coalition, attaining power through electoral means, effectively makes peace with capitalism (though not neoliberalism). It accepts private-property rights, the rule of law, the limitations of the liberal-democratic framework and the obligation to discipline followers who transgress the limits of democratic reformism. The government pays compensation for any nationalized companies or landholdings. And the party cautiously responds to its promise of participatory democracy by decentralizing limited powers, participatory institutions and resources to local governments, while buffering itself from populist pressures at the center. Capital and its allies, for their part, implicitly agree to some state regulation of markets to advance egalitarian goals, in addition to progressive and other taxes that expand the revenues needed to support universal and targeted social programs. An expanding welfare state incrementally enhances income equality, equality of opportunity, poverty reduction and the economic security of all citizens. The social-market economy expands with the partial decommodification of labor, land and money, and support for cooperative ventures. Finally, state developmentalism is widely practiced; this approach entails a state that promotes local business to augment good jobs, though usually such promotion is less extensive than that of developmental states such as South Korea in the 1970s and 1980s. The state also assists in the democratization of markets by providing microenterprises with physical infrastructure, sources of credit, and expertise. All these measures are intended to advance growth with equity.

The rationale for this approach is that no more desirable and practicable alternative is available. Patience, moderation and astute politics will allow the progressive government to mediate between the liberal movement and the societal counter-movement without suffering devastating accumulation crises. This path will gradually bring major benefits to the Left's constituencies, its advocates would contend. Certainly, the development of a welfare state and cash transfers, improved and more widely accessible essential services (education, health, housing, transit) and the creation of good jobs are important gains.

Equal freedom, however, demands more in hierarchical, class-divided societies; it requires tackling the concentration of wealth and the hoarding of opportunities that has long characterized capitalism in many countries. But such confrontation runs contrary to the modus operandi of moderate social democracy. For now, the latter must live not only with neoliberal globalization but also with the oligopolistic structure of the domestic economy and media empires. The wealthy thus continue to wield dispro-portionate political influence, while elite private schools and elite (local and foreign) universities remain largely the preserve of the wealthy, pro-viding their offspring with the qualifications and social contacts to main-tain their class position. The danger also arises that a pressured leadership will settle for too little in the class compromise, claiming that the Third Way/social liberalism is actually the left wing of the possible. These stark realities introduce an inevitable tension between the rank and file of the social-democratic movement, mobilized by early hopes of fundamental change, and its leadership. If structural change occurs, it happens only in the longer term.

In sum, moderate social democracy, in adapting to the exigencies of capital accumulation, shows promise of steady though limited progress, partly through the stimulation of economic growth. The radical Left is more ambitious in its goals, but its confrontational approach runs up against entrenched power structures and the continued influence of global neoliberalism. Power equations are not static, however. If there is to be a durable and democratic socialism in the future, it will probably be achieved through a radical social-democratic transition.

The national level is only one of three levels at which the Left practices the politics of the possible. Experiments in equitable cooperation at the local level are important either as harbingers of a new national order, as complementary initiatives that strengthen national-level solidarity, or as survival mechanisms in hard times. Reconstructing globalization is also a critical long-term goal, insofar as global regimes continue to hinder leftist experiments. I consider each level in turn.

Small-scale experiments in equitable cooperation

Solidarity allows people to work together to attain goals they could not otherwise achieve. Solidarity, in forging community, is also an end in itself. These are the main reasons that experiments in equitable coopera-tion matter to the Left.

Small-scale experiments fall into two types. The first involves community self-help among people who share a particularistic identity deriving from kinship, ethnicity, clan, caste or religious beliefs. Face-to-face interaction promotes mutual trust and cooperation among members of the community, but separates the group from other primary communities. This form of solidarity is now often labeled "bonding social capital." It provides members not only with warm interpersonal ties, but also mutual assistance and cooperation in the common good. Its downsides are several, notably its exclusive nature. The second type of small-scale equitable cooperation involves "bridging" social capital – inclusive norms and networks that buttress solidarity among people across cultural lines.[4] People cooperate as peasants, farmers, landless laborers, industrial workers, managers, businessmen, neighbors, citizens, and so on, rather than as members of a particularistic group. Of course, the Left is primarily interested in the latter form of solidarity – though not exclusively in today's multicultural societies. More specifically, the democratic Left can be expected to promote and celebrate inclusive local experiments that prefigure a future socialist or cooperative society. But it is a mistake merely to dismiss parochial cooperation as outdated traditional networks. Although the cooperation and survival mechanisms underpinned by bonding social capital are rarely harbingers of a new society, they nevertheless play an important role, as we shall see, where economic insecurity, political disorder, climatic disasters and mass poverty abound.

Yet anyone who ventures onto the terrain of community does well to avoid the romanticism that often attaches to the concept. "Community development," "participatory development" and "people-centered development" are old ideas. The early enthusiasm for these approaches was soon tempered by the reality that many projects founder (for reviews of the literature, see Berner and Phillips 2005; Harvey and Langdon 2010; Majee and Hoyt 2011). The main assumption appears sound: projects designed for the betterment of people in villages or urban squatter settlements must respond to local needs as identified in public meetings, as well as draw upon local knowledge and enthusiasm. The participation of local people in defining needs and shaping the projects, it was believed, would not only improve their effectiveness, but also empower the poor and socially marginalized. In practice, however, power relations have frequently deformed the participatory process. "Top-down" experiments fail because external animators (non-governmental organizations, aid agencies or political parties), though rhetorically committed to participatory development, actually give short shrift to genuine participation when decisions conflict with their own agenda and their need to demonstrate tangible results to head office.

But even more genuinely "bottom-up" community experiments have failed as well. Why? The reasons are several (see Mosse 2005). Many "communities" are not really communities at all: that is, not solidarity but conflict and mistrust characterize the relationships among those in a village, a neighborhood or other unit. Moreover, elites within stratified communities bend the rules to control the participatory process and capture many of the benefits – thus buttressing inequality. Also, existing social exclusion on a gender, ethnic or caste basis may vitiate any genuine participation on the part of these groups. Or communities may exist, but the organizational capacity within them to cooperate and reach a consensus on what needs to be done is lacking. In short, local experiments in equitable cooperation face many well-known problems.

One failed experiment is agricultural cooperatives in Africa, which proliferated in the 1960s and 1970s.[5] Most cooperatives in this period were established by governments rather than the farmers, sometimes with the assistance of aid donors. Maladministration bedeviled many cooperatives whose members regarded them as extensions of government services rather than their own creations. In addition, cooperatives that commanded financial resources and large memberships were often politicized as factional leaders vied for support and access to resources. In the late 1980s and early 1990s, many of these cooperatives collapsed. Since then, hundreds of new cooperatives have appeared, mainly in the form of marketing cooperatives in the rural areas and savings and credit unions. In accordance with neoliberal precepts, these cooperatives operate as autonomous associations with clearly delineated tasks. But even an upbeat assessment recently concluded that Africa's cooperative movement was "still weak," constrained by a "lack of voice" and "effective representation" (Allen and Maghimi 2009: 8, 15). Such realities should temper any tendency to romanticize community.

Nonetheless, where livelihoods are insecure or disorder is widespread, and where the state is unable or unwilling to deal with local problems, people contrive to establish their own forms of mutual insurance and social economy. In such circumstances, communal attachments may provide a haven in the storm. Consider the case of Africa.

Mutual assistance in parochial communities

Not the market or the state, but the community generates the governing structure for a range of local activities in Africa. These small-scale efforts harness and consolidate norms of trust, cooperation and mutual help to solve local problems. Cooperation, where solidarity survives, flows from face-to-face interactions among people with a special relationship to each other – for example, as members of a clan, a village, a caste, or a religious community. Where social attachments remain strong, where the exemplary fulfillment of one's social obligations brings high social standing, bonding social capital provides the basis for mutual assistance in difficult circumstances.

Although social dislocation and the culture of possessive individualism have eroded social capital, relations of trust and cooperation still often survive at the grassroots, especially in the rural areas. Goran Hyden argues that an "economy of affection" – a "network of support, communication and interaction among structurally defined groups connected by blood, kin, community or other affinities" (Hyden 1983: 8) – obtains quite widely in Africa, though in decline (Hyden 2006: 72, 153–4; see also Sugimura 2008; Bernard et al. 2008; Schaffer 1998: 80–1). The report of the Commission for Africa (2005: 127–8), commissioned by the British government, marvels at the capacity of Africans "to operate through an apparent anarchy," identifying "social networks" that, though "invisible" to outsiders, are nonetheless crucial to the functioning of many communities. Indeed, the report contends that "Africa's strength lies in these networks" (of family, clan, tribe, etc.). "Africans survive – and some prosper – in the face of low incomes and few formal economy jobs. The networks create social capital, which is crucial in [African] survival strategies." A study of Sahelian cereal producers in Senegal pinpoints the normative basis of communities underpinned by reciprocity: "I receive, therefore I exist. I give, therefore I am respected." The act of giving, a way of redistributing the surplus, thus "confers respectability and prestige. What is determinant is the social context which legitimizes the gift so that it is never an isolated act: the gift creates or reinforces the social ties; it calls for a counter-gift which is never spelt out, either for its content or for its expiry date" (N'Dione et al. 1995: 371). Reciprocity thus acts as a kind of informal social insurance, as Polanyi contends.

A World Bank-financed study of peasant villages in Senegal and Burkina Faso (Bernard et al. 2008) discovered a remarkable degree of social solidarity. The study, based on a vast trove of interviews and surveys, shows (a) that villagers deliberately employ equality considerations in allocating resources, (b) that voluntary organizations (VOs) at the village level are usually inclusive of poor households, and (c) that the solidarity ethos has blocked corruption and prevented elites from capturing the VOs for their own advantage. However, rather than accepting this mutuality as a valuable resource to be nurtured, the report recommends that market considerations should override solidarity principles. "Recognizing differential entrepreneurial abilities across members, could be a source of efficiency gains for MOs [market-oriented organizations] in the typical West African village environment" (p. 2,197). But it is not at all obvious that, given the insecurity afflicting these villagers and their own preference for a solidarity economy, outsiders know better than the people themselves in proposing a market-based alternative for them.

Critics rightly point out that the problems plaguing Africa cannot be solved at the community level, but this truth does not obviate the importance of the Left's support for grassroots initiatives. Certainly, remedies for mass poverty, vast inequalities, political disorder and environmental decline require a national if not global response. In reality, however, states are either unable or unwilling to act on these problems, while the global response is wholly inadequate. Hence, people are thrown back on their own resources. And social capital, even bonding social capital, is *one of the few resources they can draw on.*

Consider the contributions to well-being attributable to communally based reciprocity.

I have already alluded to the rural economies of affection that persist to varying degrees in Africa, where the norms and networks of solidarity provide subsistence insurance to vulnerable people. Additional examples of mutual self-help on a parochial basis include:

- Urban mutual aid associations, formed on the basis of descent, operating as ethnic associations, burial societies, sports and dance clubs, secret societies or hometown associations (Hyden 2006: 76–7; see also Tsuruta 2006).
- Informal credit schemes, whereby people pool their resources in rotating credit arrangements or savings associations so that each member has an opportunity to accumulate the financial capital he or she needs to improve productivity or pursue new ventures (Vermaak 2009: 406).
- Cooperative village enterprises to create employment for women in, for example, handicrafts, tree planting, or telecommunication services, and often including micro-credit facilities (Vermaak 2009: 407).
- Local communities that engage in the cooperative management of a common resource, such as a game park, grazing pasture, forest or fishery, in order to enhance ecological sustainability and local livelihoods (Gibbes and Keys 2010).[6]
- Networks among the urban poor, mainly in West Africa, that give rise to informal health insurance plans for their members in a context where only about 10 percent of the population (employed in the formal sector) have formal health plans (Lacey 2005).[7]
- Religious communities, especially Islamic sects and evangelical churches, which create an alternative moral universe and mutuality for members in a context of systemic clientelism, corruption and ethnic

favoritism. Faith-based organizations are "often the only locally organized groups working among the destitute, filling in for governments where governments are too feeble to provide even basic schooling and health care" (Kaplan 2009: 22; see also Maxwell 2005; Booyens and Crause 2009).

Cooperative networks thus advance the welfare of the poor and vulnerable in small-scale communities; but do they have a broader significance?

Communitarian experiments pose dilemmas for those concerned with national-level alternatives. On the one hand, they generate, via solidarity, the resources for households to subsist in circumstances of extreme poverty, marginality, drought or war. Community also provides people with the consolation of warm personal relationships, even when their personal problems are daunting. On the other hand, in reaffirming parochial norms, communitarian responses may reinforce patriarchal power structures, local inequalities, autocratic decision-making and exclusive communal identities, thus obstructing equal freedom in the broader society.

Even if a leftist movement can overcome these regressive features, can locally based solidarities be "scaled up" to the culturally diverse regional or national levels? Scaling up is crucial because problems of unemployment, poverty, inequality and disorder can be resolved only at the national (or global) level. It has been the dream of many socialists to extend existing, subnational solidarities to encompass the entire nation. Chapter 6 refers to President Julius Nyerere's abortive dream of leapfrogging from a communal society to socialism, bypassing the divisive and exploitative capitalist phase altogether. But bonding social capital arises among people who not only share a particularistic identity, but also build trust through interacting with one another over a considerable time. Moving from this localized solidarity to the bridging social capital of occupation, class, region or citizenship is a difficult transition. It has proven possible in rare cases: for instance, various indigenous communities in Bolivia, Ecuador and elsewhere in Latin America have joined social movements dedicated to advancing common interests. However, even without scaling up, community-based alternatives are an important end in themselves in reducing insecurity and helping meet the basic needs of community members.

Harbingers of a new solidarity

Other small-scale initiatives can be seen as prefiguring a new cooperative society. They construct bridging social capital, foreshadow equitable cooperation in multicultural societies, foster self-governing institutional arrangements on a non-parochial basis and empower subordinate groups through the practice of democratic decision-making. Such local experiments arise either at the instigation of leftist movements at the national level or as stand-alone or spontaneous initiatives of a locally based group. In either case, they are instances of what Antonio Gramsci (1971) terms *counter-hegemonic movements*. The construction of alternative societies within the confines of civil society are part of a long-term "war of position," according to Gramsci, aiming to undermine the hegemonic capitalist order. However, these projects, like the parochial examples already discussed, suffer from a major limitation: they usually depend for their survival upon the support of a sympathetic regional or national government.

I briefly refer to three diverse cases: the Zapatistas in Mexico, participatory budgeting in Porto Alegre, Brazil, and worker-recovered companies in Argentina. These cases illustrate the wide range of local experiments.

At first glance, the suggestion that the Zapatistas prefigure a new society is puzzling. The Ejercito Zapatista de Liberación Nacional (EZLN) is, after all, a liberation movement based on the Mayan people of Chiapas state in Mexico, located near the border with Guatemala. It thus builds on bonding, not bridging, social capital. Nevertheless, the EZLN is a long-running experiment in indigenous self-government, as well as a front designed to rally support against neoliberal agricultural policies. The Zapatistas forcefully confront the Left with the issue of how it should adjust to the realities of multicultural societies. Progressives feel more comfortable using the language of class and universal human rights than ethnicity and cultural rights. Now they must come to terms with plural societies in which groups assert their cultural rights – in this case, the demands of a long-marginalized indigenous people to attain local autonomy and protect their ancestral lands, crops and culture from invasive market forces. Mexico is only one among several Latin American countries in which assertive movements of indigenous people have come to the fore. They are also strong in Bolivia, Ecuador and Peru. By articulating demands on behalf of indigenous peoples, the Zapatistas challenge not only the nationalist discourse of the Right and Center, but also the Left's class-based discourse. They have forced the Left as well as the Right to take indigenous rights and local autonomy seriously.

As the Zapatistas' rebellion is well known, I will only sketch the key events. The EZLN seized several municipalities in the Chiapas highlands on January 1, 1994, the day that the North American Free Trade Agreement came into force. A violent struggle then ensued as the Mexican army engaged the insurgents; within two weeks, a ceasefire brought an end to the fighting and the commencement of long negotiations. Thereafter, only sporadic violent confrontations occurred. Negotiations produced the San Andrés Accords in February 1996. This agreement recognized the rights of indigenous communities to natural resources, land tenure, self-governance and the administration of justice. But the government reneged on this agreement, purportedly to assert the federal government's determination to retain control of the oil reserves discovered in the area. Instead, it unilaterally reformed indigenous rights in 2001. This law restricted indigenous autonomy to the municipal level. It denied the constitutional recognition of indigenous people as collective subjects with the right to determine their own form of self-government and control their own resources. And it stated that the federal government would continue to provide social services to indigenous people. The EZLN, rejecting these terms, proceeded unilaterally to establish five autonomous regional zones. A stalemate followed.

The Zapatistas reached out to other communities and to supporters worldwide, in an attempt to transform Mexico's gendered and ethnic inequalities into "a national campaign for building another way of doing politics" (Mora 2007: 65). Other indigenous communities began to emulate the Mayan movement. The Zapatistas also received strong support from international NGOs, who provided many services in EZLN regions (Andrews 2010). Each autonomous zone runs clinics, hospitals and educational facilities. However, the movement became quiescent in the late 2000s, though it is not moribund. It was still strong enough in December 2012 to mount major marches simultaneously in five Chiapas towns.

Although the Zapatistas have a range of genuine economic and cultural grievances (Brass 2005) and elicited significant support globally, the hostility of the federal government vitiated the movement's momentum. The government was loath to suppress the movement through force of arms owing to the negative worldwide media coverage that such action would engender. Instead, it responded with enticements to motivate Mayans to break with the EZLN. It invested heavily in the provision of infrastructure and services in Chiapas, especially schools. The lure of superior government-supported schools, together with conditional cash transfers to poor families through the government's Progresa program, led many Mayan parents to accept the authority of the federal government (Barmeyer 2008). Defections from the Zapatistas have weakened the movement's credibility among domestic and foreign supporters. Yet the counter-hegemonic movement has not disappeared.

Consider next the prototypical case of participatory budgeting in Porto Alegre, Brazil. It illustrates both the challenges of empowering people at the local level and the centrality of a sympathetic higher-level government to the flourishing of innovative community experiments.

Participatory budgeting is a complex process of establishing priorities for the allocation of infrastructural investments and monitoring outcomes through a combination of participatory and representative democracy. It initially represented a radical initiative of the Workers Party (PT) in Brazil, aiming not only to displace traditional clientelism, but also to buttress a "counter-hegemonic strategy to overcome capitalism" through the progressive extension of participatory democracy to the regional and national levels (Novy and Leubolt 2005: 2,026). Although it never came close to realizing this radical goal, in Porto Alegre or elsewhere in Brazil, participatory budgeting did contribute to empowering marginalized segments of the population, negating clientelism, improving accountability and reallocating public investment to poor and under-serviced neighborhoods. This is no small achievement. However, the resources available to participatory budgeting were too limited to make a discernible impact on poverty, unemployment and inequality (Leubolt, Novy and Becker 2008: 443).

From 1989 to the mid 2000s, previously marginalized people in Porto Alegre – especially the poor with limited literacy and women in this patriarchal society – learned how to participate in the deliberative process through observing proceedings and practicing their rhetorical skills (Baiocchi 2005: 145–7). Participatory budgeting engaged people because the elected city council rarely rejected project proposals emanating from the participatory decision-making processs. In addition, "thematic forums" on education, health, social services, transport and economic development encouraged middle-class people to take part in policy debates. Yet participatory budgeting at Brazil's state level never achieved more than a consultative status. The PT's original plan of radical democracy as part of a class struggle gave way to a strategy of class compromise, with the party catering to the middle class as well as the poor and working class.

Participatory budgeting in Porto Alegre, the most widely touted case, built on unusually advantageous conditions. This city of 1.3 million people had a relatively prosperous, well-educated population. It also manifested a relatively robust civil society, including well-organized urban movements, stronger democratic traditions than elsewhere in Brazil, and a history of left-of-center government (Leubolt, Novy and Becker 2008: 436–7; Baiocchi 2005: 149). Most important, a PT mayor won power in 1988. He could count on the support of the state government of Rio Grande do Sul, which was also under PT control, in establishing participatory budgeting. But if conditions in Porto Alegre were unusually positive, they were not unique: participatory budgeting has successfully operated in many other Brazilian cities, and indeed in cities throughout the world (with the World Bank's backing of the tamed participatory budgeting model).[8]

After the PT lost power in Rio Grande do Sul (2002) and in Porto Alegre (2004), participatory budgeting languished. It was terminated at the state level, but the new city administration did not dare to attack openly such a renowned institution. Instead, it allowed participatory budgeting slowly to decline, a result of the indifference of the city's administration and its introduction of a new consultative system (Fox 2008). The right-wing administration also turned to "Private–Public Partnerships" to solve problems through philanthropy rather than tax revenues.

Though participatory budgeting never fulfilled the initial vision of radical democracy, it nonetheless played a role in undermining traditional power structures and highlighting the possibility of participatory development. The participatory budgeting system in Porto Alegre thus raises an important issue: how can promising local initiatives in building equitable cooperation survive long enough to realize their promise?

Worker-recovered companies in Argentina, the third example, constitute an important experiment in economic democracy. Their significance lies not in the number of workers involved (probably fewer than twenty thousand at any point), but in the counter-hegemonic model they introduced. The workers' experience in seizing their bankrupt workplaces, running them, fending off eviction and seeking legal status has fostered solidarity and a workplace culture very different from that found in conventional capitalist enterprises (see especially W. Evans 2008: 34–5). The "success" of some worker-managed enterprises and, in particular, their low rate of failure have demonstrated the potential viability of worker self-management.[9]

The tumultuous year of 2001 marked a sharp break in Argentina's development model. Between the austerity program of March 1991 and the mass uprising in December 2001, Argentina had been a textbook case of neoliberal reform. Its peso was even fixed at parity with the US dollar to build investors' confidence. But the collapse of the economy in 2001, precipitated by a default on the foreign debt in December, led to conditions akin to the Great Depression, with 20 percent unemployment, 14 million of the country's 57 million people falling into poverty, and a rapid decline in purchasing power (Gabetta 2002). Little wonder that this economic crisis produced a political crisis in the form of urban riots, looting, the destruction of sections of Argentina's cities, the declaration of a State of Siege and the rapid fall of three presidents (see Schaumberg 2008). Militant forms of popular mobilization appeared in the form of neighborhood assemblies and associations of the unemployed, in addition to the workers' seizure of their failed firms. The workers' action met with widespread approval in this atmosphere.

Most of the worker-managed firms emerged during the severe economic crisis of 2001–4.[10] They originated not as part of a radical movement but as a defensive measure; employees of bankrupt firms occupied their workplaces and desperately strove, through cooperative management and help from longer-established cooperatives, to keep their plants operating and preserve their jobs. Significantly, further worker-recovered firms have emerged during the country's strong recovery in 2004–9 – about 14 percent of the total (Palomino et al. 2010: 262) – suggesting that workers' cooperatives in Argentina have come to represent more than an act of desperation.

"Recovered" companies are quite heterogeneous. Most of them are small and medium enterprises, with 70 percent of them employing fewer than 50 workers and only 4 percent more than 200 workers (Palomino et al. 2010: 259–60). Most of the firms are engaged in manufacturing – in the food industry, steel, textiles, footwear and plastics, meat packing, ceramics, glass and rubber goods – and one-third are located in Greater Buenos Aires. Many of the worker-recovered companies have attained legal status as cooperatives while the status of others remains ambiguous (Palomino et al. 2010: 263). No single model of workers' self-management exists, though there are commonalities from one enterprise to the next.

After seizing their workplaces, the employees had to devise cooperative management systems and equitable rules for determining wages. Some studies depict worker-recovered companies as pervaded by an egalitarian ethos (Sitrin 2012). It appears that about 70 percent of the firms have adopted egalitarian remuneration practices. Many have a system for rotating tasks among the workers. The vast majority hold regular (weekly or monthly) assemblies of all the workers, though more specialized committees often make routine decisions in the various units (Sitrin 2012: 131). Yet a quasi-anthropological study of a worker-managed hotel paints a more complex and contradictory picture (W. T. Evans 2008). On the one hand, the hotel's workers, when asked, describe an idealized workplace governed by egalitarian and democratic norms. On the other hand, the daily reality (perhaps not surprisingly) is one of hierarchy and inequalities in decision-making power; some workers are more equal than others. Nevertheless, the counter-hegemonic discourse in this hotel and other worker-managed enterprises challenges the neoliberal order.

The challenge arises from the popular approval and support these firms receive. Many worker-recovered companies have survived because of assistance from people in the communities in which the workplaces are located and from other workers. These outsiders have often assisted workers resisting eviction by the police. Some workplaces come to resemble community centers, where various community events take place in the facilities in the evenings and at weekends. In addition, well-established worker-recovered companies have offered financial assistance to struggling worker-managed enterprises in the early weeks (see the case studies in Sitrin 2012: chap. 6). These firms tend to be well-integrated and widely accepted.

The future of worker-managed firms is nevertheless unclear. Can they become productive alternatives to conventional private firms? Worker-managed firms manifest similar weaknesses: difficulty in obtaining credit owing to ambiguous legal status, a lack of technical, administrative and professional staff, and outdated machinery. There is also a division between those who interpret worker-recovered companies as a harbinger of a non-capitalist development path, and those who associate workers' management with traditional cooperatives operating within a capitalist economy. Although the obstacles to the success of producers' cooperatives within a capitalist economy are many, sympathetic Peronist federal governments and some provincial governments have eased their plight. A Law of Expropriation in 2004 allowed the state to expropriate firms on behalf of their workers, though it obliged the collective owners to repay their firms' debts at the time of bankruptcy. Also, employees legally have the first bid to purchase bankrupt companies. And a minority of the worker-managed firms have received public subsidies. Difficulties remain, and the advent of unsympathetic governments would create further obstacles to the success of this experiment.

The central issue concerns whether workers' cooperatives adapt to the existing capitalist order or spearhead an alternative, solidarity economy. As Marx well understood, worker-managed enterprises that operate according to the logic of profit-seeking and competition would not contribute to liberation. They would simply "become their own capitalists," co-opted by the existing capitalist order.[11] Although the critique is accurate, it implicitly expects an unrealistic willingness for self-sacrifice on the part of the relevant workers in the midst of an economic boom and lacking the support of a strong socialist movement.

In sum, small-scale experiments in equitable cooperation exist widely in the Global South, but they are subject to certain common limitations. Parochial forms of cooperation serve as survival or collective-advancement mechanisms; however, they sometimes rest on hierarchical and patriarchal foundations, and their exclusive, particularistic basis makes it difficult to scale up such solidarities to the regional or national level. Moreover, community-based development is a fragile system that is easily subverted by outside agents. Another type of small-scale experiment nurtures the seeds of a new mutuality and a new society; yet they usually depend for their survival on the sympathy of higher levels of government. Changing political circumstances may thus quickly undermine these ventures. The politics of the possible at the local level, as at the national and global levels, is constrained in typical ways.

Reconstructing globalization

The term *neoliberal globalization* refers to a pattern of economic integration inspired by the vision of a self-regulating global market economy. The removal of national barriers to the cross-border flows of capital, finance, goods and services, and technology underpins this integration. In Polanyi's terms, neoliberal globalization thus represents the global dimension of the liberal movement. This movement not only reduces the policy autonomy of leftist (as well as other) governments, but also exacerbates worldwide trends toward high inequality, economic volatility and ecological destruction, as I discussed earlier.[12]

When the global economic crisis struck in 2008, neoliberal commentators voiced concern that it would stimulate a new protectionism. Certainly, moves in that direction have occurred. Yet even such a stalwart defender of free trade as *The Economist* reported, in 2013, that the worst had not happened. Protectionist walls had not been erected. Instead, a "gated" globalization had emerged, with "more state intervention in the flow of money and goods, more regionalisation of trade as countries gravitate towards like-minded neighbours, and more friction as national self-interest wins out over international cooperation" (Ip 2013). In light of the fact that the crisis spread out from the centers of neoliberalism (Wall Street and the City of London) and that the state-capitalist economies weathered the crisis relatively well, the limited degree of systemic change is remarkable. Several factors averted the overturning of neoliberal globalization: the absence of a ready-made alternative, the unwillingness of the rising BRIC powers to champion more substantial institutional change, and the continued allegiance to neoliberalism on the part of powerful business interests, technocrats and politicians worldwide.[13] Thus, the prevailing global order continues to restrict the capacity of leftist governments to undertake the redistributive policies that their people demand and equal freedom requires.

To promote their programs in this restrictive context, leftist governments have selected one or more of three defensive strategies. The first involves *individual state action*. Adaptation to the existing rules of the game, principally through adherence to orthodox monetary and fiscal policy, is a common response. To avoid dependence on the IMF, World Bank and Western powers and retain the confidence of foreign and local investors, governments buttress their foreign exchange reserves, avoid large budget or current account deficits, maintain low inflation, and impose moderate tax burdens. Moderate social democracies have adopted this strategy, I suggested in Chapter 5. Redistribution then mainly involves creating productive jobs, extending cash transfers, and expanding the welfare state with the revenues derived from economic growth. But this adaptive strategy can prove costly. Cautious macroeconomic policy runs against the grain of a bold redistributive, job-creating strategy. It undercuts the Left's distinctive egalitarian vision, lending credence to the critics' claim that a government has sold out.

Instead of, or in addition to, adaptation, individual national governments have undertaken hidden or overt protectionist measures to enhance their control of economic life. Chávez's Venezuela, as mentioned in Chapter 6, used the policy leeway generated by the country's ample oil reserves to increase the state's regulatory direction. Chávez nationalized many large firms, removed the independence of Venezuela's central bank, issued strict regulations governing foreign investment, harnessed the state oil company to his program, and imposed exchange-rate, price and capital controls. Unfortunate by-products of these controls included a high rate of price inflation recently (at least 25 percent per annum), a rapidly growing debt, limited domestic investment, widespread complaints about shortages and high prices, and an apparent rise in corruption. Other governments have used a less intrusive combination of hidden and overt protectionist measures. "State developmentalism," an aspect of the moderate socialist-democratic strategy, entails hidden protectionism in the form of an industrial policy. It promotes domestic firms in strategic sectors through subsidies, including low-interest loans, tax breaks and reduced utility charges. Brazil has, in addition, increased tariffs on certain imported goods, such as automobiles, thus encouraging importers to establish factories in the country (Habel 2013: 4). It also requires foreign oil companies to collaborate with Brazil's state oil company in exploiting newly discovered offshore oil fields: Petrobras must receive a 30 percent stake in offshore production as well as act as the operator and strategic decision maker.

Furthermore, leftist governments (among others) have installed "speed bumps" since 2009 to stem rapid inflows and outflows of "hot" money. Capital controls are now a widely accepted defensive measure.[14] China and Malaysia – countries that weathered the East Asian crisis of 1997 and the 2008–9 crisis relatively unscathed owing to their currency controls – spurred renewed interest in this mechanism. In the aftermath of the financial crisis, money has massively flowed to the emerging markets in search of higher returns as interest rates in advanced industrial countries fell. The appreciation of national currencies in recipient countries, such as Brazil, rendered their exports uncompetitive. Capital-account regulation has been a "moderately effective" tool in responding to this destructive volatility (Baumann and Gallagher 2012). In Brazil, for example, the imposition of capital controls after 2009 shifted the composition (though not the volume) of financial inflows from short- to longer-term investments. Controls also mitigated exchange-rate volatility and "modestly" increased the government's capacity to pursue an independent monetary policy (Baumann and Gallagher 2012).

By 2012, even the IMF had accepted the efficacy of capital management tools in emergency situations. However, many existing trade and investment treaties, especially those negotiated with the United States, legally hinder the use of capital controls. These treaties will need to be renegotiated.

Governments have also expanded their policy autonomy by turning to China and, to a lesser extent, India as markets for their exports and suppliers of imports, finance, foreign investment and even foreign aid. Venezuela, followed by Bolivia and Ecuador, has developed close financial and trade relations with China, expanded links with Russia, and expressed solidarity with such "pariah" regimes as those in Iran and Cuba. These options reduce reliance on Western markets, suppliers and military security.

A second defensive option involves *regional or South–South cooperation*. A recent example of the latter is the Group of 20 developing countries, which emerged from a trade initiative of the governments of Brazil, India and South Africa (and should not be confused with the G20 of the largest industrial powers). The Group of 20, taking its name from the date of its inception on August 20, 2003, is a loose bloc of countries within the World Trade Organization. It is dedicated to fighting protectionist and trade-distorting policies in the United States and the European Union, especially in agriculture. Accounting collectively for 60 percent of the world's population, it carries some weight in the World Trade Organization's negotiating bodies (Golub 2013).

The aim of regional organizations is to promote mutual assistance among like-minded states and eventually to bypass neoliberal global institutions, such as the IMF, the World Bank, and regional development banks, which are dominated by the West. A prominent case, discussed in Chapter 6, involves South America and the Caribbean. The regional associations include, in particular, ALBA (Bolivarian Alliance for the Peoples of Our America), UNASUR (Union of South American

Nations) and BancoSur. Though too recent in origin to assess their effectiveness, they may provide some insulation for member governments from the pressures of global neoliberalism. ALBA, to recall, is a political alliance (including social movements from non-member countries) aimed at safeguarding South America and the Caribbean from neoliberal policies and imperialism. The organization's initiatives to buttress regional solidarity include providing subsidized oil to poorer members, building food security, assisting in adult literacy campaigns, and promoting public health and educational opportunities. In addition, ALBA has built links to such non-Western powers as Iran, Russia and China. Developing countries can gain some insulation from neoliberal globalization through regional organizations and external linkages such as these.

The third defensive strategy is long term and holistic: *reshaping the rules of the global market economy*. Without structural change at this level, policy options will remain constrained (for an elaboration, see Evans 2009). The problem is not globalization as such but neoliberal globalization. Enhancing international trade and cross-border flows of capital, scarce skills and technologies can support the attainment of equal freedom, depending on the rules that govern such flows. To restrict the power of corporate capital, ensure more egalitarian outcomes, reduce market volatility and ecological damage, and advance labor standards what is required is the *remaking* of economic globalization, not its termination. However, the two conflicting imperatives – to reshape the global order in the longer run and adapt to the neoliberal order in the short and medium term – doubtless produce a major tactical challenge.[15]

Proposals to place restrictions on global markets and democratize global governance are actually not so radical. Every country, even the most market-fundamentalist, shapes national market forces by means of some moral and regulatory norms. Labor markets, for instance, are usually subject to regulations that outlaw child and slave labor, protect the health and safety of workers, prevent outright exploitation, allow for collective bargaining and ban discriminatory hiring or promotion policies. It is not outlandish to propose that similar norms should constrain *global* market forces or to contend that treaty-protected property rights should not be allowed to trump all other rights.

We might use the term "social-democratic globalization" to stand for a civilized global order. The shift would involve structural changes that quell the negative tendencies of global neoliberalism and improve the possibility of realizing equal freedom globally. In other words, institutional, legal and regulatory reforms would subordinate the logic of global markets (private ownership, efficiency) to the norms of social equity, social solidarity, economic security, and health and environmental protection. How concretely this goal might be achieved would take us too far afield.[16] It must suffice to mention four essential principles that should govern change in the global economic order:

- Fundamental rights and freedoms must take priority over rules governing international trade, investment and intellectual property. Hence, existing and prospective conventions protecting human rights, labor and trade-union rights, economic, social and cultural rights and environmental and health regulations would have precedence.
- Financial markets must be regulated to limit the destructiveness arising from massive pools of financial capital seeking speculative profits through short-term cross-border investments in currencies, bonds, derivatives and equities.
- Mechanisms are needed to redistribute a share of the economic gains of global integration to populations in the Global South who bear the brunt of globalization and climate change. This redistribution would preferably depend on taxes on activities that should be discouraged anyway, especially cross-border speculative currency movements (a currency transaction tax or Tobin tax) and the generation of greenhouse gas emissions (a carbon tax).
- The reorientation and democratization of the Bretton Woods institutions, especially the IMF and World Bank, should be undertaken. The IMF, for example, should return to its original function of preventing financial crises rather than universalizing an idealized version of free-market economies. Democratization would aim at rebalancing governance to ensure that institutions do not simply serve Western, or specifically US, interests.

Additional complexity arises because all these changes need to be negotiated simultaneously. Success in negotiating in one area – the rules of international commerce, the mechanisms for sharing the benefits of globalization, or global governance reform – depends on progress on the other issues as well. The issues are indissolubly linked.

How might change in the international order come about? What we are discussing is a "counter-hegemonic globalization": "a globally organized project of transformation aimed at replacing the dominant … global regime with one that maximizes democratic political control and makes the equitable development of human capabilities and environmental stewardship its priorities" (P. Evans 2008: 272). Karl Polanyi, in studying the Great Transformation that occurred in the nineteenth and twentieth centuries, focused on the double movement only at the national and local levels. Today, the double movement also plays out at the global level. The liberal movement toward a self-regulating global market economy has, through accruing damaging side effects, provoked the formation of a societally protective global counter-movement. Without the revolutions in communications, transport and information processing, this counter-movement would hardly be possible. The internet, in particular, is critical in coordinating the activities of allied social movements throughout the world.[17] This counter-movement, which usually refers to itself as the global democracy or justice movement, is highly disparate, including such organizations as trade unions, peasant and farmer associations, religious organizations, feminist groups, environmental and conservation associations, human rights organizations, and intellectual bodies. It is obviously difficult to harmonize the concerns of single-issue organizations in a single program of change.

To succeed, a synergy needs to develop between progressive national governments, on the one hand, and transnational social movements dedicated to reshaping the global order, on the other. "More progressive state actors provide transnational movements with potential allies at the global level, strengthening these transnational movements and enhancing their ability to act as allies for [progressive] domestic movements" (P. Evans 2008: 295; see also Faux 2004). These more powerful national movements will then have increased leverage with their national governments, and hence more influence on their governments' position on global restructuring.

Realistically, however, this global restructuring will not happen soon. Major shifts in global institutions have generally followed severe economic crises and the inability of conventional policy measures to resolve them. This failure undermines the legitimacy of the dominant policy paradigm; it provides an opening for those advocating a fresh approach. Both the Great Depression of the 1930s and stagflation in the 1970s led to the rise of alternative policy paradigms. Yet the 2009–10 global crisis and its dismal aftermath have not instigated such a shift. Instead, the purveyors of neoliberal doctrine have responded by adopting a few heterodox policies (such as capital controls) and adopting a more humble and open-minded approach.

What explains this puzzling result? For one thing, neoliberalism is a moving target. The national Third Ways since the 1990s present a more ambiguous face than the market fundamentalism of the earlier Washington Consensus. And the decisive, pragmatic response to the immediate crisis on the part of leading governments – effectively employing Keynesian measures to deal with a neoliberal crisis – forestalled an outright depression. Furthermore, it is not clear that an authoritative alternative policy paradigm actually exists. One might eventually emerge from an energized global counter-movement. And what is the strength of this counter-movement? Although Polanyi conceives of the counter-movement as a spontaneous development, it must be united behind a common program to be effective. Peter Evans (2008, 2014) points out two major obstacles in forging a strong counter-movement. First, it must unite action at the local, national and global levels, transcending borders and the North–South divide in particular. Second, the leaders of the counter-movement must coordinate the diverse strands of the opposition to neoliberal globalization into a single "movement of movements." This unity depends on the articulation of ideological themes, such as rights, democracy and social justice, which can serve as an overarching program behind which all single-issue organizations can come together. It is evident that these organizational challenges cannot be easily surmounted.

Power relations, in short, do not currently favor a paradigm shift. A new international regime requires that the major economic powers back the change. Progress cannot be made against the opposition of the United States government, which presides over what is still the world's largest economy and military. Yet the US is the main sponsor of neoliberal globalization. The administration of George W. Bush (2000–8) was highly unilateral in its foreign policy. Even if subsequent presidents were more amenable to advancing a just, broadly prosperous and environmentally sustainable global order, vested interests play a powerful role in US politics. The liberal wing of the Democratic Party, together with a substantial minority of the US electorate, might support such an agenda. But the influential financial elite, as the main beneficiaries of the current order, would fight hard to protect their privileged position in alliance with other large corporations. In a plutocracy, this opposition usually prevails in normal times.

It isn't just a matter of opposition from the United States, or even from the Global North. The rising economic powers, especially China and India, are not championing an alternative; they are doing relatively well under the prevailing rules. Many other smaller developing countries, struggling to survive and expand their economies within the global market system, do not have much influence on global negotiations. Powerful business elites in emerging economies such as India, Brazil, Russia, South Africa and China are also invested in the existing neoliberal order. Indeed, one may speak of an emergent global class – "cosmopolitans" – who share a common interest in neoliberal globalization, based on proficiency in English, a shared system of meaning, and control of a mobile factor of production such as specialized knowledge or capital (Bowles and Pangano 2006). Though a small minority globally, they are powerful nationally owing to the high international demand for the assets they control. Consequently, the prevailing paradigm persists with only minor revisions.

In sum, global neoliberalism constrains the Left's options, yet the global order is unlikely to change significantly in the near future. Consequently, leftist regimes will have to rely mainly on national and regional defensive strategies to extend their room for heterodox policies. Adaptive, rather than disruptive, approaches on the Left will remain the norm, unless some major calamity such as massive climatic change disrupts the international order.

The Left and climate change

Nowhere is the challenge to "make the impossible possible" clearer than in reducing the greenhouse gas emissions that are leading to climate change.[18] The Copenhagen Accord of 2010 stated the goal as holding the global mean surface temperature to an increase of 2 degrees Celsius above the preindustrial level. Even this apparently small increase would lead to major disruptions; it translates into an increase of 6 degrees at the poles and well above 2 degrees in certain regions of Africa. Climate scientists generally believe that an increase in mean global temperatures of 4 degrees would lead to catastrophic climatic change, perhaps to the collapse of "an organized, equitable and civilized global community" (Anderson 2012: 29). Yet, despite all the warnings, earth summits and conferences, greenhouse gas emissions continue to climb – indeed, even the rate of growth of emissions is increasing. In 2013, the world passed a milestone as the level of carbon dioxide in the atmosphere reached 400 parts per million – with 450 parts per million considered the threshold of catastrophic climate change. The UN's Fifth Intergovernmental Panel on Climate Change (reflecting a consensus of more than eight hundred scientists) reported in September 2013 that the atmospheric concentration of greenhouse gases had reached levels not seen in 800,000 years and that the probability that human activities were the main cause was 95 percent.

In the Global South, the situation is particularly dire (as I discussed in Chapter 3). Global warming is one important aspect of a larger ecological problem. In many countries, populations have doubled in less than thirty years. Meanwhile, rising incomes have vastly expanded the level of consumption (and hence energy usage) of national populations. When climate change results, various unfortunate consequences follow. They include a precipitous decline in groundwater, the shrinking of lakes and rivers, pressures on rainforests, periodic failures of crops with the attendant spikes in food prices, and population movements as a result of desertification and soil erosion. Economically, these trends will undercut potential economic growth. And politically, shrinking resources, especially of fresh water, and population shifts are conducive to conflict, both civil wars and interstate hostilities. The stresses push already fragile states closer to state collapse.

What needs to be done? If we assume that emissions will peak in 2020 (an unlikely scenario in light of the current rate of increase), they would then have to fall by 10–20 percent each year thereafter to limit the rise in temperature to 2 degrees Celsius. Total emissions would have to decrease to 20 percent of the benchmark 1990 levels by 2050, according to many experts (Bello 2008). Each year, it becomes more improbable that we will be able to hold the rise in temperatures to 2 degrees.

Can the Left deal with this crisis any better than the neoliberals? I analyzed in Chapter 3 the ways in which neoliberalism has aggravated ecological problems, through the extensive commodification of nature, the spread of the culture of possessive individualism and the "grow or die" logic of the market system. I will not repeat those arguments here. On the surface, however, it does not appear that the democratic Left will do much better. The Left in the Global South has embraced economic growth and job creation as fervently as the Right (see chapters 5 and 6). For the post-development critics, the word "development" connotes a pernicious discourse that perpetuates the domination of the "developing" world by the core capitalist countries. But plenty of evidence suggests that the vast majority in the developing world endorses development as the path to social progress. If, in the Global North, this is an age of pessimism aroused by economic crisis, decline and climate change, optimism seems to abound in the economically dynamic regions of the Global South (Kapoor 2011). Environmentalists view the growth ideology as the major problem, but the Left aligns itself with economic growth or risks losing support. This orientation toward rapidly raising production and consumption has led to significant growth in emissions and environmental damage.[19]

Nevertheless, in *comparative* terms, leftist governments have a superior environmental record. Yale University's "environmental performance index" (Yale University 2011) indicates that, among 163 countries ranked on 25 environmental indicators in 2010, the top six are social democracies from Northern Europe and the Global South. Remarkably, Costa Rica ranks third, Mauritius sixth and Chile sixteenth, far ahead of the United States, which is tied with Brazil in sixty-first place. The countries in which neoliberalism is most heavily entrenched tend to have the worst environmental records, especially per capita carbon emissions (Jackson 2009: 165). Why is this so?

There are several possible explanations. One reason may simply be that left-of-center regimes arise and survive in countries with relatively strong institutions. Effective state developmentalism, a feature of such regimes, depends on a moderately strong state apparatus. Thus, contemporary leftist governments, when they decide on sustainable development, can actually implement their environmental regulations and incentives. Moreover, with the growth of a middle class, the demand for such regulation normally grows (along with their consumption), according to the World Bank. Also where eco-tourism or luxury, beach-oriented tourism is a mainstay of the economy, as in Costa Rica and Mauritius, a pristine environment is a requirement. Thus, economic growth in some cases requires environmental rectitude.

Finally, in countries with large indigenous or peasant populations supporting leftist governments, deference to this base and its way of life may dictate attention to environmental concerns. Indigenous and peasant movements have been foremost environmental activists since the 1980s, opposing the construction of dams, mining projects, biomass extraction and what is commonly referred to as "land grabbing." Consequently, progressive governments in Bolivia and Ecuador, for instance, have embraced the notion of nature having rights. In Bolivia, the "Laws of Mother Earth" in 2011 assigned to nature "the right to continue vital cycles and processes free from human alterations." Ecuador amended its constitution about the same time to declare that nature had "the right to exist, persist, maintain and regenerate its vital cycles, structure, functions and its processes in evolution." Yet both governments face a difficult dilemma because their economies depend on environmentally destructive oil and mineral extraction for raising living standards and state revenue. Pragmatism sometimes trumps Mother Earth.

The Left has a comparatively good environmental record, but forestalling catastrophic climate change demands more from governments than simply ensuring greater efficiency in conducting business as usual. It necessitates the emergence of a new paradigm or vision that breaks with the high-growth, high-consumption model in favor of a new, austere paradigm aiming at sufficiency for all. It is unlikely that the drastic reductions in greenhouse gas emissions, which are clearly needed, can be achieved in the absence of such paradigmatic change. Yet such a paradigm is distant from current preoccupations in the Global South and in much of the Global North. That is why effectively confronting climate change means making the impossible possible.

Despite its current growth orientation, the Left may yet become a strong partner of green movements. The alternative paradigm, to have any chance of prevailing, must include equality and justice at its core, in addition to low growth and a leveling off of overall consumption. Not only will equity allow for an increased quality of life for the vast majority, but also without justice there is no cooperation and hence no solution to the climate conundrum. Justice refers to the equitable sharing of costs at both the global and national levels. The Left is well placed to handle this transition owing both to its critical stance vis-à-vis neoliberalism and capitalism, and its fundamental mooring in solidarity and equality values.

The latter are sorely needed. At the global level, a climate agreement must fairly allocate burdens to win acceptance. The negotiation of such an agreement depends on the rich countries bearing a heavier reduction in their carbon emissions than the populations of the Global South. As the Cochabamba Declaration of the World People's Conference on Climate Change noted in 2010, the Global North's payment of their "climate debt" is the only basis for a fair and effective solution (Ross 2013). The postindustrial countries are disproportionately responsible for generating the accumulated carbon emissions in the atmosphere; therefore, they should pay a disproportionate share of the costs of mitigating climate change (through deep cuts in greenhouse gas emissions) and adapting to the effects of climate change worldwide. Major reductions in the North would allow some space for further growth and poverty reduction in the developing world. A "climate Marshall Plan" will also be needed to direct substantial resources to the developing world to fund green initiatives (Newell and Paterson 2010: 175; see also Mathews 2011 and Roberts and Parks 2007: 62, 97). These initiatives would lead the way to low-carbon economies by financing projects that develop renewable energy sources, invest in energy and resource efficiency, and protect the forests (important carbon "sinks") and biodiversity. Without North–South equity, an international agreement to limit greenhouse gases is unlikely, and without such an agreement, the future is bleak.

But the Global South will also need, very soon, to rein in its growth to prevent a climatic disaster. China is already the world's largest source of greenhouse gas emissions, and India is not very far behind. A similar logic of equity applies domestically as globally. About one or two percent of the world's population of 7 billion (including perhaps 200 million Chinese) is responsible for half the world's emissions (Anderson 2012: 36). It will be necessary to curb the emissions of this small, but rich and powerful, group. Both social justice and ecological survival require a drastic decrease in conspicuous consumption and inequality. Inequality skews demand toward energy-intensive luxury goods – extensive air travel, large automobiles, air conditioning – rather than basic-needs goods. Catering to luxury tastes not only places heavy demands on the environment, but also further separates the rich from the poor (Greenhalgh 2005: 1,108). In addition, the appropriation by the rich of natural assets – arable land, choice residential areas, forests, fresh water, fossil fuels, and mines – drives the poor into marginal areas; this pattern both spreads environmental destruction in the Global South and guarantees that floods, heatwaves and droughts will lead to widespread death and devastation. Above all, vastly unequal societies are unlikely to exhibit the solidarity needed to forge a consensus around a new paradigm underpinning ecological sustainability. The wealthy can use their wealth to buffer themselves against certain environmental problems, such as environmental pollution, heat and the threat of such natural disasters as floods and droughts. And high inequality means that many people are poor – and thus exposed to environmental pollution, unhealthy living conditions, and climatic disasters. Social equity and environmental sustainability are thus interlinked (Meyer 2007: 49–50; Porritt 2005: 22).

In sum, technological fixes and institutional tinkering, together with business as usual, are unlikely to suffice. We either adapt to a finite world, or its finiteness forcefully adjusts us to its reality. If we are to find a way to adapt, the Left will probably play a major role despite its current productivist inclinations.

Concluding observations

This book has sought to unravel the meaning of the Left's experience in the vast regions of the Global South since the 1960s, with special attention to the era since 1980. Any exploration of such an important and vast topic is bound to be contentious. Some readers, especially those of a Marxist or radical-socialist viewpoint, may deplore the book's "reformism," contending that the enemy of the Left is capitalism, not neoliberalism. If this is so, the solution is socialism, not a short or long-term dalliance with a social-democratic form of capitalism. Yet other readers will consider the Left's project at the national and global levels, including that of the moderate social democrats, to be wholly impracticable, if not undesirable. For them, the neoliberal global order, for all its weaknesses, still provides the best hope for the future.

Despite these sharp differences, I hope that readers will conclude that we have much to learn from the experience of the Left in the Global South. If one accepts, in whole or in part, the diagnosis of neoliberalism offered in Chapter 3, one searches for remedies. The democratic Left, chastened by the false starts of the twentieth century, is devising new strategies at the local, national and global levels for building more equitable and secure societies. This study has identified both the pitfalls and the possibilities of the various approaches.

Whether or not one sympathizes with the Left, it is likely to play an increasingly important role in the Global South. The shortcomings of the current neoliberal world order are becoming ever more apparent, and the relative power of its Western stalwarts is waning. The inequality issue is rising to the fore in many societies, stoking widespread disaffection with the existing order. Political activism has been on the rise since 2010, sparked by demands for democracy, justice and dignity – the Arab Spring, mass protests in Chile, Brazil, Guatemala and Ecuador, anti-corruption and women's rights protests in India, anti-government protests throughout sub-Saharan Africa, and large-scale labor protests in South Africa (for details, refer to Biekart and Fowler 2013). Although these actions are not specifically Left-oriented, they do reflect a widespread anger with the way things are. Moreover, climate change is a wild card in the sense that its relentless onset will unmoor all ideological certainties. Solving the climate challenge – certainly a case of making the impossible possible – will require at least the end of neoliberalism and perhaps the end of capitalism itself. This era of change provides an opportunity to the Left.

Nonetheless, even if this is so, progressive paths are strewn with dilemmas and dangers. The first article of the Universal Declaration of Human Rights asserts an eminently reasonable principle: "all human beings are born free and equal in dignity and rights. They are endowed with reason and conscience and should act towards one another in a spirit of brotherhood." And yet this simple dictum is so difficult to realize – if equality is to include, as the Declaration and its International Covenants acknowledge, social and economic, in addition to civil and political, rights. The political striving for equal freedom brings to mind Max Weber's metaphor of politics as the strong and slow boring of hard boards. Weber's somber conclusion in "Politics as a Vocation" applies with full force to those whose vocation is leftist politics: "Only he has the calling for politics who is sure that he shall not crumble when the world from his point of view is too stupid or too base for what he wants to offer. Only he who in the face of all this can say 'In spite of all!' has the calling for politics." Karl Polanyi, whose work has inspired this book, similarly cautions that freedom will depend on a clear-headed recognition of "the reality of society" – of what is attainable in light of inherent dilemmas and limitations. Polanyi's final observation in *The Great Transformation* is of broader applicability: "life springs from ultimate resignation. Uncomplaining acceptance of the reality of society gives man indomitable courage and strength to remove all removable injustice and unfreedom." The proper response to the difficult dilemmas and ever-present dangers is not paralysis of the will, but acceptance and the bold exercise of creative political imagination.

NOTES

1. In the face of tyranny, revolution may be the only way to open the possibility of equal freedom and robust democracy. What matters is how politics is organized after the violent overthrow.
2. Some would deny that Chávez actually sought to make the impossible possible, claiming that personalism, fiery rhetoric, heavy state capitalism, experiments in participatory local institutions, and the redistribution mainly of oil revenues did not add up to a unique challenge to capitalism.
3. I borrow this last term from Alperovitz and Dubb (2013), which is a very interesting discussion of how a "pluralistic commonwealth" might be constructed in the United States.
4. Robert Putnam initially drew the distinction between bonding and bridging social capital. For an extended discussion, see Svendsen and Svendsen (2004), esp. p. 30.
5. For an assessment of the fall and rise of African cooperatives, see Wanyama, Develtere and Pollett (2009).
6. Elinor Ostrom (1990) famously challenged the "tragedy of the commons" thesis propounded by Garrett Hardin, which argued that only privatization would conserve natural resources because ownership rights conveyed an incentive for their sustainable use. Ostrom demonstrated, to the contrary, that local communities, under certain conditions, can govern themselves to manage and conserve a common resource.
7. Reportedly, two hundred thousand people in West Africa belong to these informal schemes. Groups with as few as 100 beneficiaries negotiate coverage with local health clinics for members who pay a small monthly premium. The overhead of these non-profit associations is very small.
8. For an assessment of participatory budgeting in Peru, see Vincent (2010).
9. "Success" is relative in such cases. By 2010, about 90 percent of the firms were still operating. However, the output of the worker-recovered companies had generally fallen to between 20–60 percent of that attained by the former capitalist firms (Sitrin 2012: 133, 136). They faced peculiar impediments, as I shall discuss. The more productive firms did produce sufficient revenues to pay their workers above-average wages.
10. Nearly three-quarters of the 221 worker-recovered companies that existed in 2010 had arisen in this period (Palomino et al. 2010: 256).
11. For an elaboration of the Marxist critique, see Lebowitz (2010: 68–9).
12. Refer in particular to my discussion of the global opportunity structure in Chapter 4.
13. I discussed the influence of these factors in chapters 2 and 4.
14. For an argument that capital controls do not represent a "new protectionism," see Gallagher (2012).
15. A dilemma that Meyer (2007: 184–5) explores in the context of social democracies in the Global North.
16. See, for an extended treatment, Held (2004); Stiglitz (2007); Sandbrook and Guven (2014: parts 3 and 4).

17. For a case study of how information and communications technology has underpinned an increasingly effective transnational unionism, see Lambert and Webster (2014).
18. A good survey of the climatic challenge in the context of multiple crises is Dag Hammarskjold Foundation (2012).
19. For instances in Brazil and Chile, see Zibechi (2011) and Zibechi (2009) respectively.

Bibliography

Abeyratne, Sirimal. 2004. "Economic Roots of Political Conflict: The Case of Sri Lanka." *The World Economy* 27(8): 1,295–314.

Abrams, Elliott. 1986. "Pluralism and Democracy." In Dov Ronen, ed., *Democracy and Pluralism in Africa*, 61–4. Boulder: Lynne Rienner.

Adaman, F., P. Devine and B. Ozkaynak. 2003. "Re-instituting the Economic Process: (Re)embedding the Economy in Society and Nature." *International Review of Sociology* 13(2): 357–74.

"Africa's Hopeful Economies: The Sun Shines Bright." 2011. *The Economist* 401 (8,762): 83–4.

Akhtar, Aasim Sajjad. 2005. "Are We Not a Working-Class Movement?" *Socialism and Democracy* 19(2): 133–46.

Allen, Emma and Sam Maghimi. 2009. "African Cooperatives and the Financial Crisis." Paper presented at the UNRISD Conference on the Social and Political Dimensions of the Global Crisis, Geneva, November 12–13.

Alperovitz, Gar and Steve Dubb. 2013. "The Possibility of a Pluralist Commonwealth and a Community-Sustaining Economy." *The Good Society* 22(1): 1–25.

Alvarado, Marino. 2010. "Venezuela: A Democracy with Authoritarian Traits." *Libertas: Rights and Democracy Newsletter* 20(1): 1, 3.

Amann, Edmund and Werner Baer. 2006. "Economic Orthodoxy versus Social Development? The Dilemma Facing Brazil's Labour Government." *Oxford Development Studies* 34(2): 219–41.

Amarante, Verónica, Marco Colafranceschi and Andrea Vigorito. 2011. "Uruguay's Income Inequality and Political Regimes during 1981–2010." WP2011/94, UNU – WIDER, Helsinki.

Ambersley, F. 1981. "Jamaica: The Demise of 'Democratic Socialism'." *New Left Review* (July/August): 76–87.

Anderson, Kevin. 2012. "Climate Change Going Beyond Dangerous – Brutal Numbers and Tenuous Hopes." *Development Dialogue: Climate, Development and Equity* 61: 16–40.

Anderson, Perry. 2011. "Lula's Brazil." *London Review of Books* 33(7): 3–12.

Andreasson, Stefan. 2010. *Africa's Development Impasse: Rethinking the Political Economy of Transformation*. London: Zed Books.

Andrews, Abigail. 2010. "Constructing Mutuality: The Zapatista Transformation of Transnational Activist Power Dynamics." *Latin American Politics and Society* 52(1): 89–120.

Anner, Mark. 2011. *Solidarity Transformed: Labor Responses to Globalization and Crisis in Latin America*. Ithaca, NY: Cornell University Press.

Arditi, Benjamin. 2010. "Arguments about the Left: A Post-Liberal Politics?" In Maxwell Cameron and Eric Hershberg, eds., *Latin America's Left Turns*, 145–67. Boulder: Lynne Rienner.

Azam, Jean-Paul. 2001. "The Redistributive State and Conflicts in Africa." *Journal of Peace Research* 38(4): 429–44.

Bacevich, Andrew J. 2008. *The Limits of Power: The End of American Exceptionalism*. New York: Henry Holt.

Baiocchi, Gianpaolo. 2005. *Militants and Citizens: The Politics of Participatory Democracy in Porto Alegre*. Stanford University Press.

Baiocchi, Gianpaolo and Claudia Teixeira. 2013. "Pardon the Inconvenience: We Are Changing the Country." *Boston Review* (June 26).

Baldwin, Peter. 1990. *The Politics of Social Solidarity: Class Basis of the European Welfare State, 1875–1975*. Cambridge University Press.

Baran, Paul. 1957. *The Political Economy of Growth*. New York: Monthly Review Press.

Barmeyer, Niels. 2008. "Taking on the State: Resistance, Education, and Other Challenges Facing the Zapatista Autonomy Project." *Identities* 15: 506–27.

Barrientos, Armando and David Hulme. 2009. "Social Protection for the Poor and the Poorest in Developing Countries: Reflections on a Quiet Revolution." *Oxford Development Studies* 37(4): 439–56.

Barrientos, Armando, Valerie Moller, João Saboia, Peter Lloyd-Sherlock and Julia Mase. 2013. "Growing Social Protection in Developing Countries: Lessons from Brazil and South Africa." *Development Southern Africa* 30(1): 54–68.

Barros Silva, P. L., J. Carlos de Souza Braga and V. L. C. Costa. 2010. "The Difficult Combination of Stability and Development in Brazil." In Kurt Weyland, Raúl Madrid and Wendy Hunter, eds., *Leftist Governments in Latin America*, 124–39. New York: Cambridge University Press.

Bauman, Zygmunt. 1967. "The Limitations of 'Perfect Planning'." In Bertram Gross, ed., *Action under Planning*, 513–24. New York: McGraw-Hill.

Baumann, Brittany and Kevin Gallagher. 2012. "Navigating Capital Flows in Brazil and Chile." Working Paper, Initiative for Policy Dialogue, Columbia University, New York (June).

BBC. 2011. "Venezuela President Hugo Chávez in Middle Class Appeal." BBC News, Latin America and Caribbean (July 29). Access at www.bbc.co.uk/news/world-latin-america-143r1508

Beckerman, Wilfred. 1995. *Small Is Stupid: Blowing the Whistle on the Greens*. London: Duckworth.

Bell, Daniel. 2009. "Communitarianism." Stanford Encyclopedia of Philosophy 27. Accessed at http://plato.stanford.edu/entries/communitarianism

Bello, Walden. 2008. "Can Capitalism Survive Climate Change?" *Foreign Policy in Focus*. Washington, DC. April 1. Accessed at www.fpif.org/fpiftxt/5114

Benería, Lourdes. 1999. "Globalization, Gender and the Davos Man." *Feminist Economics* 5(3): 61–83.

Beresford, Alexander. 2012. "Organized Labour and the Politics of Class Formation in Post-Apartheid South Africa." *Review of African Political Economy* 39(134): 569–89.

Berman, Marshall. 1982. *All That Is Solid Melts into Air*. New York: Simon & Schuster.

Berman, Sheri. 2006. *The Primacy of Politics: Social Democracy and the Making of Europe's Twentieth Century*. Cambridge University Press.

Bernard, Tanguy, Marie-Hélene Collion, Alain de Janvry, Pierre Rondot and Elisabeth Sadoulet. 2008. "Do Village Organizations Make a Difference in African Rural Development? A Study of Senegal and Burkina Faso." *World Development* 36(11): 2,188–204.

Berner, Erhard and Benedict Phillips. 2005. "Left to their Own Devices? Community Self-Help between Alternative Development and Neo-liberalism." *Community Development Journal* 40(1): 17–29.

Bernstein, Eduard. 1961 [1909]. *Evolutionary Socialism: A Criticism and Affirmation*. New York: Schocken Books.

Berry, Albert. 2014. "The Economics of Globalization: Making Sense of the Conflicting Claims." In Richard Sandbrook and Ali Burak Guven, eds., *Civilizing Globalization: A Survival Guide*. Revised edn. Albany: SUNY Press.

Biekart, Kees and Alan Fowler. 2013. "Transforming Activism 2010+: Exploring Ways and Means." *Development and Change* 44(3): 527–46.

Bieling, Hans-Jurgen. 2007. "The Other Side of the Coin: Conceptualizing the Relationship between Business and the State in the Age of Globalization." *Business and Politics* 3, article 5, 20pp.

Bienefeld, Manfred. 1977. "Trade Unions and Peripheral Capitalism: The Case of Tanzania." Discussion Paper 112, Institute for Development Studies, Sussex (June).

Birdsall, Nancy. 2005. "Rising Inequality in the New Global Economy." 2005 WIDER Annual Lecture, World Institute for Development Economics Research, Helsinki.

Birdsall, Nancy and Francis Fukuyama. 2011. "The Post-Washington Consensus: Development after the Crisis." *Foreign Affairs* 90(2): 45–53.

Birdsall, Nancy, Nora Lustig and Darryl McLeod. 2010. "Declining Inequality in Latin America; Some Economics, Some Politics," Working Paper No. 251, Center for Global Development, Washington, DC (May).

Block, Fred 2003. "Karl Polanyi and the Writing of the Great Transformation." *Theory and Society* 32: 275–306.

Block, Fred and Margaret Somers. 1984. "Beyond the Economistic Fallacy: The Holistic Social Science of Karl Polanyi." In Theda Skocpol, ed., *Vision and Method in Historical Sociology*, 47–84. New York: Cambridge University Press.

Boo, Katharine. 2012. *Behind the Beautiful Forevers: Life, Death and Hope in a Mumbai Undercity*. New York: Random House.

Booth, David. 2011. "Working with the Grain? The African Power and Politics Programme." *Institute for Development Studies Bulletin* 42(2): 1–10.

Booth, David and Frederick Golooba-Mutebi. 2011. "Developmental Patrimonialism? The Case of Rwanda." African Power and Politics Programme, Overseas Development Institute, London (March).

Booyens, Margie and Elsa Crause. 2009. "Lessons from Andiamu, Malawi on Grassroots Development." *Development Southern Africa* 261: 157–70.

Bowles, Samuel. 1991. "What Markets Can and Cannot Do." *Challenge* 34(1): 11–16.

Bowles, Samuel and Ugo Pangano. 2006. "Economic Integration, Cultural Standardization and the Politics of Social Insurance." In Pranab Bardhan, Samuel Bowles and Michael Wallerstein, eds., *Globalization and Egalitarian Redistribution*, 289–305. Princeton University Press.

Brass, Tom. 2005. "Neoliberalism and the Rise of (Peasant) Nations within the Nation: Chiapas in Comparative and Theoretical Perspective." *Journal of Peasant Studies* 32(3/4): 651–91.

Briggs, J. 1979. "Villagization and the 1974–76 Economic Crisis in Tanzania." *Journal of Modern African Studies* 17(4): 695–702.

Brinkerhoff, D. W. 2000. "Democratic Governance and Sectoral Reform: Tracing Linkages and Exploring Synergies." *World Development* 28(4): 601–15.

Broad, Robin. 2006. "Research, Knowledge, and the Art of 'Paradigm Maintenance': The World Bank's Development Economics Vice-Presidency." *Review of International Political Economy* 13(3): 387–419.

Brooks, David. 2011. *The Social Animal: The Hidden Sources of Love, Character and Achievement*. New York: Random House.

Brown, Lester R. 2009. *Plan B 4.0: Mobilizing to Save Civilization*. New York: W. W. Norton.

Burbach, Roger, Michael Fox, and Federico Fuentes. 2013. *Latin America's Turbulent Transitions: The Future of 21st Century Socialism*. London: Zed Books.

Burger, Ronelle Caryn Bredenkamp, Christelle Grobler and Servaas van der Berg 2012. "Have Public Health Spending and Access in South Africa Become More Equitable since the End of Apartheid?" *Development Southern Africa* 29(5): 681–703.

Burke, Marshall B., Edward Miguel, Shankar Satyanath, John Dykema and David Lobell. 2009. "Warming Increases the Risk of Civil Wars in Africa." *Proceedings of the National Academy of Sciences of the United States*. Accessed at www.pnas.org/content/106/49/20670.full

Bussmann, M., G. Schneider and N. Wiesehomeier. 2005. "For Economic Liberalisation and Peace: The Case of Sub-Saharan Africa." *European Journal of International Relations* 11(4): 551–79.

Buttel, F. H. 2000. "Ecological Modernization as a Social Theory." *Geoforum* 31(1): 57–65.

Cameron, Maxwell. 2009. "Latin America's Left Turn: Beyond Good and Bad." *Third World Quarterly* 302: 331–48.

Cammack, Paul. 1997. "Cardoso's Political Project in Brazil: The Limits of Social Democracy." In Leo Panitch, ed., *The Socialist Register 1997*, 223–44. New Jersey: Humanities Press.

2012. "The G20, the Crisis, and the Rise of Global Developmental Liberalism." *Third World Quarterly* 33(1): 1–16.

Camp, Roderick. 2009. "Democracy through Latin American Lenses." In his *Citizen Views of Democracy in Latin America*. University of Pittsburg Press.

Canel, Eduardo. 2010. *Barrio Democracy in Latin America: Participatory Decentralization and Community Activism in Montevideo.* University Park: Pennsylvania State University Press.

Cardoso, Fernando Henrique. 1986. "Entrepreneurs and the Transition Process: The Brazilian Case." In Guillermo O'Donnell, Philippe Schmitter and Laurence Whitehead, eds., *Transitions from Authoritarian Rule: Comparative Perspectives,* 137–53. Baltimore: Johns Hopkins University Press.

2009. "New Paths: Globalization in Historical Perspective." *Studies in Comparative International Development* 44(4): 296–317.

Cardoso, Fernando Henrique and Enzo Faletto. 1979. *Dependency and Development in Latin America.* Trans. Mariory Mattingly Urquidi. Berkeley: University of California Press.

Carroll, Kate. 2011. "Addressing Inequality: Framing Social Protection in National Development Strategies." *IDS Bulletin* 42(6): 89–95.

Carroll, William and Jean Philippe Sapinski. 2010. "The Global Corporate Elite and the Transnational Policy-Planning Network, 1996–2006." *International Sociology* 25(4): 501–38.

Casebeer, William D. 2008. "The Stories Markets Tell." In Paul J. Zack, ed., *Moral Markets: The Critical Role of Values in the Economy,* 1–15. Princeton University Press.

Castellani, Francesca and Gwenn Parent. 2010. "Being 'Middle Class' in Latin America." Working Paper 305, Latin America Research Area, Organization of Economic Cooperation and Development, Paris.

Cessou, Sabine. 2013. "South Africa's New Apartheid." *Le Monde Diplomatique* (March): 10–11.

Chattopadhyay, Paresh. 2010. "The Myth of Twentieth Century Socialism and the Continuing Relevance of Karl Marx." *Socialism and Democracy* 24(3): 23–45.

Chen, Shaohua and Martin Ravallion. 2007. "Absolute Poverty Measures for the Developing World, 1981–2004." *Proceedings of the US National Academy of Sciences* 104(43): 16,757–62.

Christiaensen, L., L. Demery and S. Paternostro. 2002. *Growth, Distribution and Poverty in Africa.* Washington, DC: World Bank.

Clapham, Christopher. 1988. *Transformation and Continuity in Revolutionary Ethiopia.* Cambridge University Press.

1989. "State and Revolution in Ethiopia." *Review of African Political Economy* 16 (4): 5–17.

Clark, W. Edmund. 1978. *Socialist Development and Public Investment in Tanzania, 1964–73.* University of Toronto Press.

Cline, William. 2002. "Financial Crises and Poverty in Emerging Market Economies." Working Paper 8, Center for Global Development, Washington, DC.

Colburn, Forest and Dessalegn Rahmato. 1992. "Rethinking Socialism in the Third World." *Third World Quarterly* 13(1): 159–73.

Colley, Chris. 2009. "China's Reforms at Thirty and the 'Beijing Consensus.'" *Pambazuka News* 417 (January 31). Accessed at www.pambazuka.org/en/

Comaroff, Jean. 2011. "Populism and Late Liberalism." *Annals, American Academy of Political and Social Sciences* 637: 99–111.

Commission for Africa. 2005. *Our Common Interest: Report of the Commission for Africa*. London: Commission for Africa.

Conaghan, Catherine. 2011. "Ecuador: Rafael Correa and the Citizens' Revolution." In Steven Levitsky and Kenneth Roberts, eds., *The Resurgence of Latin America's Left*, 260–82. Baltimore: Johns Hopkins University Press.

Cornia, Giovanni and John Court. 2001. "Inequality, Growth and Poverty in the Era of Liberalization and Globalization." Policy Brief 4, World Institute for Development Economics Research, Helsinki.

Cornia, Giovanni and Bruno Martorano. 2009. "External Shocks, Policy Changes and Income Distribution: Latin America during the Last Decade." Kiel Institute for the World Economy, Kiel University, Germany (July 20).

Cornia, Giovanni, Tony Addison and S. Kushi 2004. "Income Distribution Changes and Their Impact in the Post-Second World War Period." In G. A. Cornia, ed., *Inequality, Growth and Poverty in an Era of Liberalization and Globalization*. Oxford University Press.

Cornwall, Andrea and Karen Brock. 2005. "What Do Buzzwords Do for Development Policy? A Critical Look at 'Participation', 'Empowerment' and 'Poverty Reduction.'" *Third World Quarterly* 26(7): 1,043–60.

Corrales, Javier. 2010. "The Repeating Revolution: Chávez's New Politics and Old Economics." In Burt Weyland, Raúl Madrid and Wendy Hunter, eds., *Leftist Governments in Latin America*, 28–56. New York: Cambridge University Press.

Cotarelo, Ramón. 2005. "Los Orígenes Literarios del Neoliberalismo." *Sistema* 186 (May): 45–52.

Craig, David and Douglas Porter. 2006. *Development beyond Neoliberalism? Governance, Poverty Reduction and Political Economy*. London: Routledge.

Crawford, Beverly. 1998. "The Causes of Cultural Conflict: An Institutional Approach." In Beverly Crawford and R. D. Lipschutz, eds., *The Myth of "Ethnic Conflict,"* 3–43. Berkeley: International and Area Studies, University of California.

Crouch, Colin. 2005. "Models of Capitalism." *New Political Economy* 10(4): 439–56.

Cruces, Guillermo and Luis Diego Battistón. 2011. "Down and Out or Up and In? Polarization-based Measures of the Middle Class for Latin America." Working Paper 113, Centro de Estudios Distributivos, Laborales y Socialies, Buenos Aires.

Cruces, Guillermos and Marcelo Bérgola. 2013. "Informality and Contributory Programs: Recent Reforms of the Social Protection System in Uruguay." *Development Policy Review* 31(5): 531–51.

Cunha Filho, Clayton and Rodrigo Santaella Gonçalves. 2010. "The National Development Plan as a Political Economic Strategy in Evo Morale's Bolivia." Trans. Ariane Dalla Déa. *Latin American Perspectives* 37(4): 177–96.

Cunningham, Frank. 1987. *Democratic Theory and Socialism*. Cambridge University Press.

2001. "Whose Socialism? Whose Democracy?" In Michael Howard, ed., *Socialism*, 263–80. New York: Humanities Books.

2005. "Market Economies and Market Societies." *Journal of Social Philosophy* 36(2): 129–42.

Cunningham, Susan. 1999. "Made in Brazil: Cardoso's Critical Path from Dependency via Neoliberal Options and the Third Way in the 1990s." *European Review of Latin America and Caribbean Studies* 67: 75–86.

Cupples, Julie and Irving Larios. 2010. "A Functional Anarchy: Love, Patriotism and Resistance to Free Trade in Costa Rica." *Latin American Perspectives* 37 (6): 93–108.

Dag Hammarskjold Foundation. 2012. "Climate, Development and Equity." *Development Dialogue* 61.

Dagnino, Eveline. 2008. "Challenges to Participation, Citizenship and Democracy: Perverse Confluence and Displacement of Meaning." In A. Bebbington, S. Hickey and D. Mitlin, eds., *Can NGOs Make a Difference? The Challenge of Development Alternatives*, 55–70. London: Zed Books.

Dale, Gareth. 2010a. *Karl Polanyi: The Limits of the Market*. Cambridge: Polity.

2010b. "Social Democracy, Embeddedness and Decommodification: On the Conceptual Innovations and Intellectual Affiliations of Karl Polanyi." *New Political Economy* 15(3): 369–93.

Daly, Herman. 1991. *Steady-State Economics*. Washington, DC: Island Press.

2007. *Ecological Economics and Sustainable Development*. Cheltenham (UK): Edward Elgar.

Davis, Mike. 2006. *Planet of Slums*. New York: Verso.

Deacon, Bob and Shana Cohen. 2011. "From the Global Politics of Poverty Alleviation to the Global Politics of Solidarity." *Global Social Policy* 11(1–2): 233–48.

De Beus, Jos and Tom Koelble. 2001. "Third Way Diffusion of Social Democracy: Western Europe and South Africa." *Politikon* 28(2): 181–94.

Decalo, Samuel. 1979. "Ideological Rhetoric and Scientific Socialism in Benin and Congo (Brazzaville)." In Carl Rosberg and Thomas Callaghy, eds., *Socialism in Sub-Saharan Africa*, 231–64. Berkeley: Institute for International Studies, University of California, Berkeley.

de Haan, Arjan. 2010. "Will China Change International Development as We Know It?" *Journal of International Development*. Published online on July 28, DOI:10.1002/jid.1732.

de la Torre, Carlos. 2007. "The Resurgence of Radical Populism in Latin America." *Constellations* 14(3): 384–97.

Demombynes, G. and B. Ozler. 2006. "Crime and Local Inequality in South Africa." *Journal of Development Economics* 76(2): 265–92.

Devine, Pat. 1992. "Market Socialism or Participatory Planning?" *Review of Radical Political Economics* 24(3/4): 67–89.

DeYoung, Karen and Greg Jaffe. 2010. "US 'Secret War' Expands Globally as Special Operations Forces Take a Larger Role." *Washington Post* (June 4).

Diamond, Larry, Juan Linz and Seymour Martin Lipset. 1988. "Introduction." In their *Democracy in Developing Societies: Africa*. Boulder: Lynne Rienner.

Dornbusch, Rudiger and Sebastian Edwards. 1990. *The Macroeconomics of Populism in Latin America*. University of Chicago Press.

Dorrien, Gary. 2010. "Michael Harrington and the 'Left-wing of the Possible.'" *CrossCurrents* 60(2): 257–82.

Duclos, J. and A. Verdier-Chouchane. 2011. "Analyzing Pro-Poor Growth in South African and Mauritius." *African Development Review* 23(2): 121–46.

Duggan, Lisa. 2003. *The Twilight of Equality? Neoliberalism, Cultural Politics and the Attack on Democracy*. Boston: Beacon Press.

Dumbrell, John. 2010. "American Power: Crisis or Renewal." *Politics* 30 (December): 15–23.

Easterly, William 2001. "The Lost Decades: Developing Countries' Stagnation in Spite of Policy Reform 1980–98," *Journal of Economic Growth* 6: 135–57.

Ebner, Alexander. 2011. "Transnational Markets and the Polanyi Problem." In Christian Calhoun and Josef Falke, eds., *Karl Polanyi: The Potential of Law in Transnational Markets*, 19–41. Oxford: Hart.

Economic Commission for Latin America and the Caribbean (CEPAL). 2011. *Statistical Yearbook for Latin America and the Caribbean*. Santiago: CEPAL.

Economist Intelligence Unit. 2011. "Asian Economy: Consumers to the Rescue?" *ViewsWire* (August 25).

Edward, P. 2005. "Examining Inequality: Who Really Benefits from Global Growth?" *World Development* 34(10): 1,667–95.

Ellner, Steve. 2003. "Introduction: The Search for Explanations." In Steve Ellner and Daniel Hellinger, eds., *Venezuelan Politics in the Chávez Period*, 7–26. Boulder: Lynne Rienner.

2008. *Rethinking Venezuelan Politics: Class Conflict and the Chávez Phenomenon*. Boulder: Lynne Rienner.

2010a. "The Perennial Debate over Socialist Goals Played Out in Venezuela." *Science and Society* 74(1): 63–84.

2010b. "Hugo Chávez's First Decade in Office." *Latin American Perspectives* 37(1): 77–96.

2011. "Venezuela's Social-Based Democratic Model: Innovation and Limitations." *Journal of Latin American Studies* 43: 421–49.

2012a. "The Distinguishing Features of Latin America's New Left in Power: the Chávez, Morales and Correa Governments." *Latin American Perspectives* 39(1): 96–114.

2012b. "The Chávez Election." *Le Monde Diplomatique* (September): 4–5.

Ellwood, Wayne. 2010. "Economic Growth is a Path to Perdition, National Prosperity." *Canadian Centre for Policy Alternatives Monitor* 17(5): 20–1.

Esping-Anderson, Gosta. 1990. *The Three Worlds of Welfare Capitalism*. Princeton University Press.

Evans, Peter 1995. *Embedded Autonomy: States and Industrial Transformation*. Princeton University Press.

2008. "Is an Alternative Globalization Possible?" *Politics and Society* 36(2): 271–305.

2009. "From Situations of Dependency to Globalized Social Democracy." *Studies in Comparative International Development* 44(4): 318–36.

2014. "Constructing Counter-Hegemonic Globalization: Braiding Mobilizations and Linking Levels." In Richard Sandbrook and Ali Burak Guven, *Civilizing Globalization: A Survival Guide*. Revised edn. Albany: SUNY Press.

Evans, W. T. 2008. "Counter-Hegemony at Work: Resistance, Contradiction and Emergent Culture inside a Worker-Occupied Hotel." *Berkeley Journal of Sociology* 51: 33–88.

Faber, Malte, Thomas Pedersen and Johannes Schiller 2002. "Homo Oeconomicus and Homo Politicus in Ecological Economics." *Ecological Economics* 40: 323–33.

Farias, Flávio Bezerra. 2003. "Na Direção de Uma Nova Economia: Para a Crítica ao Social-liberalismo Brasileiro." *Outubro* 9: 91–112.

Faux, Jeff. 2004. "Without Consent: Global Capital Mobility and Democracy." *Dissent* (Winter): 43–50.

Fernandez, Adriela and Marisol Vera. 2012. "The Bachelet Presidency and the End of Chile's Concertación Era." *Latin American Perspectives* 39(4): 5–18.

Ferreira, Francisco and Branko Milanovic. 2009. "Knowledge in Development Notes: Global Inequalities." World Bank. http://go.worldbank.org/97H7X37SLO

Field, Alexander J. 2004. *Altruistically Inclined? The Behavioral Sciences, Evolutionary Theory and the Origin of Reciprocity*. Ann Arbor: University of Michigan Press.

Fine, Ben. 2001. "Neither the Washington nor the Post-Washington Consensus." In B. Fine, C. Lapavitsas and J. Pincus, eds., *Development Policy in the Twenty-First Century: Beyond the Post Washington Consensus*, 1–27. London: Routledge.

  2012. "Assessing South Africa's New Growth Path: Framework for Change?" *Review of African Political Economy* 39(134): 551–68.

Finlayson, A. C. et al. 2005. "The 'Invisible Hand': Neoclassical Economics and the Ordering of Society." *Critical Sociology* 21(4): 515–36.

Finn, Janet. 2006. "La Victoria Comprometida: Reflections on Neoliberalism from a Santiago Población." *Research in Economic Anthropology* 24: 207–39.

FitzGerald, Valpy. 2002. "Global Linkages, Vulnerable Economies and the Outbreak of Conflict." In E. Wayne Nafziger and R. Vayrenen, eds., *Prevention of Humanitarian Emergencies*, 62–84. Houndmills, Basingstoke: Palgrave-Macmillan.

Folbre, Nancy. 2001. *The Invisible Heart: Economics and Family Values*. New York: The Free Press.

Fox, Michael. 2008. "Port Alegre's Participatory Budgeting at a Crossroads." *NACLA: Knowledge Beyond Borders* (April 11). Accessed at http://nacla.org/print/4566

Franzoni, Martínez Juliana and Diego Sánchez-Ancochea. 2013. *Good Jobs and Social Services: How Costa Rica Achieved the Elusive Double Incorporation*. London: Palgrave-Macmillan.

Fraser, Nancy. 2011. "Marketization, Social Protection, Emancipation: Towards a Neo-Polanyian Conception of Capitalist Crisis." In Craig Calhoun and G. Derlugian, eds., *Business as Usual: The Roots of the Global Financial Meltdown*. 135–57. New York University Press.

Fried, Brian. 2012. "Distributive Politics and Conditional Cash Transfers: The Case of Brazil's *Bolsa Família*." *World Development* 40(5): 1,042–53.

Friedman, Milton. 1953. "The Methodology of Positive Economics." In his *Essays in Positive Economics*. University of Chicago Press.

  1962. *Capitalism and Freedom*. University of Chicago Press.

Friedman, Milton and Rose Friedman. 1960. *Free to Choose: A Personal Statement*. New York: Harcourt Brace Jovanovich.

Fukuyama, Francis. 1992. *The End of History and the Last Man*. New York: The Free Press.

Fulong Wu. 2008. "China's Great Transformation: Neoliberalization as Establishing a Market Society." *Geoforum* 19(3): 1,096.

Fund for Peace. 2010. "Failed States Index Scores 2010." Accessed at www.fundfor peace.org/web/

Gabetta, Carlos. 2002. "Argentina: IMF's Show State Revolts." *Le Monde Diplomatique* (January).

Gallagher, John and Ronald Robinson. 1953. "The Imperialism of Free Trade." *Economic History Review* 6(1): 1–15.

Gallagher, Kevin. 2009. "NAFTA and the Environment: Lessons from Mexico and Beyond." Pardee Center Task Force on the Future of North American Trade Policy, Report 1 (November).

2011. "The End of the 'Washington Consensus.'" *The Guardian* (March 7). www.guardian.co.uk/commentisfree/cifamerica/2011/mar07/china-usa/

2012. "The Myth of Financial Protectionism: The New (and Old) Economics of Capital Controls." Working Paper 278. Political Economy Research Institute, University of Massachusetts, Amherst (January).

Garrett, Geoffrey. 2003. "Global Markets and National Politics." In David Held and Anthony McGrew, eds., *The Global Transformations Reader*. 2nd edn., Cambridge: Polity Press.

Gasparini, L., G. Cruces, L. Tornarolli and M. Marchionni. 2009. "A Turning Point? Recent Developments in Inequality in Latin America and the Caribbean." Working Paper 81, Centro de Estudios Distributivos Laborales y Sociales, Universidad Nacional de la Plata, Buenos Aires.

Gentle, Leonard. 2013. "A Week in August." *South African Civil Society Information Service* (September 2). Accessed at sacsis.org.za/site/article/1771

Ghosh, Jayati. 2010. "Global Crisis and Beyond; Sustainable Growth Trajectories for the Developing World." *International Labour Review* 149(2): 210–25.

Giarracca, N. and M. Teubal. 2004. "Neoliberal Collapse and Social Protest in Argentina." In J. Demmers, A. Fernández Jilberto and B. Hogenboom, eds., *Good Governance in the Era of Global Neoliberalism*, 66–90. London: Routledge.

Gibbes, Cerian and Eric Keys. 2010. "The Illusion of Equity: An Examination of Community Based Natural Resource Management and Inequality in Africa." *Geography Compass* 4(9): 1,324–38.

Giddens, Anthony. 2000. *The Third Way and Its Critics*. Cambridge: Polity Press.

Gillespie, Wayne. 2006. "Capitalist World Economy, Globalization and Violence: Implications for Criminology and Social Justice." *International Criminal Justice Review* 16(1): 24–44.

Gintis, Herbert. 2000. "Beyond Homo Economicus: Evidence from Experimental Economics." *Ecological Economics* 353: 311–22.

Gintis, Herbert and Rakesh Khurana. 2008. "Corporate Honesty and Business Education: A Behavioral Model." In Paul Zack, ed., *Moral Markets: The Critical Role of Values in the Economy*, 300–27. Princeton University Press.

Gledhill, John. 2006. "Resisting the Global Slums: Politics, Religion and Consumption in the Remaking of Life Worlds in the 21st Century." *Bulletin of Latin American Research* 25(3): 322–39.

Goering, Laurie. 2011. "World Not Prepared for Climate Conflicts – Security Experts." AlertNet – A Thomson Reuters Foundation Service (April 28). Accessed at www.trust.org/alertnet/news/

Goldfrank, Benjamin. 2011. "The Left and Participatory Democracy." In Steven Levitsky and Kenneth Roberts, eds., *The Resurgence of the Latin American Left*, 162–83. Baltimore: Johns Hopkins University Press.

Goldman, Michael. 2004. "Eco-governmentality and Other Transnational Practices of a 'Green' World Bank." In Richard Peet and Michael Watts, eds., *Liberation Ecologies: Environment, Development, Social Movements*. 2nd edn., 166–92. New York: Routledge.

Golub, Philip. 2013. "From the New International Economic Order to the G20: How the Global South is Restructuring World Capitalism from Within." *Third World Quarterly* 34(6): 1,000–15.

Gómez Calcaño, Luis. 1993. "Venezuelan Social Democracy: From Populism to Pragmatism." In Menno Vellinga, ed., *Social Democracy in Latin America*, 186–201. Boulder: Westview.

González Bustelo, Mabel. 2008. "Climate Change: A New Source of Armed Conflict." Safe Democracy Foundation (July 8). Accessed at http://english.safe-democracy.org/2008/07/88/

Gore, Charles. 2000. "The Rise and Fall of the Washington Consensus as a Paradigm for Developing Countries." *World Development* 28(5): 789–804.

Gore, Charles and Zeljka Kozul-Wright. 2011. "An Overview of UNCTAD's Least Development Countries Report 2010: Toward a New International Development Architecture." *European Journal of Development Research* 23 (1): 3–11.

Gott, Richard. 2008. "Venezuela under Hugo Chávez: The Originality of the 'Bolivarian' Project." *New Political Economy* 13(4): 475–90.

Gould, Carol. 1988. *Rethinking Democracy: Freedom and Social Cooperation in Politics, Economy and Society*. New York: Cambridge University Press.

Gould, Kenneth, David Pellow and Alan Schnaiberg. 2008. *The Treadmill of Production: Injustice and Unsustainability in the Global Economy*. Boulder: Paradigm.

Goulet, Denis. 1979. "Development as Liberation: Policy Lessons from Case Studies." *World Development* 7(6): 555–66.

Gramsci, Antonio. 1971. *Selections from the Prison Notebooks*. Ed. Quintin Hoare and Geoffrey Smith. New York: International Publishers.

Green, Reginald. 1983. "'No Worst There Is None:' Tanzania's Political Economic Crises, 1978–????" In Jerker Carlsson, ed., *Recession in Africa*. Uppsala: Scandinavia Institute of African Studies.

Greenfield, Patricia. 2009. "Linking Social Change and Developmental Change: Shifting Pathways of Human Development." *Developmental Psychology* 45(2): 401–18.

Greenhalgh, C. 2005. "Why Does Market Capitalism Fail to Deliver a Sustainable Environment and Greater Equality of Incomes?" *Cambridge Journal of Economics* 29: 1,091–109.

Grun, Carola and Kenneth Harttgen. 2009. "An Assessment of South Africa's Reform Post-Apartheid for Education and Mobility." Background Paper for the Education for All Meeting Report, document 2010/ED/EFA//MRT/PI/02

Guerreiro, Osório and Pedro Ferreiro de Souza. 2013. "*Bolsa Família* after *Brasil Carinhoso.*" Research Brief 41, International Policy Centre for Inclusive Growth, Brazilia (March).

Guven, Ali Burak. 2012. "The IMF, the World Bank and the Global Economic Crisis: Exploring Paradigm Continuity." *Development and Change* 43(4): 869–98.

Habel, Janette. 2013. "We Want a Different Brazil." *Le Monde Diplomatique* (July): 4.

Hahnel, Robin. 2005. *Economic Justice and Democracy: From Competition to Cooperation.* New York: Routledge.

2007. "The Case against Markets." *Journal of Economic Issues* 41(4): 1,139–59.

Hailu, Degal. 2009. "Is the Washington Consensus Dead?" Working Paper 82, International Policy Centre for Inclusive Growth, United Nations Development Programme, Brasilia (April).

Hall, Peter. 1993. "Policy Paradigms, Social Learning and the State: The Case of Economic Planning in Britain." *Comparative Politics* 25(3): 275–96.

Hancock, John. 2011. "The Capitalist Revolution." *Literary Review of Canada* 19(10): 3–6.

Hanson, Margaret and James Hentz. 1999. "Neocolonialism and Neoliberalism in South Africa and Zambia." *Political Science Quarterly* 114(3): 479–502.

Harbom, Lotta and Peter Wallensteen. 2009. "Armed Conflicts, 1946–2008." *Journal of Peace Research* 46(4): 577–87.

Harmer, Tanya. 2011. *Allende's Chile and the Inter-American Cold War.* Chapel Hill: University of North Carolina Press.

Harnecker, Marta. 2010. "Latin America and 21st Century Socialism: Inventing to Avoid Mistakes." *Monthly Review* 62(3): 3–83.

2013. "Chávez's Chief Legacy: Building, with People, an Alternative Society to Capitalism." *MRZINE* (March 6). Accessed at: mrzine.monthlyreview.org/2013/harnecker060313.html

Harper, Peter. 2000. "The End in Sight? Some Speculations on Environmental Trends in the Twenty-first Century." *Futures* 32(2/3): 361–84.

Harrington, Michael. 1972. *Socialism.* New York: Bantam Books.

Harvey, Blane and Jonathan Langdon. 2010. "Re-imagining Capacity and Collective Change: Experiences from Senegal and Ghana." *IDS Bulletin* 41(3): 79–86.

Harvey, David. 1998. "Marxism, Metaphors and Ecological Politics." *Monthly Review* 49(11): 17–31.

2005. *A Brief History of Neoliberalism.* Oxford University Press.

Hawken, Paul, A. Lovine and L. H. Lovine. 1999. *Natural Capitalism: The Next Industrial Revolution.* London: Earthscan.

Hawkins, Kirk. 2003. "Populism in Venezuela." *Third World Quarterly* 24(6): 1,137–60.

Hejeebu, Santhi and Deidre McCloskey. 1999. "The Reproving of Karl Polanyi." *Critical Review* 13(3/4): 285–314.

Held, David. 2004. *Global Covenant: The Social Democratic Alternative to the Washington Consensus.* Cambridge: Polity Press.

Heller, Patrick. 1999. *The Labor of Development: Workers and the Transformation of Capitalism in Kerala, India*. Ithaca, NY: Cornell University Press.

2012. "Movement, Politics and Democracy: Kerala in Comparative Perspective." In Atul Kohli and Prerna Singh, eds., *Routledge Handbook of Indian Politics*. New York: Routledge.

Hellman, Joel. 1998. "Winners Take All: The Politics of Partial Reform in Postcommunist Transitions." *World Politics* 50(2): 203–34.

Hellsten, Sirkku. 2004. "Human Rights in Africa: From Communitarian to Utilitarian Practice." *Human Rights Review* 5(2): 61–85.

Hettne, Bjorn. 1994. "The Future of Development Studies." *Forum for Development Studies* 1–2: 41–71.

Hibou, Beatrice. 1999. "The 'Social Capital' of the State as an Agent of Deception." In Jean-François Bayart, Stephen Ellis and Beatrice Hibou, *The Criminalization of the State in Africa*. Chapter 4. Oxford: James Currey.

Hickey, Sam. 2010. "The Government of Chronic Poverty: from Exclusion to Citizenship." *Journal of Development Studies* 46(7): 1,139–55.

Hindmoor, Andrew. 2010. "'Major Combat Operations Have Ended?' Arguing about Rational Choice." *British Journal of Political Science* 41(1): 191–210.

Hirschman, Albert O. 1973. "The Changing Tolerance for Income Inequality in the Course of Economic Development." *Quarterly Journal of Economics* 87(3): 544–65.

Hoaglan, Jim. 1998. "Financial Community Contributed to the Mess, Too." *International Herald-Tribune* (January 10–11).

Hochstetler, Kathryn and Alfred Montero. 2013. "The Renewed Developmental State: The National Development Bank and the Brazil Model." *Journal of Development Studies* 49(11): 1,484–99.

Holmstrom, Nancy and Richard Smith. 2000. "The Necessity of Gangster Capitalism: Primitive Accumulation in Russia and China." *Monthly Review* 519: 1–15.

Howe, H. and M. Ottaway. 1987. "State Power Consolidation in Mozambique." In E. J. Keller and Donald Rothchild, eds., *Afro-Marxist Regimes*, 43–66. Boulder: Lynne Rienner.

Huber, Evelyn. 2009. "Politics and Inequality in Latin America." *PS: Political Science and Politics* 42(4): 651–5.

Huber, Evelyn, Jennifer Pribble and John Stephens. 2010. "The Chilean Left in Power." In K. Weyland, R. Madrid and W. Hunter, eds., *Latin America's Left Turns*, 77–97. New York: Cambridge University Press.

Hugon, Philippe. 2010. "La crise va-t-elle conduire à un nouveau paradigme du développement?" *Mondes en Development* 38(150): 53–67.

Hunter, Wendy. 2010. *The Transformation of the Workers Party in Brazil, 1989–2009*. New York: Cambridge University Press.

Huntington, Samuel P. 1968. *Political Order in Changing Societies*. New Haven; Yale University Press.

Hyden, Goran. 1983. *No Shortcuts to Progress: African Development Management in Perspective*. London: Heinemann.

2006. *African Politics in Comparative Perspective*. Cambridge University Press.

Hyden, Goran and B. Karlstrom. 1993. "Structural Adjustment as Policy Process: The Case of Tanzania." *World Development* 21(9): 1,395–404.

Hyslop, Jonathan. 2005. "Political Corruption: Before and After Apartheid." *Journal of Southern Africa* 31(4): 773–89.

ILO (International Labour Organization). 2011. *Social Protection Floor for a Fair and Inclusive Globalization: Report of the Advisory Group Chaired by Michelle Bachelet*. Geneva: ILO.

IMF (International Monetary Fund). 2011. "Recent Experiences in Managing Capital Inflows: Cross-cutting Themes and Possible Policy Frameworks." Strategy, Policy and Review Department, Washington, DC (February 14).

2012. *Brazil: Staff Report for the 2012 Article IV Consultation*. Washington: IMF (June).

2013. *World Economic Outlook Database* (July 16) www.imf.org/external/pubs/ft/weodata/weorept.aspx?sy/

Intergovernmental Panel on Climate Change. 2007. *Fourth Assessment Report* (April).

Internal Displacement Monitoring Centre (IDMC). 2009. *Global Overview of Trends and Development in 2008*. Geneva: IDMC.

International Crisis Group. Accessed at www.crisisgroup.org/

International Fund for Agricultural Development, United Nations. 2011. *The Rural Poverty Report 2011*. Accessed at www.ifad.org/rpr2011

Ip, Greg. 2013. "World Economy: The Gated Globalisation." *The Economist* (October 10).

Isaac, T., M. Thomas and Richard W. Franke. 2002. *Local Democracy and Development: The Kerala People's Campaign for Decentralized Planning*. Lanham, MD: Rowman & Littlefield.

Jackson, Tim. 2009. *Prosperity without Growth; Economics for a Finite Planet*. London: Earthscan.

Jacque, Laurent. 2010. "The Currency Wars." *Le Monde Diplomatique* 1,012 (December): 1, 3.

Jacobs, M. 1997. "Sustainability and Markets: On the Neoclassical Model of Environmental Economics." *New Political Economy* 2(3): 365–85.

Jansen, Robert. 2011. "Populist Mobilization: A New Theoretical Approach to Populism." *Sociological Theory* 29(2): 75–96.

Jessop, Bob. 2007. "Knowledge as a Fictitious Commodity: Insights and Limits of a Polanyian Perspective." In Ayse Bugra and Kaan Agartan, eds., *Reading Karl Polanyi for the 21st Century*, 115–33. New York: Palgrave Macmillan.

Jiménez, Marina. 2006. "Venezuelans Hit the Malls with Revolutionary Zeal." *Globe and Mail* (November 27).

Johnson, Chalmers. 1987. "Political Institutions and Economic Performance: The Government–Business Relationship in Japan, South Korea and Taiwan." In F. C. Deyo, ed., *The Political Economy of the New Asian Industrialism*, 136–64. Ithaca, NY: Cornell University Press.

Johnson, Steven. 2010. "Innovation: It Isn't a Matter of Left and Right." *New York Times* (October 31): 7.

Kai, Hisakio and Shigeyuki Hamori. 2009. "Globalization, Financial Depth and Inequality in Sub-Saharan Africa." *Economics Bulletin* 29(3): 2,025–37.

Kanbur, Ravi and Anthony J. Venables. 2005. "Spatial Inequality and Development: Overview of UNU-WIDER Project." Working paper, Economics Department, Cornell University, Ithaca, NY.

Kaplan, Seth. 2009. "Faith and Fragile States: Why the Development Community Needs Religion." *Harvard International Review* (Spring): 22–6.

Kapoor, Aditi. 2007. "The SEWA Way: Shaping another Future for Informal Labour." *Futures* 39(5): 554–68.

Kapoor, Rakesh. 2011. "Is There a Postnormal Time? From the Illusion of Normality to the Design of a New Normality." *Futures* 43(2): 216–20.

Kaztman, R. F. Filgueira and M. Furtado. 2000. "New Challenges for Equity in Uruguay." *CEPAL Review* 72 (December): 79–97.

Keen, David. 2005. "Liberalization and Conflict." *International Political Science Review* 26(1): 73–89.

Keith, N. W. and N. Z. Keith. 1992. *The Social Origins of Democratic Socialism in Jamaica*. Philadelphia: Temple University Press.

Kettel, Steven and Alex Sutton. 2013. "New Imperialism: Toward a Holistic Approach." *International Studies Review* 15(2): 342–58.

Kim, Andrew and Innwon Park. 2006. "Changing Trends of Work in South Korea." *Asian Survey* 46(3): 437–56.

Kingstone, Peter and Aldo Ponce. 2010. "From Cardoso to Lula: The Triumph of Pragmatism in Brazil." In Kurt Weyland, Raúl L. Madrid and Wendy Hunter, eds., *Leftist Governments in Latin America*, 98–123. New York: Cambridge University Press.

Kitching, Gavin. 1983. *Rethinking Socialism*. London: Methuen.

Klare, Michael. 2008. "'2025 Report': A World of Resource Strife." *Foreign Policy in Focus*. Accessed at www.fpif.org/fpifxt/5708

Kliksberg, Bernardo. 2006. "Insecure Democracies: Five Myths about Crime in Latin America." Safe Democracy Foundation, Washington, DC. Accessed at http://english.safe-democracy.org/2006/12/2

Kohl, Benjamin and Rosalind Bresnahan. 2010. "Bolivia under Morales: Consolidating Power, Initiating Decolonization." *Latin American Perspectives* 37(3): 5–17.

Kohli, Atul. 1987. *The State and Poverty in India*. Cambridge University Press.

    2004. *State-Directed Development; Political Power and Industrialization in the Global Periphery*. New York: Cambridge University Press.

    2012. *Poverty amid Plenty in the New India*. New York: Cambridge University Press.

Kovel, Joel. 2002. *The Enemy of Nature: The End of Capitalism or the End of the World?* London: Zed Books.

Kroger, Markus. 2012. "Neo-Mercantilist Capitalism and Post-2008 Cleavages in Economic Decision-making Power in Brazil." *Third World Quarterly* 33(5): 887–901.

Kurtz, Geoffrey. 2013. "An Apprenticeship for Life in Common: Jean Jaurès on Social Democracy and the Modern Republic." *New Political Science* 35(1): 65–83.

Kurtz, Marcus and Sarah Brooks. 2008. "Embedding Neoliberal Reform in Latin America." *World Politics* 60(2): 231–80.

Lacey, Marc. 2005. "Neglected Poor in Africa Make their Own Safety Nets." *New York Times* (August 26).

Lacher, Hannes. 1999. "Embedded Liberalism, Disembedded Markets: Reconceptualizing the Pax Americana." *New Political Economy* 4(3): 343–60.

Laclau, Ernesto. 2005. *On Populist Reasoning.* London: Verso.

Lakshman, W. D. 1997. "Introduction." In W. D. Lakshman, ed., *Dilemmas of Development: 50 Years of Economic Change in Sri Lanka,* 1–27. Colombo: Sri Lanka Association of Economists.

Lal, Deepak. 2008. *Reviving the Invisible Hand: The Case for Classical Liberalism in the Twenty-first Century.* Princeton University Press.

Lambert, Renaud. 2013a. "Whose Free Press?" *Le Monde Diplomatique* (February): 14–15.

 2013b. "Brazil Looms Larger." *Le Monde Diplomatique* (June): 12–13.

Lambert, Rob and Edward Webster. 2014. "Transnational Unionism in the Global South." In Richard Sandbrook and Ali Burak Guven, eds., *Civilizing Globalization: A Survival Guide.* Revised edn. Albany: SUNY Press.

Lanzaro, Jorge. 2008. "La socialdemocracia criolla." *Nueva Sociedad* 217: 41–58.

 2011. "Uruguay: A Social Democratic Government in Latin America." In Steven Levitsky and Kenneth Roberts, eds., *The Resurgence of the Latin American Left,* 348–74. Baltimore: Johns Hopkins University Press.

Lawn, Philip. 2005. "Is a Democratic-Capitalist System Compatible with a Low-Growth or Steady-State Economy?" *Socio-economic Review* 3: 209–32.

Leahy, Stephen. 2010. "Climate Change: As the World Warms, Southern Africa Swelters." *Inter Press Service, Africa.* Accessed at www.ips.org/africa/2010/climate-change-as-world-warms/

Lebowitz, Michael. 2007. "Venezuela: A Good Example of the Bad Left in Latin America." *Monthly Review* 59(3): 38–54.

 2010. *The Socialist Alternative: Real Human Development.* New York: Monthly Review Press.

Lee, Seung-Ook, Joel Wainwright and Sook-Jin Kim. 2010. "Mad Cow Militance: Neoliberal Hegemony and Social Resistance in South Korea." *Political Geography* 29(7): 359–69.

Lemoine, Maurice. 2012. "Why Nicaragua Chose Ortega." *Le Monde Diplomatique* (June): 10–11.

Leubolt, Bernhard, Andreas Novy and Joachim Becker. 2008. "Changing Patterns of Participation in Porto Alegre." *International Social Science Journal* 59(193–4): 435–48.

Le Velly, Ronan. 2007. "Encastrement et déencastrement de l'économie." *La revue du MAUSS* 29: 241–56.

Leiva, Fernando. 2006. "Neoliberal and Neostructuralist Perspectives on Labour Flexibility, Poverty and Inequality: A Critical Appraisal." *New Political Economy* 11(3): 337–59.

Levien, Michael. 2007. "India's Double Movement: Polanyi and the National Alliance of Peoples Movements." *Berkeley Journal of Sociology* 51: 119–49.

Levitsky, Steven and Kenneth Roberts. 2011. "Introduction: Latin America's 'Left Turn'." In Steven Levitsky and Kenneth Roberts, eds., *The Resurgence of the Latin American Left,* 1–29. Baltimore: Johns Hopkins University Press.

Li, Quan and Drew Schaub. 2004. "Economic Globalization and Transnational Terrorism: A Pooled Time-Series Analysis." *Journal of Conflict Resolution* 48 (2): 230–58.

Lieberman, Evan. 2003. *Race and Regionalism in the Politics of Taxation in Brazil and South Africa*. New York: Cambridge University Press.

Lin, Justin Yifu. 2012. *The Quest for Prosperity: How Developing Economies Can Take Off*. Princeton University Press.

Lin, Justin Yifu and Célestin Monga. 2010. "The Growth Report and New Structural Economics." Policy Research Working Paper 5,336, World Bank, Washington, DC.

Lindbeck, Assar. 2002. "European Social Model: Lessons for Developing Countries." *Asian Development Review* 19(1): 1–13.

Lofchie, Michael. 1978. "Agrarian Crisis and Economic Liberalisation in Tanzania." *Journal of Modern African Studies* 16(3): 451–75.

Lopes, Paulo S. 2005. "The Disconcerting Pyramids of Poverty and Inequality of Sub-Saharan Africa." Working Paper 05/47, African Department, International Monetary Fund, Washington, DC (March).

Lopez-Calva, Luis and Nora Lustig. 2009. "The Recent Decline of Inequality in Latin America: Argentina, Brazil, Mexico and Peru." Occasional Paper, Center for International Development, Harvard University, Cambridge, MA (September 3).

López Levy, Marcelo. 2004. *We are Millions: Neo-liberalism and New Forms of Political Action in Argentina*. London: Latin American Bureau.

López Maya, Margarita. 2011. "Venezuela: Hugo Chávez and the Popular Left." In Steven Levitsky and Kenneth Roberts, eds., *The Resurgence of the Latin American Left*, 260–82. Baltimore: Johns Hopkins University Press.

Luna, Juan Pablo. 2007. "Frente Amplio and the Crafting of a Social-Democratic Alternative in Uruguay." *Latin American Politics and Society* 49(4): 1–30.

Lupu, Noam. 2010. "Who Votes for *Chavismo?* Class Voting in Hugo Chávez's Venezuela." *Latin American Research Review* 45(1): 7–32.

Luttwak, Edward. 1999. *Turbo-Capitalism: Winners and Losers in the Global Economy*. New York: HarperCollins.

MacLean, Lauren M. 2010. *Informal Institutions and Citizenship in Rural Africa: Risk and Reciprocity in Ghana and Côte d'Ivoire*. Cambridge University Press.

Macpherson, C. B. 1973. *Democratic Theory: Essays in Retrieval*. Oxford: Clarendon Press.

Madrid, Raúl. 2011. "Bolivia: Origins and Policies of the Movimiento al Socialismo." In S. Levitsky and K. Roberts, eds., *The Resurgence of the Latin American Left*, 239–59. Baltimore: Johns Hopkins University Press.

Majee, Wilson and Ann Hoyt. 2011. "Cooperatives and Community Development." *Journal of Community Practice* 19(1): 418–61.

Malleson, Tom. 2012. "The Theory and Practice of Economic Democracy." Ph.D. thesis, University of Toronto.

Mannathukkaren, Nissam. 2010a. "The Conjuncture of 'Late Socialism' in Kerala: A Critique of the Narrative of Social Democracy." In K. Ravi Raman, ed., *Development, Democracy and the State: Critiquing the Kerala Model of Development*, 157–73. London: Routledge.

2010b. "The 'Poverty' of Political Society: Partha Chatterjee and the People's Plan Campaign in Kerala, India." *Third World Quarterly* 31(2): 295–314.

March, Luke. 2007. "From Vanguard of the Proletariat to *Vox Populi*: Left-populism as a 'Shadow' of Contemporary Socialism." *SAIS Review* 27(1): 63–77.

Marx, Karl. 1971. *The Grundrisse*. Trans. David McLellan. New York: Harper & Row.

Mathews, John A. 2011. "Naturalizing Capitalism: The Next Great Transformation." *Futures* 43: 868–79.

Mauritius, Republic of. 2010. *Mauritius Strategy for Implementation: National Assessment Report*. Port Louis: Ministry of Environment and National Development.

Maxwell, David. 2005. "The Durawall of Faith: Pentecostal Spirituality in Neoliberal Zimbabwe." *Journal of Religion in Africa* 35(1): 4–31.

May, Julian and Charles Meth. 2007. "Dualism or Underdevelopment in South Africa: What Does a Quantitative Assessment of Poverty, Inequality and Employment Reveal?" *Development: Southern Africa* 24(2): 271–87.

McCulloch, Neil and Andy Sumner. 2009. "Will the Global Financial Crisis Change the Developmental Paradigm?" *Institute for Development Studies Bulletin* 40(5): 101–8.

McHenry, Donald. 1979. "The Struggle for Rural Socialism in Tanzania." In Carl Rosberg and Thomas Callaghy, eds., *Socialism in Sub-Saharan Africa*, 37–60. Berkeley, CA: Institute of International Studies.

McKee, Arnold. 1992. "What Adam Smith Really Meant." *Forum for Social Economics* 22: 12–21.

Mehta, Jal. 2011. "The Varied Role of Ideas in Politics: From 'Whether' to 'How'." In Daniel Béland and Robert Henry Cox, eds., *Ideas and Politics in Social Science Research*, 28–63. Oxford University Press.

Meintjies, Frank. 2013. "Can COSATU"s Former Glory Be Restored?" South African Civil Society Information Service (August 6, 2013). sacsis.org.za

Mejido Costoya, Manuel. 2011. "Politics of Trade in Post-neoliberal Latin America: The Case of Bolivia." *Bulletin of Latin American Research* 30(1): 80–95.

Mendell, Marguerite. 2007. "Karl Polanyi and the Instituted Process of Economic Democratisation." In Mark Harvey, Sally Randles and Ronnie Ramlogan, eds., *Market, State and Society at the End of the Twentieth Century*. Manchester University Press.

Meyer, Thomas, with Lewis Hinchman. 2007. *The Theory of Social Democracy*. Cambridge: Polity Press.

Michels, Robert. 1968 [1911]. *Political Parties; A Sociological Study of the Oligarchical Tendencies of Modern Democracy*. Trans. Eden and Cedar Paul. New York: Free Press.

Mideksa, Torben. 2010. "Economic and Distributional Impacts of Climate Change: Case of Ethiopia." *Global Environmental Change* 20(2): 278–86.

Milanovic, Branko. 2002. "True World Income Distribution, 1988 and 1993." *Economic Journal* 112 (January): 51–92.

2003. "The Two Faces of Globalization: Against Globalization as We Know It." *World Development* 31(4): 667–83.

Miller, David. 1989. *Market, State and Community: Theoretical Foundations of Market Socialism*. London: Oxford University Press.

Mitra, Aparna and Pooja Singh. 2007. "Human Capital Attainment and Gender Empowerment: The Kerala Paradox." *Social Science Quarterly* 88(5): 1,227–42.

Mittal, Anuradha. 2001. "Land Loss, Poverty and Hunger." In D. Barker and J. Mander, eds., *Does Globalization Help the Poor?* San Francisco: International Forum on Globalization.

Mol, Andrew P. J. 2001. *Globalization and Environmental Reform: The Ecological Modernization of the Global Economy*. Cambridge, MA: MIT Press.

Molero Simarro, Ricardo and Maria José Paz Antolín. 2012. "Development Strategy and the MAS in Bolivia." *Development and Change* 43(2): 531–6.

Moore, Barrington. 1966. *Social Origins of Dictatorship and Democracy: Lord and Peasant in the Making of the Modern World*. Boston, MA: Beacon Press.

Mora, Mariana. 2007. "Zapatista Anticapitalist Politics in the 'Other Campaign'." *Latin American Perspectives* 34(2): 64–77.

Morais, Lecio and Alfredo Saad-Filho. 2011. "Brazil beyond Lula: Forging Ahead or Pausing for Breath?" *Latin American Perspectives* 38(2): 31–44.

Morgan, D. R. 2009. "World on Fire: Two Scenarios of the Destruction of Human Civilization and the Possible Extinction of the Human Race." *Futures* 41: 683–93.

Mosse, D. 2005. "'People's Knowledge,' Participation and Patronage: Operations and Representations in Rural Development." In Bill Cooke and Uma Kothari, eds., *Participation: The New Tyranny?* 16–35. London: Zed Books.

Motta, Sara. 2011. "Populism's Achilles Heel: Popular Democracy beyond the Liberal State and the Market Economy in Venezuela." *Latin American Perspectives* 38(1): 28–46.

Muir, Rick. 2011. "Social Democracy Reborn? The Latin American Left in Government." *Renewal* 19(1): 55–61.

Muller, Jerry. 2006. "The Neglected Moral Benefits of the Market." *Society* 43(2): 12–14.

Munck, Gerardo. 2013. "The Precariat: A View from the South." *Third World Quarterly* 34(5): 747–62.

Mwansasu, Bismarch and Cranford Pratt, eds. 1979. *Toward Socialism in Tanzania*. University of Toronto Press.

Myers, David. 2006. "The Social Psychology of Sustainability." In Ervin Laszlo and Peter Seidel, eds., *Global Survival*, 101–13. New York: Select Books.

Nafziger, E. Wayne and Juha Auvinen. 2002. "Economic Development, Inequality, War and State Violence." *World Development* 30(7): 153–63.

Naim, Moisés. 2013. "The Nation Must Reverse Course." *New York Times* (January 13).

Narayan, Deepa. 2000. *Voices of the Poor: Can Anyone Hear Us?* Oxford University Press.

N'Dione, E. P., de Leener, J.-P., Perier, M. Ndiaye and P. Jacolin. 1995. "Reinventing the Present: The Chodak Experience in Senegal." In M. Rahnema and V. Bawtree, eds., *The Post-Development Reader*, 227–37. London: Zed Books.

Nel, Philip. 2006. "The Return of Inequality." *Third World Quarterly* 27(4): 689–706.
Nelson, Richard. 2003. "On the Complexities and Limits of Market Organization." *Review of International Political Economy* 10(4): 697–710.
Nesvetailova, Anastasia and Ronen Palan. 2010. "The End of Liberal Finance? The Changing Paradigm of Global Financial Governance." *Millennium* 38(3): 797–825.
Neuman, William. 2012. "Fear of Losing Benefits Affects Venezuelan Vote." *New York Times* (October 6): 1+.
Newell, Peter and Matthew Paterson. 2010. *Climate Capitalism; Global Warming and the Transformation of the Global Economy.* Cambridge University Press.
Nkrumah, Kwame. 1970. *Consciencism.* London: Panaf Books.
Norberg-Hodge, Helena. 2009. *Ancient Futures: Lessons from Ladakh for a Globalizing World.* 2nd edn. San Francisco: Sierra Club Books.
Novy, Andreas and Bernhard Leubolt. 2005. "Participatory Budgeting in Porto Alegre: Social Innovation and the Dialectical Relationship of State and Civil Society." *Urban Studies* 42(11): 2,023–36.
Nowak, Martin, with Roger Highfield. 2011. *Supercooperators: Altruism, Evolution and Why We Need Each Other to Succeed.* New York: The Free Press.
Nyerere, Julius. 1968. *Ujamaa: Essays on Socialism.* Dar es Salaam: Oxford University Press.
O'Boyle, Edward. 2007. "Requiem for *Homo Economicus.*" *Journal of Markets and Morality* 10(2): 321–37.
O'Connor, James. 1998. *Natural Causes: Essays in Ecological Marxism.* New York: Guilford Press.
Organization for Economic Cooperation and Development (OECD). 1997. *Economic Globalization and the Environment.* Paris: OECD.
Orhangazi, Ozgur. 2011. "Contours of Alternative Policy Making in Venezuela." Working Paper Series No. 275, Political Economy Research Institute, University of Massachusetts, Amherst (November).
Ostby, Gudren, Ragnheld Nordast and Jan Ketil Rod. 2009. "Regional Inequalities and Civil Conflict in Sub-Saharan Africa." *International Studies Quarterly* 53(2): 301–24.
Ostrom, Elinor. 1990. *Governing the Commons: The Evolution of Institutions for Collective Action.* Cambridge University Press.
Ostry, Jonathan D., Atish Ghosh, Karl Habermeier, Marcos Chamon, Mahvish Qureshi and Dennis Reinhardt. 2010. "Capital Inflows: The Role of Controls." IMF Staff Position Note 10/04, International Monetary Fund, Washington, DC (February 19).
Owusu, Francis. 2003. "Pragmatism and the Gradual Shift from Dependency to Neoliberalism: The World Bank, African Leaders and Development Policy in Africa." *World Development* 31(10): 1,655–72.
Paes-Sousa, Rômula. 2013. "New Strategy for Poverty Eradication in Brazil: The Emergence of *Plano Brasil Sem Miséria.*" Working Paper 214, International Policy Centre for Inclusive Growth, Brasilia (Aug.).
Palomino, Héctor, Ivanna Bleynat, Silvia Curro and Caria Giacomuzzi. 2010. "The Universe of Worker-Recovered Companies in Argentina, 2002–2008: Continuity and Change inside the Movement." *Affinities* 4(1): 252–87.

Panizza, Francisco. 2009. *Contemporary Latin America: Development and Democracy beyond the Washington Consensus*. New York and London: Zed Books.

Park, Juyoung and Jai Mah. 2011. "Neoliberal Reform and the Bipolarization of Income in Korea." *Journal of Contemporary Asia* 41(2): 249–65.

Pausewang, S. 1988. "Local Democracy and Central Control in Ethiopia." Paper presented to the Conference on Post-Revolutionary Ethiopian Society, Oxford University (September 7–9).

Pearce, Jenny. 2009. "Beyond Shock: Does Latin America Offer a New Doctrine?" *New Political Economy* 143: 417–21.

Peet, Richard. 2002. "Ideology, Discourse and the Geography of Hegemony: From Socialist to Neoliberal Development in Post-Apartheid South Africa." *Antipode* 34(1): 54–84.

  2009. *Unholy Trinity: The IMF, World Bank and WTO*. 2nd edn. London: Zed Books.

Pepper, David. 2010. "On Contemporary Eco-Socialism." In Qingzhi Huan, ed., *Eco-Socialism as Politics: Rebuilding the Basis of Our Modern Civilization*, 33–44. New York: Springer Science.

Pereira, Carlos and Marcus Andre Melo. 2010. "Tax Policy in Brazil: The Reform that Never Was." Brookings Institution, Washington, DC (September)

Pesendorfer, Wolfgang. 2006. "Behavioral Economics Comes of Age." *Journal of Economics Literature* 44(1): 712–21.

Peters, Pauline. 2004. "Inequality and Social Conflict over Land in Africa." *Journal of Agrarian Change* 4(3): 269–314.

Piachaud, David. 2013. "Social Protection, Redistribution and Economic Growth." *Development Southern Africa* 30(1): 24–38.

Pieterse, Jan Nederveen. 1998. "My Paradigm or Yours? Alternative Development, Post-Development, Reflexive Development." *Development and Change* 29: 343–73.

  2014. "Crisis and the East–South Turn." In Richard Sandbrook and Ali Burak Guven, eds., *Civilizing Globalization: A Survival Guide*. Revised edn. Albany: SUNY Press.

Piñeiro Harnecker, Camila 2009. "Workplace Democracy and Social Consciousness: A Study of Venezuelan Cooperatives." *Science and Society* 73(3): 309–39.

Polanyi, Karl. 1947. "Our Obsolete Market Mentality". *Commentary* 3(2): 109–17.

  1957. "The Economy as an Instituted Process." In Karl Polanyi, M. Arensburg and H. W. Pearson, eds., *Trade and Markets in the Early Empires*, 243–70. Glencoe: The Free Press.

  1977. *The Livelihood of Man*. Ed. Harry Pearson. New York: Academic Press.

  2001 [1944]. *The Great Transformation: The Political and Economic Origins of Our Time*. Boston, MA: Beacon Press.

"Polanyi Symposium: Conversation on Embeddedness." 2004. *Socio-economic Review* 22.

Polgreen, Lydia. 2012. "Unfulfilled Promises Are Replacing Prospects of a Better Life in South Africa." *New York Times* (October 14): 5.

Porritt, Jonathon. 2005. *Capitalism as if the World Matters*. London: Earthscan.

Porzecanski, Rafael. 2005. "Types of Democracy, Economic Policies and Social Equality in Latin America." *Revista de Ciencias Sociales* 22: 67–94.

Posner, Paul. 2012. "Targeted Assistance and Social Capital: Housing Policy and Chile's Neoliberal Democracy." *International Journal of Urban and Regional Research* 36(1): 49–70.

Prasch, Robert. 2005. "Neoliberalism and Empire: How Are They Related?" *Review of Radical Political Economics* 37(3): 281–7.

Pratt, Cranford. 2000. "Julius Nyerere: The Ethical Foundations of His Legacy." *The Round Table* 355: 365–74.

Pribble, Jennifer and Evelyne Huber. 2011. "Social Policy and Redistribution: Chile and Uruguay." In Steven Levitsky and Kenneth Roberts, eds., *The Resurgence of the Latin American Left*, 117–38. Baltimore: Johns Hopkins University Press.

Przeworski, Adam. 1985. *Capitalism and Social Democracy*. New York: Cambridge University Press.

Putzell, James. 2005. "Globalization, Liberalization and Prospects for the State." *International Political Science Review* 26(1): 5–16.

Raman, K. Ravi. 2009. "Asian Development Bank, Policy Conditionalities and the Social Democratic Governance: Kerala Model under Pressure?" *Review of International Political Economy* 16(2): 284–308.

Rao, J. Mohan. 1998. "Agricultural Development under State Planning." In Terrence Byres, ed., *The State, Development Planning and Liberalisation in India*. New Delhi: Oxford University Press.

Rénique, Gerardo. 2005. "Latin America Today: The Revolt against Neoliberalism." *Socialism and Democracy* 193: 1–12.

Reno, William. 1998. *Warlord Politics and African States*. Boulder: Lynne Rienner.

Reygadas, Luis and Fernando Filgueira. 2010. "Inequality and the Incorporation Crisis: The Left's Social Policy Toolkit." In Maxwell Cameron and Eric Hershburg, eds., *America's Left Turns*, 171–91. Boulder: Lynne Rienner.

Riesco, Manuel. 2009. "Latin America: A New Developmental Welfare State in the Making?" *International Journal of Social Welfare* 18(s1): s22–36.

Riggirozzi, Pia. 2012. "Region, Regionness and Regionalism in Latin America." *New Political Economy* 17(4): 421–43.

Riskin, Carl, Zhao Renwei and Li Shi, eds. 2001. *China's Retreat from Equality*. New York: M. E. Sharpe.

Rist, Gilbert. 2006. "Before Thinking about *What Next*: Prerequisites for Alternatives." *Development Dialogue* 47: 65–95.

Robert, J. T. 2001. "Global Inequality and Climate Change." *Society and Natural Resources* 14(6): 501–9.

Roberts, J. Timmons and Bradley Parks. 2007. *A Climate of Injustice: Global Inequality, North–South Politics and Climate Policy*. Cambridge, MA: MIT Press.

Roberts, Kenneth. 2011. "Chile: The Left after Neoliberalism." In Steven Levitsky and Kenneth Roberts, eds., *The Resurgence of the Latin American Left*, 325–47. Baltimore: Johns Hopkins University Press.

Rodrik, Dani. 2006. "Goodbye Washington Consensus, Hello Washington Confusion?" *Journal of Economic Literature* 44(4): 973–87.

Rodriquez, Francisco. 2008. "An Empty Revolution: The Unfulfilled Promise of Hugo Chávez." *Foreign Affairs* 87(2): 49–56.

Roemer, John. 1996. "A Future for Socialism." In Erik Olin Wright, ed., *Equal Shares: Making Market Socialism Work*, 7–39. London: Verso.

Rohter, Larry. 2013. "Brazil's Leader Is on the Defensive as Attempts to Placate Protesters Misfire." *New York Times* (July 14): 10.

Roncallo, Alejandra. 2013. "Cosmologies and Regionalisms from 'Above' and 'Below' in the Post-Cold War Americas: The Relevance of Karl Polanyi for the 21st Century." *Third World Quarterly* 34(7): 1,145–58.

Rondier, Phillip, Benjamin Sultan, Philippe Quirion and Alexis Berg. 2011. "The Impact of Future Climate Change on West African Crop Yields." *Global Environmental Change* 21(3): 1,073–83.

Ross, Andrew. 2013. "Climate Debt Denial." *Dissent* (Summer). www.dissent-magazine.org/article/climate-debt-denial

Rovira Koltwasser, Cristóbal. 2010. "Moving beyond the Washington Consensus: The Resurgence of the Left in Latin America." *Internationale Politik und Gesellschaft* 3: 52–62.

Rowe, Tom. 2010. "Guinea Waits for Change." *Le Monde Diplomatique* (English edn.) (April 1).

Ruckett, Arne. 2010. "The Forgotten Dimension of Social Reproduction: The World Bank and the Poverty Reduction Strategy Paradigm." *Review of International Political Economy* 17(5): 816–39.

Rudd, Murray. 2000. "Live Long and Prosper: Collective Action, Social Capital and Social Vision." *Ecological Economics* 34(234): 131–44.

Rueschemeyer, Dietrich. 2004. "Addressing Inequality." *Journal of Democracy* 15(4): 79–90.

Ruggie, John. 1982. "International Regimes, Transactions and Change: Embedded Liberalism in the Postwar Economic Order." *International Organization* 362: 195–231.

Ruiz, Carlos. 2012. "New Social Conflicts under Bachelet." *Latin American Perspectives* 39(4): 71–84.

Saad Filho, Alfredo. 2013. "The Mass Protests in Brazil in June–July 2013." *The Bullet: The Socialist Project* e-bulletin 851 (July 15).

Sahn, David and David Stifel. 2003. "Urban–Rural Inequality in Living Standards in Africa." *Journal of African Economies* 12(4): 564–97.

Samoff, Joel. 1979. "The Bureaucracy and the Bourgeoisie: Decentralization and Class Structure in Tanzania." *Comparative Studies in Society and History* 21(1): 30–62.

Samuels, David. 2004. "From Socialism to Social Democracy: Party Organization and the Transformation of the Workers Party." *Comparative Political Studies* 37(9): 999–1,024.

Sánchez-Ancochea, Diego. 2009. "States, Firms and the Process of Industrial Upgrading: Latin America's Variety of Capitalism and the Costa Rica Experience." *Economy and Society* 38(1): 62–86.

Sandberg, Johan. 2012. "Conditional Cash Transfers and Social Mobility: The Role of Asymmetric Structures and Segmentation Processes." *Development and Change* 43(6): 1,337–59.

Sandbrook, Richard 2000a. "Globalization and the Limits of Neoliberal Development Doctrine." *Third World Quarterly* 2(16): 1,071–80.

2000b. *Closing the Circle: Democratization and Development in Africa*. London: Zed Books.

2005. "Origins of the Democratic Developmental State: Interrogating Mauritius." *Canadian Journal of African Studies* 39(3): 517–48.

Sandbrook, Richard and Ali Burak Guven. 2014. *Civilizing Globalization: A Survival Guide*. Revised edn. Albany: State University of New York Press.

Sandbrook, Richard, Marc Edelman, Patrick Heller and Judith Teichman. 2007. *Social Democracy in the Global Periphery: Origins, Challenges, Prospects*. Cambridge University Press.

Sanyal, Sanjeev. 2012. "Who are Tomorrow's Consumers?" *Globe and Mail* (Toronto) (August 11).

Schaffer, Frederic C. 1998. *Democracy in Translation: Understanding Politics in an Unfamiliar Culture*. Ithaca, NY: Cornell University Press.

Schaniel, William and Walter Neale. 2000. "Karl Polanyi's Forms of Integration as Ways of Mapping." *Journal of Economic Issues* 341.

Schaumberg, Heike. 2008. "In Search of Alternatives: The Making of Grassroots Politics and Power in Argentina." *Bulletin of Latin American Research* 27(3): 368–87.

Schlyter, Charlotte. 2003. "International Labour Standards in the Informal Sector: Developments and Dilemmas." Working Paper on the Informal Economy, Employment Sector, International Labour Organization, Geneva.

Schneider, Leander. 2004. "Freedom and Unfreedom in Rural Development: Julius Nyerere, Ujamaa Vijijini and Villagization." *Canadian Journal of African Studies* 382: 344–92.

Schwartz, Peter and Doug Randall. 2003. "An Abrupt Climate Change Scenario and Its Implications for United States National Security." Unpublished report to the Pentagon, Washington, DC (October). Accessed at eesc.columbia.edu/courses/v1003/reading/Pentagon.pdf

Seekings, Jeremy. 2004. "Trade Unions, Social Policy and Class Compromise in Post-Apartheid South Africa." *Review of African Political Economy* 100: 299–312.

2008. "Deserving Individuals and Groups: The Post-Apartheid State's Justification of the Shape of South Africa's System of Social Assistance." *Transformations* 68: 28–52.

2013. "Democracy, Poverty and Inclusive Growth in South Africa since 1994." Paper presented at Centre for Development Economics, University of Cape Town (March 19).

Seekings, Jeremy and Nicoli Nattrass. 2002. "Class, Distribution and Redistribution in Post-Apartheid South Africa." *Transformation* 50: 1–30.

Seidel, Peter. 2011. "To Achieve Sustainability." *World Futures* 67(1): 11–29.

Selassie, Abebe. 2011. "What Ails South Africa." *Finance and Development* 48(4): 6 pp. www.imf.org/external/pubs/ft/fandd/12/

Sen, Amaryta. 1977. "Rational Fools: A Critique of the Behavioral Foundations of Economic Theory." *Philosophy and Public Affairs* 6(4): 317–44.

1999. *Development as Freedom*. New York: Alfred A. Knopf.

2009. *The Idea of Justice*. London: Allen Lane.

Sengupta, Mitu. 2011. "A Tale of Two Indias: 20 Years of Liberalization." *Dissent* (15 August). Accessed at http://dissentmagazine.org/online.php? id=519

2012. "The Organized Poor and *Behind the Beautiful Forevers*." *Dissent* (January), 4 pp. Accessed at http://dissentmagazine.org/online.php?id=603

Servet, Jean-Michel. 2007. "Le Principe de réciprocité chez Karl Polanyi." *Revue Tiers Monde* 190 (April–June): 255–73.

Shapiro, Ian. 2010. "On Non-Domination." Inaugural Brian Berry Lecture, London School of Economics, London (May 7).

Shivji, Issa. 1991. "The Democracy Debate in Africa: Tanzania." *Review of African Political Economy* 50: 79–91.

Silva, Eduardo. 2012. "Exchange Rising? Karl Polanyi and Contentious Politics in Latin America." *Latin American Politics and Society* 54(3): 1–32.

Sitrin, Marina. 2012. *Everyday Revolutions: Horizontalism and Autonomy in Argentina*. London: Zed Books.

Smith, Adam. 1863 [1776]. *The Wealth of Nations*. London: A. & C. Black.

2010 [1759]. *The Theory of Moral Sentiments*. London: Penguin.

Smith, W. C. and N. Messari. 1998. "Democracy and Reform in Cardoso's Brazil: Caught between Clientelism and Global Markets?" Agenda Paper 33, North–South Center, University of Miami (September).

Snyder, Jack. 2000. *From Voting to Violence: Democratization and Nationalist Conflict*. New York: W. W. Norton.

Soares, Sergei. 2012. "*Bolsa Família*: Its Design, Its Impacts and Possibilities for the Future." Working Paper 89, International Policy Centre for inclusive Growth, Brasilia (February)

"Socialism on the Never-Never: Venezuela's Oil Dependent Economy." 2009. *The Economist* 391(8,636): 53.

South Africa, Republic of. 2007. *Development Indicators: Mid-Term Review*. Johannesburg: The Presidency.

Sseguya, Haroon, Robert Mazur and Dorothy Masinde. 2009. "Harnessing Community Capital for Livelihood Enhancement: Experience from a Livelihood Programme in Rural Uganda." *Community Development* 40(2): 123–38.

Standing, Guy. 2007. "Labour Recommodification in the Global Transformation." In Ayse Bugra and Kaan Agartan, eds., *Reading Karl Polanyi for the 21st Century*, 67–93. New York: Palgrave Macmillan.

2011. *The Precariat: The New Dangerous Class*. London: Bloomsbury.

Stanfield, J. R. 1986. *The Economic Thought of Karl Polanyi: Lives and Livelihoods*. New York: St Martin's Press.

Stephen, Matthew. 2010. "Globalisation and Resistance: Struggles over Common Sense in the Global Political Economy." *Review of International Studies* 37(1): 209–28.

Stephens, Evelyn H. and John D. Stephens. 1983. "Democratic Socialism in Dependent Capitalism: An Analysis of the Manley Government in Jamaica." *Politics and Society* 12(3): 373–411

Stiglitz, Joseph. 1998. "More Instruments and Broader Goals: Moving toward the Post-Washington Consensus." WIDER Annual Lecture No. 2, United Nations University, Helsinki (January)

2002. *Globalization and Its Discontents*. New York: W. W. Norton.

2007. *Making Globalization Work*. New York: W. W. Norton.

2008. "A Global Lesson in Market Failure." *Globe and Mail* (Toronto) (July 8).

2010. "Contagion, Liberalization, and the Optimal Structure of Globalization." *Journal of Globalization and Development* 1(2): article 2.

Stiglitz, Joseph and Andrew Charlton. 2005. *Fair Trade for All: How Trade Can Promote Development*. New York: Oxford University Press.

Stone, C. 1989. "Running Out of Options in Jamaica: Seaga and Manley Compared." *Caribbean Review* 15(3): 10–12.

Stroup, Michael D. 2007. "Economic Freedom, Democracy, and the Quality of Life." *World Development* 35(1): 52–66.

Sugimura, Kazuhiko. 2008. "Les paysans Africaines et l'économie morale." *Revue du MAUSS* 30. revuedumauss.com

Sundar, Aparna. 2012. "Capitalist Transformation and the Evolution of Civil Society in a South Indian Fishery." Ph.D. thesis, University of Toronto.

Svendsen, Gunnar and Gert Svendsen. 2004. *The Creation and Destruction of Social Capital*. Cheltenham, UK: Ashgate.

Swenarchuk, Michelle and Scott Sinclair. 2014. "Protecting the Environment from Trade Agreements." In Sandbrook and Guven, 75–86.

Tavolaro, S. B. F. and L. G. M. Tavolaro. 2007. "Accounting for Lula's Second Term Electoral Victory." *Constellations* 14(3): 426–44.

Taye, Meron Teferi and Patrick Willems. 2011. "Influence of Climate Variability on Representative QDF Prediction on the Upper Blue Nile Basin." *Journal of Hydrology* 411(3/4): 355–65.

Taylor, Ian and Paul Williams. 2000. "Neoliberalism and the Political Economy of the 'New' South Africa." *New Political Economy* 5(1): 21–40.

Teichman, Judith. 2012. *Social Forces and States: Poverty and Distributional Outcomes in South Korea, Chile and Mexico*. Stanford University Press.

Thaler, Richard H. 2000. "From Homo Economicus to Homo Sapiens." *Journal of Economic Perspectives* 14(1): 133–41.

Tharamangalam, Joseph. 1998. "The Perils of Social Development without Economic Growth: The Development Debacle of Kerala, India." *Bulletin of Concerned Asian Scholars* 30(1): 23–34.

2010. "Human Development as Transformational Practice: Lessons from Kerala and Cuba." *Critical Asian Studies* 42(3): 363–402.

Thorbecke, Erik and Chutatong Charumilund. 2002. "Economic Inequality and Its Socioeconomic Impact." *World Development* 30(9): 1,477–95.

Tirman, John. 2005. "The Washington Consensus and Armed Conflict." *Development* 48(3): 35–40.

Torche, Florencia and Luis Lopez-Calva. 2013, "Stability and Vulnerability of the Latin American Middle Class." *Oxford Development Studies* 41(4): 409–35.

Tokman, Victor. 2007. "The Informal Economy, Insecurity and Social Cohesion in Latin America." *International Labour Review* 146(1): 81–109.

Toro, Francesco. 2012. "How Hugo Chávez Became Irrelevant." *New York Times* (October 6): A17.

Tschirgi, Dan. 1999. "Marginalized Violent Internal Conflict in the Age of Globalization: Mexico and Egypt." *Arab Studies Quarterly* 21(3): 13–34.

Tsuruta, Tadasu. 2006. "African Imaginations of Moral Economy: Notes on Indigenous Economic Concepts and Practices in Tanzania." *African Studies Quarterly* 91(2).

Ulriksen, Marianne. 2011. "Social Policy Development and Global Crisis in the Open Economies of Botswana and Mauritius." *Global Social Policy* 11(2–3): 194–213.

UN (United Nations). 2010. "Africa's Hard Road to the Millennium Development Goals." *Africa Renewal* (August): 4–7.

UNCTAD (United Nations Conference on Trade and Development). 2012. *World Investment Report 2012: Toward a New Generation of Investment Policies*. Geneva: UNCTAD.

UNDP (United Nations Development Programme). 2000. *Human Development Report 2000: Human Rights and Human Development*. New York: Oxford University Press.

2006. *Human Development Report 2006: Beyond Scarcity: Power, Poverty and the Global Water Crisis*. New York: Oxford University Press.

2010. *Human Development Index 2010: The Real Wealth of Nations*. New York: UNDP.

United Nations Economic and Social Affairs Department. 2005. *Report on the World Social Situation 2005: The Inequality Predicament*. New York: United Nations Publications.

United Nations Environmental Programme (UNEP). 2006. *Africa's Lakes: Atlas of Our Changing Environment*. Nairobi: UNEP.

United Nations University. 2007. *UNU Update* 44 (December 2006–February 2007). Accessed at http://update.unu.edu/archives/issue44_22.htm

UNRISD (United Nations Research Institute in Social Development). 2010. *Combating Poverty and Inequality: Structural Change, Social Policy and Politics*. Geneva: UNRISD.

Uppsala Conflict Data Program. Uppsala University, Uppsala, Sweden. Accessed at www.pcs.uu.se/

Urioste, Miguel. 2009. "La 'revolución agraria' de Evo Morales: desafíos de un proceso complejo." *Nueva Sociedad* 223: 113–27.

Valencia Ramírez, C. 2006. "Venezuela in the Eye of the Hurricane." *Journal of Latin American Anthropology* 11(1): 173–86.

Valli, Vittorio. 2009. "The Three Waves of the Fordist Model of Growth and the Case of China." Working Paper 5/2009, Department of Economics, Università di Torino, Turin.

Van Binsberger, Wim. 2001. "Ubuntu and the Globalisation of Southern African Thought and Society." *Quest* 15(1/2): 53–84.

van der Westhuizen, Janis. 2013. "Class Compromise as Middle Power Activism? Comparing Brazil and South Africa." *Government and Opposition* 48(1): 80–100.

Van Waeyenberge, Hannah and Terry McKinley. 2013. "The IMF, Crisis and Low-Income Countries: Evidence of Change." *Review of Political Economy* 25(1): 69–90.

Varughese, Anil. 2012. "Democracy and the Politics of Social Citizenship: A Comparative Study of Pro-Poor States in India." Ph.D. thesis, University of Toronto.

Vermaak, Jaco. 2009. "Reassessing the Concept of 'Social Capital': Considering Resources for Satisfying the Needs of Rural Communities." *Development Southern Africa* 263: 399–412.

Vidal, John. 2010. "How Food and Water are Driving a 21st Century African Land Grab." *The Observer* (London) (March 7).

Vincent, Susan. 2010. "Participatory Budgeting in Peru: Democratization, State Control, or Community Autonomy." *Journal of Global and Historical Anthropology* 56: 65–77.

Visagie, Justin and Dorrit Posel. 2013. "A Reconsideration of What and Who is Middle Class in South Africa." *Development Southern Africa* 30(2): 149–67.

Wade, Robert. 2001. "Making the WDR 2000: Attacking Poverty." *World Development* 29(8): 1,435–41.

2004. "The World Bank and the Environment." In Morton Boas and Desmond McNeill, eds., *Global Institutions and Development: Framing the World?* 72–94. London: Routledge.

2010. "After the Crisis: Industrial Policy and the Developmental State in Low-Income Countries." *Global Policy* 1(2): 150–61.

Wagle, U. 2007. "Are Economic Liberalization and Equality Compatible? Evidence from South Asia." *World Development* 35(11): 1,836–57.

Wallerstein, Immanuel. 1999. "Ecology and Capitalist Costs of Production: No Exit." In W. Goldfrank, D. Goodman and Andrew Szasz, eds., *Ecology and the World System,* 3–11. Westport, CT: Greenwood Press.

Walzer, Michael. 1999. "Rescuing Civil Society." *Dissent* 46(1): 62–9.

2010. "Which Socialism?" *Dissent* 57(3): 37–43.

Wan, Guanghua (ed.). 2008. *Inequality and Growth in Modern China.* London: Oxford University Press.

Wang Shaoguang. 2008. "The Great Transformation: The Double Movement in China." *Boundary* 2(35): 15–47.

Wanyama, Frederick, Patrick Develtere and Ignace Pollett. 2009. "Reinventing the Wheel? African Cooperatives in a Liberalized Economic Environment." Co-operative Facility for Africa, International Labour Office, Dar es Salaam.

Webber, Jeffery. 2011. *From Rebellion to Reform in Bolivia: Class Struggle, Indigenous Liberation, and the Politics of Evo Morales.* Chicago: Haymarket Books.

Webster, Edward and Glenn Adler. 1999. "South Africa's 'Double Transition': Bargained Liberalization and the Consolidation of Democracy." *Politics and Society* 27(3): 347–85.

Weinstein, Martin. 1975. *Uruguay: The Politics of Failure.* Westport, CT: Greenwood Press.

Weisskopf, Thomas. 1992. "Toward a Socialism for the Future, in the Wake of the Demise of the Socialism of the Past." *Review of Radical Political Economics* 24(3/4): 1–28.

West Bengal, Government of. 2004. *West Bengal: Human Development Report*. Government Printer.

Weyland, Kurt. 2010. "The Performance of Leftist Governments in Latin America." In K. Weyland, R. Madrid and W. Hunter, eds., *Leftist Governments in Latin America*, 1–27. New York: Cambridge University Press.

2011. "The Left: Destroyer or Savior of the Market Model?" In Steven Levitsky and Kenneth Roberts, eds., *The Resurgence of the Latin American Left*, 71–92. Baltimore: Johns Hopkins University Press.

White, Rodney and Joseph Whitney. 2014. "Financing the Transition to a Low-Carbon Future." In Sandbrook and Guven.

Wilkinson, Richard. 2004. "Why is Violence More Common Where Inequality is Greater?" *Annals of the New York Academy of Sciences* 1,036 (December): 1–12.

Wilkinson, Richard and Kate Pickett. 2010. *The Spirit Level: Why Greater Equality Makes Societies Stronger*. New York: Bloomsbury Press.

Williams, William Appleman. 1972. *The Tragedy of American Diplomacy*. New edn. New York: W. W. Norton.

Williamson, John. 1990. "What Washington Means by Policy Reform." In his *Latin American Adjustment: How Much Has Happened?* 7–38. Washington, DC: Institute for Development Economics.

Wilpert, Gregory. 2013. "Unity and Succession in Venezuela after the Death of Chávez." *Le Monde Diplomatique* (April): 2.

Wiredu, Kwasi. 2008. "Social Philosophy in Postcolonial Africa: Some Preliminaries concerning Communalism and Communitarianism." *South African Journal of Philosophy* 27(4): 332–9.

Wolf, Martin. 1998. "Flows and Blows." *Financial Times* (March 3).

Wolfensohn, James D. 1999. "A Proposal for a Comprehensive Development Framework." Address to the Board, Management and Staff of the World Bank Group. Washington, DC: World Bank (January 21).

World Bank. 1981. *Accelerated Development in Sub-Saharan Africa: An Agenda for Action*. Washington, DC: World Bank.

1989. *Sub-Saharan Africa: From Crisis to Sustainable Development*. Washington, DC: World Bank.

1992. *World Development Report 1992; Development and the Environment*. New York: Oxford University Press.

1997. *World Development Report 1997: The State in a Changing World*. New York: Oxford University Press.

2001. *World Development Report 2000/2001: Attacking Poverty*. New York: Oxford University Press.

2002. *World Development Report 2002: Building Institutions for Markets*. New York: Oxford University Press.

2005a. *Economic Growth in the 1990s: Learning from a Decade of Reform*. Washington, DC: World Bank.

2005b. *Educational Change in South Africa 1994–2003*. Washington, DC: World Bank.

2006. *World Development Report 2006: Equity and Development*. New York: Oxford University Press.

2007a. *Development Results in Middle-Income Countries: An Evaluation of the World Bank's Support*. Washington, DC: World Bank.

2007b. *An Evaluation of World Bank Research, 1998–2005*. Washington, DC: World Bank (January).

2007c. Disasters, Climate Change and Economic Development in Sub-Saharan Africa: Lessons and Future Directions. Independent Evaluation Group, Brief No. 3. World Bank, Washington, DC (June 1).

2008. *The Growth Report: Strategies for Sustained Growth and Inclusive Development*. Washington, DC: World Bank Commission on Growth and Development.

2009. *World Development Indicators 2009*. Washington, DC: World Bank.

2010. *World Development Report 2010: Development and Climate Change*. Washington, DC: World Bank.

World Commission on the Social Dimensions of Development. 2004. *A Fair Globalization: Creating Opportunities for All*. Geneva: International Labour Organization.

Wright, Erik Olin (ed.). 1996. *Equal Shares: Making Market Socialism Work*. London: Verso.

2010. *Envisioning Real Utopias*. London: Verso.

Yale University. 2011. *Environmental Performance Index 2010: Country Scores*. Accessed at http://epi.yale.edu/Countries

Yashar, Deborah. 2011. "The Left and Citizenship Rights." In Steven Levitsky and Kenneth Roberts, eds., *The Resurgence of the Latin American Left*, 184–210. Baltimore: Johns Hopkins University Press.

York, Geoffrey. 2009. "Financial Crisis Pushed Millions More into Hunger." *Globe and Mail* (June 12), F5.

2011. "India is Competing with China to Wield Influence in Africa." *Globe and Mail* (May 23).

2012. "The House that Mandela Built, Divided." *Globe and Mail* (October 13): F7.

York, Richard and Eugene Rosa. 2003. "Key Challenges to Ecological Modernization Theory." *Organization and Environment* 16(3): 273–88.

Zack, Paul, ed., *Moral Markets: The Critical Role of Values in the Economy*. Princeton University Press.

Zibechi, Raúl. 2009. "Consequences of the 'Chilean Miracle': Salmon Farms and the Privatization of the Sea." Center for International Policy, Americas Program, Washington, DC. www.cipamericas.org/

2011. "Rebellion in the Brazilian Amazon." Center for International Policy, Americas Program, Washington, DC. www.cipamericas.org/

2013. "The Twenty Cent Revolt." Center for International Policy, Americas Program, Washington, DC. www.cipamericas.org/

Zuazo, Moira. 2010. "¿Los movimientos sociales en el poder? El gobierno del MAS en Bolivia." *Nueva Sociedad* 227: 120–35.

Index

accumulation
  crisis, 20, 136, 178, 223, 225, 235, 236
  as imperative, 11, 13–14, 21, 135, 136,
    146, 171, 182
African National Congress (ANC), 148–55,
  163, 184, 185
African socialism, 54, 58, 193; *see also*
  Nyerere, Julius
Allende, Salvador, 20, 165, 168, 169, 179,
  216
Allianza Bolivariana para los Pueblos de
  Nuestra América (ALBA), 210, 213, 251
Andean Community of Nations (CAN),
  210, 214
Angola, 191
Argentina, 22, 37–8, 39, 41, 246–7
  and financial crisis, 66, 69, 96
  and the left turn, 39, 167, 228
  and old-style populism, 22, 105
Asian Development Bank (ADB), 223
Australia, 107

Bachelet, Michelle, 105, 169
Banco Nacional de Desenvolvimento
  Econônomico e Social (BNDES),
  160, 174
BancoSur, 213, 252
Baran, Paul, 119
Beckerman, Wilfred, 84
Bernstein, Eduard, 19–20, 214
Berry, Albert, 78
black economic empowerment, 149
Block, Fred, 112
Bolivia, 23, 100, 212, 216, 224, 225, 227,
  229; *see also* Left populism
  and the environment, 258
  and inequality, 80
  and policy autonomy, 23, 212, 251
  and regional integration, 213–14
  and the role of social movements, 39, 108,
    209–12, 235, 242, 243

Bolsa Família, 157, 159, 161
Botswana, 66, 94
Brasil Carinhoso, 161
Brazil, 41, 131, 170, 174, 182, 184, 185, 255
  Cardoso government, 150, 155–7
  civil society and protests, 109, 163–4, 261
  compared to South Africa, 147–8, 171–63
  and consumerism, 129
  and crime, 93
  and decentralization, 179, 180–1, 233,
    243, 244–6
  and economic crisis, 37, 69
  and the environment, 86, 257
  and inequality, 76, 80
  and the left-turn, 39
  Lula da Silva government, 157–61
  as a moderate social democracy, 15, 18,
    21, 167
  and old-style populism, 22, 105
  and organized labour, 106, 107
  and regional organizations, 213–14
  rise of, 46, 47, 251
  and role of the media, 123
  Rousseff government, 161, 176
  and state developmentalism, 72, 173, 251
BRIC (Brazil, Russia, India, China) group,
  91, 115
bureaucratic collectivism, 119, 124, 187,
  188, 190–2, 200; *see also* socialism, state
  socialism
Bush, George W., 72, 114, 116, 255

Canada, 160
Capriles, Henrique, 202
Cardoso, Fernando Henrique, 56, 147, 155
Castro, Raúl, 124, 226
Chávez, Hugo, 51, 144, 188, 197–209, 210,
  212–13, 227, 231, 250; *see also* Left
  populism; twenty-first-century
  socialism
Chiapas, 39